Nationalization

Nationalization

A BOOK OF READINGS

EDITED BY

A. H. HANSON

*Reader in Public Administration
in the University of Leeds*

*Published for The Royal Institute
of Public Administration*

LONDON . GEORGE ALLEN AND UNWIN LTD

PRINTED IN GREAT BRITAIN
in 10 point Times Roman type
BY SIMSON SHAND LTD
LONDON, HERTFORD AND HARLOW

PREFACE

This collection of readings, I hope, will be of use to all interested in the development of publicly-owned industry; but it is primarily designed as an aid to the student. Of the enormous amount written on this subject, that portion contained in the surprisingly few books is readily accessible. It is the literature buried in a mass of periodicals, pamphlets and reports that presents a serious problem both of accessibility and of selection, which this volume aims at easing if not solving. Even the fortunate few with access to university libraries are daunted by the quantity of material apparently demanding their attention; others are often compelled to content themselves with the reading of a few well-known texts. I trust that the following pages will be of use to both.

This is not an 'anthologized' textbook. Many of the extracts will be barely intelligible to those without a good general knowledge of the subject. Fortunately, such knowledge may now be easily and pleasurably acquired from Professor William A. Robson's *Nationalized Industry and Public Ownership*, which has become indispensable to the serious student. To help the reader orient himself, however, I have preceded the chapters dealing with special aspects of nationalization by an introduction which briefly surveys the whole field. This is a slightly modified version of an article which I contributed to the Italian journal *Civilta delle Macchine*.

The main purpose of the extracts, which are arranged under topics, is not to provide factual information but to acquaint the reader with the many controversies to which the nationalization of industry has given rise and with the various solutions attempted or proposed for the constitutional, organizational and economic problems of the 'public sector'. The result, I would hope, is a classified anthology of creative thought.

The brief introduction at the head of each chapter is intended to indicate the problems with which the extracts deal and to put each of them into a comprehensible setting.

Only occasionally has it been possible or necessary to reproduce an article, pamphlet or report in full. Most extracts attempt to isolate what is original, essential or characteristic in their authors' approaches to the topics under discussion. Hence, in spite of the care taken in selecting passages for reproduction, it is possible that some of the writers herein represented will feel that justice has not been done to them. To any such I offer my apologies, while expressing the hope that the truncated versions of their thought will stimulate the reader to seek the full argument in his nearest library.

My best thanks are due to Mr D. N. Chester, CBE, Warden of Nuffield College, Oxford, for his advice, and to Mr I. D. Shelley, of the Royal Institute of Public Administration, for his assistance in obtaining permissions to reprint and in seeing this book through the press.

University of Leeds   A. H. HANSON

CONTENTS

CHAPTER I

Introduction

THE NATIONALIZED INDUSTRIES—THEIR SCOPE AND ROLE

The nationalized industries do not cover the whole of the 'public sector' of the British economy, which includes—for instance—a considerable amount of municipal enterprise. With that we are not here concerned, except to the extent that certain services providing for municipal needs, such as London Transport, are nationally owned and managed by government-appointed boards. Nor are we concerned with public bodies whose main function is the financing of private or 'mixed' enterprise, such as the Colonial Development Corporation, or with its regulation, such as the Marketing Boards. Our business is entirely with nationally-owned productive enterprises. These are now of major economic importance. They are responsible for about 12 per cent of the gross national product. The services provided by them are basic to the whole British economy.

Their most rapid expansion took place during the immediate postwar years, when a Labour Government with a socialist programme was in office. But it would be wrong to stress their 'ideological' inspiration. Many of the services nationalized between 1945 and 1950 were already partly under municipal control, such as gas and electricity, or administered by trusts of a public kind, such as harbours. Railways had become increasingly subject to public regulation, while the coal industry, under-capitalized and bedevilled by bad labour relations, demanded a 'rescue operation' which no government, of whatever political complexion, could have afforded not to undertake.

It should also be noted that, before 1945, a considerable amount of nationalization had been undertaken by non-socialist and anti-socialist governments. After 1880, when the High Court ruled that telephones were a state monopoly, the Post Office steadily extended its telephone services, at the expense of those run by private companies under licence, until in 1912 a nation-wide public service had been established. In 1908, a Liberal Government passed the Act constituting the great Port of London Authority, which in some respects provided the model for future public corporations. Between

the two World Wars, Conservative governments set up the Central
Electricity Board (responsible for the nation-wide distribution of
electrical energy through a 'grid'), the British Broadcasting Corporation (with a monopoly of broadcasting services), the London Passenger Transport Board (which took over all the London passenger
transport services previously run by municipalities and private companies), and the British Overseas Airways Corporation (by merger of
the two private companies, Imperial Airways and British Airways).
Hence it was difficult for the Conservatives of 1945–50 to object to
nationalization on principle—although they did protest most
vigorously both at the Labour Government's selection of industries
for nationalization and at the manner in which it was carried out.

It may be argued, in fact, that none of the industries brought into
the public sector (with the exception of Iron and Steel, which was
subsequently restored to private ownership) was nationalized
primarily for 'socialistic' reasons. In some cases, it seemed undesirable to leave a monopoly, however well regulated, in private hands;
in others, it appeared that the further development of a particular
service, in accordance with presumed national needs, could not be
undertaken in the most efficient manner by the private entrepreneur.
These considerations applied as much to the Labour nationalizations
of 1945–50 as to the previous Conservative and Liberal ones. The
result is our present 'mixed economy'.

THE LEGAL STRUCTURE OF THE NATIONALIZED INDUSTRIES

The phrase 'mixed economy', however, must not be taken as implying that any of the British nationalized industries are 'mixed' enterprises. Unlike many continental governments, the British Government has not chosen to extend the public sector of the economy by
taking up shares in enterprises organized as limited companies. Share
participations, as in the British Petroleum Company and the Agricultural Mortgage Corporation, are of comparatively limited importance. The nationalized industries themselves may be divided into
those run on the normal 'departmental' pattern and those organized
as public corporations. The Post Office is the chief example of the
former, although one might also mention the Royal Ordnance
Factories and the Admiralty Dockyards. The Post Office, although—
as befits a trading concern—having a highly distinctive form of
organization and special financial arrangements, is a department of
the central government, subject to Treasury control and Civil Service
regulations, and headed by a Minister, the Postmaster-General, who
is fully responsible to the House of Commons for its performance. All
the other major nationalized industries are public corporations.

The characteristics of the public corporation, which is very largely a British invention, are as follows: (*a*) it is wholly owned by the state, even though it may raise all or some of its capital by the issue of bonds to the public; (*b*) it is created by special law, and is not subject —except to such extent as may be prescribed—to the ordinary company law; (*c*) it is a body corporate, i.e. a separate legal entity which can sue and be sued, enter into contracts, and acquire property in its own name; (*d*) it is independently financed, obtaining its funds by borrowing, either from the Treasury or from the public, and deriving its revenues from the sale of its goods or services; (*e*) it is exempt from the forms of parliamentary financial control applicable to government departments; (*f*) its employees are not civil servants, and are recruited and remunerated on terms and conditions that the corporation itself determines.

The last four of these characteristics are intended to give the public corporation a 'business flexibility' which an ordinary government department, whatever special 'immunities' may be conferred upon it, usually finds difficulty in achieving. In the conduct of its day-to-day business, the public corporation is expected to behave 'commercially', i.e. in very much the same manner as a private company.

The problem universally experienced is to combine such business flexibility with an adequate measure of public control over general policy, without which there would be little point in having the enterprise in the public sector. In Britain this is attempted by statutorily conferring certain powers on the 'responsible Minister', i.e. the Minister of Power for the coal, gas and electricity industries, the Minister of Transport for the Transport Commission, and the Minister of Aviation for the civil airways enterprises. This Minister appoints the Board, or governing body, of the corporation, which is required to consult him in devising its capital investment programmes and in formulating its plans for research, training and education. Any capital finance which the corporation wishes to raise externally (e.g. from the Treasury or from the public) requires the sanction both of the responsible Minister and of the Treasury. The Minister receives the corporation's annual Report and Accounts, which he lays before Parliament, prescribes the form of the Accounts, and appoints qualified commercial firms to audit them. He may require the corporation to provide him with information, and, after consultation with its governing Board, is empowered to give it any 'directions of a general character as to the exercise of performance by the Board of their functions in relation to matters appearing to the Minister to affect the public interest'. Generally, there is supposed to be a distinction between 'day-to-day administration', in respect of which the corporation possesses autonomy, and 'general policy', over which the Minister exercises more or less continuous supervision.

This distinction, in its turn, determines the relationship between the nationalized industry and Parliament. The Minister is responsible to Parliament only for his statutory functions *vis-à-vis* the public corporation, and consequently will normally refuse to accept responsibility for policies and decisions not subject to his intervention, although he will often provide Parliament with information on such matters. Nevertheless, Parliament enjoys fairly frequent opportunities to discuss the affairs of the corporations. Many questions about them are asked and answered; three days are allocated annually for debating their Reports and Accounts; sometimes they are discussed, on a Supply Day, in connection with the Vote of the relevant Ministry; occasionally they are the subject of a Private Member's resolution; and further opportunities occur, from time to time, when the House is asked to sanction capital advances, give its approval to a major reorganization plan, or confer additional powers on a corporation.

The corporation-minister-parliament relationship, however, is not susceptible to precise legal definition, and many difficulties have arisen in its interpretation. Although only two 'general directions' of any political importance have ever been issued (both to the Transport Commission) it can hardly be said that the corporations enjoy that freedom from ministerial interference which was originally envisaged for them. Contact between Minister and corporation is, in most cases, close and continuous, and many consider that the latter's 'autonomy' has been considerably eroded. In practice, for instance, neither the Coal Board nor the Transport Commission has been able to determine its own prices, although ministerial intervention in this respect has been mostly of an informal kind. This type of intervention tends to create, in the minds of Members of Parliament, the suspicion that the Minister is using the Board as a 'screen', and there have been periodical demands that the extent of formal ministerial responsibility should be increased, to correspond with the reality of the minister-board relationship which is thought to prevail.

Another difficulty has arisen from the interpretation of the statutory requirement that the corporation shall pay its way, i.e. 'that the revenues of the Board shall not be less than sufficient for meeting all their outgoings properly chargeable to revenue account . . . on an average of good and bad years'. What is to happen if the Minister, either by informal representations or by the issue of a general direction, causes the corporation to pursue unremunerative policies? This issue has arisen on several occasions when Ministers, by refusing permission for price increases, have involved corporations in heavier deficits than they would otherwise have probably incurred. It has never been brought to any legal test, however, nor is it likely to be; for, as with much else in the nationalization laws, the relevant provisions are so vague and general that one can hardly imagine their becoming the subject of argument before a court of law.

For several years, a frequent complaint from Members of Parliament was that the information they obtained about the nationalized industries was neither objective enough nor of sufficient quantity, with the result that the House was hampered in the exercise of its supervisory functions. Since 1956, an attempt has been made to remedy this defect, through the establishment of a special parliamentary committee of inquiry, known as the Select Committee on the Nationalized Industries. At first regarded as highly experimental, this body has produced a series of Reports (e.g. on the Coal Board, the Civil Airways Corporations, British Railways and the Gas Boards) which are generally regarded as of great value.

People with complaints against a nationalized industry sometimes communicate their grievances to their Member of Parliament, who will attempt to obtain rectification by writing to the Chairman of the Board or to the Minister, or in the last resort by asking a Question in the House of Commons. An alternative method, not as yet much used, is to get in touch with one of the Consumers' Advisory Councils established by law for the industry concerned. These have an advisory role only, but their recommendations can, in certain circumstances, lead to executive action, in so far as the Minister may give a specific direction to the corporation to remedy any defect in its 'general plans and arrangements' revealed by consumers' council representations made to him. This type of consumers' representation, however, has not worked as well as its originators hoped.

In Britain, there is no legal provision for workers' representation on the Boards of the corporations, but each Board is required by law to devise a system of joint consultation and to operate a satisfactory procedure for collective bargaining. Although some of the trade unions concerned favour direct workers' representation on the Boards, most consider it desirable to maintain their complete independence of the managerial hierarchy.

THE BOARDS

Each public corporation has a collective leadership known as a Board, appointed by the responsible Minister. Boards vary in size according to the requirements of the industry, and their members are drawn from many different walks of life. Only Ministers of the Crown and Members of Parliament are specifically excluded from membership. Apart from this limitation, the discretion of the Minister in making appointments is very nearly absolute, for the law does little more than particularize the types of experience which board members would in any case need to have. Thus, for instance, the Gas Act, 1948, provides that the members of the Area Gas Boards shall be

> appointed by the Minister from amongst persons appearing to him to
> · be qualified as having had experience of, and shown capacity, in gas
> supply, local government, industrial, commercial or financial matters,
> applied science, administration, or the organization of workers.

All boards have part-time as well as full-time members, although in different proportions. Most of the full-time members, as might be expected, have had previous experience of the industry concerned, as directors, managers, engineers, accountants or trade union officials. Most of the part-timers are drawn from other industries, and are expected to bring the light of varied experiences to bear on the problems of the corporation. The Board of a public corporation, therefore, is very similar to that of a private company. Its responsibility, however, is not to an annual shareholders' meeting but to the Minister and, through him, to Parliament and the public.

A frequently-discussed problem is that of the organization of a Board. Should it be solely responsible for taking top-level policy decisions and for making key executive appointments, or should certain members of it be responsible, in addition, for specific managerial functions? No generally-acceptable answer can be given, or has been attempted, to this question. The practice varies from one corporation to another, and even from time to time, as experience accumulates. The National Coal Board, for instance, was given a predominantly 'functional' organization in 1946; subsequently most of its members lost their specific executive responsibilities; then, in 1955, the functional principle was reintroduced.

Another problem is security of tenure. Board members are appointed for a limited period only, although they are always eligible for reappointment. In practice, changes of personnel on certain boards have been rather frequent, as perhaps was inevitable during the 'settling-down' process. Although it is obvious that inefficient or unco-operative members cannot be allowed to retain their appointments, opinion is now veering strongly in favour of making full-time service on the Board the culmination of a successful career in the industry, with expectation of continuing membership until retiring age. Some authorities on nationalization, however, emphasize the dangers of 'in-breeding'.

Remuneration of Board members has also caused controversy. The general tendency has been to pay them salaries lower than those which people of comparable qualifications and experience could obtain in private industry. As salaries all the way down the managerial hierarchy are, in the last resort, determined by those of the men at the top, there is a danger that the nationalized industries will recruit only the second-best talent. Already, in conditions of keen competition for the services of qualified managers and technicians, some of the industries are finding difficulty in recruiting an adequate number of graduates and other suitable trainees. This problem is one that is likely to become more rather than less acute.

ORGANIZATION FOR MANAGEMENT

It would be futile to attempt to prescribe, by law, a common organizational pattern on a series of industries so different in their characteristics. Each nationalization Act gives the industry concerned a specific pattern of the broadest kind. The Coal Industry Nationalization Act, indeed, simply gave the National Coal Board the responsibility for organizing the whole industry, leaving the Board entirely free to devise whatever forms of subordinate and decentralized bodies it saw fit; but this was not repeated in subsequent Acts. The Gas Act, for instance, prescribed a structure of fourteen Area Gas Boards, with responsibility for both production and distribution, and a central Gas Council with functions mainly of an advisory and co-ordinating character. The Electricity Supply Industry, as reorganized under the 1958 Act, consists of an Electricity Generating Board, responsible for generation and main-line transmission, twelve Area Boards, with responsibility for distribution to consumers, and an Electricity Council, mainly composed of representatives of the Generating Board and the Area Boards, for advice, co-ordination and the provision of certain common services.

As the major nationalized industries are very large, organizational problems of an almost unique kind have arisen, and no-one pretends that the best possible solution has been found in every case. Already, coal, electricity and rail transport have undergone major reorganizations, which are by no means likely to be the last ones. At present, there is a strong demand in some quarters for a radical decentralization of the structure of the coal industry, and at the moment of writing a government-appointed committee is reviewing railway organization. The periodical appointment of advisory committees on organization has become almost standing practice. Sometimes they are appointed by the Government, sometimes by the industry itself. Two of them, the 'Herbert' Committee on the Electricity Supply Industry and the 'Fleck' Committee on the coal industry, have given rise to major organizational changes. It should also be noted that, within the industries themselves, operational research and organization and methods studies have been increasingly employed to improve managerial efficiency.

FINANCE

As the part of the public sector with which we are concerned consists of 'nationalized' industries (i.e. enterprises transferred from private ownership), the servicing of the stock issued as compensation to the former owners of their assets has been one of their first financial obligations. New capital, except for the coal industry, was originally raised by the issue of further stock (at fixed interest rates, bearing Treasury guarantee, and without voting rights). From the beginning, the Coal Board raised its capital through loans from the Exchequer, and since 1956 this method of financing has been adopted for all the public corporations. The amount of capital issued to each industry (together with the timing and terms of the loans) is at the discretion of the responsible Minister in consultation with the Treasury, and ultimately subject to the approval of Parliament, which periodically raises the 'ceiling' on permitted capital advances. Capital requirements are, of course, considered by the Government in relation to approved development plans.

The Government has been more generous in meeting the financial needs of some of the industries than those of others. Electricity and coal, for instance, have had their very heavy capital demands more or less fully met. The railways, on the other hand, were starved of funds until about six years ago, when their critical condition compelled the Government to take drastic action. In 1956, it undertook to provide the finances for the Transport Commission's comprehensive and expensive modernization plan, and early in 1957, by the Transport (Railway Finances) Act, empowered the Transport Commission to borrow, by means of advances from the Minister, a sum, not exceeding £250 million in aggregate (i) to meet any deficit on revenue account of British Railways for 1956 or any of the next six years, and (ii) to pay interest on the money so borrowed. Although the Government insisted that this was not a subsidy, as the Commission would ultimately be responsible for repaying this sum, with interest, there was justified scepticism whether it was likely to succeed in doing so. The expectation, then officially expressed, that the Commission would be in balance by 1961 or 1962 was not realized. At present (1962) railway finances are undergoing a further and even more radical reorganization, along the lines laid down by the Government's White Paper on Nationalized Transport Undertakings (Cmnd 1248).

For industries such as coal and transport, which have aggregate losses on revenue account, the question of self-financing does not arise. For profitable ones, such as electricity, it does. Should they aim merely at 'breaking even', or at making profits sufficiently large to contribute substantially to their own capital expenditure? On this, divergent views have been expressed. The 'Herbert' Committee was strongly of the opinion that such self-financing would involve improperly taking advantage of a quasi-monopoly position to exploit the current consumers for the benefit of the consumers of future years, and that the Electricity Supply Industry should raise its capital by 'going to the market'. Others have argued, however, that this policy involves the creation of artificial and harmful divergencies in the average price-levels of the public and private sectors respectively, inflates the profitability of private at the expense of public industry, and unjustifiably increases the burden of loan charges on the latter. Professor Arthur Lewis, for instance, believes that it is folly to keep prices down in the nationalized industries, thereby raising 'private sector profits', and then 'to have to borrow these profits to finance investment in the nationalized industries'. The whole controversy, of course, is complicated by arguments among the economists as to what is, theoretically, the correct pricing policy for the public sector to pursue. Into this we have no space to enter. Nor can we do more than mention the question whether the prices charged by public corporations should be subject to review and confirmation by an independent tribunal. At present, the Transport Tribunal, the successor of the old Railway Rates Tribunal, is the only body of this kind.

PERFORMANCE

Nationalized industries in Britain have been fiercely criticized, particularly by anti-socialists. In a recent, much-publicized book, *Nationalization in Britain: the End of a Dogma*, Mr Kelf-Cohen can find virtually nothing to say on their behalf. They are accused of being slow-moving, bureaucratic, extravagant, and contemptuous of the consumer. Much of this criticism, however, is politically inspired and totally lacking in objectivity. That the railways have done badly, for instance, is by no means entirely or even mainly the fault of the Transport Commission. The assets it took over were in very bad condition; until recent years it has been starved of funds; and the problem of making rail transport 'pay' is one that few countries have successfully solved. The coal industry, likewise, has had tremendous leeway to make up in respect of productive efficiency, and since 1956 has been confronted by the very difficult problem of adjusting itself to contracting demand. Where circumstances have been more favourable, nationalized industries have performed satisfactorily. Of the Electricity Supply Industry, for instance, the 'Herbert' Committee wrote:

> ... in our opinion it would be quite wrong to call the industry inefficient, nor can the organization which has produced the results it has produced be described as a bad organization.

Evidence of satisfaction with the Gas Industry is the lack of controversy about it. The Civil Airlines, better than their foreign competitors in some respects and worse in others, are generally admitted to be enterprising and commercially-minded. Significantly, they are omitted from Mr Kelf-Cohen's survey.

The difficulty about assessing efficiency in an industry which is not fully competitive and subject to the normal 'capitalist' incentives is to discover adequate units of measurement. The industries themselves have developed, and are developing, certain indices, such as 'output per manshift' (coal), 'gas made per ton of coal carbonized' (gas), and 'kilowatts generated per ton of coal burnt' (electricity). In some of the industries, an attempt is being made to bring together a number of separate indices in such a way as to provide a generalized efficiency assessment. The National Coal Board, for instance, produces 'colliery profiles', in which many standard indices are entered on punch cards, one for each of the 900 coal mines, so that valid comparisons of relative efficiency may be made. Too little credit is given to the public corporations for these efforts at self-criticism.

It should also be said that the critics of nationalization tend to assume, quite arbitrarily, that the industries concerned would have done better under private ownership. There is no evidence that this is so; nor, in the nature of things, is there much evidence to the contrary. But at least the Conservative Party, among whose members such assumptions abound, has confined its denationalization efforts to Iron and Steel and Road Haulage, and has made no suggestion that it hopes to return coal, railways, electricity, gas and civil airlines to private (or private and municipal) ownership.

THE FUTURE

Nevertheless, it cannot be said that the nationalization of industry is a popular principle in Britain today, and it is most unlikely that further nationalizations will take place in the near future. The Conservatives are committed to 'free enterprise' principles, although by no means averse to assisting certain private industries (such as aircraft construction and shipbuilding) with massive subsidies. The Labour Party, while committed to the renationalization of Iron and Steel, has uncertain prospects of coming into office, and is studiedly vague about the possibility of its engaging in further extensions of the public sector. No-one knows precisely what it means when it says that it will subject to public control the 'commanding heights' of the economy.

As for the existing nationalized industries, it is probable that some of them will undergo extensive reorganization. There is also some demand, particularly in Conservative circles, for the splitting up of the great Coal Board monopoly—although this would meet with the most determined resistance from the miners. Some people would like to experiment with more effective methods of consumer representation; others (particularly on the socialist side) feel that the nationalized industries will not work satisfactorily until their workers are given a substantial share in the management.

Nationalization is no longer a panacea for socialists, nor an object of unreasoning hatred for Conservatives. All agree that our economy must be a 'mixed' one. Remaining disagreements, in this field, are about the constitution of the mixture and the organization of its 'public' element.

(Originally published in Italian in *Civilta delle Macchine*, Anno VIII, No. 5. Settembre-Ottobre 1960 as 'L'Impresa Pubblica in Gran Bretagna'.)

CHAPTER II

Motives for Nationalization

The inclusion of an enterprise in the public sector may be motivated by principle, by expediency, or by a combination of the two. In England, the Labour Party has traditionally stood for 'the nationalization of the means of production, distribution and exchange' for reasons of principle clearly set out by Mr Hugh Gaitskell in *Extract 1*. However, the Party has never interpreted this slogan literally, and many of its leading members, as the same extract shows, nowadays interpret it less literally than ever.

In any case, evolutionary socialism implies a series of *priorities* for nationalization, which means that it has to give specific reasons for the taking into the public sector at a particular time of one industry rather than another. The criteria applied have varied, but have usually included such factors as (*a*) the 'basic' character of the industry concerned, (*b*) the extent to which it is monopolized, (*c*) the condition of its internal organization, and (*d*) the quality of its labour relations. Some of these factors are brought out in *Extract 2* from the Trades Union Congress's *Interim Report on Post-War Reconstruction*, which considered, from the point of view of organized labour, how far nationalization should be extended during the period following the Second World War.

When 'cases' are thus under discussion, there is the possibility of fruitful dialogue between socialists and non-socialists. Some of the latter, of course, have a principled dislike of nationalization as such, but even the most anti-nationalizing Conservative is prepared to accept, on grounds of expediency, the need for public ownership and control of certain types of enterprises. *Extract 3* provides a moderately-argued statement of Conservative attitudes.

Strong empirical arguments, of course, underlay the nationalizations effected by Conservative or Conservative-dominated governments during the inter-war period, i.e. the British Broadcasting Corporation, the Central Electricity Board, the London Passenger Transport Board and the British Overseas Airways Corporation. Similarly strong arguments provided support for some of the nationalizations effected by the Labour Government between 1945 and 1950, in so far as these were preceded by the publication of expert reports which pointed to nationalization, sometimes explicitly and sometimes by inference, as the only way to effect necessary reorganizations. Such 'specific' reasons for nationalization are illustrated by *Extract 4*, from the 'Reid' Report on the Coal Industry, and by *Extract 5*, from the 'Heyworth' Report on the Gas Industry. The earlier 'MacGowan' Report on Electricity Distribution, from which *Extract 6* is taken, rejected nationalization, but advocated radical structural reforms which the Labour Government considered could best be effected by nationalization rather than by the methods which the Report recommended. These extracts show why the Conservative Party opposed the nationalization of these industries less heatedly than they opposed the nationalization of, for instance, iron and steel, which was a much less obvious candidate for the public sector except from the standpoint of principles which no Conservative could accept. The clash of principle between the Conservative Party and the Labour Party on the issue of iron and steel nationalization is illustrated by excerpts from speeches by Mr Duncan Sandys, the Minister of Supply, and Mr G. R. Strauss in the Second Reading of the 1952 'denationalization' Bill. (*Extract 7*.)

1. TRADITIONAL AND 'REVISIONIST' SOCIALISM*

Anybody who thinks about it for a moment will agree that nationalization, which is an institutional change in the ownership and control of industry, must be treated as a *means* and not grouped with the ultimate aims which I have just described. The fact that it is nevertheless often treated as an end, as, indeed, more or less identical with Socialism, is because it has been regarded not as *a* means to achieve the ideals of Socialism but as the *only possible* means *which could not fail to produce the desired ends*. This applies both to *nationalization*, which is generally understood to mean the taking over by the State of a complete industry so that it is owned by and managed and controlled for the community, and *public ownership*, which strictly speaking means the ownership by the community of any property whether industrial or not, whether embracing the whole of an industry or only part of it. This is an important distinction to which I shall return later.

* From Hugh Gaitskell: *Socialism and Nationalization*, Fabian Tract 300, 1956, pp. 5–7 and 31–36. Reprinted by permission of the author and publishers. Those readers who are interested in pursuing further the Labour Party views on this subject are advised to read the whole of this pamphlet.

Why, however, was it supposed that these ultimate Socialist objectives were regarded as attainable only through the nationalization of the means of production, distribution and exchange? To this vital question there are four answers, broadly corresponding to our four objectives. . .

The first is in essence a Marxist argument, based upon the Labour theory of value. The flow of unearned income—of rent, interest and profits—is the root evil of capitalism; it represents the toll laid upon the workers by the owners of capital, who thereby deprive them of their rightful earnings. The existence of unearned income is wrong in itself, irrespective of how it is distributed. In any case it all goes to one class—property owners—and not at all to the other—the workers—and, by a natural historical process, its distribution becomes more and more unequal. . .

The second main argument relates to the working of the capitalist system. Both in the light of experience and on theoretical grounds, it is claimed that the free individualist economy leads perpetually to the unnatural result of 'poverty in the midst of plenty'. Artificial scarcity is imposed through the existence of unemployed workers and unused factory space. Thus while consumers are left hungry, cold and poor, producers are complaining of gluts and surpluses. They are even driven into deliberately curtailing production, despite the vast unsatisfied needs of the world. . .

Thirdly, it was argued that the private possession of capital inevitably gave too much power to those who own it, too much power over their employees, too much power to take, on their own, decisions of vital economic importance to the community, too much power and influence in society generally. . .

Fourthly, it was held that the capitalist system, based upon competition—the survival of the fittest, the desire to do down your neighbour, whether as a competitor or employee or consumer—was fundamentally unchristian, and would always prevent a real spirit of co-operation. Only in a co-operative economy, where men and women worked for the community, would the new spirit prevail. The rivalry between firms, the hostility between employer and worker, the greed for the maximum profit, would thus all be replaced by new and better relationships. . .

Let us take the Socialist ideals one by one.

First, . . . the experience of the last fifteen years suggests that it may be possible to maintain full employment in a mixed economy without having to extend the scope of the nationalized sector. Although such an extension would be of value in any attempt at better economic planning, it cannot be said to provide either an automatic or a unique solution. The real problem is how to maintain a very high degree of employment without inflation; and the answer in a democracy where free Trade Unions flourish must be a combination of controls and voluntary restraints, which are not easy to maintain unless there is already a fair distribution of wealth and income.

Secondly, while a better framework may be constructed under nationalization for the development of democracy in industry, its progress can certainly be carried very much further even within the private sector than now. Both the differences between different firms in Britain and more democratic practices in certain other countries suggest that this must be so.

Thirdly, as regards the closely associated question of economic power there can be no doubt that nationalization does involve a significant transfer and diffusion of power; but . . . this is not such a simple issue as it is sometimes supposed, and . . . the gain to society of the transfer, though real, is not always obvious to all. Here again a more even distribution of wealth would make a big difference to the whole question.

EQUALITY THE TOUCHSTONE

One is, therefore, driven to the conclusion that the most vital question is how far greater social and economic equality can be achieved without more nationalization and public ownership. So far, as has been pointed out earlier in this pamphlet, greater equality has been brought about in Britain not so much by nationalization as by the growth of social services, severe taxation on high incomes partly resulting from war, and an increase in the share of the national income enjoyed by wage and salary earners, resulting from the power of the Trade Unions exercised during a period of mild inflation. Can we expect a further advance on these same lines? And is such a further advance compatible with rising production if the greater part of the economy is still owned and controlled by private individuals? No doubt financial, monetary and physical controls will be available to the Government. But will these be enough, in circumstances where fiscal policy and the power of the Trade Unions are both used to redistribute wealth and income more evenly, to secure a steady increase in the national income, a mastery of the foreign trade problem and generally prosperous conditions?

The answers to these questions clearly depend upon which lines of policy it is proposed to adopt in order to produce social and economic equality and upon the repercussions on the economy which will follow from this adoption. Two such lines are of special importance. One is educational reform. I do not propose to discuss it here. But this at least can be said—that apart from the extra public expenditure involved in providing better schools, better teaching, etc., there is no reason why advance on this particular front should lead to major economic difficulties.

The second line of policy is a fairer distribution of wealth; it is this which presents by far the greater problem. . . . Whatever fiscal or other measures are used, the dangers which they might involve in a still predominantly private enterprise economy (which is assumed here) really all converge at the same point. They all amount to the same danger of too little saving and too little investment. By too little saving I mean a disposition for the community as a whole to spend too much on consumption. . . .

By too little investment I mean not the consequences of too little saving to which I have just referred, but an unwillingness on the part of the business community to invest, i.e. to install new equipment, machinery and plant, to spend money in research, to do those very things which are in a large part the basis of rising productivity in the future. . . .

NATIONALIZATION AND SAVING

But how far can these two dangers which lie in the path of the advance to equality be averted by more nationalization and public ownership? We must distinguish between them. First as to saving, it can be said that the larger the public sector the easier it would be for the Government to insist upon a high rate of saving. It would simply direct the nationalized boards to fix their prices at such a level that they would make very large profits, all of which would be saved. There are good grounds for saying that up to now the nationalized industries have, if anything, been encouraged to do the opposite, and the policy should be deliberately changed so that they may finance more of their investment themselves. This would extend public ownership more rapidly as well as increasing saving.

But it is no use pretending that this would be very easy. The fact that since 1945 the public sector of industry, far from financing its development out of its own profits, has been borrowing extensively from private sources is not just accidental. While one reason for this is that the nationalized industries happened for the most part to be in a weak financial and physical condition when they were taken over, even more important are the economic and political obstacles in the way of higher prices and profits in these industries. One must be exceedingly careful not to ascribe to public ownership, as such, possibilities which really spring from a different *political* system which we have no intention of adopting. In a democracy it is not so easy for the nationalized undertakings to charge high prices in order to provide a larger volume of saving. It is as difficult as it is for the Government to impose taxes, earn a budget surplus and thus reach the same objective—namely a rise in public saving—by a slightly different path.

Indeed of the two methods of increasing saving—by taxation and a budget surplus or by high prices, profits and reserves in the nationalized industries, the first is rather to be preferred. It is more certain— for the high profits in the nationalized industries will very probably invite higher wage claims. It is fairer—because the Government does not have to concentrate on the products of the nationalized industries only, or even on commodity taxation in raising the extra revenue; and it is less disturbing, because the wider choice available to the Government makes it possible to avoid increases in the prices of particular products which might cause demand to fall off too sharply, and create local unemployment.

We cannot therefore be sure that more nationalization in itself will contribute very much to the problem of combining egalitarian policies with a high rate of saving, though undoubtedly it could, provided the appropriate policies were followed. Other devices will certainly also be important; they might include dividend limitation so as to ensure a high rate of company saving, and they will almost certainly have to involve fiscal measures of one kind or another.

THE RATE OF INVESTMENT

On the other hand if the danger to be expected arises more from unwillingness to invest, then the case for nationalization as a countermeasure is certainly much stronger. For though the nationalized boards may not always see eye to eye with a government proposal for higher investment expenditure and may take a more cautious or pessimistic view of a particular project, nevertheless the Government does have much more prospect of speeding up investment in the public than in the private sector. In the last resort the Government can insist and ride out any political storm that may arise through disagreement with the Board. This is simply not open to them in dealing with private firms.

The problem here is likely to be administrative and technical rather than political—the difficulty of the Government having sufficiently experienced and expert advice to match the technical knowledge and judgment of the nationalized boards. But with a strong planning machine this is not an insuperable obstacle.

But which is likely to be the greater difficulty? Unwillingness to save or failure to invest sufficiently? A few years ago more stress would have been laid on the failure to invest. But recent experience suggests on the whole that partly because of the divorce between ownership and control in industry, partly because of fiscal incentives, it may not be so difficult to ensure a continued readiness to invest by business executives even if the Government is pursuing egalitarian policies. At the same time the problem of keeping down consumption so as to finance a high rate of investment is obviously not yet solved—as the experience of the last eighteen months clearly shows.

ALTERING THE DISTRIBUTION OF WEALTH

Can we then really envisage a continued further advance towards a more even distribution of wealth without a simultaneous sweeping extension of nationalization and public ownership?

Here I believe we must draw a distinction, to which I referred earlier, between public ownership—the ownership by the community of assets and property of any kind—and the nationalization of particular industries as this has been carried out in recent years. If it is nationalization of which we speak, no definite answer can yet be given; but if it is the extension of public ownership then it seems to me that this is almost certainly necessary if we are to have a much more equal distribution of wealth.

The argument which leads up to this conclusion is simple enough. The distribution of privately owned wealth today is still very uneven —about 3 per cent of the population own two-thirds of it. Although distribution was even more unfair in the past, the effect of high death duties and income and surtax is slow in its operation, chiefly because of a rise in the value of equity capital—a form of property which tends to be concentrated in the hands of wealthier people. If wealth is to be more fairly shared there are only two ways of doing it—either to arrange for the redistribution of the existing privately-owned wealth among more people or to increase the proportion of wealth owned by the community, the income from which is also available for the use of the community.

Some steps towards the first could be taken by a change in the incidence of death duties, whereby the size of the tax was dependent on the wealth of the beneficiary instead of the value of the estate as a whole. But in practice the only effect of this would be to spread wealth a little more evenly among people who are already comfortably off. More drastic measures could, of course, be adopted to share out existing wealth. In theory there could be a capital levy with the proceeds distributed evenly among the whole population. From a Socialist angle such policies have two drawbacks. First, in the early stages at least, simple redistribution after a capital levy—quite apart from the political objections—would almost certainly increase consumption and reduce saving. Secondly, although for the time being such a move would profoundly affect the class structure, if the economy continued to be conducted on the lines of private ownership and inheritance a new class structure based on property ownership would before long emerge.

While, therefore, there is much to be said for privately-owned property being widely spread, it is certainly not along this path alone that we can proceed. The second course—a high proportion of publicly-owned property—must also be adopted.

ALTERNATIVE FORMS OF PUBLIC OWNERSHIP

As I have said, this is not necessarily the same as nationalization. There are several differences between them. Industries can be taken over and run by local authorities as well as by the nation through its central government, even if there are strict limits to the possibilities— especially with the existing structure of local government. But there is another and far more important distinction, which is especially important when the transfer to public ownership is gradual. The State may become the owner of industrial, commercial or agricultural property without necessarily exercising detailed control even over an individual firm—much less a whole industry. This can be done either by taking in death duties—not cash or bonds but equity shares and real estate—or by using the proceeds of a budget surplus to purchase equity shares; or, if political conditions allowed, by a capital levy which again could either be paid in shares or land and buildings, or if paid in cash could be used to purchase these assets.

One can envisage in this way a gradual extension of the public ownership of property, the income from which would be available for the community and which might itself for a time be set aside for further purchases. This could undoubtedly be carried through without a great extension of the list of nationalized industries. It would no doubt be necessary to set up one or two new public Corporations which would in effect be large investment trusts—not so different in their operation from the insurance companies or some other financial institution. But they would be owned by the whole community to which their profits would accrue, and their operation would be ultimately subject to ministerial control. How far they would exercise control over the companies in which they held shares is not a matter on which it would be wise to be dogmatic now. Although as the process continued the possibilities of control in this way would become greater, this would be—as it were—a by-product of the operation, the fundamental purpose of which would be to produce more social justice. Another incidental advantage of developing institutions of

this kind would be to make available a plentiful supply of risk capital
and to make it easier to stimulate more investment.

Here, I must add, more direct action might be necessary, different
from either the complete nationalization of a whole industry or the
mere acquisition of equity shares. Such action might include either
the establishment of 100 per cent State enterprises to carry out a
project where private firms would not undertake the risk, or of some
form of mixed enterprise involving a partnership between the State
and private firms. There are other possibilities. One is the purchase by
the State of certain selected firms and their grouping together under a
holding company to form a single efficient unit—within an industry;
another is the extension of the activities of the existing nationalized
industries into other fields. For example, the Coal Board might
follow the example of the Dutch State Mines and operate chemical
plants.

There is no need to elaborate further. The differences between these
various forms of State ownership and control are matters of degree
only. The point is that we need not conceive of public ownership as
always a matter of taking over a whole industry, making a structural
change within that one industry and setting up a single large organization, but as embracing also many other types of change: in some of
these the State will be a passive and in others an active participant; in
some, completely new public or semi-public enterprises will be
launched; in others, existing firms may come into public ownership
and management.

In this way over the years, while more industries may be nationalized as circumstances require . . . we can envisage simultaneously the
community becoming the owner, not of whole industries, but of
many different shareholdings and other forms of property. It is
already the owner of millions of houses, large forest areas, thousands
of acres of land, valuable atomic energy plants, defence factories and
dockyards and much besides, in addition to the nationalized industries. The Labour Party have proposed that it should also become the
owner of some six million older rent-controlled tenanted houses.
There is no reason why it should not become the owner of more and
more industrial and commercial capital, replacing the passive shareholder, receiving dividends, and reaping the capital gains.

A NEW ALLIANCE OF POLICIES

The process of transition, during which the public ownership of
property is thus gradually extended, will bring with it many diffi-

culties, especially of fiscal policy. But as far as the working of the economy is concerned, the divorce of control from ownership in the private sector, and the change in the character of management, will greatly facilitate progress on those lines. The fact that shareholders nowadays are purely passive and virtually without function, and that managements can manage without them so easily, means that the transfer of shares to public ownership will bring with it no serious administrative or economic problems comparable to those presented by the full nationalization of a complete industry. If, as I believe, the major weaknesses of nationalization be not the elimination of the profit incentive, but the creation of units which are too large to get the best response from those employed in them, and in the weakening of competitive attitudes in management, that is another argument for being careful about 'structural' changes which do just this. It is another argument for distinguishing between the transfer of land and capital to public ownership on the one hand, and the public control of management, industry by industry, on the other. Thus in the next phase public ownership achieved by an alliance with fiscal policy, and not just nationalization as conceived in these last twenty years, may well become a major instrument of Socialist policy.

2. CANDIDATES FOR THE PUBLIC SECTOR*

THE REASONS FOR PUBLIC CONTROL

26. It is not only the Trade Union Movement . . . which recognizes the importance of establishing some measure of public control over industry and trade. Full employment; price stability; the protection of the people, either as workers or consumers, against exploitation; the equitable distribution of income and economic opportunity, and the promotion of national development and national security are all aims widely acknowledged to be a responsibility of government which demand some measure of planning, regulation and control if they are to be fulfilled.

27. The modern economic system bears little resemblance to the *laissez faire* form of capitalism of a century ago. Before the present war it was a system subject to a considerable amount of control exercised in many cases by private individuals and organizations and not infrequently in a manner in which public responsibility was not clearly defined or accepted. Technical development and the greater

* From Trades Union Congress: *Interim Report on Post-War Reconstruction*, 1944, paras. 26–36. Reprinted by permission of the authors.

complexity of economic relationships have made higher forms of business organization advantageous and, indeed, inevitable, but the concentration of economic power in private hands, which so far has been a consequence of this development, brings with it dangers of which the whole community is now acutely aware. Although the supporters of private enterprise still frequently plead their cases in the name of freedom, it is now abundantly clear that the liberty of the individual is most endangered by a system of unrestrained private enterprise.

28. Equally fallacious is the claim that only free private enterprise can provide a rising level of industrial efficiency. On the contrary the development of scientific research and productive technique and, even more, their full utilization to meet the needs of the people, have been continually hampered on the one hand by lack of industrial co-ordination and organization, and, on the other hand, by the restrictive policies of private monopolies. One of the strongest arguments for the transfer to public ownership of key industries and for the introduction of those other forms of public control which we propose is that these changes are essential for efficient industrial organization and to ensure that industrial efficiency serves its proper purpose of improving the standard of life of the community. A controlled economic system is a modern necessity in advanced industrial communities. The choice before us is not between control or no control, but, in principle, between control by public authority responsible to the community, or control by private groups and persons owning a final responsibility to themselves alone and, in detail, between degrees of control and types of control.

THE TRANSITION TO PUBLIC OWNERSHIP

29. The attitude of the Trades Union Congress towards the Public Control and Regulation of Industry and Trade was broadly defined in the report issued under that title submitted to Congress in 1932. The report opened by calling attention to the fact that:

> Labour policy . . . is tending to emphasize the transitional forms of public control and the immediate steps to be taken rather than the more ideal programme of complete socialization with the entire elimination of private enterprise. As a practical policy this would appear to be inevitable, given present conditions and the existing psychology of the British people. We may therefore expect that the change from undiluted private enterprise in many industries and services will be by way of general governmental regulation leading to operation by public corporations.

This conception of a gradual transition of the economic system

involves more than a change in the organization of separate industries. There are certain minimum objectives of Trade Unionism
which coincide with the general public interest and whose fulfilment
ought not to wait upon the complete realization of any long-term
policy. The abolition of unemployment, the provision of an adequate
number of good houses, reduced hours of labour, better working
conditions and progressive improvements in the standard of living
generally, for example, are objectives which must be achieved in the
post-war world even if private ownership continues in a substantial
section of the economic system. The achievement of such objectives,
moreover, prepares the ground for further developments in the scope
and form of public ownership; and all forms of public control and
regulation can be examined according to the contribution which they
can make to that development.

30. The 1932 Report defined three categories into which industries
and services fell:

(*a*) Those immediately ripe for socialization.

(*b*) Those less important or less unified but needing some measure
of regulation in the public interest.

(*c*) Those of minor importance which can be left for the time being
under completely private enterprise.

31. The report did not consider it possible to say 'with any exact-
ness or finality' into which of those categories the various industries
and services fell but that amongst the criteria of fitness of an industry
or service for socialization or public control were:

(*a*) The importance of the industry to the life and safety of the
community.

(*b*) The existence of monopoly or unification in an industry serving
a wide demand.

(*c*) The importance of an industry as a source of demand for new
investment.

The Priority of Certain Industries

32. There are some industries which are of vital importance to the
life and well-being of the community in that all other industries
depend to a greater or less extent upon the goods or services they
supply. It is to these industries that the first criteria of the 1932 report
particularly applies. They are notably two groups of industries
namely:

(*a*) Fuel and power (including coal, gas and electricity); and

(*b*) Transport (including railways, canals, road transport, coastwise shipping, and internal airways).

33. The public ownership of these industries is not only desirable

B

for their own development but as an essential condition for any effective economic planning because of the influence which they exert on the location and efficient working of many major industries. Furthermore, their internal co-ordination is equally essential for the effective and orderly development of their constituent parts which are uniquely related to each other. This latter point has been fully recognized during the war by the setting up of the Ministry of Fuel and Power and the Ministry of War Transport.

34. In both of these groups of industries there is one industry—coalmining in the case of fuel and power and the railways in the case of transport—on which public opinion is most strongly prepared for their transfer to public ownership. We think that there are unchallengeable economic reasons for the complete co-ordination of both of these groups of industries though it may well increase political opposition and the legislative difficulties to link them together and insist upon their complete transference to public ownership under one Act of Parliament. We would emphasize, therefore, that in the matter of priorities the public ownership of the coal-mines and the railways is a matter of immediate urgency, which should on no account be delayed. If it should prove not possible to nationalize the other sections of the two industries immediately, it would at least be imperative to secure the co-ordination of fuel and power as a whole and transport as a whole by bringing those other sections under public control at the same time as coalmining and rail transport are nationalized.

We propose to make each of these groups of industries the subject of a special detailed report.

35. Next in urgency and importance for public ownership is the iron and steel industry which is already highly integrated under private ownership. For the nationalization of this industry the TUC has already published a detailed programme.

36. The cotton industry is of considerable importance, especially in relation to exports of which Great Britain will, after the war, stand in very great need. The industry is also recognized to be in need of unification and more centralized control. Ultimately it must be brought under public ownership but it is doubtful if that could or should be done immediately. In the meantime it is obviously an industry which should immediately be brought under a form of public control, possibly in association with rayon, which would prepare the way for complete public ownership. Our subsequent proposal for the formation of Industrial Boards has particular application to this industry.

3. BRITISH CONSERVATIVES AND STATE
OWNERSHIP*

In theory, the British Conservative Party opposes nationalization as a principle, as a philosophy, as a policy and as a programme. Conversely, the British Labour Party has consistently supported nationalization in all four contexts, although the zeal of some of its members has dimmed in recent months. It was the nationalization party throughout its long periods in opposition, notably, and with increasing force, between 1931 and 1939, and more recently, during its six and a half years in power. Nationalization in one form or another is the essential ingredient, the fundamental technique, in the establishment of state ownership and in the fulfilment of the hallowed Socialist aspiration—public control of the means of production, distribution and exchange. However, many of the devices and precedents for Socialist action in Great Britain in 1945–51 were created by the Conservative and Conservative-dominated governments of the inter-war years, more particularly after the reversion to protection through the Import Duties Act of February 1932 and the Ottawa Agreements Act of November 1932. The restraints and restrictions of a new mercantilism were no small help to the collectivist propaganda of the inter-war period—the era of the retreat from liberty.

A representative example of such thinking was Mr Harold Macmillan, now Prime Minister, a man of integrity and high intellectual calibre, who wrote in his book, *The Middle Way*, published in 1938, 'The Socialist remedy should . . . be accepted . . . where it is obvious that its social usefulness or where the general welfare of the economy requires that certain basic industries need now to be conducted in the light of broader social considerations that the profit motive provides'. Eleven years later, at Gainsborough, on June 18, 1949, Mr Macmillan opined, 'Socialist enterprises—nationalized industries and utilities—lose money. Profits turn into losses. Outputs fall. Costs increase.' And in 1933, Professor Harold Laski, a future Chairman of the Labour Party National Executive, warned the nation in his work on *Democracy in Crisis* that 'a Labour Government would build upon the amplitude of the National Government's precedent!' So, indeed, it did. That, too, was the age in which collectivist writers vied in devising means whereby their own favoured variants of state ownership could be achieved constitutionally. Sir Stafford Cripps asked: 'Can Socialism come by constitutional means?' He replied with an

* From Deryck Abel: 'British Conservatives and State Ownership', *Journal of Politics*, Vol. 19, 1957, pp. 227–39. Reprinted by permission of the author and the editors of the *Journal of Politics* and the *Quarterly Review*.

emphatic 'Yes'. How, if policy dictated such a course, to curtail the
liberty of the subject, how to supersede the rule of law by bureaucratic ordinance, how to confer upon the Executive—the Government of the day—powers more properly belonging to legislature or
courts, how to enable the Executive to arrogate to itself a monopoly
of such powers—these were the lessons. Such were the lessons
involved, too, in promulgating a coherent programme of socialization.

Mr Attlee, Mr Morrison and their colleagues were ready learners.
Returned to power in 1945, the Socialist Government carried through
a series of nationalization measures in nine Acts of Parliament within
four and a half years:

		Royal Assent	*Vesting Date*
1.	Bank of England	Feb. 14, 1946	March 1, 1946
2.	Civil Aviation	Aug. 1, 1946	Aug. 1, 1946
3.	Coal	July 12, 1946	Jan. 1, 1947
4.	Cable and Wireless (entrusted to Post Office)	Nov. 6, 1946	Jan. 1, 1947
5.	Transport	Aug. 6, 1947	Jan. 1, 1948
6.	Land Development Rights (Town & County Planning Act)	Aug. 6, 1947	July 1, 1948
7.	Electricity	Aug. 13, 1947	Apr. 1, 1948
8.	Gas	July 30, 1948	May 1, 1949
9.	Iron and Steel	Nov. 24, 1949	Feb. 15, 1951

The route had long ago been mapped. The rapid tempo of Britain's
progress towards 'rationalization' and the chain of authoritative
wartime and pre-war Reports, the Sankey Commission Minority
Report on coal mining, the Royal Commission on Transport, the
McGowan and Heyworth Reports on electricity and gas—had prepared a mental and psychological climate kindly to Socialists and
socialism. The railways and the mines had already been entrusted to
the State for the duration of two world wars. Moreover, the minority
Labour Government's Coal Mines Act of 1930 had meanwhile provided (despite clauses on the buying and selling of quotas) that price
and output regulation should maintain the existing pattern of production. 'This is the endowment and entrenchment of inefficiency,'
Sir Herbert (now Viscount) Samuel had said on the Second Reading;
'This is the irrationalization of the coal mines.' It could be argued,
and was argued, in the case of mines and railways, that the purport of
post-1945 legislation was only to accord legal validity to (more or
less) accomplished facts.

Let us now consider, in detail, four or five examples of post-war
state ownership in practice and the representative Conservative
approach to each specific issue—the Bank of England, Civil Aviation,

Coal, Transport, and Iron and Steel. The first measure, the Bank of England Act, caused, curiously enough, the least acute controversy. Its main provisions can be succinctly stated as follows. First, the entire stock of the Bank of England, hitherto possessed by some 17,000 private stockholders, of whom 10,000 owned less than £500 each, was taken over by the Treasury, with powers, after consultation with the Governor, to give directions to the Bank. Secondly, the Court of Governors was reduced from a Deputy-Governor and twenty-four Directors to a Deputy-Governor and sixteen Directors, all of whom were appointed by the Crown—that is, in practice, by the Chancellor of the Exchequer. Opposition to the Bill was ineffective, because a great many Conservatives, and even some Liberals, took the view that, as Mr Hugh Dalton put it, it would bring the law 'into accord with the facts of the situation as they have developed'.[1] Lord Pethick-Lawrence averred: 'The Bank of England is already very largely a department of the Treasury, and its nationalization will not make a pennyworth of difference to the bulk of the people in this country.'[2] It must be confessed, as a matter of historical objectivity, that what opposition emerged to the Bank of England nationalization was feeble and fitful. 'A Conservative Government,' said the Party's official *Industrial Charter*, 'will not repeal the whole of the Bank of England Act, but will examine the powers of the Bank to give directives to the commercial banks.'

Socialists and Conservatives could argue that civil aviation was a very different kettle of fish—all the more so because the Socialist Government's Civil Aviation Act, 1946, heralded by the White Paper of December 1945,[3] embellished the wartime Conservative-dominated Coalition Government's White Paper, 'British Air Transport'.[4] The latter was, very substantially, a product of Conservative wartime thinking. The Civil Aviation Act brought all regular air transport services under national ownership and control, eliminated competition, provided Government finance for the three corporations, and authorized the Minister to tell the corporations what aircraft to use—and where. A consolidating measure, amalgamating the British Overseas Airways Corporation and the British South American Airways Corporation, was carried by the Attlee Ministry against Conservative opposition in 1949. The Act of 1946 had empowered the Minister to reimburse the national corporations for losses at the rate of £10 million per year for 1946–47 and 1947–48

[1] *Parliamentary Debates* (Hansard), Fifth Series, Vol. 413 (1945), p. 495.
[2] Edinburgh *Evening Dispatch*, June 26, 1945.
[3] 'British Air Services', House of Commons Sessional Papers, Cmd 6712, Vol. 15 (1945–46).
[4] House of Commons Sessional Papers, Cmd 6605, Vol. 7 (1945).

and £8 million per year for 1948–49, and each subsequent year till 1956—a total maximum liability of £84 million over ten years. Speaking in the House of Commons on July 6, 1950, Mr A. T. Lennox-Boyd (Conservative, Mid-Bedfordshire), presented the official Conservative attitude to this facet of the state ownership programme:

> It might interest the House to hear this brief comparison of nation-alized British European Airways' operating costs with what would be the operating costs of charter companies using similar aircraft on the same routes. In 1949 . . . we are told that BEA flew 15½ million miles and that its revenue was £6,400,000. This shows that the revenue per aircraft mile was 8s 3d. The corporation flew Vikings, Dakotas and Rapides. All three types of aircraft may be hired from the charter industry for less than 8s 3d per mile, so it is safe to say that if the whole business had been contracted out there would have been a profit. We have not had the accounts for this year, but we have them for last year, and with the same aircraft and with the same mileage, private operators claim that they would have made a profit of £472,000—instead of a loss of £2½ million. Therefore, the Exchequer would have had £3 million more, quite apart from the ordinary taxes for the private operators' profits. I do not claim that a single private operator could have achieved that successful result, but a series of small manageable units of some 15 to 25 aircraft could achieve results of that kind. The taxpayers of Great Britain, sorely tried now, and to be still more sorely tried by the in-escapable obligations of the British Empire throughout the world, cannot afford to reject any chance of economy, coupled, as it would be, with highly efficient management.

Marked improvements in the financial and administrative structure have been achieved during the past four years, but the principles of 1946 remain strong in civil aviation. 'It would be Conservative policy,' proclaimed *The Right Road for Britain*, 'to give the fullest encouragement to the orderly expansion of air transport by private enterprise for every class of load (passenger, mail or freight), both by regular scheduled services and by individual charter. It is only in this way that British mercantile aviation can match the achieve-ments of our Merchant Navy . . . We shall . . . review the structure of the Corporations and of the Ministry itself, so as to eliminate un-necessary functions and restore as wide a measure of private enter-prise as possible.'

Likewise, on the vexed question of state ownership of coal, the same authorized programme adumbrated the Conservative philo-sophy in terms no less robust. Push back the area of monopoly to its narrowest limits, it demanded; decentralize the hierarchical structure of the central national authority, the National Coal Board; stimulate local enthusiasm by conferring real responsibility upon individual pit management; abolish the old divisional boards; establish new area boards; restrict the functions of the National Coal Board to such matters as national wage negotiations, co-ordinating selling prices, raising capital, and performing common services like research. In other words, realign the Socialist mosaic of 1946. It is reasonable to assume that, confronted with the atmosphere of the times, Conservatives, had they been in power immediately after the war, would have reinforced, or, at least, maintained the wartime Coal Control of the Ministry of Fuel and Power with its twelve-section regional structure. The argument would have been that, however bleak the economic and financial case for nationalization, there was a sociological case. The miners had long ago persuaded themselves of its merits. The Socialist structure had turned the eight coal-producing regions into eight divisions, each with a divisional board appointed by the National Coal Board, with each division broken into forty-nine areas, each with an average of twenty collieries. Such was the pilot plant for socialization in practice. The National Coal Board members were specialists, each assuming responsibility for the functions of a department, for example, production, finance, marketing, or relations with labour. In May 1948, Sir Charles Reid, a mining engineer and production director of the highest distinction, who had represented production on the National Coal Board in London since 1946, resigned from the Board, explaining that he had no faith in the structure. Eight more important resignations followed in the same year.

The Technical Advisory Committee on Coal Mining, presided over by Sir Charles Reid, had, in March 1945, already strongly urged decentralization in a passage which commanded Conservative support: 'This is not an industry which can be conducted on any stereotyped plan. It is our conviction that whatever degree of integration is decided upon, and the greater the degree the more important this becomes, scope must be provided within each unit for the fullest opportunity for and encouragement of individual initiative. Without this, the full benefits of planned production and technical improvement cannot be secured.'[1] On another and all-important aspect, namely, the provision in the Coal Nationalization Act for consumer representation, *Change Is Our Ally*, a new, lively, stimulating and provocative booklet by ten Conservative MPs of the 'One Nation' group, rightly commented: 'It is significant that, in the first six years of its operation, the Domestic Coal Consumers' Council received only 300 letters. That is partly because the work—indeed the very existence—of these Councils is inadequately publicized, but

[1] 'Coal Mining', House of Commons Sessional Papers, Cmd 6610, Vol. 4 (1945).

more because there is a general feeling that they are impotent to protect the interests of consumers.' That is, in itself, a powerful indictment which has so far attracted too little political attention, and no political action.

The two nationalized enterprises which the Conservative Government has decentralized since the general election of 1951 furnish the fairest and most illuminating examples of the Conservative approach to state ownership. First, in transport, the Railways Act (1921) was Britain's earliest essay in 'rationalization'. During the next few years, the struggle between this industry and free and ever-expanding road transport accentuated, and accelerated, propaganda for nationalization. Mr Herbert Morrison, Minister of Transport in the Labour Government of 1929–31, willingly responded by fathering the Road Transport Act of 1930, in which Part IV forbade the provision of passenger road transport except by holders of road service licences, which the traffic commissioners could refuse, or grant, subject to certain detailed conditions. The essential feature was the grant of semi-monopolies or protection against competition in order to achieve 'co-ordination of all forms of passenger transport'. The London Passenger Transport Act, initiated by the Labour Government in the spring of 1931, which became law in 1933 under the Conservative-dominated National Government, consolidated and strengthened earlier measures of voluntary amalgamation already effected between the London General Omnibus Company and the underground group. It now gave legislative sanction to a 100 per cent monopoly. In the same year (1933), the Conservative-dominated National Government, in its Road and Rail Traffic Act, extended to road haulage the principle of licensed semi-monopoly, which road passenger traffic had 'enjoyed' since the 1930 Act. Men and women already well set up in the road haulage business were encouraged to oppose new applicants for licences on the ground that 'suitable transport facilities . . . are, or if the application were granted, would be, in excess of requirements'. The project attracted the distinguished patronage of such Conservative leaders as Mr Oliver Stanley, who expatiated upon the theme that 'unless you have some system where people who provide transport do take the rough with the smooth, you will have everyone taking the smooth and no one prepared to take the rough'. The next major event was the 1947 Act. The Transport Act of 1947, passed by the post-war Labour Government, presented a solution diametrically opposed to the conclusions of the Road Haulage Report presented to Parliament in 1944 by the three-party Select Committee on National Expenditure.[1] That Report had

---

[1] 'Rail and Road Transport', Part II; House of Commons Sessional Papers, No. 58, Vol. 2 (1944).

been uncompromisingly adverse to the wartime working of Government haulage control. The framework of the new Transport Act was delineated in more meticulous detail than that of the Coal Nationalization Act of the previous year. It created the British Transport Commission, with a chairman and four to eight members to be appointed by the Minister. The Chairman and at least four other members were required to give full-time service. It further created five 'public authorities known as Executives to assist the Commission in the discharge of their functions': Railway, Docks and Inland Waterways, Road Transport, London Transport and Hotels. The Railway Executive was conceived as a triple-tiered organization, divided into regions corresponding to the old-time railway companies. Such, then, was the new structure for state ownership of transport. It is worth recalling, in passing, that as many as 1,137,000 members of the public had owned the 'big four' railway companies, and that, of the total railway stocks of £1,109,000, one-third represented holdings not exceeding £200.

The Right Road for Britain, the most important Conservative Central Office policy pamphlet of the post-war years, forthwith promised the public and the road haulers that 'A Conservative Government will proceed to sell back to free enterprise those sections of the road haulage industry which have been nationalized. Operators will have to obtain "A" or "B" licences under the Road and Rail Traffic Act, 1933. But new entrants will have to prove that business is available and that it cannot be as cheaply and effectively handled by existing carriers of goods whether by road or rail. The limitation of distance on private road hauliers will be progressively eliminated. The present freedom of "C" licences will remain untouched.' Concerning passenger road transport, it likewise added, 'A Conservative Government will stop any further plans for nationalizing omnibus and tram undertakings and wherever possible will return those already nationalized at the time of the General Election to their former owners, whether local authorities or private enterprise.' And, yet again, discussing the railways, it advanced the view that ' "British Railways" should be reorganized into an appropriate number of regional railway systems, each with its own pride of identity, and co-ordinated as to broad policy alone by a central body. The present top-heaviness due to excessive central staff should be corrected, and each railway system should be administered by its own Board of Direction, which should include a strong part-time element of persons with varied practical experience of serving public needs.'

In May 1953, the new Conservative administration's Transport Bill became the law of the land. It incorporated the fundamental principle that the alternative forms of transport should be 'co-ordi-

nated' by consumers' choice and that its appropriate charges should
be related to the cost of the selective service. That was almost revolutionary in our time. The road haulage undertaking of the British
Transport Commission was to be sold to private enterprise. As
railway operator, the Commission could, however, 'provide, continue or develop any services or facilities for the carriage of goods by
road otherwise than as a part of the operations of the existing road
haulage'. The Minister was further 'empowered' to direct the Commission to abandon any *controlling* interest in an omnibus company
which it might have acquired since inception. It could retain minority
shareholdings. The Commission must henceforth secure Transport
Tribunal confirmation of *maximum* charges. Power was also entrusted to the Tribunal to intervene if the Commission charges 'place
coastal carriers at an undue or unfair disadvantage in the competition
or are inadequate having regard to the cost of affording the service',
thereby injuring 'the interest of coastwise shipping' to the detriment
of 'the national interest'.

The main implications of the new Act concern, however, the return
to competition. Three illustrations may be cited. First, transport units
for disposal were not to exceed fifty vehicles without ministerial
approval, and, in assembling them, the Commission was 'to have
regard to the desirability of securing that persons desirous of entering
or re-entering the road haulage industry have a reasonable opportunity of doing so notwithstanding that their resources permit them
to do so only if their operations are on a small scale'. Secondly, the
Act made the granting of licences under the 1933 Act a little easier.
Henceforth, instead of an applicant having to prove that new service
was needed, an objector would have to prove that it was not needed,
and consumer interests were given specific priority over 'provider'
interests in such assessments. Thirdly, with the decentralization of
the Railway Executive into its component parts, the railways were
emancipated from the legal restrictions imposed upon them in the old
monopoly days and were duly accorded legal freedom to relate
charges to costs. Fourthly, road and rail transport were to be 'co-
ordinated' through the natural interplay of economic forces—
perhaps, in the mid-twentieth century, an unusually radical answer.

In this context, a constructive criticism from the ten Conservative
MPs of the 'One Nation' group in their admirably documented
manifesto, *Change is Our Ally*, merits full quotation:

> The Transport Act, 1953, did not exhaust the application of the
> principle which it enshrines. One of the avowed purposes of the Road
> Traffic Act, 1930, and the Road and Rail Traffic Act, 1933, was to
> protect a railway system, still handicapped commercially, against un-
> limited competition from road transport. Now that the commercial

handicaps have been removed and co-ordination entrusted to the user's choice, the limitations of the 1930 and 1933 Acts, so far as they are not justified on any other grounds—for example, safety—have lost their basis. The Acts need a critical overhaul.

The same applies to London Transport Executive. This is the London Passenger Transport Board of old, swallowed whole by the Act of 1947 and swallowed again by that of 1953. Why losses incurred by London's railways should be made good by those who use its 'buses, or *vice versa*—has never yet been explained. *Prima facie*, the continued existence in London of a monopoly embracing alternative forms of transport is inconsistent with legislation designed to eliminate or prevent this in the provinces.

This is, indeed, well said. This comment almost (but not quite) crystallizes the traditional Liberal view, and it cannot be denied that the Transport Act of 1953 represents a huge advance in the forward road to economic freedom.

Iron and steel denationalization exemplifies a similar trend in mid-twentieth-century Conservative economic thinking. The fiscal revolution of 1932, the overthrow of free trade and the revival of the pre-1846 policy of protection, stimulated, in iron and steel, as in transport, a new phase of government intervention in industrial organization. Way back in 1932, 'rationalization' was the order of the day. Under the Import Duties Act, the Import Duties Advisory Committee recommended $33\frac{1}{3}$ per cent duties on iron and steel imports, contingent, of course, upon adequate 'reorganization'. In June 1932, despite opposition from both the Liberal and Socialist parties, these duties were forthwith enacted. The new economic alliance between the Import Duties Advisory Committee and the British Iron and Steel Federation (1934) fixed prices, controlled competition and development, subsidized high-cost producers, administered the cartel, and secured, by a bout of tariff-skirmishing and a heavy temporary increase in duties, the concurrence of the continental cartel that iron and steel imports from cartel members should be pegged at approximately half a million tons a year. In the amusing, but amazingly naïve words of the Conservative Central Office *Campaign Guide* of 1950, 'It is important to note that the majority of criticisms relate to things which happened a long time ago, even twenty or thirty years ago. The first is that the introduction of tariffs in 1932 and the formation of the British Iron and Steel Federation in 1934 produced a radical change in the industry. The majority of Socialist arguments, therefore, clearly have no more relevance to the problems of the industry than what may have happened after the Napoleonic Wars.' The 'One Nation' group of Conservative MPs, be it said to its credit, has taken a different, and infinitely less complacent, view. The measures of 1932 and 1934 set the stage for the Socialist offensive of 1949.

The Iron and Steel Nationalization Act of 1949 provided that the securities of ninety-six firms either working 50,000 tons or more of iron ore, or producing 20,000 tons or more of pig-iron, or 20,000 tons or more of ingot steel or hot rolled steel per annum, should be transferred, together with their subsidiaries, whether steel-producing or not, to a new corporation, comprising a chairman and between six and ten members appointed by the Minister of Supply. The Iron and Steel Corporation thus enjoyed the powers of a holding company over its nationalized subsidiaries. It could found, or acquire an interest in, further subsidiaries. Private enterprise company names were very sensibly retained—partly no doubt because of the gains accruing to the export drive.

Iron and steel denationalization proved a more complex and intricate 'unscrambling' operation for the incoming Conservative Government than had transport denationalization. First, there is, for all practical purposes, hardly any competition with iron and steel from outside the industry. This comment applies not only to the heavy sections, but indeed to the majority of iron and steel manufactures. Secondly, whereas exceedingly efficient road haulage businesses are frequently quite tiny, the vast integrated plants, with net assets ranging from £21 million to £36 million, dominate the texture of iron and steel organization. Thirdly, overseas competition is limited by the extraordinarily high iron and steel prices prevalent outside the United Kingdom, although, more recently, the prices quoted by the European Iron and Steel Community are appreciably below current British prices.

The Churchill Government's Iron and Steel Act of 1953 is not nearly as revolutionary or as libertarian in tone as its Transport Act. True, the main purport was to revive the profit motive as the tonic to efficiency and to restore to private ownership the sections nationalized, or threatened with nationalization, by the Attlee Government. But it contented itself with retaining much of the Socialist administrative machinery and with forming an independent Iron and Steel Board, charged with the primary task of fixing maximum prices. To the double appeal that internal domestic restrictions must be eschewed and that the highest costs must not determine the Board's price-fixing policy, Conservatives reply, first, that 'competitive conditions' are prescribed in the very terms of the Act, and, secondly, that, in any case, there is always ultimate recourse to the Monopolies and Restrictive Practices (Enquiry and Control) Act, 1948—a fair enough argument, if limited in scope. The group of Conservative MPs, to which we have referred, is disposed both to question and to deplore some of the powers of the new Board. 'The further powers are by no means so easy to justify,' they comment in *Change is Our Ally*. 'For example, the Iron and Steel Board, informed by the Minister of general economic or other national considerations, is enjoined to keep the productive capacity of the industry under review; to consult with the industry to secure any development required for "the efficient, economic and adequate supply of iron and steel products"; and to disapprove any major development schemes which would "seriously prejudice the efficient and economic development of production facilities". The Government are given a residual power themselves to promote any development, required in the national interest, which the industry itself is not prepared to take on.' The old-time strategic argument, coupled with the 'possible fluctuations in the economy' argument, are the themes most commonly invoked to justify these excessive powers. Moreover, the Board's 'general duty' to supervise the supply of raw materials to the industry formed a pretext for bringing beneath its aegis the foundries —a large number of iron and steel users, who had not hitherto been nationalized, but who consumed a quarter of the industry's materials. This, too, is a very questionable procedure and as such has been challenged by Mr Angus Maude, Conservative MP for Ealing South, Mr Enoch Powell, Conservative MP for Wolverhampton South-West, and their colleagues. On balance, this denationalization measure represents a limited advance towards economic freedom—an advance considerably less substantial than that accomplished by the Transport Act.

Thus the modern British Conservative approach towards state ownership is strictly empirical. It is conditioned by the times and by the political pulse of the people. As befits Conservative thinking, it rejects doctrine and dogma. It interprets state ownership, in given circumstances, as only one of several solutions—if, indeed it is proven a solution. Conservatives and Liberals forthwith announced their resolute opposition to new Labour Party proposals for the 'mutualization' of life insurance and the nationalization of certain branches of the chemical industry, sugar-refining, the water supply and the wholesale meat trade. In 1950, 1951 and 1955, the British electorate called a halt to nationalization and there is no reason yet to believe that it wants further instalments. In the closing days of the Orléans Monarchy, Lamartine said that France was bored. After the ever-accelerating tempo of the nationalization measures of 1946–49, Britain likewise was tired of this fifty-year-old refrain, as most 1951 and 1955 general election parliamentary candidates will testify. The Socialists soon recognized the prevailing mood of the nation and transformed their agitation into a campaign for encouraging and developing competition between state enterprise and private enterprise. The formula befitted the climate.

4. THE COAL INDUSTRY*

749. . . . we have come to the conclusion that it is not enough simply to recommend technical changes which we believe to be fully practicable, when it is evident to us, as mining engineers, that they cannot be satisfactorily carried through by the Industry organized as it is today.

750. It is vital that these technical changes should be carried through if the cost of production is to be so reduced as to enable the coal industry to meet all the needs of the country, and especially of the export trades. It follows that every practicable economy in costs must be sought, and that the volume of new investment should not be unnecessarily inflated. In addition, all this must be done in a manner compatible with careful regard to the national coal resources.

751. Very great significance must, therefore, be attached to the following basic facts of the situation:

752. There are mines on the point of exhausting their reserves; mines which should be closed down altogether and their reserves worked from adjoining collieries; mines where the remaining reserves can, under no scheme of reconstruction, be worked profitably; mines between which valuable coal has been sterilized to form barriers; and mines which, for a period of their reconstruction, will have to be completely closed down.

753. There are undertakings which have a lease of coal that could be worked to better advantage by another undertaking; and undertakings whose mines are widely spread through a district, and even among several districts.

754. There are new sinkings required where the reserves which should be worked from them are leased to two or more undertakings; and new sinkings where, by reason of the depth to be reached, so long a view has to be taken and such heavy interest payments incurred, that the cost of the shafts, plant and development is likely to be beyond the resources of the undertaking owning the leasehold.

755. There are surface plants to be erected which should serve a number of mines, which may be under different ownership.

756. There are districts where the reconstruction of certain mines

* From *Report of the Technical Advisory Committee on Coal Mining*, 1945, Cmd 6610, paras. 749–60.

would enable the output required to be maintained, leaving for the time being at least, no place for the remaining mines in these districts.

757. There are many other spheres also, including systematic research into methods of work, and a wide range of problems from mine drainage to the training of the personnel of the Industry, in which combined action upon a broad basis presents the only satisfactory solution.

758. Unfortunately, there is a serious dearth of mining engineers who possess the knowledge and experience necessary to undertake the far-reaching schemes of reorganization which are essential. The services of those who are so qualified will consequently be required for the wider benefit of the Industry.

759. In these circumstances, it is evident to us that it is not possible to provide for the soundest and most efficient development and working of an area unless the conflicting interests of the individual colliery companies working the area are merged together into one compact and unified command of manageable size, with full responsibility, financially and otherwise, for the development of the area. We are not in a position to suggest what size of unit would provide the best foundation upon which to reconstruct the Industry. Indeed, there would necessarily be variations in the optimum size according to local conditions. It is essential, however, the geological, geographical and other technical considerations should be the determining factors.

760. Moreover, if a comprehensive scheme of reorganization along the lines we have recommended is to be carried through, we consider that an Authority must be established which would have the duty of ensuring that the Industry is merged into units of such sizes as would provide the maximum advantages of planned production, of stimulating the preparation and execution of the broad plans of reorganization made by these units, and of conserving the coal resources of the country. The existence of such an Authority, endowed by Parliament with really effective powers for these purposes, is, we are satisfied, a cardinal necessity.

5. THE GAS INDUSTRY*

231. The main objects which grouping into larger units can be expected to promote are:

(1) Some further reduction of production costs—

* From *Report of the Committee of Enquiry into the Gas Industry*, 1945, Cmd 6699, paras. 231–8, 245 and 247.

(*a*) through higher carbonizing efficiency;

(*b*) through better labour utilization and reduction in maintenance costs; and

(*c*) through improvement in load factor.

The overall scope for improvement in these directions is
relatively limited and will arise through reduction in number of
production units and a general raising of technical efficiency in
undertakings which are at present too small to provide
adequate scientific control.

(2) Improvement in labour conditions.

One aspect of this arises in small units in which the necessary
mechanization to reduce the amount of manual physical effort
cannot be justified on cost considerations alone, or which do
not possess the necessary capital resources.

(3) Further economy in capital charges.

This can reasonably be expected to flow from the better use
of production and distribution plant made possible by treating
large areas as one. One aspect of this general question is
already demanding attention, viz., where a highly developed
but relatively restricted urban area is losing population through
slum clearance, thus bringing about redundant production
capacity.

(4) More intensive study of distribution problems.

Large groupings would permit a higher level of technical
skill, facilitating the planning of development on the best
possible long term projections of future demand.

(5) Further concentration on sales policy—

(*a*) to ensure provision of improved appliances on attractive
terms;

(*b*) to ensure intensive development of new uses, both domestic
and industrial, involving further study of and bold experimentation with tariffs; and

(*c*) the raising of the general level of consumer service to the
standard of the most progressive undertakings.

(6) Greater concentration of development of 'fringe' and rural
areas.

(7) Further extension of coke grading and selling effort.

(8) Expansion of research and its application.

232. It is not possible to quantify the results likely to be achieved
under any one of these headings, or, indeed, to express an opinion as
to their overall potentialities. The improvement will certainly not be
dramatic, and achievement will necessarily be a matter of some years.
The mere formation of larger groupings will not of itself bring about
the improvement; it can only provide the opportunity.

233. The next consideration is how larger units are to be brought into being. No voluntary process is likely to be sufficiently speedy to satisfy present and future requirements. The reason for this is that the difference in structure between the statutory companies and the municipal undertakings is a basic one, and it is unrealistic to expect such a change of climate as will make possible fusion between them in any form which is likely to be effective.

234. It is possible to envisage machinery which would bring about further fusions between statutory companies, but this would involve some form of arbitration to overcome the differing opinions as to price which always exist between a willing seller and a willing buyer. It is also possible to envisage further progress through the instrument of the Holding Company in bringing about groupings, but, again, without arbitration it is difficult to resist the thought that the bargaining power is unduly weighted in favour of the unit which it is desired to absorb, and, therefore, that resultant economies would be undesirably discounted by excessive capital charges.

235. In the municipal field the instrument of the Joint Board provides an obvious line of approach, but history provides little ground for optimism. Furthermore, the larger the grouping brought about by this method, the more complex would its control structure become, with consequent handicap to bold policy formation.

236. But, in fact, it is not necessary to decide whether or not the provision of additional machinery would, or would not, bring about acceleration of integration within the different forms of structure. A glance at the map of the structure of the Industry as it is today will make it clear that no degree of success along this line of approach could produce a pattern of grouping even approximating to the ideal.

237. Predetermination of boundaries is the only approach which will produce a workable pattern. Although the discussions within the Industry itself did not actually lead to this recommendation, it is consistent with the main content of their evidence.

238. The main considerations which, in our view, should determine the form of the new and larger units which are required, are the following:

(1) The units should be able to attract personnel at least the equal in imagination, initiative, judgment and energy of those of other fuel industries;

(2) they should provide conditions conducive to continuing efficiency in management;

(3) they should be able to compete freely with other fuel industries; and

(4) they should have a capital structure which does not handicap

them competitively and should be able to obtain new capital on attractive terms.

245. Regional Boards should be set up by Act of Parliament covering the whole of England, Scotland and Wales. Each Board should acquire all the existing undertakings—municipal, joint board, statutory company and non-statutory company—in its area, and should have the responsibility of initiating any new development which is found to be commercially desirable in areas within its regional boundary which are not at present included within the boundaries of any existing undertaking.

247. The Boards should have the responsibility of promoting on progressive commercial principles the maximum development of the Gas Industry within their Regions. Their policy should be directed towards serving the interests of the Regions as a whole, rather than any particular local or sectional interests. Normal cost and commercial considerations should determine price in different districts of the Regions and for different uses.

6. THE ELECTRICITY INDUSTRY*

84. In all the circumstances and having regard to the evidence placed before us there can, in our opinion, be no question that an improvement in the present organization can and must be effected.

85. In practically every case the Associations and witnesses who have appeared before us have stated that the present organization is unsatisfactory and calls for improvement. As might be expected, however, there is considerable divergence of opinion as to the nature and extent of the action which ought to be taken.

86. For example, it was suggested that the supply of electricity should be placed on a national basis comparable to the Post Office organization, by the establishment of one National Electricity Board to which would be transferred all authorized electricity undertakings, the grid system, railway and traction generating stations and certain non-statutory undertakings; and that the new Board should also take the place of the Electricity Commissioners and the Central Electricity Board and become responsible for the direction and for securing the efficient management of the nationally-owned undertaking.

87. It was also suggested that all that was necessary was the elimination of what were described as 'weak spots'.

* From Ministry of Transport: *Report of the Committee on Electricity Distribution*, May 1936, paras. 84–93, 96–133 and 137–40. Reprinted by permission of the Controller of H.M. Stationery Office.

88. As a result of the evidence we have taken, it appears to us that, broadly speaking, any scheme for the improvement of distribution must, in principle, involve the adoption of one or other of the following alternatives:

(1) Immediate and complete reorganization on a regional basis under public control, by the setting up of regional boards which would buy out all the existing undertakings;

(2) The retention and utilization, where possible, of the larger and more efficient of the existing undertakings (both public authorities and companies) and the absorption by such undertakings of the smaller and less efficient undertakings.

89. We have come to the conclusion that a scheme of complete reorganization which would involve the vesting of all electricity undertakings in a number of regional boards must result in a serious and unnecessary dislocation of the supply industry.

90. Moreover, as fair compensation would have to be paid for the acquired undertakings, there must necessarily be great uncertainty as to the actual amount which would be payable, even if Parliament were to lay down certain broad principles. It must be borne in mind that in addition to Distribution Companies whose terms of purchase at the end of their franchise are already defined, it would be necessary to deal with Power Companies with rights in perpetuity for which no defined basis of purchase exists at the present time, and with Local Authorities both large and small. Whether such amount might not impose an undue burden on the new authorities by way of capital charges, which would be detrimental to existing consumers and to future development, must necessarily be a matter for conjecture.

91. The fact that it has been found possible to vest the control of *generation and main transmission* throughout the United Kingdom in the Central Electricity Board (operating for administrative convenience on the basis of a small number of regional areas) is not, in our opinion, conclusive evidence that the *distribution of electricity* should be organized on a similar basis.

92. We are of opinion that a reorganization of such a revolutionary character would only be justified if it were beyond doubt that the constituent bodies in the Electricity Supply Industry, as distinct from the organization of the Industry as a whole, were generally inefficient and unprogressive, and incapable of being improved on a more evolutionary basis.

93. On the contrary, there has been abundant evidence to show that, taken as a whole, the Electricity Supply Industry has made remarkable progress, particularly during the last ten years, notwithstanding its complicated and, in many cases, uneconomic structure and the trade depression from which the country is now emerging, and that a

progressive and enterprising policy has been adopted by many
undertakings. . .

96. The progress which is being made today by individual undertakings is, however, uneven and there is no uniform standard of
efficiency among either the large or the small undertakings.

97. We are satisfied that a substantial measure of simplification
and co-ordination of the present structure is necessary if the fullest
measure of development is to be achieved throughout the country
in the future.

98. We therefore recommend that the basis of reorganization which
should be adopted should be that outlined in the second of the two
alternatives referred to in paragraph 88, namely, the retention and
utilization where possible of the larger and more efficient of the
existing undertakings, and the absorption by such undertakings of
those which are smaller and less efficient.

99. The essential objects of any such scheme must include:
   (1) A substantial reduction in the present number of undertakings
       by the substitution, where appropriate, of larger and more
       economic units.
   (2) The prevention of the splitting up of comprehensive under-
       takings in consequence of the exercise of rights of purchase by
       individual local authorities.
   (3) The elimination of duplicate powers wherever they exist in the
       same area.

100. While size alone is admittedly no criterion of efficiency, there
can be no question that a large electricity supply undertaking
efficiently operated and managed has inherent advantages which the
small undertaking cannot enjoy.

101. Among the advantages which accrue to a large undertaking
operating over a comprehensive area, when compared with the
operation of the same area by a number of smaller units, reference
may be made to the following:

(a) Improved Technical Layout and Economy of Capital Expenditure

102. While low voltage distribution from high voltage sub-stations
is similar in both large and small undertakings, the elimination of a
multiplicity of boundaries, between small undertakings, and the
development of an area on a comprehensive scale, enables the high
voltage system to be laid out more efficiently from the point of view
of continuity of supply, and at a considerable economy in cost.

103. Evidence has been given to show that even though expenditure
incurred on existing development has to be taken into account,
substantial savings can be realized in all future development by plan-

ning on a wider scale. Furthermore, the removal of a multiplicity of boundaries would enable low voltage distribution to be carried out on a more flexible basis, and would avoid many of the difficulties which arise both where low voltage mains are carried out by two adjacent undertakings to dead ends on opposite sides of a boundary and also where one undertaking carries a low voltage main to its boundary and cannot supply premises just beyond because they are in the area of another authority.

(b) Diversity of Load

104. A general advantage results when an area is sufficiently comprehensive to include supplies for all the principal purposes for which electricity can be utilized such as industrial power, domestic and commercial requirements, public lighting and traction. In such cases there is always a diversity between the times when the maximum demands in kilowatts for these various classes of supply occur, with a resultant high load factor.

105. From the evidence it is clear that many of the smaller undertakings have not the benefit of such diversity. In some cases this is due to the fact that owing to the small extent of the area it does not contain the different classes of load.

106. In other cases an important part of the load such as, for example, industrial supplies, is lost to the small undertaking either because:

(a) it is being served by a Power Company (the small undertaking only distributing for domestic or similar purposes); or

(b) the small undertaking is unable to secure such load either because of its inability, owing to high distribution costs, to quote a sufficiently attractive price, or because of its reluctance to incur capital commitments which, if for any reason the supplies are subsequently discontinued, would impose a serious burden on the undertaking.

The result under any of the foregoing conditions is the same, namely, a low load factor.

107. We are aware that in certain cases it is possible for the smaller undertakings to come to a special arrangement with the Central Electricity Board in regard to bulk supply terms so as to enable them to deal with large demands of a special character, which may arise in their areas, but this course is only practicable where the load is of an exceptional nature.

108. Judicious grouping of many of the existing undertakings into larger units and the elimination of duplicate powers of supply should undoubtedly result in greater diversity of load being obtained

in the consolidated area. This in turn would result in a considerably improved load factor which is an important and necessary contribution to the attainment of reduced costs, since more units of electricity are sold for each kilowatt of demand, on which the capital investment of any undertaking depends.

(c) Financial Resources

109. The financial resources of large undertakings enable them to take a long view and to take certain risks in proceeding with schemes of development such as standardization of systems or extensions of mains, which though possibly unremunerative for a period are expected eventually to show improved results.

110. Small undertakings must necessarily adopt a more cautious policy in such matters since any loss on a particular scheme of development would impose a proportionately more serious burden on the undertaking than would be the case where such a scheme was carried out by a larger undertaking.

111. Furthermore, small undertakings are in some cases reluctant to adopt a progressive scheme of commercial development by offering facilities for hire, hire purchase and assisted wiring and low tariffs possibly because the cost of providing mains and apparatus to meet the increased demand which arises from the offer of such facilities, may be felt to be beyond the financial capacity of the undertaking.

(d) Central Purchasing

112. The larger undertakings are clearly in a more favourable position than the small undertakings to negotiate contracts and obtain trade discounts in connection with the purchase of cables, apparatus, etc.

113. In the case of individual purchases by a number of small Authorities there is almost a custom, we are told, for each Authority to require some special modification of a particular type of cable or apparatus, thereby increasing the cost of production to the manufacturers. If the purchasing is concentrated in the hands of a smaller number of larger undertakings, there will be a greater tendency towards standardization of type, thereby reducing the cost of production.

(e) Personnel

114. It is of the utmost importance that, with a view to ensuring that undertakings are operated and managed on the most efficient

basis, the chief executive officers of the undertakings should be men of the highest qualifications.

115. There can also be no question that to secure a substantial demand for electricity it is essential that all undertakings should adopt a progressive sales and development policy, and that for such a policy to be effective the undertakings must employ expert and well-paid technical and commercial staffs.

116. This is particularly necessary at the present time when the uses to which electricity is being put take so many new forms, often of a highly technical nature. Many of the larger undertakings (particularly in industrial areas) employ individual experts to deal with different classes of supply.

117. The larger undertakings have the financial resources to pay salaries which will attract the right type of man with the necessary qualifications for these various expert positions. In the case of the smaller undertakings all the duties have to be concentrated in the hands of the senior executive officer, and in many cases the undertakings appear to be unable to pay the salary necessary, not only to attract, but also to retain a man with the qualifications necessary to enable him to deal with all the varied aspects of electricity supply.

118. In general and apart from the advantages outlined in the preceding paragraphs, we are satisfied that from the point of view of future development the elimination of a large number of the smaller undertakings and their amalgamation or co-ordination with larger units is the only practical means whereby substantial progress can be made towards standardization of systems and methods of charge, and also towards greater uniformity in actual charges.

119. In support of the foregoing considerations, evidence shows that in certain cases undertakers (both public authorities and companies) have themselves effected voluntary amalgamations from which substantial advantages have materialized. This has resulted in a standardization of tariffs and other advantages of centralized control, together with a substantial reduction of price to consumers.

120. Even where geographically separated undertakings are under the control of a single company, we are satisfied that certain advantages have accrued to the consumers in the several areas. These advantages have resulted from the provision of a more highly skilled and better paid technical management; a uniform direction of policy in the framing of tariffs; a greater ability to standardize systems and voltages on account of the greater resources arising from the combination; and the consequential economy of centralized purchasing of stores and materials.

121. Evidence has been adduced to show that in certain cases small undertakings have adopted a progressive policy, and, owing to

particularly favourable local conditions, are able to charge lower prices for certain classes of supply than some of the larger undertakings.

122. While, however, the fullest recognition should be given to the good work which has been carried out by many small undertakings, often under difficult circumstances, we feel bound to endorse the view expressed by the Electric Power Supply Committee in 1918 that the object to be kept in view is not merely to have exceptionally low costs in a few small and specially favoured areas, but rather to have the same or lower costs available over wider areas. For this reason we emphasize the necessity that any regrouping of undertakings should be carried out on a reasonably comprehensive scale.

123. The necessity for a wider outlook is, in our opinion, particularly important in connection with the development of supplies of electricity in rural areas.

124. Owing to the low density of population and to the scattered location of premises, the supply of electricity in rural areas gives rise to problems of some difficulty from the point of view of carrying out development on an economic basis and at attractive tariffs. The position has been rendered still more difficult by the prior independent development of the urban areas.

125. We regard the problem of bringing a supply into the rural areas and extending it as widely as possible as being one of primary importance from a national point of view, for reasons which are dealt with more fully in a later part of the Report (see paragraph 372 *et seq.*).

126. There can be no doubt that if instead of having to deal with the present complex structure a system of distribution were being planned anew, adequate provision would be made to associate rural with urban areas.

127. The difficulties experienced in providing supplies in many rural areas under existing conditions are due to the fact that the development of such areas has in many cases been divorced from the development of the urban areas. We are satisfied that any scheme of reorganization for the country as a whole must provide, as far as possible, for the rural areas being developed in conjunction with the urban areas.

128. Circumstances will obviously vary in different cases, but evidence has shown that it would by no means follow that the association of rural with urban areas would be detrimental to the urban areas. Owing to the different types of load such an association should result in a greater diversity of load with a consequent increase of load factor, thereby reducing the cost of electricity over the area as a whole.

129. The technical and administrative personnel required for the management of the urban area can be expanded to deal also with the rural area at less cost than would be necessary to set up a separate personnel for the rural area. Furthermore, while owing to the lower density of population in the rural area the capital charges on mains, transformers and other apparatus might be expected to form a larger proportion of the total distribution costs, this can to a large extent be offset by the cheaper forms of construction which can be adopted in such areas, e.g. by the provision of overhead lines instead of underground cables. Even where in the initial stages of development the urban area may have to carry some of the charges in respect of the rural area, there would seem to be no reason to anticipate that when the rural area has been developed it need be a liability on the urban area. In the course of evidence, instances have been brought to our notice which support this view.

130. With regard to our major recommendations we recognize that the conditions on which the full development of electricity depends vary widely even in adjacent areas. A careful local investigation of each area is, in our opinion, a necessary preliminary to the preparation of a scheme of improvement. We feel strongly that it would neither be equitable nor practicable to prescribe what particular undertakings or even what particular size of undertaking should be amalgamated under such a scheme until after a survey which has taken into account the circumstances of each undertaking has been made.

131. It is, however, important that after a local investigation has been held and a scheme for improvement has been drawn up, simple machinery should be available for giving effect to the scheme without undue delay.

132. Past experience has demonstrated beyond question that any attempt to carry through on a voluntary basis a scheme of reorganization on the general lines we have recommended, would be bound to fail.

133. We would emphasize, therefore, the necessity that legislation should confer definite and adequate compulsory powers to enable our recommendations to be carried out effectively. . .

137. The consideration and approval of the schemes of reorganization, when prepared, and the carrying into effect of the other recommendations contained in this Report will . . . involve a considerable amount of administrative work on the part of some central authority.

138. We consider that the Commissioners should be entrusted with these further duties and that it is unnecessary and would in fact be undesirable to envisage the establishment of any new central body for that purpose. We have received from all sections of the Industry

evidence of the confidence felt in the ability and impartiality of the Commissioners which justifies us in recommending this course.

139. We must emphasize that the rapid discharge of such further administrative duties is vital to the success of our proposals. These proposals will necessarily involve a substantial increase in both the volume and the importance of the duties falling upon the Commissioners, and notwithstanding the delegation of the local investigations to specially appointed persons to whom we refer later in this Report, considerable pressure of work on the Commissioners is bound to ensue.

140. It is essential, therefore, that the Commissioners should be enabled to provide themselves with officers, both administrative and technical, on a scale suitable to meet the new demands without any unavoidable delay—otherwise the effect of our recommendations may be stultified.

7. THE IRON AND STEEL INDUSTRY*

The Minister of Supply (Mr Duncan Sandys): This Bill has two main objectives. The first is to establish a comprehensive system of public supervision embracing the whole iron and steel industry, and so bring to an end the extremely harmful split created by the 1949 Act. The second is to restore independence, initiative and financial responsibility to the companies and so ensure that they have the strongest incentives to produce as cheaply and efficiently as possible.

In short, we seek to preserve the stimulus of private enterprise, subject to the safeguards of public supervision. This policy has been consistently advocated by the Conservative Party for years past. Our outlook was very well summed up by my right hon. Friend the Colonial Secretary in a debate in this House as far back as 1946, when he said that the companies should be allowed to spend their own money, run their own business and take their own risks, but should be subject to such amount of Government supervision as will secure that the national interest and that of the steel industry march together in harmony. That is precisely what this Bill sets out to do.

Even hon. Members opposite have at times felt obliged to recognize that free enterprise has a contribution to make to the vitality and efficiency of industry. In fact, the right hon. Member for Vauxhall (Mr G. R. Strauss), when he was commending his steel nationalization Bill to the House on Second Reading, claimed as a point in its favour that it would

* From *H.C. Deb.*, 508, c. 266–7, 268–71, 281–2.

'combine all that is best in private enterprise with public ownership'.

What he did not seem to appreciate was that you cannot combine private enterprise with monopolistic public ownership any more than you can mix fire with water. By removing from the individual companies real financial responsibility and incentives, State ownership quenches the very spirit of private initiative.

On the same occasion the right hon. Gentleman went on to say rather ingenuously:

> 'we propose to keep intact the identity of the individual concerns. . . . Indeed, on the morning of Vesting Day the only difference for them will be that the ownership of the securities has changed hands'.*

But of course it makes all the difference in the world for the ownership of the companies to change from the hands of thousands of separate shareholders into the single hand of a State monopoly. By retaining the brass nameplates of the companies, it may be possible to keep up the appearance but not the reality of private enterprise. The facade of separate management may for a while be preserved, but let us make no mistake: financial control by the State Corporation carries with it control of the policy of the companies and must progressively stifle their individual initiative and their sense of responsibility.

I think it is common ground between us, on both sides of the House, that some measure of public supervision and control is necessary in the iron and steel industry. The main question is whether that necessary supervision and control can be obtained without State ownership.

We on this side of the House challenge that assumption. We maintain that the effectiveness of public supervision has nothing whatever to do with the question of ownership. It can be made equally, if not more, effective under conditions of private enterprise.

There are three fields in which some measure of public supervision is necessary: prices, development, and raw materials. Let us take prices first. Can it really be said that it is necessary for the State to own the steel works in order to prevent excessive prices from being charged? The history of the industry itself provides the answer. Nationalization has been operating for about twenty months, yet iron and steel prices have been under effective public supervision for no less than twenty years. I would say that of all the various methods of control adopted at different times, the one provided by the 1949 Act is by far the least efficient.

If prices are to be controlled, it is quite obvious that the control

* *Official Report*, November 15, 1947, Vol. 458, c. 60-3.

must apply to all products of the same kind irrespective of who makes them. But that is just what the Corporation cannot do; for it has no power to control the prices charged by any company that it does not own. In order to control iron and steel prices effectively through ownership, one would have to nationalize hundreds more companies in many other industries. This, in turn, would no doubt create further anomalies and a call for further nationalization until, step by step, one had nationalized almost the whole of our economy.

Public ownership, is, I submit to the House, the most unpractical and the most cumbersome method of exercising public control that has ever been devised. How much simpler and how much more straightforward it is to entrust this task to a Board such as we now propose whose authority is defined in terms of a list of specific products, irrespective of the ownership of the companies that make them.

Much the same difficulty arises over raw materials. Here again, we see the grave disadvantages of the split in the industry created by the 1949 Act, and, above all, the absence of any co-ordinating machinery. Problems of material supplies inevitably raise issues which affect both the nationalized and the privately-owned companies. These require to be dealt with by a body which is able to take an objective view over the whole industry. Since the Corporation is not in a position to do that, the task of co-ordination falls upon the Government.

For example, it was necessary for me a few months ago to reconcile differences between steel makers and founders on the question of the distribution of pig iron and coke. This type of industrial problem should, in our opinion, not have to be referred in the first instance to the Government. However, this will, I am glad to say, be to a large extent remedied when the new Board is set up.

I turn now to the question of development. The right hon. Member for Lewisham, South (Mr H. Morrison) complained that we were giving the Board negative, destructive bureaucratic powers of veto. One hon. Member opposite said that the steel industry was being put into the clammy clasp of my dead hand. That was the charming expression used by the hon. and learned Member for Brigg (Mr E. L. Mallalieu).

But these arguments and criticisms come strangely from the party opposite, who were responsible for the 1949 Act, which gave to the Corporation, as the sole shareholder, unrestricted control over the affairs of every nationalized company. We, on the other hand, are deliberately limiting the powers of the intervention of the Board to cases in which a major scheme might seriously prejudice the balanced development of the industry.

In addition, we are providing two important safeguards. The first is that the Board must consult the trade associations representing the branch of the industry concerned before exercising its powers—even before exercising its powers to call for the submission of schemes. The second is the right of appeal from the Board's decision to the Government. In short, my reply to the charge of bureaucracy is that the carefully defined powers with which we are providing the Board are the bare minimum necessary to ensure balanced development of the industry and to avoid waste of national resources on a large scale.

The party opposite have also criticized this Bill for not providing adequate positive powers of development. The right hon. Gentleman the Member for Vauxhall said that we were providing a brake but no accelerator. In my opinion, too much emphasis has been put on this question of positive powers. The real power of the Board will depend not on its right to give orders, but on its ability to lead and to persuade. The Board will have the duty of keeping itself informed about the industry's plans for expansion and modernization, and of satisfying itself that they are adequate.

Personally, I have little doubt that normally the plans prepared by the companies on their own initiative will be sufficient to meet any forseeable demands for iron and steel. But should the Board, at any time, consider that more is required, it will, under Clause 4 of the Bill, discuss the matter with the industry. I believe that those discussions, to which we attach the greatest importance, will almost always result either in the Board's persuading the industry to carry out the desired expansion or in the industry's convincing the Board that its existing development plans are adequate.

It is, of course, true that, in the rare case where a difference of opinion persists, the Board will have no power to order the carrying out of a development scheme which the industry considers to be economically unsound. The Board will, however, have the right to report the matter to the Government, who are, by this Bill, given the power, which does not exist at present, to provide additional capacity if the national interest requires it.

Mr G. R. Strauss (Vauxhall): Before I come to the details of the Bill, I want to make quite clear—although I think it is already quite clear—that we on this side of the House are opposed to the Bill in principle because we believe it is contrary to the national interest to transfer this iron and steel industry from public to private ownership. This principle has been argued in the House so often before that I do not intend to take up any time arguing it again today. I must, however, say this. In our view it is indefensible for the control of this industry—on which depends our economy, the fate of townships and the livelihood of hundreds of thousands of employees—to rest in the hands of people with no public responsibility.

For example, when the people of Jarrow were suffering from widespread unemployment and all the demoralization and malnutrition which goes with it, it was morally and socially wrong that a decision as to whether a new steel works should be built there should have been made by directors of other steel works responsible only to their shareholders rather than by the Government of the day, responsible to Parliament. We believe that it is equally wrong that people with no public responsibility should have the power to decide where and when steel works are to be closed and whole communities rendered derelict. It is wrong that decisions on such matters should be dictated by private profit interests.

It is our belief, also, that the defects of our iron and steel industry —and they are serious—can only be removed through common ownership of all the large plants. These defects have been clearly stated in the conclusions of the Iron and Steel Team of the Anglo-American Council for Productivity. They report at considerable length that in their view in this country there is too great a dispersal of production facilities and that the production units are too small.

We consider, and I think it is plain, that these defects cannot be removed without eliminating the conflicting vested interests of the companies concerned, large and small. Only then can reorganization take place based on national plans, unhindered by sectional obstruction. That, of course, means single ownership and I think it is accepted, even on the other side of the House, that a single ownership of this great industry is only tolerable under full Parliamentary control.

Next, we say that denationalization, which is bound to disturb and dislocate this industry, cannot possibly be justified without evidence to show that the industry has in some way suffered from nationalization. No such evidence has been produced in any debate on this industry—it has not been produced by the Minister of Supply today —for the simple reason that there is no such evidence. On the contrary, the industry, as we know, is flourishing. Its production is greater than ever; it will be greater, we are told, next year. Its profits are greater than ever and it is in a more prosperous condition than at any time in its history. So far from nationalization having damaged the industry, I have on several occasions recounted to the House facts showing how the industry has benefited already—in small ways it is true but in significant ways—from nationalization, and these facts no one has denied.

Moreover, the iron and steel industry has adapted itself to the new machinery established by the Nationalization Act. That machinery is working well. I believe, and I do not say this without some knowledge of the industry and those who work in it, that, by and large, managements—relieved, perhaps to find that the tiresome interference in their affairs which they were told by Conservative spokesmen would follow nationalization has not happened—are content with the new set-up. In any case, I am certain that most of them would far rather that the industry should be left in peace than that it should suffer from the upsetting and long-term uncertainty that will follow the enactment of this denationalization Bill.

It is for these reasons that we oppose the Bill in principle irrespective of the demerits of the detailed provisions in it, which are many, and we say that the Government, in bringing it forward, are sacrificing the true interests of the iron and steel industry to please their political supporters.

CHAPTER III

Types

Apart from municipal enterprises, with which we are not here concerned, the three main types of nationalized industry are (*a*) the government department, (*b*) the public corporation and (*c*) the public or 'mixed' company. In England, the public corporation has been the chosen vehicle, although examples of the other two are not lacking. The Post Office, of course, is the outstanding instance of a departmental enterprise, while the 'company' type is represented by the British Petroleum Company and the Agricultural Mortgage Corporation.

Reasons for preferring the public corporation have been stated so often that repetition here would be superfluous. Much more useful is the careful account of the evolution of the public corporation idea and the sceptical examination of its alleged virtues provided by Mr D. N. Chester in his paper read before the Manchester Statistical Society (*Extract 8*).

Although by the 1930's all three political parties were substantially agreed that, should further nationalization be necessary, the public corporation provided the most suitable organizational form, it was the Liberal Party that had the distinction of first expressing itself on the subject with some clarity and precision (*Extract 9*). The fullest pre-war statement of the case from a Labour source was Mr Herbert Morrison's *Socialization and Transport* (1933). A very brief expression of the same view, taken from the TUC's *Interim Report on Post-War Reconstruction*, is here reproduced as *Extract 10*.

The popularity of the public corporation idea gave rise to proposals (e.g. in Lord Wolmer's *Post Office Reform*) to change the constitutional status and organizational pattern of the Post Office itself. These were rejected by the 'Bridgeman' Committee of 1932, for reasons explained by the Committee itself in *Extract 11*. This Committee nevertheless proposed certain changes in the management of the Post Office and in its relations with the Treasury which, when put into effect, made it more like a public corporation in its *modus operandi*. Further developments in the same direction took place in 1961, as explained by Professor William A. Robson in *Extract 12*.

Many now hold that there is no clear dividing line, except in a purely legal sense, between the government department and the public corporation. Modifications of 'normal' departmental organization, designed to facilitate the conduct of commercial transactions, can be sufficient to blur the distinction between the two forms. Moreover, the public corporation may be used, for reasons of pure expediency, to conduct operations which are by no means fully or even predominantly commercial in character. Of the latter situation, a good example is provided by the Atomic Energy Authority, whose special position in the government structure is analysed by Mr R. Darcy Best in *Extract 13*.

There are some who suggest that, in certain fields of nationalized industry, we are moving away from the 'pure' public corporation to an intermediate type of organization. Mr Ernest Davies (*Extract 14*) sees the Government's latest proposals for publicly-owned transport in this light, and deplores the development. On the other hand, there are authors who believe that this process may be inevitable and desirable, in so far as the *ad hoc* organization, brought into existence to perform functions with which 'normal' governmental machinery is temporarily unable to cope, has always proved ephemeral. This suggestion is made by Professor E. C. S. Wade in *Extract 15*.

8. MANAGEMENT AND ACCOUNTABILITY
IN THE NATIONALIZED INDUSTRIES*

The nationalized industries—coal, transport, gas, electricity and iron and steel—are managed by public corporations. In many quarters the public corporation is hailed as the pattern of a brave new world superseding the joint stock company on the one hand and the Ministerial department on the other. In Mr Herbert Morrison's words, 'a public corporation gives us the best of both worlds' for with it 'we can combine progressive modern business management with a proper degree of public accountability . . .'[1] When in 1933 President Roosevelt presented to Congress the Bill to establish the Tennessee Valley Authority he asked for 'a corporation clothed with the power of Government, but possessed of the flexibility and initiative of a private enterprise'.[2] And Lord Wolmer has referred to 'the organ to which men both of socialistic and individualistic predispositions are

---

* From D. N. Chester: 'Management in the Nationalized Industries', *Public Administration*, Vol. XXX, Spring 1952, pp. 27–47. Reprinted by permission of the author and editor.
[1] *H.C. Deb.*, May 6, 1946, 422, c. 604–5.
[2] Message to Congress, April 10, 1933.

C

turning to conduct such services as are agreed to be best conducted by monopolies'.[1]

The best of both possible worlds—of public and of private enterprise—is the phrase which sums up most of the support for the public corporation. It is a most attractive slogan. Indeed we are so used to compromises which give us much less than the best of both possible worlds that it is no wonder that an institution which claims to give us the best should have widespread support—and induce, in some, a degree of scepticism.

As might be expected of something which appears to satisfy very diverse political views, the public corporation is a creature with a mixed and interesting ancestry. Though it is now thought of as the chosen instrument of the Labour Party for the management of nationalized industries, and though it might not have reached its present vigour without the continual and painstaking advocacy of Mr Herbert Morrison, the Labour Party cannot claim the device to be all its own work. Conservatives and Liberals have strong ancestral claims and there are others without close party ties who have contributed.

I propose, therefore, first of all to indicate the way in which the main ideas have come together, clashed and been refined; what the different contributions were and what kind of problems the contributors thought they were solving. We can then look a little more closely at this creature which counts among its ancestors and supporters men of such diverse opinions and see whether it is likely to live up to their early hopes. But it is still very young as institutions go and I do not think any definitive judgment is yet anywhere near possible.

SOME HISTORY

It would be very nice to be able to show a clear and logical development of an idea: to show it becoming generally accepted and replacing or refining an older idea which had been subjected to scrutiny and reasoned argument. But that is not how ideas develop, at least not when a comparatively short period is put under the microscope. Though my main approach is historical I have not stuck to a strictly chronological order of narrative. The literature of the period is extensive and one can almost always find some reference either to a new proposal earlier than I have indicated or to an idea being strongly held after it had been generally discarded. My quotations, therefore, are more often representative, than exactly-dated landmarks in public opinion.

[1] Post Office Reform (1932), p. 281.

EARLY DISCUSSIONS ABOUT COAL NATIONALIZATION

It is convenient to start with the discussions that took place about coal. The Nationalization of Mines, Canals, Railways and Tramways Bill (No. 103 of 1906) had twenty clauses. (Clause 20 rather hopefully read 'This Act shall come into operation on the first day of January 1907'.) The Local Government Board was to be given powers to serve notice, within five years, on the owners of any railway, tramway, canal or mine (but not to a Local Authority working the property themselves) of intention to purchase at a price provided. Four possible forms of management were contemplated: The Local Government Board (*a*) could use and manage the properties themselves; or (*b*) depute all their powers to a Board of Control of not less than fifty nor more than a hundred members; or (*c*) resell the property to any Local Authority; or (*d*) lease any of the property for seven, fourteen, or twenty-one years—the existing owners to have certain preferential claims as lessees.

The same Bill was introduced in 1907. In 1908, 1909, 1911 and 1912 similar Bills were introduced except that they were confined to railways and canals. At this stage no single form of management had been decided upon.

In 1913 however the Nationalization of Mines and Minerals Bill (No. 244 of 1913) was introduced into the House of Commons after being approved at the Annual Conference of the Miners' Federation of Great Britain at Swansea in October 1912. The main managerial provisions were as follows:

A Minister for Mines was to be appointed to whom would be transferred (*a*) every colliery and coal mine and all coal and other minerals used for fuel, whether being worked or not; and (*b*) the responsibilities of the Home Secretary for the hours of work and conditions in the mines. The Minister had to cause 'full and faithful accounts to be kept' and laid annually before Parliament. He also had to have prepared an annual balance sheet and profit and loss account for each mine. All expenditure was to be met 'out of moneys provided by Parliament' but moneys received in respect of the sale or supply of coal should be directly expended for carrying out the purposes of the Act. If the income in the National Coal Mines Account was insufficient to meet the 3 per cent guaranteed on the compensation stock the interest was to be payable out of the Consolidated Fund. Comments[1] on the Bill made it clear that the miners wished the Minister to be fully responsible to Parliament. The Minister would be answerable to Parliament 'for all these deplorable acci-

[1] See Fabian Tract No. 171 (1913) for text of the Bill and a short commentary.

dents' and 'The effect of paying out of "moneys provided by Parliament" is to make parliamentary criticism more effective . . .'.

Though the next Bill was not introduced into the House of Commons until 1923[1] it was drafted in 1919 and formed part of the miners' evidence to the Sankey Commission.[2] It contained very different proposals.

Instead of the industry being vested in and operated by a Government Department the mines and minerals were to be transferred to a Mining Council which was to be a Corporation having perpetual succession, with power to hold land without licence in mortmain, could sue and be sued and had the powers of appointing managers, miners, etc., operating pits, selling coal, etc. A Minister of Mines was to be appointed and he was to be President of the Mining Council. The twenty other members of the Council were to be appointed half by His Majesty and half by the Miners' Federation of Great Britain. The members were to be full time and to be appointed for five years but eligible for reappointment. They could be removed by those responsible for the appointment, in other words the Miners' Federation could remove any of their appointees and replace them by others of their choice.

The Bill also provided for District Mining Councils (of ten members, five to be appointed by the Miners' Federation) and Pit Councils for each mine or group of mines (of ten members appointed by the District Councils, half were to be members of the Miners' Federation nominated by the workers in the mine or mines concerned). The District Mining Councils were to exercise such powers as the Mining Council delegated to them and they in turn could delegate some of these powers to the Pit Councils. Thus the representatives of the Miners' Federation were to constitute half the total membership of this hierarchy of Councils. These bodies were managerial not advisory. The only mention of the miners in the 1913 Bill, a Bill also produced by the Miners' Federation it must be remembered, was that the employees should have the right to join a trade union and be free to engage in political activities. What was the explanation of this new conception?

The main explanation must be found in the conversion of the miners' leaders to joint control.[3] Apparently the process of conversion was going on during the drafting discussions for I have been

---

[1] This Bill was introduced into the House of Commons in 1923, 1924 and early 1925. For the Bill submitted to the Samuel Commission late in 1925 see p. 72.

[2] Coal Industry Commission, 1919; Cmd. 359, 360, 361.

[3] Industrial Unionism and Syndicalism had been particularly strong among the South Wales miners and a section of the Scottish miners in the years immediately before 1914.

fortunate enough to see the papers on coal-mining which Professor
G. D. H. Cole[1] collected about this period. Among them is a first
draft of the 1919 Bill, dated March 7, 1919, which is very much
nearer to the 1913 Bill than the draft put before the Coal Industry
Commission. In this first draft the mines were to be vested in the
Minister for Mines.[2] There was already mention of a Mining
Council (of ten members, five appointed by the Miners' Federation)
but it was to act on behalf of the Minister. There were also to be
District and Pit Councils to whom the Mining Council could dele-
gate functions. It is not clear from this draft quite what was envisaged;
for example, Clause 7 (5) gave 'the Mining Council, on behalf of the
Minister for Mines' power to appoint managers, engineers, etc.
Presumably 'on behalf of' implies that they were to be agents for the
Minister, but just who was responsible for any decision was uncertain.

Professor Cole's copy of this draft contains a number of pencilled
corrections in his handwriting. These were made for the discussion
of the draft—their significance is that they were all designed to make
the Mining Council the real management body and most found their
way into the draft put before the Royal Commission on May 23,
1919. The tide was running strongly in the direction of workers'
management. For example, a draft dated May 7, 1919, does not contain the provision whereby the Miners' Federation could remove
their representatives on the Mining Council, a power which obviously
increases the Unions' control of the Council: yet this was only sixteen
days before the Bill was put before the Commission.

G. D. H. Cole was at this time a leading member of the National
Guilds League. His evidence[3] to the Commission is therefore of
special interest. He supported the ideas in the Miners' Bill by saying
that as a result of the war, labour was now so strong that its active
co-operation must be enlisted. This meant going beyond discussion of
wages and conditions, 'it includes the whole conduct of the industry,
both in its productive and in its business aspects'. Industrial democracy involves that when a worker receives orders 'he must, if he is to
be free, feel that these orders come from himself, or from some group
of which he feels himself to be a part, or from some person whose
right to give orders is recognized and sustained by himself and by

[1] The 1919 Bill was drafted by Slesser and Cole in consultation with the miners'
leaders, especially R. Smillie, F. Hodges and W. Straker.

[2] Mr Sidney Webb had put forward a scheme for transferring the mines to a
Minister of Mines in 1916 in the Fabian pamphlet *How to Pay for the War*. Webb
was a member of the Sankey Commission and also gave evidence before it.

[3] Coal Industry Commission, Vol. II, pp. 548–50. He had already stated his
views in his *Self Government in Industry* (1917)—see in particular Chapter VI on
State Ownership and Control.

such a group'. He went on '. . . national management by itself will not secure the full co-operation of the workers. State management means in practice management by a State Department; and a State Department is not "a group of which the ordinary man feels himself to be a part". The workers under State *management* are no more free, so far as the conditions of their working life are concerned, than the workers under capitalistic management.'

In explaining why the State should appoint half the membership of the Mining Council he said: 'The reasons for State participation in actual management are, to a considerable extent, of only temporary validity. If the whole effective working personnel of the mining industry were combined in a single group possessed of a feeling of community . . . direct participation by the State in the normal work of management would be unnecessary. It is my hope that this position will gradually be reached. . . .'

Mr W. Straker, a leading member of the Miners' Federation, in earlier evidence to the Commission had said that since 1912 'thought has been growing and maturing on the subject, so that now the miners are not only asking for Nationalization, but also for joint control of the mines'. He said 'nationalization with bureaucratic administration' would not prevent unrest, and stressed 'the necessity of the worker controlling the industry in which he is, otherwise you never get clear of labour unrest'. Appearing before the Commission on a second occasion he said: 'If the miners had proposed to nationalize the mines and set up a system of bureaucratic management, I would have understood all the criticism of State control. I want to say that the miners are just as strongly opposed to such bureaucracy as the mine-owners are.'

Undoubtedly there was considerable fear of bureaucratic administration among the supporters of nationalization. Mr Arthur Greenwood, for example, in his evidence to the Commission said:

> There are certain dangers to be avoided in a nationalized system of coal mines. In the first place a whole industry under a single ownership lends itself to centralization and bureaucracy—a defect which is not wholly absent from very large enterprises, whether under private or public control. In this respect a coal trust might not be greatly different from a public monopoly. This danger is to be met by decentralization. Secondly, Government administration tends to become conservative and inelastic. This danger might be overcome by attaching to the central administration for a term of years, men with experience of 'provincial administration' in the coal mining industry and by the pressure of public opinion, for the coal mining industry will be closely watched by the whole industrial community. (Vol. II, p. 546.)

Mr Frank Hodges, a member of the Commission and Secretary of the Miners' Federation, in his *Nationalization of the Mines* (1920) found himself in agreement:

> with those who think that a Governmental body, composed of politically-minded people, or an administration composed of Civil Servants, educated and trained for the administration of things, would be incompetent and unfit for the great work of industry, and it is because of such unfitness that lack of initiative has characterized Government activities in the past. If it were proposed that this great industry, so vital to the well-being of the nation, should be handed over to politicians or those nominated by them, of the civil servant class, we could agree that the last state of the industry would be worse than the first (pp. 104–5).

It was never quite clear in the public discussion just what would have been the responsibility of the Minister. Slesser, who drafted both Bills on the instructions of the Miners' Federation, thought the Minister's position would be very like that of the Secretary of State for War in relation to the Army Council[1] but it is not clear from his evidence that he quite understood the constitutional position of that Council. Mr Straker (at Q. 23570) envisaged that the Minister might be outvoted in the Council, in which case he would have to carry out the wishes of the majority. Yet at Q. 23590–2 he said that the Mining Council would be just as completely under Parliamentary control as was, for example, the Home Office. Mr Frank Hodges[2] saw the Minister of Mines as the link between the Mining Council and the Government, the Minister's function being to provide the channel through which the desires of the nation would be expressed to the Council.

In passing it should be noticed that the Nationalization of Railways Bill of 1914 (No. 212 of 1914) contained a provision whereby the nationalized railways were to be operated by a Railway Board of four members 'on behalf of and subject to the absolute control of' a Minister of Posts and Railways. For the first five years two of the members were to be appointed by the Minister of Posts and Railways and one each by the Board of Trade and the Treasury. Thereafter appointments were to be made by a Railway Council composed of six members appointed by the Associated Chambers of Commerce and Trade and six by the Associated Chambers of Agriculture, twelve by the Trades Union Congress and one by each County and County Borough Council served by a State railway. (This is perhaps a strange ancestor of the device of Appointing Trustees found in the London Transport Act, 1933.) A draft Railway Nationalization Bill circulated in 1918[3] shifted the emphasis to a Transport Council of

[1] See his answer to Q. 22068.
[2] *Nationalization of the Mines*, p. 120.
[3] For the text of the 1918 Bill see A. E. Davies, *The Case for Nationalization*

seven members whose duty 'on behalf of and subject to the absolute control of the Transport Council' was 'to maintain and work the railway system'. The Chairman was, however, to be a Minister for Transport and Communications, the railway assets were vested in the Minister and the Council could not incur expenditure without the Minister's sanction. Four of the members were to be appointed by the Minister for Transport, and one each by the Board of Trade and the Treasury. Three of the members appointed by the Minister for Transport were to be chosen from a panel of twelve names nominated by the Executive Committees of the twenty principal Trade Unions concerned with transport services.

There was no serious discussion of the problem of management and organization in the reports of the members of the Sankey Commission. Each group seemed content to state its views and proposals as briefly and as categorically as possible. But when a somewhat similar plan was submitted to the Samuel Commission in 1925 the Commission pointed out the impossible constitutional position of the Minister of Mines in these words:

> The essential contradiction which is embodied in the scheme proposed to us is clearly seen if the position assigned to the Minister of Mines is considered. Like other Ministers he is responsible to Parliament. If the representatives of the tax-payers should disapprove of the manner in which the industry is administered, whether on financial grounds or on any others, they can secure the resignation of the Minister or a change in his policy. But under this scheme the Minister is also to be the Chairman of two bodies,[1] by whom questions of wages and prices are to be settled. These bodies are not appointed or controlled by him; their members are almost all elected by independent constituencies. The Minister therefore may receive the instructions of Parliament, but he has no power to give effect to them. If, however, the scheme were to be modified in order to meet this criticism, and were to give him that power, then, we repeat, its essential character would be changed, and it would become a plan for direct State control. As it stands, the position in which the Minister for Mines is to be placed leaves him as the embodiment of the inconsistency of one authority being given the right to manage, another being left with the liability to pay.

(1920), pp. 265–81. See also Bill 53 of 1921 for the proposal that the nationalized railways should be vested in a Minister of Transport but conducted, subject to his overriding authority, by seven Railway Commissioners, all appointed by the Minister, three from persons nominated by the recognized railway unions.

[1] The Labour Party's 1925 proposals covered coal, electricity and transport. The two bodies were a National Coal and Power Production Council and a Consumers' Council. See R.C. on the Coal Industry, 1926, Report pp. 68–9. This scheme was drawn up by a joint Committee representative of the Miners' Federation, the TUC, the Labour Party and the Parliamentary Labour Party.

THE COAL INDUSTRY NATIONALIZATION ACT, 1946

By 1925, therefore, the Labour Party and Trade Unions were still some way off the form of organization in the Labour Government's Coal Industry Nationalization Act, 1946. There are three major differences in the organization of the industry between the 1946 Act and the Bills I have just been describing. First, the members of the National Coal Board are all appointed by the Minister, none is representative of the miners nor of any other interest. Second, the Minister and the Board are clearly separate entities each with powers defined in the Act. The Board is an independent management body and is neither an executive agent of the Minister nor an advisory body. Third, there is no provision in the Act for District or Pit Councils with statutory powers and responsibilities, though in practice the National Coal Board has set up a hierarchy of Divisional, Area and Pit management units and a scheme of this kind was promised by the Minister of Fuel and Power during the passage of the Bill through the House of Commons. This third difference is not important for the subject of this paper. How did the other two changes come to be accepted?

WORKER PARTICIPATION

The idea of direct worker management of a nationalized industry has a long and interesting history and has taken many forms. In 1918 it was strongest among the miners and certain other trade unions. There are several reasons why it did not take a stronger hold and why what strength it had faded so that it was no longer a major element by the time of the Labour legislation of 1945–50. The movement was strong in 1918–19 because of the greatly increased strength and status of the trade unions as a result of wartime conditions. Mass unemployment, the General Strike and other large-scale stoppages left the trade unions, particularly the miners, very weak and this combined with the growth of Labour Party strength in the House of Commons turned Socialist eyes to political instead of trade union methods.

To many people there was a conflict between the idea of the mines for the miners and that of the mines for the community. As one of the critics said to the Sankey Commission, the Miners' Federation proposed 'the purchase of the mines by the Government and the management of the mines by the miners for the miners'.[1] Could the miners be relied upon to be fair to the consumers? Was there not also the general interest and the interest of workers in other industries?

[1] Mr Wallace Thorneycroft at Vol. II, p. 888.

The miners partly recognized this objection and during the later stages of the drafting of the 1919 Bill a new section[1] was inserted providing for the establishment of a Fuel Consumers' Council appointed by the Minister to represent the interests of consumers. Mr Straker in his evidence claimed that the Chairman and the ten Government appointees would 'take special care of the consumer and all the rest of the community'. (Q. 23270.) But on the whole there was little discussion of the consumer before the Sankey Commission or in the Commission's reports. On the Labour and Trade Union side this was no doubt partly due to the belief that private enterprise exploited the consumer to earn a profit, whereas under nationalization there would be no profits and therefore no incentive for exploitation.

Consumer representation and consumer councils appear in most of the later Bills. The 1936 Bill[2] (No. 11 of 1936–7) provided that members of the Coal Corporation 'shall include representatives of consumers organizations and of those employed in the coal mining industry'. There could also be a Fuel Consumers' Council, but this like the one in the 1919 Bill was optional and had no stated powers or functions. Strangely enough in the Bill presented in the following year (No. 15 of 1937) there is no mention of the Corporation containing representatives of consumers but the Fuel Council had to be convoked by the Corporation at least once in every three months.

Another influence was the growing appreciation on the part of the trade union movement of the difficulties for themselves inherent in direct trade union representation. What in fact was to be the position of the trade union representatives in the dealings between the Board and the trade union? Whose side would they be on in cases of dispute and for wage negotiations? Speaking in 1926 of the two representatives of labour interests in the Port of London Authority, Sir Joseph Broodbank said: 'They are placed in an intolerable position ... no man can act as an employer one day and as his own employee the next day.'[3] During the discussions in the 1930s stimulated by the London Passenger Transport Bill, some of the TUC leaders began to stress the danger of representation to trade union activities. In Russia the trade unions had by then become adjuncts of management with little or no power of independent negotiation. In 1933 a joint memorandum of the Labour Party and the TUC stated that trade

[1] The draft dated March 7, 1919, stipulated that two of the five members to be appointed by the Minister were 'to represent the interests of consumers', but this was left out of the final version.

[2] The 1936 and 1937 Bills provided for worker representation at the national, regional and pit level. Their backers were mining MPs.

[3] *Public Administration*, Vol. IV, 1926, p. 313. Writing in 1937 Dr Lincoln Gordon took a more favourable view, based on the period after 1926, *Public Enterprise*, p. 27.

union rights, including the right to strike, must be fully maintained in nationalized industries. At the 1934 Conference the General Council of the TUC, in putting forward a scheme for the nationalization of the Iron and Steel Industry, suggested that members of the Board should be appointed for their competence and that 'Any person holding office in his Trade Union . . . should be required to relinquish such office on appointment to the Board'. This was also to apply to any sectional boards.

The TUC in their Interim Report on Post-War Reconstruction (1944) made their attitude quite clear:

> It does not seem by any means certain that it would be in the best interest of the workpeople of a nationalized industry to have, as directly representative of them, members of the controlling board who would be committed to its joint decisions. It will be essential, not only for the maintenance and improvement of the standards and conditions of the workpeople, but because of the power of the independent criticism that they can exert, that the trade unions shall maintain their complete independence. They can hardly do so if they are compromised in regard to Board decisions which are not considered to be in their members' interests by the fact of their representatives' participation in them.

Increasing emphasis came to be placed on joint consultation as the best method of worker participation and most of the nationalization Acts make it obligatory for machinery of this kind to be established.

Another argument, particularly important in the case of the London Passenger Transport Bill, was that direct worker representation would make it difficult, if not impossible, to withstand the claims of other interests. There were the consumers, Local Authorities and possibly the owners of the compensation Stock, who had claims. The Labour movement would not have accepted representation of Stock holders as being consistent with public ownership. There were the difficulties of arranging direct representation, particularly in the case of the consumer. It was also argued that a board composed of different interests could not give single-minded attention to management.

Finally, there was the growing appreciation of the importance of efficient management and a realization that directors and top level management performed specialized functions. The business management view of nationalization strongly propagated by Mr Morrison came to win the day. This view attracted many who would otherwise have opposed nationalization. In part it is a view which reflects the growth of the manager as a profession and no doubt is evidence of what Mr Burnham has called the Managerial Revolution.

It was comparatively easy to throw cold water on the idea of direct election of managers by their employees. Allegations of the in-

efficiency and indiscipline that would occur if the miners controlled
the mines were quite common. There was, however, a more positive
side. People of different political views and many more without any
strong party allegiance saw the problem of coal or electricity or some
other major industry under public control as a problem of securing
the greatest efficiency. Fuel and power and transport were used by all
industries—Britain's industrial interests demanded that they should
be managed as efficiently and provided as cheaply as possible. Some
found the answer in competition, others in any form of public ownership—but an increasing number saw the answer in able management.
This was particularly the case after the 1924 slump had hit the coal
industry. Support came from those on both sides of the industry who
wanted 'rationalization'.

The Liberal Party Report—*Britain's Industrial Future* (the Yellow
Book) published in 1928—put the point as follows:

> Efficiency in management is what matters most to the miner, to the
> consumer, and to the owner, whether the owner be the community or
> the shareholders . . .
> The essence of industrial administration is executive decision.
> Nobody proposes that engineers or accountants should be elected by the
> personnel in a business. They are appointed by reason of their pro-
> fessional qualifications, and their record in results actually produced.
> The controllers of business and industry are, or ought to be, chosen for
> their business capacity. The only test of this is their success in 'getting
> results' in the shape of those prices, wages, and profits which are
> necessary to the prosperity, health, and peace of any industry. The real
> problem in Government-owned, as in private, industry is that of picking
> directors. When you have found the right directors, the only practical
> course is to equip them with the right organs through which they can
> consult workers, consumers, or others who are affected by their actions,
> and to leave them a free hand, subject to a yearly or half-yearly account
> of their stewardship to the ultimate owners of the business. How are a
> million 'electors' within the industry to choose such men? Even if
> candidates of that type are put forward, are they likely to be elected in
> competition with others who have long been known for their sympathy
> with the electors' particular point of view? How would the candidates
> be nominated—by 'parties', by Trade Unions, or by individuals? How
> would the 'campaign' for election be conducted, so that the electors
> should judge of the rival candidates and listen to their rival policies?
> And as to the outcome, is it probable that election would produce just
> that proportion of administrative experience, financial knowledge,
> understanding of the needs of industry and labour at home and abroad,
> which the directors of a nationalized coal industry must possess if they
> are to have the least chance of making a success of their business? (pp
> 348–9).

Business efficiency was very much one of the points stressed time and time again by Mr Morrison. In the Bill he introduced in 1931 into the House of Commons to establish a London Passenger Transport Board he rejected the idea of a representative Board and claimed he was setting up a business Board. The Board should be composed of 'the best business brains that we can secure': 'we must insist upon all the members being persons of business ability and capacity', and 'the people in charge, certainly the Chairman of the Board, must have great industrial and managerial ability, and we must be prepared to pay what is necessary in order to secure that ability, if the undertaking is to be efficient, and if the ordinary work-people are not to be let down by incompetent management at the top'.[1]

The Labour Party Executive Report on the National Planning of Transport put before the Leicester Conference of the Party in 1932 said 'a Board appointed on grounds of ability is likely to be far more efficient; [i.e. than a representative Board] and Socialists, above all, must keep the communal interest to the fore ... it is vital to Socialism that national ownership should show itself superior to private enterprise in all-round efficiency'.

Thus for various reasons[2] the idea of worker representation on the board of management had come to be translated into joint consultation by the time that a Labour Government came into office powerful enough to put through legislation for the nationalization of the coal industry. The general ideas which led to the demand for worker participation are still, however, quite strong though they may be searching for new forms of expression.[3]

THE OPPOSITION TO THE MINISTERIAL DEPARTMENT

The opposition to nationalization made a great deal of the argument that the Civil Service and the normal Government Department were quite unsuited for the efficient management of a large industrial undertaking.[4] The supporters, not helped by the views of the miners'

[1] See his speech opening the Second Reading Debate, March 23, 1931. *H.C. Deb.*, 250, c. 54–9.

[2] For another and fuller account of the trend in Labour Party opinion on the subject of Workers' Control, see *Workers' Control of Industry and the British Labour Party* by Robert A. Dahl in the *American Political Science Review*, 1947, pp. 875–900. Professor Dahl emphasizes the growth of the idea of a planned economy as a factor unfavourable to the acceptance of the idea of workers' control.

[3] See *Industrial Democracy and Nationalization* by Hugh Clegg (1951) and the two Fabian Pamphlets: *National Coal Board* by G. D. H. Cole and *Consultation or Joint Management* by J. M. Chalmers, I. Mikardo and G. D. H. Cole.

[4] Some of the early criticism of the Civil Service was due to the feeling that the higher grades were part of a 'governing class' that was opposed to nationalization. (See A. E. Davies, *The Case for Nationalization*, 1920, pp. 34–6.)

leaders or of the Guild Socialists, could put forward no strong case
against this line of criticism. The experience of 1914–18 was quoted to
support both sides. Even Lord Haldane who was clearly trying to
be helpful said that 'Unless you grow up in an atmosphere where it is
encouraged you do not have initiative. That is where the business
man has the strength and the advantage. He is in an atmosphere of
initiative. The Civil Servant is not . . .'[1]

Mr Justice Sankey, the Chairman of the Commission, in recommending nationalization of the mines under a Minister of Mines,
thought these difficulties could be overcome. Though civil servants
had not been trained to run an industry he thought they could be so
trained. Moreover there existed a class of men who were just as keen
to serve the State as they were to serve a private employer and who
had been shown to possess courage and initiative. (Here he was
mainly referring to the business men recruited by the Government
during the war.) Nevertheless he was moved to recommend that:

> The Treasury shall not be entitled to interfere with or to have any
> control over the appropriation of moneys derived from the industry.
> The said moneys shall be kept entirely separate and apart from other
> national moneys, until the profit accruing from the industry is periodically
> ascertained and paid into the Exchequer,

and again:

> It being of vital importance that the Mines Department should be
> managed with the freedom of a private business, the present Civil
> Service system of selection and promotion by length of service, of
> grades of servants, of minuting opinions and reports from one servant to
> another, and of salaries and pensions, shall not apply to the servants
> attached to the Mines Department.

There was also the fear of political influence if the industry were to
be managed by a Minister. As the report of anti-nationalization members of the Royal Commission stated:

> It is an inseparable feature of departmental Government that each
> man instead of taking responsibility for any proposed action should
> pass it on to his superior; and the final responsibility of the Department
> must always be [to] Parliament. Its actions are thus inevitably governed
> by political considerations and the interests of political parties.

In various forms and with various degrees of emphasis these
criticisms of departmental administration are to be found in such
diverse writings (diverse at least so far as party affiliations are concerned) as the Liberal Yellow Book (1928), *Post Office Reform* by

[1] Coal Industry Commission (1919). Q. 25598.

Lord Wolmer (1932) and *Socialization and Transport* by Mr Herbert
Morrison (1933).

The Liberal Yellow Book stated quite bluntly:

> We think that Ministers should be directly responsible for commercial
> operations and the employment of labour to the least possible extent,
> and that the financial side of these operations should be kept separate
> from the State Budget to the greatest possible extent. The great Depart-
> ments of State are not organized for business administration (p. 76).

Lord Wolmer summed up his indictment of Post Office administration in these terms:

> The Post Office is a great business which is organized not as a business
> but as a Government Department. House of Commons control results
> in over-centralization of the Post Office and timidity in its development,
> without enabling Members to secure reforms. Treasury control results
> in excessive charges to the public, and pettifogging interference with the
> Department without securing economy in administration. The fact that
> the Postmaster-General is a promising junior Minister generally results
> in his promotion before he has mastered his job. Civil Service conditions
> result in inadequate salaries for the important posts and absence of
> financial stimulus to the lower ranks. Entrance and promotion by
> examination results in a preponderance of theoretical over practical
> ability. The combined result of all these factors is to produce a Service
> which is extravagantly and inefficiently administered, whose charges to the
> public are consequently excessive, and which is therefore prevented
> from expanding as it should. Since this service is a State monopoly no
> efficient rival can supplant it, and the industries dependent upon it are
> stifled (p. 249).

Mr Morrison, though very much on guard against critics of the
Civil and Local Government Services, was nevertheless clear that he
did not want the Ministerial department for his nationalization
measures. The management must be free to pay the salaries and wages
necessary to command the type of ability needed and these could not
be tied down by Civil Service methods or Treasury control. The
management must also be:

> sufficiently free from those undesirable pressures associated with both
> public and private Parliamentary strategy, political lobbying, and
> electoral 'blackmail'. Subject to whatever Ministerial or other checks or
> appeals may be provided in the public interest, the management must be
> a responsible management and must be able to stand its ground in the
> interests of the undertaking which is committed to its charge.[1]

If there were to be a Minister in charge of an industry 'there would
be a great temptation on the part of competing candidates to make

[1] *Socialization and Transport*, p. 137.

irresponsible promises of support for better and better labour conditions' in the industry. MPs would:

> receive large numbers of letters from persons seeking employment or promotion in the publicly-owned industries and complaining about wrongful disciplinary action or dismissal.[1]

Finally,

> the Board must have autonomy and freedom of business management. It must not only be allowed to enjoy responsibility: it must even have responsibility thrust down its throat. . . . With the exception of the limited duties legally imposed upon him, the Minister will have no right to interfere with the work of the Board. . . . A mischievous and not too competent Minister could easily ruin any business undertaking if that were permitted . . .[2]

Criticisms of this kind are quite common among the literature against nationalization and go back a long time. (See, for example, *Contemporary Socialism* by John Rae (1891), p. 411.) Their acceptance by most supporters of public ownership is much more recent and coincides with the growing acceptance of the alternative offered by the public corporation. In 1931–32, G. D. H. Cole could write '. . . most people nowadays, including the majority of Socialists, do appear to hold that the direct conduct of industries through Civil Service departments is not the best method of industrial organization . . . Socialists have for a long time been veering towards the idea that publicly administered forms of enterprise ought to be conducted through some sort of *ad hoc* trading body, with accounts clearly separated from the national Budget, and with methods of administration conferring a wider discretion than can easily be reconciled either with the Civil Service tradition or with the present forms of parliamentary control through a responsible Minister.'[3]

It thus came about that neither the supporters of nationalization nor those who saw that sometimes there was a case on other grounds for publicly-owned monopolies were in favour of management by a Minister and a normal Civil Service department. What other form of management was possible?

THE PUBLIC CORPORATION

We have seen that the Bills for nationalizing coal and railways proposed to establish a Council or Board to manage the industry.

---

[1] P. 142.
[2] Pp. 169–71.
[3] *Economic Tracts for the Times* (1932), p. 270. See also Hugh Dalton, *Practical Socialism for Britain* (1935), p. 93 *et seq.*

Usually, however, a Minister was to be Chairman and the relative powers of the Minister and the members of the Council were not always clear. The Council might, of course, have been an advisory body, but this would not have satisfied those who wanted worker participation. The miners had had experience of an advisory committee during the war—the Coal Controllers' Committee—and wanted a much more responsible share in the management of the industry. If therefore there was to be a managerial board the problem was to settle satisfactorily its constitutional relations with the Minister. This could be achieved either by stressing the independence of the Board and excluding the Minister from participating in its affairs or by separating Minister and Board and giving different statutory functions to each. It could not be done by making the Board simply the agent of the Minister. Acceptance of a non-Ministerial independent board would still leave the method of appointment or election to the Board to be settled.

It is possible to find many references to the public board[1] as a possible form of management scattered throughout the early literature. For example, in his *World of Labour*, first published in 1913, G. D. H. Cole wrote that a nationalized industry 'should be run, not directly through a Department of State, but by semi-independent Commissioners with powers similar to those of the Development Commissioners or the Road Board; Parliament should of course have the power of raising questions in the House about the conduct of the industry, and should, by periodic vote, control its expenditure; but it should not interfere normally in the conduct of the enterprise, which should not be under the direct control of the Government—in its ordinary working' (pp. 380-1). But it was not until after Mr Morrison's Bill for establishing a London Passenger Transport Board (March 1931) that the idea in any clear form emerged and was accepted by the Labour movement.

Nowadays it is usual to cite the Port of London Authority, the British Broadcasting Corporation and the Central Electricity Board as the forerunners of the present Boards. Strangely enough, though the Sankey Commission heard evidence from the Chairman of the Port of London Authority, there is no indication that this form of organization influenced any of the members. I say strangely, for the Port of London Act, 1908, provided that two[2] of the ten appointed

---

[1] There was a certain amount of Australian and foreign experience of administration by independent Boards. The French CGT had put forward proposals for a tripartite board composed of representatives of workers, consumers and the general public. There was also the so-called Plumb Plan for the United States railways which attracted attention in this country.

[2] In 1924 and 1925 the Transport and General Workers' Union, through a Private Member's Bill, tried to increase the size and alter the composition of the

representatives should be appointed to the Board—one by the President of the Board of Trade and one by the London County Council—after consultation with organizations representative of labour.

On one occasion, Mr Baldwin, in supporting the establishment of a Central Electricity Board, said that the Government had in mind 'a board managed by practical men closely in touch with the industry on the lines of such an authority as the Mersey Docks and Harbour Board or the Port of London . . .'.[1] But the Port of London Authority is primarily a representative board. As such it was criticized in the Liberal Yellow Book. During the passage of the Electricity Supply Bill (1926) efforts were made to secure representation of various interests on the Board but were rejected. Nevertheless the Act (unlike later Acts) prescribed that in making appointments to the Board the Minister should consult such representatives or bodies representative of the following interests as he thought fit, i.e. local government, electricity, commerce, industry, transport, agriculture and labour.

The Crawford Committee on Broadcasting (1925) which proposed the establishment of a 'public corporation . . . to act as a Trustee for the national interest . . .' suggested that a body of this kind could be set up by Act of Parliament (and if so the Pacific Cable Act, 1901, which set up the Pacific Cable Board, might be the model) or under the Companies Acts. In the latter case the company would be limited by guarantee, the word 'limited' in the title being dispensed with and the subscribers to the Memorandum of Association should be nominees of the Postmaster-General. Members of the Commission should be appointed by the Crown and should be persons 'of judgment and independence' and 'of business acumen and experienced in affairs'.

Though the BBC and CEB are now extensively held up as desirable models for the management of nationalized enterprise, and though their experience has greatly influenced political thought, neither body was established as the clearly-thought-out answer to the general problems of public management set by nationalization. Each was designed to meet a particular situation.

There is little evidence that in 1926–27 the BBC and CEB were regarded as a possible pattern for the management of nationalized industry or even that the main ideas were understood. Mr W. Graham, the chief Labour spokesman in the debate on the BBC

Authority to include nine representatives of labour. It was not until after the establishment of the British Broadcasting Corporation and the Central Electricity Board in 1926–7 that the Port of London Authority begins to be generally quoted as a desirable or possible ancestor.

[1] Quoted by Lincoln Gordon. *The Public Corporation in Great Britain*, p. 100.

(and a member of the Crawford Committee), expressed the doubt whether the Government's proposals would not make the BBC 'a mere creature of the Postmaster-General', whereas Mr Ammon, a more typical Labour speaker, said 'it would have been much better if they had gone the whole road and handed the administration over entirely to the Post Office as a national concern'.

Once established, however, the BBC and the CEB, along with the PLA, were used as arguments for a new form of public management —the public corporation. The Liberal Yellow Book (1928) talked of the Public Concern and thought that 'for the administrative and executive management of public concerns, the *ad hoc* Public Board points to the right line of evolution'.[1] Lord Wolmer held up these three bodies as the model for the reform of the Post Office. The main strength of these bodies to him was the absence of direct political control. They could operate by business methods and yet they had a legal responsibility to the public. Mr Morrison used the example of the three bodies to support his proposal[2] for a London Passenger Transport Board, and then in his *Socialization and Transport* (1933) and in his general advocacy in the Labour Party did more than anybody else to get the idea of the public corporation fully accepted in labour and trade union circles.[3]

THE LIMITED LIABILITY COMPANY

To many people nationalization was an attack on the private ownership of capital and on the profit motive. At one time these people assumed that management was the same as ownership and was, therefore, rewarded by profits. It became increasingly apparent that the development of the limited liability company had modified these assumptions. On the one hand it had facilitated a distinction between ownership and management. In the large firms in particular there was a body of shareholders who owned and had rights but did not manage; instead they appointed a Board of Directors to do this for them. On the other hand, again in the larger firms, much of the top management was remunerated mainly by salary and only very par-

[1] P. 77. It used the term Public Corporation to mean a special category of public limited liability company (broadly large-scale private monopolies) which were to be subjected to more stringent control.

[2] In his Second Reading Speech on the London Passenger Transport Bill, Mr Morrison said he had been influenced in his choice of the public corporation form by the Liberal Yellow Book and by the Central Electricity Board. As Minister of Transport he was the Minister most concerned with the CEB and therefore had had direct experience of the main body of this kind.

[3] See G. D. H. Cole, *The Essentials of Socialization* (*Political Quarterly*, July 1931, expanded in his *Economic Tracts for the Times*) for an examination of whether the CEB and the proposed LPTB were examples of socialization.

tially by a share in the profits. These developments in association with the growth of the idea of management as a thing in itself made an important contribution to the public corporation as a form of industrial management.

The separation of ownership from management opened the way for State ownership without State management. In its simplest form this could mean just the purchase by the Government or other public body of all or part of the shares in a private firm. The Government would then be in the position to exercise the rights of the shareholder, e.g. take part in the election of Directors. If it had a majority holding then it could dominate the concern. The mixed undertaking, popular on the Continent, is found here only in a few cases, e.g. the Anglo-Iranian Oil Company and the Manchester Ship Canal Company. The mixed undertaking associated as it was with private profit was not acceptable to Socialists. The limited liability company had, however, opened the way to wider possibilities. For control over the management was a right normally given only to those holding risk bearing shares. Holders of debentures and fixed interest stock normally could exercise their powers only should the interest not be paid promptly. If, therefore, the capital of a public concern could be composed wholly of fixed interest securities, two results would be achieved. On the one hand, the 'profit motive' could be eliminated and on the other the holders of the capital would not have rights of control.[1] But who would then elect the directors and exercise the powers normally exercised by the shareholders? After much discussion on the Bills for establishing the Central Electricity Board and the London Passenger Transport Board, the answer came to be the Minister.

Thus some people saw the public corporation as a joint stock company, non-profit making (and non-risk bearing), financed by fixed interest securities with the rights of the shareholders exercised in the first instance by the Minister and ultimately by Parliament. These people saw the relationship between the Corporation and the Minister (and Parliament) as being the same as that between the private Board of Directors and the shareholders.

As the Liberal Yellow Book put it, '. . . a Board . . . appointed by and ultimately responsible to some public authority, national or local —but only in the sense in which a company is responsible to its shareholders—is a better model to follow than that of direct public trading . . . We see no inherent reason why such Boards, merely

---

[1] See G. D. H. Cole, *The Essentials of Socialization* (1931) for a discussion of the relation between different forms of capital holding and 'socialization'. R. H. Tawney in his *Acquisitive Society* (1921) has a chapter headed 'The Liberation of Industry' devoted to freeing industrial management from shareholder control.

because they have no private shareholders and are functioning entirely in the public interest, need be any less efficient than the Boards of large public companies, which are managed by salaried directors and officials subject to no real and effective control by their shareholders' (p. 77).

SOME IMPLICATIONS

I think it is too early as yet to reach definite conclusions about whether the public corporation can give us the best of both possible worlds or even whether the two worlds are altogether reconcilable. But we can at least ask certain questions and indicate certain implications.

First, if the criticisms against the Ministerial departments are valid (and they are criticisms which have been accepted by all Parties), why should the public corporation not be substituted for a good deal of present day Ministerial administration? If political management is so inimical to good management, the Civil Service so bureaucratic, and the Treasury such a dead hand, why, for example, should the Ministries of Food, Materials and Supply and the Post Office be left in such hands? I mention only departments with large commercial and industrial activities for the public corporation has mainly been suggested for the management of such activities. But many of the criticisms of the Ministerial department must, if true, be equally valid for the non-trading services.

It is possible, of course, that the supporters of nationalization did not wholly accept these criticisms but accepted the public corporation because it enabled them to get a measure of nationalization without having to try to answer the criticisms. Or it may be that these criticisms are based on either an imperfect or an out of date knowledge of the Civil Service.

But if these criticisms are wholly or mainly justified, should we not ask whether we cannot secure some of the good results claimed for business management, e.g. initiative, by modification of existing departmental practice or attitude? Or is it possible that the necessary conditions or prerequisites are lacking in the Ministerial department?

Second, what are the conditions which allow 'business management' to thrive and how are they provided in the public corporation but not in the Ministerial department? As I see it there are two main conditions stressed by the supporters of the corporation: freedom from financial control and freedom from political control. These two freedoms are more closely associated than many realize. Let us look again at business management as it is found in the limited company.

In the limited company the shareholders do not attempt to manage but confine themselves to seeing that good directors are appointed and that certain changes of policy, e.g. raising of new capital, are not made without their approval. If things are going well the board and the management are normally left very largely to their own devices. This relationship is sustained by two factors. On the one hand, and most important, it is usually fairly easy to tell whether the directors are doing a good job—that test is the dividend or at most an examination of the Balance Sheet. On the other hand, the shareholders in a large concern are so numerous and unorganized that it would be virtually impossible for them to exercise any detailed or continuous control over the management. The same relationship could be sustained in the public corporation if there was a ready acceptance of a similar simple test and if the Minister and Parliament were ready to accept the role of shareholder. The 'business' supporters of the corporations assume the existence of these conditions. In doing so they are partly being optimistic, and partly being misled by a too simple analogy.

In place of the 'size of dividend' test the pre-war supporters of the public corporation put the 'absence of loss'. These bodies were to be required to pay their way and this included meeting the interest on their capital. The post-war nationalization legislation prescribes that the Board must arrange its affairs so that its receipts should not be less than outgoings over a period of years. One possible approach of Parliament to its responsibilities would be to wait until the annual accounts of the Board appeared and be happy if a loss had been avoided but get anxious and ask questions if the accounts showed a deficit.

This simple approach is under attack from several quarters. First, as to the validity of the 'break even' test: (1) Certain theoretical economists are arguing that a proper distribution of resources requires the nationalized boards to fix their prices to cover marginal and not average cost. If adopted, this rule might cause a Board to make a large loss or a large profit according to whether the marginal cost of its service or product was below or above average cost. (2) As the Boards usually operate as monopolies it is argued that balanced accounts cannot be a certain indication of efficiency, they may merely reflect high prices obtained by monopoly exploitation. (3) There are some who see these industries as public services little different from services wholly or partly met out of taxation. These people are prepared to subordinate the 'break even' test to social needs as they see them. Usually this means they wish the Board to make a loss for some reason or other—possibly in order that higher wages can be paid.

The first, and probably the last, of these three sets of critics have not a great deal of general political support, but the second group undoubtedly voices a feeling fairly strong in all Parties. If for any reason the confidence of a company's shareholders in the profit and loss and balance sheet test were undermined, their task of controlling the directors would be very much more difficult. In the case of the public Board any nonacceptance of this financial test means the application of other tests which would probably be less simple and might well involve detailed investigation into the Board's affairs.

Second, these considerations are reinforced when it is appreciated that the Minister and Parliament to whom the Board is accountable are not merely in almost continuous session but represent not only the shareholders but also the consumers and the workers. What is a simple relationship in the limited company thus becomes highly complicated. The shareholders may be satisfied by the financial results and they do not have to ask whether the consumers or the workers are satisfied. It is assumed that if they are not they will either go elsewhere or profits will fall. But if a Board is operating a monopoly can the consumer be altogether happy that the absence of an annual financial loss is the test of an efficient service, providing cheap and adequate supplies? May he not want to enquire more deeply into the Board's operations—whether prices could be lowered or the quality of service improved.

Conclusions drawn from the experiences of joint stock companies in private hands and operating in a competitive market may, therefore, not be applicable to public monopolies in whatever form these are managed. In so far as this is so those who saw the public corporation as conferring the benefits of independent commercial management will have to change their ideas. For should the idea ever be accepted that any of the everyday actions of the Boards may be subjected to detailed Parliamentary or departmental scrutiny, then we may have moved into having the worst of both worlds.

As I understand the business argument, it is precisely this kind of detailed outside investigation which is inimical to initiative, experimentation and vigorous management. For the manager must, during the course of the years, take hundreds of decisions. The good manager is the man who makes a smaller number of mistakes than other managers, but even an outstanding manager is likely to make some mistakes. If there is a straightforward overall test, e.g. the profit earned during the year, the few mistakes may be more than counterbalanced by the many good decisions and so the general results are favourable. But a detailed scrutiny of most or all the decisions, such as might be carried out by a Parliamentary Committee, would reveal many of these errors. Moreover, they would be scrutinized by people wise after the event, possibly armed with data which came available only after the decision had been taken. In the absence of any overall test, and with the possibility of party politics playing a part, it is inevitable that some of these errors and the authors of them would be held up to public ridicule. Good decisions tend to be passed over or accepted as a matter of course. These are the circumstances which may cause managers to play for safety or at least not to accept responsibility for something which with all the good intention in the world they may not be able to explain satisfactorily in public.

Moreover, public criticism falls on the senior people and not necessarily on the man who actually made the mistake. As a result there is a tendency for headquarters to be unwilling to allow local discretion and for those who exercise discretion to avoid risky decisions for which their seniors will be blamed.

Finally, there is a wider issue which has so far not been clarified. The supporters of the business principle see management as a technical service and as such hardly the subject for 'lay' intervention. Just as the layman should not interfere in the work of the surgeon or doctor in treating a patient or of the engineer in designing a bridge so he should not interfere in the work of the manager in managing an industry. Many supporters of the public corporation find it more possible to accept this attitude because the manager is not working for 'profit'. It is the 'acquisitive society' which perverts the manager: free him from the rapacity of the shareholders and industrial management becomes a vocation or profession, and a profession is concerned with the service it could perform, not with the gains it could amass. 'They (i.e. members of a profession) may, as in the case of a successful doctor, grow rich; but the meaning of their profession, both for themselves and for the public, is not that they make money but that they make health, or safety, or knowledge, or good government or good law. They depend on it for their income, but they do not consider that any conduct which increases their income is on that account right'.[1]

I do not wish to decry for one moment the motive of public service and standards of professional conduct. These are clearly of considerable importance in all walks of life. I merely wish to point out that many of those who strongly support nationalization do so because they want industry to be operated so as to achieve what to them are desirable social ends, and these may not flow automatically from the exercise of 'professional' conduct.

Thought of this kind has usually been indistinct or frankly sentimental or even mystical. It usually assumes that people know the public good but are prevented from following it by the search for profit. It flourishes in such slogans as 'production for service and not

[1] R. H. Tawney, *The Acquisitive Society* (1921), p. 108.

for profit'. It seems to me, however, that the basis of efficient business management is the production of what people want for the lowest cost. The avoidance of loss is as important as the making of a profit. Many of those who talk about industry being run as a public service have in mind the achievement of social ends which are uneconomic in the sense that they may involve the firm or the industry in making a loss or raising production costs. Private firms may, of course, disregard costs on occasion in order to further some public aim. But were the business manager to be told that as a general rule he must be guided by something called 'social' or 'public' policy rather than by production costs I cannot but feel that he would be rather out of his depth. The Civil Service is organized for that kind of decision, business management is not.

Sometimes the relative functions of the Minister and the Board are described as general policy on the one hand and day-to-day management on the other. If by general policy is meant the kind of decisions which are normally taken by a Board of Directors it would seem that such a division would leave the Boards with little responsibility for major managerial matters. But should it mean that the Minister supplies the viewpoint of social policy and the Board the viewpoint of business management there is a possible division of responsibility, workable if the Minister and the Board have a little of each other's viewpoint and if the objects of the two viewpoints are not too far apart.

The balance between the two may not always be easy to maintain. So far as form of management is concerned the greater the stress on running industry as part of social and political policy the less the need for the public corporation and the more suitable becomes the Ministerial department with its attendant Parliamentary control. At the moment the business principle is being preferred to the representative principle. It may continue to be so though there will almost certainly be some comeback from those whose main emphasis is on social purpose. As the late Professor Laski said in what must have been almost his last public lecture:[1]

> 'We have grown into the acceptance of the Public Corporation as the form that nationally owned industries should assume, less, I think, because everyone is agreed that this is their appropriate way of organization, than because business men have said, so long and so loudly, that you could not run an industry in national hands as the Post Office has been run for a century or so, that the business men's attitude has been taken for granted.'

It would seem that the distinction between public and private

[1] *Reflections on the Constitution* (1951), pp. 199–200.

enterprise is rapidly growing less clear. The private firm is subject to Ministerial control and has to have regard to the main trends of public policy. The public Board is trying to operate on principles of management well established in private industry. Nevertheless, there is considerable confusion about the factors which produce good or bad management and about the form of managerial body suitable for achieving different purposes. My impression is that we have not yet given sufficient thought to the problems of management and public control set by the large-scale monopoly. Much of our thinking is still based on the lessons derived from watching the results achieved by smaller-scale competitive units.

ACKNOWLEDGMENT

I wish to thank my colleagues Professor G. D. H. Cole and Mr Hugh Clegg, and Mr Geoffrey Ostergaard, Student of Nuffield College, for their most helpful comments and their criticisms of the first draft of this paper.

9. LIBERALS AND THE PUBLIC CORPORATION*

THE NATURE AND FUNCTION OF PUBLIC CONCERNS

When we seek to analyse in the light of experience the characteristics of the types of enterprises which tend to become Public Concerns, it is fairly clear what they are. They comprise undertakings of great national importance; which require large amounts of capital, yet may fail to attract private enterprise on an adequate scale, either because of the necessity of limiting profits or for some other reason; where unavoidable conditions of monopoly would render unregulated private enterprise dangerous; or where the private shareholder has ceased to perform a useful function. These characteristics are not only explanations, but justifications of public ownership or of regulation in the appropriate conditions.

It follows that there is a necessary and important place for the Public Concern in the national economic system. The problem is to evolve an efficient business organization for such concerns, to find room for various types intermediate between the Public and the Private Concern, and to define in the right way the field of operation appropriate to each type.

* From *Britain's Industrial Future: the Report of the Liberal Industrial Enquiry*, Ernest Benn, 1928, pp. 75–77 and pp. 80–81. Reprinted by permission of Bernard Gilpin and by courtesy of the publishers.

State Trading

As regards the mode of operating a Public Concern, we see no great advantage, and some substantial disadvantages, in direct State trading. . .

If 'the Nationalization of Industry' means this, we are decidedly opposed to it. We think that Ministers should be directly responsible for commercial operations and the employment of labour to the least possible extent, and that the financial side of these operations should be kept separate from the State Budget to the greatest possible extent. The great Departments of State are not organized for business administration. Nor are Ministers selected for their business capacity. So far, therefore, from recommending any additions to the list of State trading concerns operated by the Central Government, we are inclined to think that it would have been better if in the first instance the Post Office, Telephones, and Telegraphs had been in the hands of an *ad hoc* administrative body detached from the Central Administration. There are weighty arguments for requiring Government undertakings to be conducted in a form analogous to that of joint-stock companies, the capital of which is owned and the Directors appointed by the State. This is the present method of administering, for example, the Belgian and German Railways and the German Post Office. Amongst its advantages are a greater detachment from politics and from political influence.

Municipal Trading

We are in favour of municipal trading in the sense of local public ownership of local public utilities. But we are doubtful whether the right form of organization and the right geographical unit have yet been attained. As regards organization, there are often objections to direct administration by Committees of Local Authorities. As in the case of State enterprises, the right model seems to us to be one which borrows some of the machinery of large-scale private enterprise. Generally speaking, an *ad hoc* body should be set up, the executive and administrative Board of which would correspond to the Board of Directors of private concerns (though freed, we hope, from some of the grave faults of these Boards as at present constituted, to which we shall advert in the next chapter), the Local Authorities themselves corresponding to the shareholders. We elaborate this idea in further detail below. As regards the choice of geographical unit, there is no presumption that this will coincide with the boundaries of local government areas. It is a defect of many existing municipal undertakings that their operations are confined to an area too small to be worked to the best advantage. Hence existing municipal and local

enterprises should be overhauled so as to ensure for each enterprise
the optimum area. This task would be facilitated by a form of
organization analogous to that of a public company in that a single
executive could be responsible to more than one local authority as
shareholders.

THE LINE OF EVOLUTION

Thus we are of opinion that, for the administrative and executive
management of public concerns, the *ad hoc* Public Board points to
the right line of evolution. We think that a Board of this kind, appointed by and ultimately responsible to some public authority,
national or local—but only in the sense in which a company is
responsible to its shareholders—is a better model to follow than that
of direct public trading, whether national or local. We see no inherent reason why such Boards, merely because they have no private
shareholders and are functioning entirely in the public interest, need
be any less efficient than the Boards of large public companies, which
are managed by salaried directors and officials subject to no real or
effective control by their shareholders.

But it is quite another question whether the existing examples of
Public Boards ought to be imitated, or are incapable of improvement.
We have allowed Public Boards to creep into our economic system,
without enough preliminary criticism or deliberate reconsideration of
their efficiency in the light of experience. They have not come into
the limelight of public discussion. Parliament and the Press since the
War have been almost oblivious of them.

PROPOSALS

Our suggestions for the future organization of Public Boards may be
formulated as follows:
  (i) The method of appointing the executive authority of Public
      Boards should be reformed, particularly in the case of some of
      the older established bodies. Business and technical efficiency
      should be aimed at in choosing the personnel rather than the
      representation of 'interests', consumers' or other. We see no
      objection to some powers of co-option by the executive
      authority itself—which is, in practice, the method by which
      the Boards of most public companies are filled. Above all,
      large Boards, half composed of dead-heads or ex-officio
      members who never attend, are to be avoided. We doubt if it
      is in the interests of efficiency that, for example, the Chairman
      and Vice-Chairman of a vast undertaking like the Metro-
      politan Water Board should be unpaid. We think that the

appropriate Ministry should be given powers, subject to proper safeguards, to overhaul the membership of the governing bodies of Public Boards and the mode of their appointment.

(ii) We need to build up an attractive career for business admini-stration of this type open to all the talents. A regular service should be recruited for Public Concerns with a cadre and a pension scheme, with room for the rapid promotion of excep-tionally efficient officials and with satisfactory prizes for those who reach the top. We should like to see the maximum amount of interchange of the officials between different undertakings, and a practice of moving such officials about at different stages of their career from one concern to another—and not leaving them as at present to vegetate in one job for thirty years or more—wherever the requirement of special technical qualifications does not stand in the way of transfer.

(iii) In the case of concerns ultimately subject to municipal and other local authorities, it might be advisable to set up a body representative of such authorities from all parts of the country with functions covering those now performed for the Civil Service by the Civil Service Commission and the Establish-ments Division of the Treasury. By these means the prospects and attractions of a business and administrative service for local bodies might be, as they need to be, greatly improved.

(iv) Whenever possible, there should be several Public Boards, in any given type of undertaking, operating in different parts of the country in circumstances sufficiently similar to give value to comparisons between their respective results.

(v) We attach a great importance to a proper system of accounting which distinguishes on sound principles between expenditure on capital and on current account. The system should be as uniform as possible, so as to facilitate comparisons. We ought to know exactly how much new capital is being put into these enterprises year by year and how much is being written off the old capital; we ought to be able to compare the prices charged and the profits earned by Public Concerns of a similar kind in different parts of the country. It should be added that existing State-run concerns . . . whether or not they continue as they are, should also show their financial results in a proper shape, keeping business accounts and presenting clear balance sheets which distinguish expenditure on capital account and make allowance for interest and depreciation. The charge on the National Budget for the year, or, where there is a trading profit, the contribution to the Budget, should then be the net balance on income account properly chargeable to the year in question.

10. LABOUR AND THE PUBLIC CORPORATION*

37. . . . the most suitable form of public ownership is a Public Corporation of the kind proposed in the 1932 TUC report on 'Public Control and Regulation of Industry and Trade' and described in greater detail in the TUC plans for the public ownership of particular industries. The main argument for the establishment of Public Corporations was set out clearly in the 1932 Report, and is important enough to quote again in full. In the words of that Report:

> . . . it is doubtful, according to modern Socialist ideas, whether there is ever any advantage in conducting an industry or a commercial service by the method of direct State operation, i.e. by a Government Department. State activities such as the general supervision and administration of national education, public health, postal service, and trade, as well as the older functions in relation to foreign affairs, finance, and the rest, are obviously different in kind from the operation of services like Transport, Coal Mining, etc. The former are typical Governmental functions which cannot be divorced from the machinery of the State and Parliament. The latter are really commercial undertakings, whose business is production, not regulation and supervision.
>
> The idea that socialization and public control of industries necessarily mean administration directly by a Government department dies hard, but it is dying in every country. The importance of flexibility and expert management on the one hand, and of freedom from party political domination on the other hand, has so far been recognized that (as in the Labour Government's London Passenger Transport Bill) the tendency is to secure public control and the elimination of the profit motive while keeping the actual management in the hands of a body not susceptible to party political pressure and interference.

38. For those industries for which nationalization is proposed, therefore, a Public Corporation would be established by Act of Parliament to take over all the undertakings in the particular industry or group of related industries. In relation to corporations of this type, it is essential that responsibility to the public shall be maintained by the appointment of the members of its governing body by a Minister responsible to Parliament, and they should therefore be

* From Trades Union Congress: *Interim Report on Post-War Reconstruction*, 1944, paras. 37–40. Reprinted by permission of the authors.

selected on the basis of their competence and ability to administer the industry efficiently in the public interest. It is further essential that their organization shall make proper provision for the representation and participation of workpeople, and to this end statutory provision should be made for the interests of workpeople to be represented on the Governing Board.

39. It will be necessary also to provide for the ultimate responsibility of the managements of socialized industries to a Minister in order to ensure the proper co-ordination of their policies and that the industries are conducted in full accordance with the Government's general plans for the maintenance of employment, the control and the location of industry, and the furtherance of socially desirable expansions of consumption.

40. Where the policy of the industry is required to be determined in part at a sectional or regional level, it would of course be necessary to establish subsidiary Boards, similarly constituted, for the sections or regions concerned. Subsidiary Boards might also be established to perform special functions, such as marketing at home or abroad, the bulk purchase of materials or imports or products to supplement home supplies, where the organization of the industry required it.

11. A NEW DEAL FOR THE POST OFFICE*

46. At this point we shall concern ourselves only with those root causes which, in our opinion, are responsible for such defects as exist, endeavouring at the same time to furnish the reasons which have prompted us to regard as impracticable certain radical reforms suggested to us. It may be apposite here to say that several witnesses, whose opinions carry considerable weight with us, while differing as to the solution of the problem, were very largely in fundamental agreement as to the nature of these causes which give rise to the defects mentioned and militate against a higher standard in the conduct of Post Office Communications Services.

The causes may be described as:
(1) The relationship in which the Post Office stands, as a Revenue Department, to the Exchequer.
(2) The internal organization of the Post Office which is to some extent conditioned by (1).

47. It has been further contended that over-centralization inevitably results from Parliamentary intervention in regard to the day to day

* From *Report of Committee of Enquiry on the Post Office*, 1932, Cmd 4149, paras. 46–9, 54–7 and 61.

working of the machine. It has been argued that so long as the Post-master-General is liable to be questioned and cross-examined in the House of Commons on every petty detail of daily administration, so long will the devolution of responsibility be hampered, since every official feels that his actions may form the subject of Parliamentary interpellation, and that he himself may be called upon to justify his actions months, and even years, afterwards. In addition, the liability to Parliamentary questioning entails the maintenance of elaborate records and breeds in the individual a tendency to require documentary justification or authority for every action taken.

48. It has been represented from many quarters that this position would, and can only be, remedied by sweeping changes in the status of the Post Office and the transfer of the control and administration of its Communications Services, either in whole or in part, to an independent authority of the Public Utility Company or Statutory Corporation type.

49. We have examined the arguments in favour of the total transference to a body of this character of all Post Office Communications Services—Mails, Telephones and Telegraphs—and we are definitely of opinion that such transference is impracticable, nor do we believe it to be either necessary or desirable. We consider that the public have a right to the influence which Parliamentary discussion and control alone can give. . .

[*The Committee then proceeds to state its reasons for opposing also the transference to an independent Corporation of either the Telephone and Telegraph Services, or the Telephone Service by itself.*]

54. Even assuming that the total or partial transference of the Communications Services to an independent Corporation were feasible, we are by no means satisfied that the management of the Services in question by such a body would infallibly result in the disappearance of the defects to which we have alluded, while it might be withdrawn too much from the wholesome operation of public criticism. Over-centralization, absence of initiative, lack of imagination and failure to give appropriate representations to technical functions are faults which are to be found in the sphere of private as well as Government administration.

We also feel impelled to observe that those sections of the public which are most insistent upon the Communications Services of the Post Office being conducted on the lines of commercial enterprise, are not infrequently those most prone to demand services and facilities which cannot possibly pay their way. We fear that independent management would seek to develop the more remunerative business of the denser areas to the detriment of more remote and sparsely populated districts.

55. It cannot be denied that Parliamentary intervention in the minor details of daily administration may be harassing and sometimes vexatious; it indubitably involves in many instances an expenditure of time and effort quite disproportionate to the importance of the matter in question. At the same time, we are inclined to think that this insistence on the supposed results of Parliamentary intervention in matters of detail is somewhat unduly stressed and that in the long run, the advantages of the power of Parliamentary intervention outweigh its disadvantages. It seems to us that where complaints are expressed against a business so closely in contact with the everyday lives of the public as the Post Office, some means of ventilation is necessary, and on the whole we believe that the House of Commons provides the best machinery for this purpose. In effect, we do not consider the relationship in which the Post Office stands to Parliament is a factor which essentially and inevitably makes the efficient performance of its duties impossible, or that the position of the Post Office in this respect differs substantially from other Government Departments subject to Parliamentary control.

56. We do, however, consider that the main causes of such defects as may exist, are the two described in paragraph 46, viz. the relationship between the Post Office and the Exchequer, and the internal organization of the Department, and we believe that the faults to which attention has been drawn, can be eradicated by certain modifications of financial status and by changes in organization at least as effectively as by the revolutionary step of removing the Post Office Communications Services from direct Government control.

57. As we have indicated, we have formed the opinion that one of the main obstacles to the more effective performance of the Post Office is the absence of what may be termed 'self-contained' finance. So long as the existing financial arrangements continue, so long will the tendency to regard the Post Office as a revenue-producing instrument obscure and impede its primary function, which is the service of the public. By self-contained finance we mean briefly a system under which the Post Office, after making a certain agreed annual contribution to the Exchequer, would be allowed to use its surpluses, after making the necessary reserves, for the benefit of the public, the improvement of services and the development of its business. Self-contained finance would enable the management of the Post Office to concentrate upon the service of its public instead of being faced with dual and often conflicting objectives. . .

61. We consider, therefore, that the main modification in the status of the Post Office which is required is in respect of its relationship to the Exchequer.

D

12. ANOTHER NEW DEAL FOR THE
POST OFFICE*

The publication of a White Paper last year on *The Status of the Post Office*, followed by the introduction of the Post Office Bill, which received its Second Reading on January 26 of this year, carries a stage further a series of Post Office reforms which began nearly thirty years ago.

The Post Office had been for long a highly unpopular department. Jokes about Post Office pens, like those about mothers-in-law and railway sandwiches, were among the stock-in-trade of popular comedians. The department was regarded with disfavour by politicians of all parties; and in December 1931 a memorial signed by 320 MPs was addressed to the Prime Minister asking him to transfer the business of the Post Office to a public corporation. The parliamentarians who signed the memorial were mostly Conservative; but members of the Labour Party shared the view that the Post Office, as then organized, was ill fitted to attain a high degree of efficiency. Lord Attlee, who served as Postmaster-General in MacDonald's second Labour Government, wrote an article in 1931 declaring that Treasury control is wholly incompatible with the flexibility necessary for the conduct of a business concern, and urged that Treasury control over the Post Office should be abolished. He also remarked on the unfavourable effects of parliamentary interpellation on the work of the Post Office.

THE BRIDGEMAN COMMITTEE

Shortly afterwards the Government appointed the Bridgeman Committee to inquire into the Post Office. The Committee rejected the idea of a public corporation but recommended some far-reaching changes in the organization and operation of the Post Office which were promptly put into effect by the Government. In place of a small secretariat under the Permanent Secretary, which arrogated to itself authority to decide virtually everything, and which excluded important officers in charge of vital operating and staff functions, a Post Office Board was set up, with the Postmaster-General as chairman. The members include the chief officers in charge of mail services, telecommunications, engineering, finance, etc., as well as the Director-General. Boards of a similar type were set up in the Post

* From William A. Robson: 'A New Deal for the Post Office', *The Political Quarterly*, Vol. 32, No. 2, April–June 1961, pp. 139–45. Reprinted by permission of the author and the editors of *The Political Quarterly*.

Office regions. By this means the senior officers in charge of the major functions are enabled to participate fully in policy decisions at the highest level.

The Committee declared that they did not consider the relation in which the Post Office stands to Parliament to be a factor which necessarily makes efficient performance of its duties impossible. The main obstacle to efficiency in their view was the absence of self-contained finance, which would enable the management of the Post Office to concentrate on service to the public instead of being faced with conflicting objectives. The knowledge that any increase of profits would be entirely absorbed by the Exchequer had a detrimental effect on Post Office enterprise and initiative. They thought that self-contained finance would create a radically different outlook.

The relations between the Post Office and the Treasury were modified in consequence of this recommendation. The Post Office was to be required to pay an annual sum to the Treasury to cover interest on past capital expenditure, a royalty for the monopoly conferred by Parliament, a payment for Income Tax, Schedule A, and adjustments for work done for other departments by the Post Office. The new arrangement was authorized for the first time by the Finance Act, 1933. But in 1934–35, out of a surplus of £12 million earned by the Post Office, the Chancellor took the lion's share of £10¾ million; and this annual tribute was exacted from 1933 until 1939. The amount was not based on any principle but merely represented the average cash surplus which the Post Office had earned during the three years prior to the introduction of the new arrangement. The Treasury was quite unwilling to surrender any substantial part of the money it had extorted from the Post Office.

The arrangements for dividing the surplus between the Treasury and the Post Office were rescinded on the outbreak of the Second World War, and were not revived until 1956, when it was agreed that for a trial period of five years a sum of £5 million should be paid annually to the Exchequer, any remaining surplus going to the Post Office's revenue reserve.

Despite this concession, nothing approaching financial autonomy was conferred on the Post Office. Every penny of revenue had to be paid into the Exchequer and every penny required by the Post Office for its expenditure had to be voted by Parliament and doled out by the Exchequer.

SELF-CONTAINED FINANCE

The system outlined in the 1960 White Paper and now embodied in the Post Office Bill is intended to give the Post Office greater commercial and financial freedom while remaining under the direct control of the Postmaster-General. Post Office finances are to be separated from the Exchequer, and will no longer be dependent on money voted by Parliament in the annual estimates. Thus, the elaborate scrutiny and control exercised by the Treasury, by the Chancellor of the Exchequer, and by the Estimates Committee, will no longer apply to the Post Office. The justification for this is that the Post Office depends for its revenue not on taxation but on the money it receives from its customers.

Henceforth the Post Office will prepare and present only Commercial Accounts. The antiquated Appropriation Accounts and the cash accounts will be discontinued. A Post Office Fund will be established into which all revenue will be paid and from which all sums required for the purpose of ordinary Post Office business will be taken. Thus a further stage has been reached in the protracted struggle to secure self-contained finance for the Post Office.

TREASURY CONTROL

Yet the Post Office has not by any means achieved financial autonomy. First, Treasury control will continue in respect of capital developments. This includes approval of the total amount proposed to be spent each year and of borrowing for the purpose of such investment. In the event of a struggle with rival claimants in the public sector for capital in short supply, the Post Office might have to justify its investment proposals in detail. In these respects the Post Office will be in the same position as the nationalized industries. Secondly, the Treasury will control the foreign exchange operations of the Post Office. And thirdly the Treasury will regulate the pay, grading, and conditions of service of the Post Office staff, who will remain civil servants.

In my view it is right in principle that the Treasury should exercise these controls. The capital expenditure of the public sector is a matter of great importance to the whole economy, and the Chancellor, and ultimately the Cabinet, must have the final decision. But a much more liberal policy is needed on the part of the Treasury towards Post Office development, particularly in regard to telephones, than it has shown in the past. In this field we are far behind the standard set not only by the United States but by many European countries. This applies to the number of telephones in proportion to the population, the intensity of use, the standard of service, and the type of equipment in use. The disparity between the excellence of the postal service, in which the British Post Office leads the world, and the mediocrity of the telephone service, is striking and deserving of investigation. The telephone service absorbs by far the greater share of capital investment—about 88 per cent, compared with 8 per cent for post and 4 per cent for telegraphs. On the other hand, the telephones contributed nearly £17 million to the total surplus of about £21 million in 1959–60. It is frequently alleged that the Treasury is largely responsible for the stunted development of the telephone service in this country; and Lord Crook referred with some bitterness in the House of Lords on February 1 to the dead hand of Treasury control which has limited the ability of the Post Office to give us an up-to-date telephone service.

Again, in the matter of pay, grading, and conditions of service, it is necessary that the Post Office staff should be kept broadly in line with the rest of the civil service, in so far as circumstances are comparable.

SHOULD THE POST OFFICE PAY TAXES?

What is much more questionable is the obligation, as part of the new arrangement, of the Post Office to pay to the Exchequer a contribution in lieu of taxation. The 'governing principle' is that the Post Office will pay what it would pay in taxation if it were a commercial profit-making concern. 'It is not intended,' says the White Paper, 'that the Exchequer should be deprived of what would accrue to it if Post Office activities were subject to normal tax law.' What this means in practice is that the charges of the Post Office will be higher than they need be in order to include an element of taxation. In our view there is nothing to be said in favour of requiring publicly owned services to contribute to general taxation. This question was fought out long ago in the sphere of municipal trading. Joseph Chamberlain, as Lord Mayor of Birmingham, had persuaded the City Corporation to embark on municipal trading and land ownership on a large scale in order to make profits to reduce the local rates. The Webbs, Bernard Shaw, and other leading Fabians opposed the idea that the public services should be run in order to relieve the ratepayer. This view has, on the whole, prevailed in local government. It should prevail equally in nationally owned undertakings, because the analogy with private enterprise is misleading. What is taxed in private enterprise is profit, which is available for distribution to the stockholders for their personal benefit. Profit in this sense does not exist in public enterprise; there can only be a surplus, and there is no one to whom it can be distributed. The main use to which the surplus should be put is the improvement of the service. There is no more justification for imposing a tax on the use of postal services than there is in making a charge for using the highway. Both are essential means of communication;

and the mere fact that it is convenient to charge individuals who use the postal or telecommunications services does not justify requiring them to contribute to the Exchequer as customers of the Post Office.

REPAYMENT OF CAPITAL DEBT

Another feature of the new arrangement which calls for comment is that the outstanding capital indebtedness of the Post Office to the Exchequer, which amounts to about £800 million, is to be repaid by twenty-five equal portions during a similar number of years. Hitherto the outstanding debt of the Post Office to the Exchequer has been perpetual; now there is to be an obligation to repay it unless it is renewed. Here is an example of the curious distinction which is often made in this country between public and private enterprise in the treatment of their capital liabilities. The capital of a company is represented by the assets of the business, and it is illegal to repay such capital to the stockholders without the permission of the High Court. In the case of a local authority or a public corporation, and now the Post Office, the capital liabilities are to be treated as a debt to be repaid within twenty-five years. Thus, a heavy obligation is laid on the shoulders of the Post Office for which there is no parallel in private enterprise, apart from debentures or loan stock, which are seldom used today. In practice, however, the outstanding debt will almost certainly be renewed when it falls due for repayment, so the obligation is likely to result only in a review of interest rates in the light of conditions prevailing at the time when repayment is due.

The Post Office Bill places a duty on the Postmaster-General to conduct the business of his department in such a manner as to secure that its revenue is not less than sufficient, taking one year with another, to meet outgoings properly chargeable to revenue account, including 'proper allocations' to the general reserve. This resembles the obligation placed on the nationalized industries—an obligation which the British Transport Commission has not been able to fulfil for several years.

THE POSITION OF THE POSTMASTER-GENERAL

The Postmaster-General will continue to be fully responsible to Parliament for the work of his department. The total amount of Post Office borrowings of new capital will be authorized by statute, as in the past, every two or three years. The Commercial Accounts will be audited by the Comptroller and Auditor-General and examined by the Public Accounts Committee of the House of Commons. The charges and tariffs of the Post Office for postal and other services will be fixed by or under Statutory Instruments, and these will be subject to a negative resolution of Parliament. This goes further than the present practice, as not all Statutory Instruments of the Post Office are at present subject to parliamentary control. MPs will have the same scope for parliamentary questions as they have today.

The salaries of the Postmaster-General and Assistant Postmaster-General will continue to be voted annually so that a Supply Day can be devoted to discussing and criticizing the work of the department. A House of Commons resolution will also be required before the beginning of each financial year to authorize expenditure from the Post Office Fund. Parliament will receive the annual report and accounts of the Post Office after they have been examined and certified by the Comptroller and Auditor-General. Thus, all the safeguards necessary to preserve accountability to Parliament and ministerial responsibility will be maintained in full force.

THE WORK OF THE POST OFFICE

The report of the Post Office for 1959–60 (presented to Parliament last November) gives an impression of an alert, progressive, and competent department. Postings exceeded 10,000 million for the first time in its history—an increase of nearly 10 per cent over the previous year. Many improvements in the postal service are in train, including brighter post offices, the abolition of specialized counters, more and better self-service facilities, and letter sorting by electronic machines. Even the telephone service is making some headway, though the rate and quality of progress remain far too low.

The Post Office was the first government department to introduce a public relations service and its example has been followed by almost all departments. Its staff policy is good on the whole; and the ordinary postman is one of the most obliging, reliable, and trustworthy public servants. At the higher levels, an interchange of staff between the Post Office and great industrial firms like Unilever recently took place for a trial period. The more modern of the Post Office buildings are usually quite good as regards their appearance though some of them are not above reproach.

The Post Office today carries out a great variety of services for other departments. They include the sale of National Insurance stamps and the payment of insurance pensions, family allowances, and service allowances; the issue of broadcast receiving licences, dog licences, and motor-car licences; the sale of Savings Stamps and Certificates, Defence Bonds, Premium Savings Bonds, and other securities; medical prescription refundments, etc. This agency work is of great magnitude: the sale of National Insurance stamps exceeds

£500 million a year and the payment of insurance pensions and other benefits is approaching £1,000 million a year.

The telegraph service has been declining for many years and is run at a loss, amounting to £2.3 million in 1959–60 and £2.5 million in 1958–59. This is mainly due to the falling demand for telegraph services, but a contributory cause is the transmission of press telegrams at an uneconomic rate. The rate of decline is inevitable and likely to increase as telephones are more widely used. The loss on telegrams can easily be offset by the surplus on other services, in much the same way as the Labour Party intended that the loss on railways should be offset by a surplus on road haulage or road passenger services. Fortunately, everyone agrees that the Post Office should run all the telecommunication services, so there is no suggestion that telephones and telegrams should be separated.

The Post Office is at present financing about 70 per cent of its annual capital expenditure on renewals, modernization, and expansion from internal sources, i.e. from depreciation funds. This is undoubtedly the correct policy for all undertakings of this character to pursue; and we may hope that the proportion of capital expenditure raised from internal sources will increase with the greater financial independence of the Post Office in the future. The average figure for all the nationalized industries is about 30 per cent, though there are large variations among the industries. This is far less than the corresponding figure for private enterprise.

The reforms now being introduced are in general likely to prove beneficial to the Post Office and the services it provides to the public. The degree of financial independence which the new Bill permits could bring the Post Office several steps nearer to the position of one of the public corporations as regards finance. But just how much— or how little—the commercial freedom ostensibly accorded to the Post Office will mean in practice depends chiefly on the attitude of the Treasury towards the new relationship.

13. THE UNITED KINGDOM ATOMIC ENERGY AUTHORITY*

The new Atomic Energy Authority is of interest among public corporations for its treatment is most unusual. It has been declared to be

* From R. Darcy Best: 'The United Kingdom Atomic Energy Authority', *Public Administration*, Vol. XXXIV, Spring 1956, pp. 15–16. Reprinted by permission of the author and the editor of *Public Administration*.

not a Government Department but a '. . . non-departmental organization with the necessary executive power, within the framework of an
approved policy and under a financial ceiling, to settle day-to-day
problems'.[1] The Authority comprises a board of five full-time functional and five part-time members without separate technical functions. They have extensive powers for the development of atomic
energy and they act on the orders of the Government, which come to
them through the Lord President. He is fully answerable for their
activities to Parliament and his powers, which are more clearly
defined than is the case with other public corporations, give him the
last word in their affairs. The office of the Lord President is no longer
to be a sinecure for a man of long experience and party standing,
able to think ahead unburdened by the detail of business. Instead he
must now decide the course and advance the claims of the most
advanced industry in the country. Besides the Lord President, three
other Ministers have powers of control over certain aspects of the
Authority's affairs and a further committee of Ministers decide their
policy. The finances of the Authority are those of a Department of
State; there is the same system of annual estimates and votes, audit
by the Comptroller and Auditor-General, and return of unspent
balances. However, the Authority have a latitude in that they are free
from detailed Treasury control. This method of finance is similar to
that which has already been used to finance other bodies, such as the
Overseas Development Corporation, out of grants by the Government. Indeed, the wording of Section 4 (1) and (2) of the Atomic
Energy Authority Act follows that of Section 3 of the Overseas
Development Act.

Apart from these statutory provisions, the Authority differ from
the Boards of other nationalized industries in that they have no
commercial function—apart from the sale of a few isotopes—
although in the future they may have a revenue from the sale of
nuclear fuel elements and royalties from their designs. The business
of the Authority is the design of prototype nuclear power stations,
the manufacture and operation of which can be taken up by British
industry and the Electricity Authorities. Unlike other nationalized
industries, where already established public utilities and basic industries were taken over from private hands, the Atomic Energy
Authority were created out of a Government Department to pioneer
a new industry and a new science little more than a decade old.
Hitherto some critics of the public corporation have taken the view
that it is not suited to be the alert and imaginative leader of a new
technology. Although the Authority, who employ about 20,000
industrial and non-industrial staff, are not removed from the atten-

[1] *The Future Organization of the UK Atomic Energy Project*, p. 4, para. 12.

tion of Parliament, they will be outside the scope of the Select Committee set up to examine the affairs of the nationalized industries, for the committee are to report only on corporations 'whose annual receipts are not wholly or partly derived from money provided by Parliament or advanced from the Exchequer'.

Sir David Eccles has described the Authority as '. . . a curious half-way house between a Government Department and an ordinary industry,'[1] and we may agree with him that they are indeed 'a novel and exceptional Authority'.[2] For they enjoy the best of two worlds, the Act conferring on them certain powers and privileges normally reserved for the Crown, which they combine with the freedom of operation and internal structure of an industrial enterprise. It still remains to see how well these provisions will work in practice, but in the meantime we have Sir David's assurance that 'the whole of these arrangements have been thought out simply to try to get the best possible organization for developing what we all know to be the most promising of the industrial developments in our country today'.[3]

14. THE WORST OF BOTH WORLDS?*

THE GOVERNMENT'S PROPOSALS

The White Paper entitled 'Reorganization of the Nationalized Transport Undertakings', published in December 1960,[4] after the Stedeford group had made its unpublished recommendations, proposed a structure based on an increased measure of decentralization which leans towards autonomy.

The White Paper explains that the Commission will be abolished, and that statutory boards are to be established for each of the major undertakings (i.e. railways, London Transport, Docks, and Inland Waterways). The rest are to be placed under a holding company, which will control British Road Services, Tilling (Buses) Group, Scottish Omnibuses Group, the railway hotels, Road Freight, Shipping Services, Thomas Cook and Son, Ltd, etc. The process of disintegration of the national transport system will thus be completed. Paradoxically, however, the Government's proposals could result in

[1] *H.C. Deb.*, April 29, 1954, col. 1881.
[2] *H.C. Deb.*, July 1, 1954, col. 1536.
[3] *H.C. Deb.*, March 17, 1954, col. 472.
* From Ernest Davies: 'Reorganization of Nationalized Transport', *The Political Quarterly*, Vol. 32, No. 2, April–June 1961, pp. 185–9. Reprinted by permission of the author and the editors of *The Political Quarterly*.
[4] Reorganization of the Nationalized Undertakings, Cmnd 1248.

even greater ministerial control of the nationalized transport sector, as is revealed by an examination of the proposals.

A British Railways Board is to assume responsibility for the railways, but its responsibilities will be confined to those central functions essential to the running of the railways as a single entity. It will be responsible 'for such matters as national staff and wage negotiations, overall control over finance and investment, policies for safety, training and research, and the future size and shape of the railway system'. Regional Boards which are to replace the Area Boards will be responsible for all other functions: the management and operation of the regional railway systems. Each is to maintain a regional trading account. The autonomy of the Regional Boards is further advanced by the appointment of their chairmen by the Minister of Transport, who will appoint the other members after consultation with him, not, be it noted, with the Railways Board. Further, each region is to be represented on the Railways Board, whose Chairman, Vice-Chairman, and full-and part-time members will be appointed by the Minister. This arrangement could perpetuate many of the faults of the previous organization without providing any compensating advantages. In fact, confusion as to where responsibility lies will be considerable.

Under the Transport Act, 1947, the Minister appointed the members of the Railway Executive, but the responsibility for policy and planning resided in the Commission, and managerial responsibility for the railways as a whole was delegated to the Executive. This was far from satisfactory, although it may have been desirable in the early days of nationalization, in view of the need for consolidation of the acquired concerns and strong centralized control. With the abolition of the Executive by the Conservative government in 1953, the Commission itself became responsible for the central functions but delegated an increasing amount of managerial responsibility to the Regions. This was not ideal, but when Area Boards were established under the Railway Reorganization Scheme of 1954, the Commission appointed their members, all of whom were part-time, and the Commission was represented on the Boards. Final responsibility resided in the Commission. This is changed by the present proposals and the chairmen of the Regional Boards will be responsible to the Minister. It is not a case of loyalties split between the Minister and the Railways Board, as were possibly those of the Railway Executive split between the Minister and the Commission, because the Railways Board appears to have no direct control over the Regional Boards. Nor are the functions of the Railways Board clear. Its full-time members are to have 'special responsibilities', but what they are is not specified; not is it clear how the Railways Board will exercise authority to

ensure that its policy decisions are carried out. There is no provision
for their executive powers to be implemented.

THE NEBULOUS POSITION OF THE RAILWAYS BOARD

The powers of the Railways Board and its responsibilities, and the
means to carry them through, are thus ill-defined, and it is difficult
to appreciate what advantage this vague structure of central and
Regional Boards, each appointed and responsible to the Minister,
can possibly have over either the old structure of the Commission
and Executive or over the Commission and the Area Boards.

It is easy to envisage, for instance, difficulty arising over the
all-important matter of finance since the Railways Board is responsible for this but the Regional Boards have complete managerial
responsibility. Further, since the chief executive, the General Manager, sits on his Regional Board, and there is to be a strong element of
full-time members, all these presumably will be high-calibre executives exercising their responsibility and authority to the full and
unlikely to be easily amenable to the dictate of the central board. It is
significant also that whereas the Commission was represented on the
Area Boards, the reverse is now to be the case: the Regional Boards
are to be represented on the Railways Board.

This proposed structure is no solution to the difficulties of the
Commission, nor will it necessarily result in greater efficiency if
conflict develops between the centre and the periphery, as seems
probable. Delay in implementation of policy decided at the centre is
likely to result.

GREATER POWER FOR THE MINISTER

This already confused situation is further confounded by the decision to establish a Nationalized Transport Advisory Council consisting of the Chairmen of the Boards of British Railways, London
Transport, Inland Waterways, Docks and the holding company, and
members from outside the nationalized industry. This will have no
executive functions and its task is only to advise the Minister on
co-ordination of the various boards and the holding company, all of
which he appoints and which are responsible directly to him. It
would seem that since he is to be the Chairman of this Council, he
will have greater authority over the nationalized industry than has
previously been statutorily provided. The fact that the Council has no
executive powers confirms this because it means that all matters concerning relationships between the various undertakings, with their
separate boards or under the holding company's umbrella, will ultimately be his responsibility. It would be difficult to exclude questions

of management from the Council's consideration and from the Minister's final responsibility. The White Paper claims that the Minister's powers will not be extended, but with the abolition of the Commission there will be no other central body with responsibility for linking the respective undertakings; and because responsibility for carrying out the policies recommended by the Council must rest with the Minister, there is little doubt that his powers will become very considerable. This is further confirmed by the declaration that the organization is intended to provide for direct contact between the Minister and the main component parts of the nationalized transport industry. Presumably, each of the segregated undertakings will be able to state its case to the Minister in regard to any matters arising between them and any one of the other undertakings, and it will be for the Minister to decide.

With the Minister's responsibilities increased to this extent, he will become correspondingly accountable to Parliament over a wider range than previously. Probably, it will not take long for ingenious Members of Parliament to table questions on detailed matters of management by linking them to this added responsibility, as, for instance, on co-ordination between the British Railways and the London Transport Board which is to replace the London Transport Executive.

UNDERMINING THE PUBLIC CORPORATION

The new proposals in these aspects remove further the organization of nationalized transport from the public corporation inasmuch as its managerial and commercial independence is diminished. Not only are the Minister's responsibilities in regard to management enhanced, but his opportunities to intervene in the affairs of the nationalized concerns for social or political reasons are increased. This may or may not be desirable when an undertaking is in financial difficulties, but one main purpose of the public corporation was to leave the maximum possible independence to boards appointed by the Minister and for him to intervene only where the national interest was concerned, or where he had special responsibilities statutorily allocated to him.

There is every reason for the Minister of Transport, or the Minister of Power, to have final responsibility in their respective spheres for overall policy so far as co-ordinating the different industries is concerned; but, heretofore, such responsibility has been constitutionally limited to matters of general policy and the accepted procedure is that beyond this the responsibility rests with the responsible boards. This principle has been greatly undermined in recent years, largely due to the greater dependence of the nationalized undertakings upon the state for capital investment and finance; but, as the Select Committee on Nationalized Industries has reported in regard to all the nationalized concerns into which it has inquired, the Minister has required policies to be followed which have conflicted with the commercial operation of the public corporations. In regard to the British Transport Commission, the Select Committee states that 'the Commission are open to the influence of the Minister over a greater area than the statutes lay down', and it mentions the Minister calling upon the Commission to make economies amounting to £20 million a year. The Committee have consistently recommended that the principle be accepted that where government action has affected a corporation's commercial operations, the Minister should give the board a direction which should be made public, and that where a nationalized industry incurs a specific loss or specific expenditure owing to ministerial intervention which it would not otherwise incur, the Government should compensate the industry.

In regard to prices, services, and other matters, such intervention has frequently affected the successful commercial operation of the industries and often the Minister's actions have not been disclosed; consequently he could not be called to account in Parliament in regard to them. The present transport proposals carry this process a stage further, and while it may be difficult for the Minister to deny responsibility as frequently as has been the case in the past, he will be in a position to diminish the responsibility of the Boards, which may make it difficult to obtain persons of sufficient calibre to serve on them. Further, since the principle of the public corporation is thus undermined, it can be fairly asked what advantage this amalgam of the public corporation and government department has over the direct operation of the industry by a government department, as is the case with the Post Office.

15. A TRANSITORY FORM?*

The Public Corporation, though under another name, such as Commissioners for this or Board of that (e.g. Sewers, Paving, Turnpike, School Boards, Health Boards), has a long history as an autonomous organ of government, especially in the field now covered by local government. Holdsworth and others have written of the *ad hoc*

* From E. C. S. Wade: 'The Constitutional Aspect of the Public Corporation', *Current Legal Problems*, Vol. 2, 1949, pp. 173–7. Reprinted by permission of the publishers, Messrs Stevens & Sons.

body usually created by statute, but sometimes lacking any direct legal sanction which, in the eighteenth century, was neither controlled nor inspected by the central government. The golden age of the constitution from the point of view of balance of power in central government would have meant stagnation indeed but for the growth of local autonomous bodies to give effect to the needs created by the rapid industrialization of the country. What in the nineteenth century became the public health services of the general purpose authorities— the local elected councils—had their origin, as did highway, police and education services, in the *ad hoc* statutory commissioners of the previous century. The Port of London Authority and the London Passenger Transport Board, the immediate forebears of the post-war corporations for nationalized services, were less novel than is sometimes supposed. Nor is it without significance to the problem of constitutional control of the modern corporation to recall that often those bodies engaged in experiments in developments which, had they been subjected to central administrative or judicial control, would have been restrained. Moreover, the autonomy and independence of these bodies were influenced by the fact that those who served on them were apt to be the same persons as served, or were served by their nominees, in eighteenth-century parliaments. This secured an informal separation of powers, such as no formally enacted relationship between the central government and parliament and the local autonomous bodies could have achieved. I need not remind this audience, which has learned to recognize the Reform Act of 1832 as ushering in the era of ministerial responsibility, as we understand it in modern constitutional law, that the early examples of the Poor Law Commissioners and the General Board of Health furnished examples of the administration of public services without any real ministerial responsibility to Parliament, although in the latter case there was an ineffectual attempt to maintain it. That they failed, where a hundred years later the Unemployment Assistance Board, as it was first styled, succeeded, may have been due to other factors rather than to the inherent unsoundness of their constitutional structure. In particular the Unemployment Assistance Board never operated on a falling level of employment.

It is often said by Scotsmen that the English constitutional lawyer assumes that nothing of importance happens north of the Border, but Scotland can teach us something about government by boards where until comparatively recently they were a prominent feature of public administration. The difficulty of administering a country 400 miles and more from the seat of government was partly responsible for this. Another factor relevant to our topic was that a board was supposed to supply expert knowledge necessary for the management of affairs which were largely technical more adequately than could a government department. The board system in Scotland was criticized by the Royal Commission on the Civil Service in 1914 because it proved ineffective in securing responsibility for official action and also because it left no room for the employment of civil servants of the administrative class. This latter difficulty has not prevented the national boards which were set up in the years between the two world wars from recruiting adequate administrative staffs, though at a high cost. The board system in Scotland was much reduced in the reorganization of 1928 and, after further condemnation by a departmental committee, finally disappeared in 1937 when all the Scottish departments were brought under the Secretary of State. In the nineteenth century in Ireland, too, public business was largely conducted by boards, few of which came under the full and direct control of Dublin Castle. Here again in 1907 Parliament increased the control of the Chief Secretary over the more important of the boards.

Mention may also be made of the two early twentieth-century experiments in the field of autonomous authorities—the Insurance Commissions and the Road Board. At its inception in 1911, the National Health Insurance Organization was entrusted to four Insurance Commissions (one for each country in the United Kingdom) and to a National Health Insurance Joint Committee. The functions of the Commissions for England and Wales were transferred to the Ministry of Health on its formation in 1919. At a later date the Department of Health for Scotland became responsible for the work of the Scottish Commission. The Road Board was set up in 1909 under the Board of Trade to make advances out of motor taxation to highway authorities for construction and improvement of roads; the Board also had power, which it was reluctant to exercise, to construct and maintain new roads. The Ministry of Transport formed ten years later took over these powers. It cannot be said either of the Insurance Commissions or of the Road Board that they were superseded because they showed too much independence. They seem to have been sacrificed to the objective of making comprehensive the functions of the new Departments, the Ministry of Health and the Ministry of Transport. But their fate suggests that Boards and Commissions may have their part to play in extensions of State control which do not at the start fit readily into the sphere of any existing Department of State. This is not, however, a necessary guarantee of permanence. In support of this view the year, 1919, which saw the disappearance of the Insurance Commissions and the Road Board was also the date of the formation of the Electricity Commissioners and of the Forestry Commission. The latter has now passed under the control of the Minister of Agriculture, though it maintains a separate corporate existence. The functions of the former have passed to the British Electricity Authority—one of the new public utility corporations.

Thus history until 1919 does not support the view that independent authorities have any very permanent place in the machinery of central government. Sooner or later they are absorbed by a Government Department. On the other hand, they have played their part in extending governmental control to new spheres in an age which, generally speaking, regarded direct State control as objectionable.

I have given this condensed historical review because it shows that independent agencies of government have hitherto had only a transient value. Sooner or later they have disappeared and their responsibilities have passed into the hands of a Department under a Minister to be administered by civil servants or in the case of *ad hoc* local authorities to the general purpose elected authorities with their local government officers and staff. So far then ministerial responsibility has always triumphed. This naturally suggests the question, Will the National Coal Board give way to a new Ministry of Coal on the lines of the GPO, or an enlarged Ministry of Fuel and Power? I will only say as to this that it is politically as likely an event as the devolution of the Coal Board's powers to a large number of autonomous coal-producing agencies whether publicly owned or not. But politics and economics do not always make easy bedfellows.

CHAPTER IV

Organization and Management

If only for reasons of space, it is impossible here to provide more than a few extracts from the voluminous literature dealing with organization and management in the nationalized industries. We have therefore chosen to concentrate on those problems that arise *because* an industry is nationalized, rather than on those common to the public and the private sectors of the economy.

Among the most discussed are those arising from the sheer size of certain nationalized undertakings, such as the National Coal Board and British Railways. Significantly, those industries where technical factors dictated, or at least indicated a clear statutory division of functions between a central organization and a number of regional organizations (e.g. gas and electricity) have presented far fewer problems of this kind. Changing techniques, however, may at any time demand a reconsideration of these organizational patterns, as in the gas industry at present (*Extract 16*).

Extract 17, from another article by Mr D. N. Chester, deals in a general way with the problem of size. *Extract 18*, in which the late Sir Charles Reid (the mining expert who was one of the original members of the National Coal Board) presents his 1948 proposals for the reorganization of the coal industry, carries the argument for the break-up of monopoly and for 'co-ordination through competition' to extreme lengths. The 'Fleck' Report of 1953 (important because most of its recommendations were adopted) presents a contrary view (*Extract 19*)—that bigness is not incompatible with efficiency and enterprise, so long as leadership is positive and the meaning of managerial decentralization is properly understood. This is followed (*Extract 20*) by passages from the National Coal Board's directive giving effect to some of the major 'Fleck' recommendations, and by a criticism of their 'authoritarian' bias by Mr Hugh Clegg, a distinguished student of labour relations (*Extract 21*). It should be read in conjunction with some of Mr Clegg's other writings about nationalization, represented here by a passage from the article on the North of Scotland Hydro-Electric Board which he wrote in collaboration with Professor T. E. Chester, of Manchester University (*Extract 22*). The arguments of these two authors are developed at greater length in the book entitled *The Future of Nationalization*. For a criticism of their views, see Professor William A. Robson's *Nationalized Industry and Public Ownership* (pp. 115–17).

An allied problem, much discussed in connection with the nationalized coal industry, is that of 'functionalism'. Under this heading, different views have been advanced about the related questions of (*a*) the extent to which members of the Board should have 'functional' responsibilities (which involves also the question of how many should be full-time and how many part-time) and (*b*) the proper way of regulating the 'use of the functional channels' all the way down the administrative hierarchy. The 'Fleck' Committee came down heavily on the side of functionalism (and full-time service) at the Board level (*Extract 23*) and expressed very definite views about 'the duties and responsibilities of functional heads in relation to the functional level below' (*Extract 24*). These views, particularly in so far as they relate to the composition of the Board, do not command universal assent, nor do they necessarily apply with equal force to a nationalized industry with a basic organizational structure radically different from that of the coal industry. The 'Herbert' Committee, as will be seen from *Extract 25*, recommended a very different type of organization for the Area Boards of the electricity supply industry.

Except in the coal industry, recent tendencies have been in the direction of statutory decentralization (e.g. the Electricity Supply Act of 1956 and the Transport Bill of 1961). This, however, may be reversed in the case of the gas industry, for reasons already explained in *Extract 16*. In transport, the decision to abolish the Commission and to decentralize railway administration to six area boards has been subject to criticism such as that expressed by Mr Ernest Davies in his *Political Quarterly* article (see above, Chapter III, *Extract 14*). Some support for his attack is supplied by the Select Committee on Nationalized Industries, in its massive Report on British Railways. Although highly critical of certain aspects of railway management, the Committee consider that the existing balance between centralization and decentralization is about right (*Extract 26*). The same passage from the Committee's Report also contains views on (*a*) the question of part-time versus full-time Board service, (*b*) the relationship between a part-time Chairman and a full-time General Manager and (*c*) the limitations on decentralization imposed by a nationalized industry's 'political sensitivity'.

Extract 27 brings the light of sociological theory to bear on some of the questions discussed in this chapter, with particular reference to the frictions which develop when, through nationalization, many small units lose their independence on incorporation in a large-scale enterprise.

The final passage (*Extract 28*), from the Report of the 'Ridley' Committee, is also concerned with centralization and decentralization, but from a different angle. An unresolved question is how far the decision-taking process can and ought to be centralized above the level of the Board responsible for the individual industry, in order to achieve better inter-industry co-ordination. This is discussed with special reference to the group of nationalized fuel and power industries. At present, with a government committed to the promotion of competition rather than co-ordination, it is not perhaps a very live issue, but the views of the 'Ridley' Committee are a reminder that it still exists.

16. A NEW STRUCTURE FOR GAS*

465. Your Committee now answer the question, posed above (paragraph 459), which asked whether the existing statutory powers were enough to bring about the successful introduction of a national gas system. They have already expressed their opinion that the present structure of the industry is not suitable for developing and establishing large-scale production and distribution facilities. This, they think, is due to the practical difficulty of getting a number of independent Chairmen to fall in with the lead of a Council of limited powers. While the existing statutory powers may in theory be adequate, in practice they are not so.

466. For however good has been the initiative of and planning by the Gas Council, there has in fact been no single authority armed with powers and responsibility for developing the production of gas on a national scale, and the investigation of Lurgi has suffered from a lack of the drive which such an authority would have given. It has been different with the development of the project to import methane. In that case, the requirements of the interested Boards were given to the North Thames Board, who were to act as the agents of the Gas Council and thus, as the authority responsible for the development of the project, would bring the necessary drive to its realization.

467. This does not necessarily imply that additional powers should be given to the Gas Council. One possibility (which the Council's memorandum did not discuss) is that a thirteenth Board should be set up to develop and carry out the large-scale manufacture of cheaper gas which would then be sold to all or some of the Area Boards. This arrangement would be somewhat analogous to the

* From *Report from the Select Committee on Nationalized Industries: The Gas Industry*, Vol. I, Report and Proceedings, 1961, HC 280, paras. 465–75.

position of the Central Electricity Generating Board and the Electricity Council, with the difference that at any rate in the early years, and perhaps for longer, the Area Gas Boards would continue to operate such of the existing gas-making plants in their Areas as were needed. The case for a generating Board is that they would make gas cheaply and therefore find no difficulty in selling it to Area Boards, but they would have the right (which they would not normally have to use) to insist, with the Gas Council's agreement, on the Area Boards' taking certain quantities of gas under certain conditions (in the same way as, under the Gas Council's plan, the Council would themselves be able to insist) (Q. 3140–1).

468. The Gas Council urged that, if a new Board were set up now to control new large plants, it would have little or nothing to do for some while (Q. 3209); and an alternative plan, that the new Board should take over some of the existing gas works, was described by them as 'a cumbersome operation' (Q. 3139). Nevertheless, they themselves agree that a thirteenth Board of this kind might eventually be needed; their own plan, giving increased powers to themselves, is said to be only for a transitional period (Q. 3133, 3175). So the idea of a thirteenth Board, though it presents some difficulties, is acknowledged as a practical possibility. It has two important advantages: first, the Board would have responsibility for production and distribution on a national scale but no other responsibilities; secondly, the Gas Council would retain their impartiality and disinterestedness in any conflict between large scale production and Area Board production, and so would not lose their present characteristic of objectivity. Thus the answer to the second question posed above (paragraph 459)—if additional powers are needed, must they necessarily be given to the Council?—is No, not necessarily.

469. Your Committee have said that they believe the structure of the industry is relevant to the speed of the development of a national system of gas supply, which itself offers the best hope of cheaper gas in the future. In answering the two questions above, they have shown the three possibilities which, on the evidence given to them, are open to Parliament if it should wish to legislate anew for the gas industry in future.

470. First, the present structure of the industry could be left unchanged, in the hope that the spirit of collective co-operation which Board Chairmen have shown in their attitude to the methane project should extend to other problems on a national scale. Your Committee have noted (paragraphs 460 to 466) the advantages of and drawbacks to this scheme, which is the one the Ministry prefer.

471. Secondly, the Gas Council's own plan (see paragraph 455) under which they themselves are given powers to manufacture and

supply gas, could be implemented. It has, it was said, the unanimous
support of the Area Board Chairmen, although it would lead eventually to a derogation of their powers. This is what the Gas Council
would prefer.

472. Thirdly, a thirteenth Board could be set up, to undertake all
new gas generation on a large scale; and to control such aspects of
national gas supply as a national grid, and underground storage. The
twelve Area Boards would retain their responsibility for internal
distribution and for production by all but large-scale processes, and
the Gas Council would still be left with their present functions; they
would, in particular, remain the Minister's advisers, and would be
able to oversee the situation in which the thirteenth Board sells gas
to the other twelve. This new Board would be able to offer a more
positive lead to the industry in developing and undertaking large new
projects leading to cheaper gas. This possibility is the one which,
after their relatively short inquiry, Your Committee prefer.

473. Whatever kind of future structure is chosen, Your Committee
wish to emphasize that the predominating factor is that of time. It
has only been in recent years that the possibility of getting cheaper
gas from larger gasworks has been realized. It was only in June 1960
that the Gas Council discussed their proposals for the first time.
These went to the Minister in November 1960, but in December 1960
the Ministry witness said, 'We have not had before us any specific
proposals. . . . The Gas Council have not yet reached that point'
(Q. 464). In June 1961, the same witness said (Q. 3585): 'We have had
no specific proposals for altering the organization.' Possibly the Gas
Council themselves were having doubts about their plan; speaking
of it in May 1961, their Chairman said (Q. 3166): 'It may be
that we have not thought right to the end of the road on this.' 'Time
is not on the side of gas,' they say (Appendix 43); but meanwhile
a year has gone by and no progress has been made towards their
reorganization.

474. To some extent, the situation is affected by the fact that the
new large-scale processes, which provide the stimulus towards a
change of structure, are still embryonic. For that reason it may be
tempting to take no decision on structure yet awhile; there is weight
in the contention that it is pointless to create new machinery to deal
with processes as yet undecided. But there are two dangers; first, that
when the processes are proved, the organization will not be there to
make the most of them; secondly, that unless the organization is
changed, the processes may not come forward as quickly as they
should.

475. Your Committee believe it is most important that decisions
should be taken soon on the form of the structure with which the gas

industry will go forward into the early years of national, rather than local, gasmaking and gas supply.

17. NATIONALIZATION AND MONOPOLY*

It seems to me that a large part of the problem is due to use of very large-scale monopolies. All our economic thinking and industrial experience is really based on comparatively small-scale competitive industry and even those who wish to abolish such conditions are still largely conditioned by the results which flow from them. We simply do not know how to control national statutory monopolies and their introduction into the field of industry raises problems for which we are nowhere near finding the solution.

A single national industrial monopoly must obviously be more powerful *vis-à-vis* the public and even the Civil Service and Parliament than can a number of smaller monopolies. It presents a solid front and has a monopoly of the expertise and technical knowledge of the industry. Glaring errors can be detected and remedied, but can it be said that the Ministry of Transport, for example, has the technical knowledge necessary to judge the British Transport Commission and the Railway and other Executives, or to stand up against it on any matter other than some outstanding popular issue? Moreover it is difficult to make comparisons, except between one country and another, and these are often invalidated by the diversity of operating conditions between the two countries. Finally, with a national monopoly there is always the danger of a single orthodox view being established. The manager or technician within the organization who has a different view may be refused the opportunity to try it out. He may not be able to move to another employer for there may be only one buyer of his particular kind of skill—the Board with a national monopoly. If he tries to express his disagreement in public disciplinary action may be taken against him, for the rule of all these large-scale bodies is that public utterances on policy are the monopoly of the Board or very top management.

If this is a reasonable diagnosis of the problem created by national industrial monopolies it follows that as far as possible nationalization schemes should avoid being national monopolies. Instead of Boards operating on a national scale there should be a number of self-contained units. Gas is already organized on this basis and so is electricity distribution but not production. The other industries are,

* From D. N. Chester: 'The Nationalized Industries', *Three Banks Review*, December 1952, No. 16, pp. 38–40. Reprinted by permission of the *Review*.

however, managed by national Boards. The existence of a number of area or local Boards does not preclude the use of some form of national Council for national wage negotiations, research and for other national matters common to a series of Boards. In other words, I find the Gas Council and the Area Gas Boards a more suitable model than most of the other organizations.

It also follows, I suggest, that we should avoid too much imposed co-ordination. Co-ordination is usually contrasted with chaos and is said to lower costs and produce all kinds of benefits for the consumer. In actual practice it is often a euphemism to conceal a restriction on consumer choice and its purpose is frequently to protect one service or product against the competition of another. I am not, of course, referring to the co-ordination which arises from consumer choice in the light of a price system based on costs, but to that based on administrative or political considerations, the underlying assumption of which is that any form of competition is wasteful.

In other words, the nature and size of the problem should be kept within more manageable limits. If there is not to be competitive enterprise between a number of comparatively small units it should be possible to reap some benefits from the spirit of emulation that would naturally occur between the different areas and enable public comparisons to be made between them. If there cannot be direct competition, the history of the gas industry and possibly of the railways is a testimony to the benefits that can accrue from competition between alternative products and services. If the size and character of the problem is limited by these means, it will be easier to tackle.

18. THE COAL BOARD AS HOLDING COMPANY*

In view of what I have said in the two previous articles, I am convinced that reorganization must begin with the structure and composition of the National Coal Board itself. I suggest, therefore, that a new Board should be formed. It should consist of a chairman and possibly three vice-chairmen, who should all be full-time members, and in addition eight members appointed on a part-time basis. These should be men of proved leadership and experience in large-scale industrial and commercial enterprise, together with men skilled in labour problems.

* From Sir Charles Reid: 'The Problem of Coal, III—New Structure proposed for the Industry'. © The Times Publishing Company Limited, 1948. All rights reserved. Reprinted, by permission, from *The Times* of November 24, 1948.

The functions of this Board would be confined to directing the national policy of the industry. It would deal with overall finance, and with the national wage policy, and exercise supervision of the corporations into which I propose that the coalfields should be divided.

The present eight divisions ought to be abandoned, since these, in my view, have tasks too big for efficient management. In their place I suggest the division of the coalfields into approximately twenty-six corporations, as follows: Scotland (three); Northumberland; Durham (three); Yorkshire (four); Notts; Derbyshire; South Derbyshire and Leicester; Kent; Forest of Dean, Somerset and Bristol; South Wales (three); Warwickshire; Cannock Chase; South Staffordshire and Shropshire; North Staffordshire; North Wales; Lancashire (two); Cumberland. Such names might be given to these corporations as would identify them with the localities in which they operate.

Each corporation, I suggest, should be managed by a board consisting of a managing director, who would have full executive power, a general mining manager, and a sales manager. All other departments are services either to production, or sales, or both. There should also be four part-time members, drawn from the district, who should be men with commercial, industrial, and labour experience. The chairman might be a part-time member.

A share of the capital of the National Coal Board might be allocated to each corporation. The cost of servicing this and any new capital it might be authorized to spend would require to be added to its production costs. The corporation would be expected to operate in a similar manner to that of the best type of private enterprise, producing its own balance-sheet each year.

CORPORATIONS IN CONTROL

All the members of the boards would be appointed by the National Board in London. They would be in complete managerial control, working to the policy of the National Board, and subject to such direction regarding policy as might from time to time be determined by it. While the staffs under the corporations would be subject to maximum salary scales, the corporations would be free to appoint these officials without control from London. Members of the staff of one corporation would be free to leave its employment for service in another. This would prove an incentive to managers and officials, for it would give a sense of freedom which is absent under the present system of one employer. Managers, labour leaders, and men would be encouraged to take a keen interest in the success of their own area.

Consultations between management and men at all levels would be essential, and frank and friendly personal relationships established. In this way I believe that a new spirit of co-operation between men and management would be secured. A lively but friendly competition between the corporations would be fostered, and might have a considerable effect on output and costs without reducing earnings. Wages, as I shall go on to say, should be decided nationally. Confidence between officials and the Board of Management would be restored. Loyalty both of officials and men would centre round the managing director, who would be available for their constant guidance and support.

Under this scheme the National Coal Board would be in the position of a holding company controlling twenty-six distinct and definite businesses, all owned by it on behalf of the nation. The organization in London would then be cut down to the minimum necessary for this purpose. The following economies would thus be made possible:

(1) The central secretariat would be drastically reduced to a staff sufficient for gathering the information which the National Board required, and providing a channel through which the Board could keep in touch with the corporations.

(2) The recruiting branch in London would be closed and responsibility for recruitment given to the corporations. Past experience has shown that permanent recruits are found for the most part in regions in and adjacent to the coalfields.

(3) The central training and educational department would act only in an advisory capacity to the corporations. Its purpose would really be to provide information on which the policy of the Board in this matter would be based.

(4) The scientific staff should merely act as advisers to the corporations. Their major work would be the management of research stations, which are outwith the corporations' control.

(5) The purchase of all plant and materials for the collieries and for any ancillaries in the control of the corporations should be made by the respective corporation buyer. The duties of any staff in London would be limited to contact between Ministries on behalf of the Coal Board.

(6) The Miners' Welfare Commission at headquarters should for the most part have its work transferred to the corporations. Such money as would be required for welfare in the corporations would be allotted to them, and be under the control of a committee composed of management and men. Only thus can welfare become an integral part of the corporations' organization, and develop the personal interest of both workmen and

officials in what is an important part of the Board's activities. The only staff required in London would be for the purpose of shaping and co-ordinating policy.

A National Wages Board would be formed in London composed of representatives of the corporations and of the workmen. A new wages structure covering the whole industry is necessary if permanent peace in the coalfields is to be assured, but the problems involved are immense. A national wage policy must mean equal pay for equal work, and this would involve a fresh assessment of tasks in many pits. One method of achieving this would be to appoint task-and-rate-fixers, who would require to be specially trained for the purpose, and time-study would clearly be essential. These men would quickly become skilled in the work and would, I believe, by honesty of purpose, win the confidence of both managements and men. If a settlement of this important question could be obtained it would mean much to the industry.

CENTRAL CONSULTANTS

At headquarters there should be a central technical service composed of competent engineers, both mining and other. This organization would act as consultants to the corporations and would be of great importance in the work of reconstruction. In addition a branch of this would be required to make and keep up to date the national reorganization plan, and would thus give the Board information upon which their policy would be based.

The three vice-chairmen of the National Board would each have executive duties to ensure that the policy determined was being carried out by the corporations. One of them, for instance, might take executive charge of the organization in London, while the other two could share the supervision of the corporations. But interference from headquarters with the work of the corporations should be reduced to a minimum, and all encouragement given to them to solve their own problems.

The national task of reconstruction is so vast that the only hope of achieving it is to break it up into manageable pieces. Therefore, while the corporations should be set an output target towards which they should be expected to work, a careful survey should be made by the mining engineers of each corporation in order to consider what mines should be remodelled, what new sinkings should be undertaken, how much it would cost, and which of the mines should be maintained or abandoned. On the basis of these surveys each corporation would submit its plan to the National Board. When this has been approved each corporation should be given full responsibility for carrying out the work.

DANGERS OF STATE MONOPOLY

The nationalization of this industry has great potential advantages, but it is certainly not without dangers. Private enterprise must depend upon its own resources for survival, and the check which shareholding makes on management keeps it up to the scratch. Under State ownership, on the other hand, with its monopoly, the price of the commodity can be raised too easily, and inefficiency and extravagance are difficult to guard against. There is the tendency to spend the nation's money without too much consideration and to look upon the cost of production as not of the first importance. Excessive demands for increased wages are more difficult to resist with the nation's purse at a Board's disposal, and the easy way of appeasement for the sake of peace is a very real temptation. The necessity, therefore, of an organization which insists upon personal responsibility at all levels so that waste in whatever form can be immediately checked and eliminated must be obvious to all. Character develops with responsibility, and a man will only give of his best when he is given complete charge of his job and is trusted to perform it. This is the hope of the new structure I advocate.

It will be appreciated that in this limited space I can only give a rough outline of my suggestions. Some will object that important aspects have been omitted. This is inevitable, but the vital point to keep in mind is the objectives which nationalization was intended to secure. These are the welfare of the producers, the satisfaction of the consumers in quantity, quality, and cost, and the direct contribution which coal can make to the exports on which our national survival depends. I am satisfied that, with the present manpower and machinery, all the coal we need can be produced; but I am convinced that only in some such way as I have outlined can an organization be created which is fitted to secure these objectives.

19. DISCIPLINE AND DECENTRALIZATION*

DISCIPLINE

298. We are not satisfied that policies and decisions emanating from the Board's Headquarters are being properly carried out in the Divisions and Areas; we shall give specific examples later (paragraphs 332 to 367).

* From National Coal Board: *Report of the Advisory Committee on Organization*, February 1955, paras. 298–318. Reprinted by permission of the National Coal Board.

299. There are various reasons for this failing. At the outset of nationalization the many undertakings were grouped together, often unwillingly; the management of some of them, now in the employ of the Board, have found it difficult to adjust themselves to the new conditions. Again, policies may be accepted by Divisions or Areas, but inertia, habit, other preoccupations or lack of staff prevent them from taking effective action. Divisions and Areas are ill-staffed for carrying out new policies and sometimes the rapport between Division and Area is insufficient. To get policies carried out, much depends on the strength and efficiency of the functional channels; and these channels are generally much weaker at and below than above Division.

300. But the main reason for the failing is the unwillingness of the topmost management—the National Coal Board themselves—to insist on their policies being carried out. From the outset, the Board have tried to control their subordinate formations with a very light touch. Some Divisions have taken advantage of this. The National Board, having adopted a policy, have too often been half-hearted in holding to it when Divisions have not liked the policy or have been slow in carrying it out.

301. As one example of this unsatisfactory state of affairs, we take stock control. The Board early took a decision that stocks throughout the industry should be kept down to an economic level. In June, 1953, one of the Board's Executive Committees reviewed progress towards this objective and found that progress was, in many respects, unsatisfactory. The Committee then considered whether Divisions should be given a further general exhortation to keep down the level of stocks or whether a directive should be issued to Divisions requiring certain steps to be taken for more effective control of stocks.

302. In any ordinary business, where the controlling Board had made a policy decision, there would be no question of choosing between exhortation or direction if the policy had not been implemented; a firm instruction would undoubtedly be issued and disciplinary action taken if it was disregarded. Weakness of this sort at the top soon communicates itself to all levels of management below and inevitably brings the top management into disrepute.

303. In consequence the tone of management is, in many places, not all that it should be. This situation is not solely due to the lack of firm and consistent direction from above. In some places it is due also to bad discipline among the rank and file of labour. Too often agreements made between the Board and the Union by means of the conciliation machinery set up by agreement between them are not properly implemented by the men. This leads to stoppages and loss

of output. But it has a worse effect in that it leads to a feeling of irritation and frustration among management and to bad labour relations. We recognize that this is a situation which the Board and the Union have taken seriously from the first. But their efforts to put matters right have not solved the problem.

304. We have stressed these matters because we believe that they are fundamental weaknesses in the coal industry, and considerable and sustained efforts will be needed by management and the Unions to bring about an improvement.

305. In general much remains to be done in order to counteract the remoteness of the top management from those who are working in the field and from the general body of the Board's employees. Members of the Board and senior members of management at all levels of the organization have, to their great credit, taken every opportunity that offers of making contact with people in the industry whom in the ordinary course of business they could not expect to meet. But the problem of remoteness still largely remains. We know that the Board have given much attention to the problem and it is one to which, in our view, they could most usefully return.

THE MEANING OF DECENTRALIZATION

At Headquarters

306. We are satisfied that the Board's decision to decentralize management as far as reasonably possible was the right one. We believe, however, that the indecisive attitude on the part of the Board, to which we have referred in paragraphs 300 to 303, stems from a wrong conception of what decentralization means. The failure to enforce policy decisions is looked upon as justified in the name of decentralization or the desire not to interfere with day-to-day management.

307. In our view, decentralization means that each level of management specifies clearly the powers which may be exercised by the level below it. Having done so, it leaves the lower formation free to exercise those powers. But each level of management must see that the policies which it lays down are punctually and effectively carried out by the level of management below it. No organization will work well unless the people who give the instructions and frame the policies also ensure that they are carried out. This should be done, not by interference in detailed or day-to-day matters, but by modern management techniques of approved programmes followed by periodical reports and reviews of progress and by physical inspections. The Board appear to have assumed that decentralization

means that they should not, or need not, impose their will on Divisions and Areas. We do not agree with this policy.

308. An illustration of what we believe to be the Board's mistaken attitude towards decentralization is to be found at paragraph 361 of their Annual Report for 1948. The subject is 'Budgets and Standards'; after indicating the need for proper control of operating expenses at collieries and after pointing to the desirability of achieving such control through modern methods of budgetary control combined with standard costs, the report continues:

> 'The Board felt that it would be wrong to force the adoption of budgetary control and standard costs on those who were reluctant to use them; full weight was given to local opinion that in some coalfields it would be impracticable to evolve a workable system of standards which would be flexible without being cumbersome. The National Board therefore left it to the Divisional Boards to decide whether or not to experiment at this stage with budgetary control and standard costs of mining operations; and this is one example of the way important decisions of management are decentralized to the coalfields.'

It is true that later on the Board adopted a more decisive policy in this matter (see paragraph 348). But the Board did not then ensure that the policy was carried out with energy. We have come across other examples of this attitude towards decentralization.

309. We have also met a wrong conception of decentralization at Divisional level and below. Each level of management tends to want full authority and powers of direction over the people at and below its own level, but at the same time to expect from management above only advice (which they would only give if asked for it)—not instructions and control. The inconsistency of this attitude does not seem to be appreciated.

310. We find that at Division to some extent, but much more so at Area, senior people think that the way to get the coal produced is for them to take a hand themselves in the detailed operations at the collieries. In fact, the task of producing coal cannot be properly carried out from a Headquarters; it is the Colliery Manager's job to produce the coal, and he must have above him a good Area General Manager and Area staff to guide, lead, direct and inspire him in the same way as the Works Manager in any large industrial concern looks to his General Manager or Managing Director. Just as we believe that the National Board should lay down the powers they will delegate to Divisions and what powers and responsibilities are to remain with Headquarters, so we believe that the National Board should lay down with precision the maximum powers that Divisions may delegate to Area General Managers and what powers and responsibilities are to remain with Divisions. More important still,

Divisions must instruct Area General Managers and their staff on the proper functions of Area Headquarters, and must see that these functions are rightly discharged.

311. If the powers to be prescribed for Area General Managers are maximum powers, Divisional Boards may think it right from time to time to give to particular Area General Managers less than the full powers. There is no objection to this—indeed flexibility is desirable—so long as the exceptions from the general rule are specific and so long as they are known to and approved by the National Board. We believe that Divisions concentrate too little on translating the National Board's policy into policies for their coalfields and on seeing that policy decisions are carried out. Similarly, it is vital to ensure that Area General Managers and the other chief Area officials concentrate on their job of running the Area instead of trying to carry out detailed operations at the colliery. Later we shall recommend that the Board's present General Directive on Organization be withdrawn and rewritten. If that recommendation is adopted, we suggest that the principles of decentralization which we have set forth should be incorporated in the new Directive.

ATTITUDES IN THE COALFIELDS

312. Some Area General Managers misunderstand the purpose and function of National Headquarters. Whereas we found them very ready to criticize National Headquarters and even to suggest that it was an unnecessary imposition, it soon became clear to us that they had no idea how National Headquarters fitted into the Board's organization. Least of all did they understand the ramifications of the coal industry. Thus, some Area General Managers thought that one of the tasks of the Division was to protect them from having to implement policy decisions and instructions emanating from National Headquarters. In the main, the complaints about the Board's organization came from men who before nationalization had been employed in small undertakings. Those who had been brought up in large companies seemed to feel at home in the new conditions and understood the needs of a large organization.

313. In our opinion it is the duty of the Board's Headquarters to see that it imprints its personality on the Area General Managers by ensuring that they understand how great a responsibility and volume of work rests on the shoulders of the Board's Headquarters and what part it has, and intends, to play in the industry.

314. Although there is agreement throughout the industry about the shortage of able people, most Divisions and Areas told us that they were satisfied with the qualities and numbers of the staff in their

own offices, and this suggests to us that at any rate some of them had not faced this issue for themselves. By the same token, Divisional Boards and Area General Managers seldom seemed to ask themselves whether their own organization was properly conceived and was working as well as it should.

315. We think that this attitude of mind is due to failure by the National Board to stimulate and supervise adequately the work of Divisions and Areas in this respect, in the mistaken belief that it would be contrary to the declared policy of decentralization to do so.

SUGGESTED REMEDIES

316. The most powerful remedies for the weaknesses we have outlined would be: first, a clear realization by the National Board and the Unions of the need for discipline, goodwill and leadership throughout the industry; secondly, precise and firm clarification at every level of management of what decentralization means and how it should work in practice; thirdly, a clear definition of the powers which are delegated to Divisions and of the maximum powers which Divisions may delegate to Areas. Lastly, we think it would make for the smoother working of the organization if the Board, before committing themselves to a policy, took greater pains to consult Divisions about it. The present main methods of consulting Divisions—correspondence, and meetings with Divisional Chairmen every two months—are not wholly satisfactory. We suggest that, in the same way as Divisional Boards have the benefit of the advice of their Area General Managers through a Divisional Advisory Committee, the National Board, when framing policy, should draw upon the advice of the Divisional Chairmen by establishing a National Advisory Committee composed of the full-time Board Members and the Divisional Chairmen.

317. There is a further remedy. We have pointed, in paragraph 118, to the need for a policy for retiring people who are not capable of filling satisfactorily the responsible positions they hold. Anyone who cannot, or will not, fit into the Board's organization properly and accept the methods and disciplines necessary in a large undertaking should be removed, either completely or at any rate to a position in which his deficiencies will not be seriously felt. But a systematic policy for retiring many ineffective people who are kept in the industry cannot be carried out unless reasonable compensation is paid. The money would be well spent.

318. We recommend:

(*a*) that the Board should insist on their policies being properly carried out by the subordinate formations and should ensure that discipline obtains;

E

(*b*) that the Board should consult with the Unions in a further endeavour to find a remedy for the problems referred to in paragraph 303;

(*c*) that, to ensure better consultation with Divisions, the Board should set up a National Advisory Committee, comprising the full-time Board Members and the Divisional Chairmen;

(*d*) that the Board should restate the principles of decentralization to be followed in the industry, on the lines indicated in paragraph 307; in particular the Board should lay down precisely the powers which they propose to delegate to Divisions and the maximum powers which Divisions may delegate to Area General Managers; the Board should also require Divisional Boards to issue instructions to Area General Managers on the proper functions of Area Headquarters;

(*e*) that the Board should be more bold in making changes in personnel where they are justified either on account of age, inefficiency or indiscipline.

20. THE COAL BOARD'S DIRECTIVE OF JULY 5, 1955*

1. This Directive is to be observed by all Members of the Board's staff.[1]

GENERAL

2. The levels of management through which the National Coal Board discharge their responsibility for the industry are—Headquarters, Division, Area, Group and Colliery.

3. The authorities in charge at the levels of management below Headquarters are—the Divisional Boards, the Area General Managers, the Group Managers and the Colliery Managers. The authorities are responsible for the general management, within the framework of the National Coal Board's policies, of their Division, Area, Group or Colliery as the case may be. Divisional Boards, Area General Managers and Group Managers must control and co-ordinate the work of subordinate authorities, must help, guide and stimulate them, and must hold them to account.

* From C. A. Roberts: 'The National Coal Board and the Fleck Report', Appendix, *Public Administration*, Vol. XXXV, Spring 1957, paras. 1–32. Reprinted by permission of the author and the editor of *Public Administration*.

[1] To staff engaged in the management of the Board's opencast activities this Directive is issued mainly for information. They are required, however, to observe the contents of paragraphs 31 to 33.

4. Policy decisions of the National Board will continue to be communicated to Divisions by the Chairman, Deputy Chairman or Secretary of the Board: detailed instructions about implementation may be issued at the same time through departmental channels (see paragraph 11 below). Policy decisions of the National Board and the Divisional Board will be communicated to Area General Managers by the Divisional Chairman, Deputy Chairman or Secretary: separate instructions about implementation may be issued through departmental channels or to the Area General Managers (see paragraph 22). Policy decisions of the National Board, Divisional Board or Area General Manager, when issued from Area Headquarters, should be signed by the Area General Manager, or on the Area General Manager's behalf by the Assistant Area General Manager or Area Secretary.

5. In discharging their responsibilities the authorities must make full use of the departmental staffs. The authorities are responsible for ensuring proper consultation and co-operation between the departments at their level of management.

6. The following are the departments:

Production.	Scientific.
Marketing.	The Medical Service.
Carbonization.	Finance.
Purchasing and Stores.	Reconstruction.
Industrial Relations.	Secretary's.
Staff.	Legal.

Not all of the twelve departments are represented at every level of management.

7. The responsibilities of each Head of department at the various levels of management are:

(*a*) To advise on the framing of policy in his field.

(*b*) To set in motion the execution of policies in his field.

(*c*) To co-ordinate the specialist work of his department, not only at his own level, but also at the next level of management below him.

(*d*) To advise, guide and stimulate the department at his own level and at all levels of management below him.

(*e*) To keep himself informed about the work of his department, and to satisfy himself that the policy in his field is being carried out punctually and efficiently both at his own level and at all levels of management below him.

8. On matters of established policy each Head of department at Headquarters is empowered by the Board to issue to the functional Head at Division instructions on the implementation of such policies. Divisional Boards will delegate corresponding powers to their

functional Heads. Area General Managers will delegate to functional Heads at Area powers to issue, on matters of established policy, instructions to Group Managers, or, if the particular matter is one for which Group Managers are not responsible (see paragraph 29 below), to Colliery Managers. If and when functional Heads at Area issue instructions direct to a Colliery Manager, they must inform the Group Manager.

9. At each level of management the functional Heads must give an effective lead in departmental matters to the functional Heads at the level of management below. The senior man's views in his departmental field will normally be accepted by the functional Head at the level next below him. The views of senior officials assisting each functional Head will normally be accepted by the corresponding officials at the next level below, in so far as the man at the higher level is acting in accordance with powers delegated to him by his functional Head.

10. On matters of policy, and on many purely departmental matters, there must be frequent and full consultation between levels, particularly when new policies not yet adopted are under discussion. Full use will be made of the National Advisory Committee and the Divisional Advisory Committees for purposes of consultation on policy.

11. Instructions issued by a functional Head should be addressed to the functional Head at the level of management next below, but a copy must go direct to the authority in the line of command at the next level below so that the authority may be kept informed. These copies should be sent to the Divisional Secretary or to the Area Secretary as the case may be. Divisional Boards will establish a system under which their functional Heads consult as necessary with them, or with their Divisional Chairman or Deputy Chairman, before taking action on instructions issued departmentally. Area General Managers will establish a system under which functional Heads at Area consult as necessary with the Area General Manager or Assistant Area General Manager before taking action on instructions which are issued departmentally.[1]

[1] The provisions in paragraph 11 will not usually be appropriate in marketing matters. The National Board will inform Divisional Boards of all important policy decisions they take in the marketing field, and Divisional Boards should see that Area General Managers are also informed as necessary of such decisions. The responsibility for implementing the Board's marketing policies rests with the Director-General of Marketing (see paragraph 14) and it will be for him and for Divisional Marketing Directors and Area Marketing Managers to see that Divisional Boards and Area General Managers are informed of, and are consulted about, any instructions issued in marketing matters, which may affect the general management of the Division or Area.

12. Where a functional Head feels that the implementation of an established policy is falling short of what is required, he will, unless he can otherwise secure that matters are put right, bring his view to the notice of the authority at his level, viz. the National Board, the Divisional Board or the Area General Manager as the case may be.

13. Internal audit is organized as a national service, attached to Finance Department. The Chief Internal Auditor will issue instructions on audit work and programmes. Divisional Chief Internal Auditors will be responsible to the Chief Internal Auditor for the execution of their duties, but will be attached to and will normally report to Divisional Finance Directors. Area Internal Auditors will be responsible to Divisional Chief Internal Auditors, but will be attached to and will normally report to Area General Managers.

14. The responsibility for implementing the Board's marketing policies rests with the Director-General of Marketing. The selling of coal on the inland market, other than coal supplied from colliery landsales, is the function of the Regional Sales Organization under the Director-General of Marketing. In addition to his other duties, each Divisional Marketing Director is responsible for maintaining liaison between his Divisional Board and the Regional Sales Organization and for keeping his Divisional Board fully informed on marketing matters generally. The Area Marketing Manager (or, where there is no Area Marketing Manager, the staff carrying out the marketing functions for the Area) will work under the instructions of the Divisional Marketing Director and will be responsible for keeping the Area General Manager and other officials in the Area informed and advised on all marketing matters affecting the management of the Area. He will also be responsible for keeping the Divisional Marketing Director and the Regional Sales Organization fully informed of the views of the Area management.

DIVISIONAL HEADQUARTERS

(a) Responsibilities of the Members of Divisional Boards

15. The Members of each Divisional Board are jointly responsible to the National Board for the general management of the National Board's business within the boundaries of their Division. (Divisional Boards are not, however, responsible for such opencast activities or Headquarters-controlled activities as are carried on within their Division.) The powers and responsibilities of members of Divisional Boards, other than the Chairman, are also governed by the provisions in paragraphs 7 to 14 above.

(b) Organization of Divisional Headquarters

16. All the functions which are represented at Divisional Head-quarters must be organized departmentally, and no small groups of staff are to report direct to the Divisional Board.

17. Apart from the usual duties of presiding over meetings of the Divisional Board and over other important meetings in the Division, the Divisional Chairman will keep a general watch over the work of Divisional Headquarters and over the more important items of work being done in the Areas. He will initiate at Divisional Board meetings important items of business, or see that such items are properly initiated. The Divisional Chairman will have no departmental responsibilities. The Divisional Deputy Chairman's primary duty is to assist, and deputize for, the Divisional Chairman. He will also be responsible for supervising certain departments which initially will include Purchasing and Stores and Scientific Departments and the Medical Service. Each of the Divisional Directors is to be responsible for one of the following departments—Production, Marketing, Industrial Relations, Staff and Finance.[1] In the Durham, North Eastern, East Midlands and South Western Divisions there will be a Divisional Director responsible for Carbonization Department.

18. Apart from his secretarial duties, the Divisional Secretary will initially be departmentally responsible for Public Relations, Patents and Common Services.

19. The Divisional Secretary and the Divisional Legal Adviser will report to the Divisional Board as a whole, through the Chairman or, as he may direct, the Deputy Chairman.

20. Divisional Boards must satisfy the National Board that, within the pattern laid down in paragraphs 16 to 19, their Divisional Headquarters is properly organized and staffed.

(c) Powers

21. Divisional Boards, in discharging their responsibility for the general management of their Division (see paragraph 3 above), have full authority to take decisions, save where the responsibility is specifically reserved by the National Board to themselves. The National Board will specify from time to time the powers which each Divisional Board is authorized or required to delegate to Area General Managers in particular matters. Divisional Boards and Area General Managers will ensure that the authorities subordinate to them are left in no doubt about the powers which they may, and the powers which they may not, exercise.

[1] In some Divisions a Reconstruction Director may be appointed and a Reconstruction Department created.

AREA HEADQUARTERS

(a) Responsibilities of the Area General Manager

22. Each Area General Manager is responsible for the general management of his Area to the Divisional Board as a whole and is at all times subordinate to the Divisional Chairman and Deputy Chairman. In addition, Divisional Boards may delegate powers to Divisional Board Members to issue instructions to Area General Managers in the Division. Area General Managers will act upon such instructions and will be held accountable to the Divisional Board.

(b) Organization of Area Headquarters

23. All departments other than Reconstruction, Legal and Carbonization Departments, are to be represented at Area Headquarters. The Production Manager, Industrial Relations Officer, Chief Accountant and Area Secretary are to be directly responsible to the Area General Manager. The Internal Auditor and Marketing Manager will have direct access to him. The responsibility for supervising the remaining departments and branches will be delegated by the Area General Manager to the Assistant Area General Manager. In the absence of the Area General Manager the Assistant Area General Manager is to be in charge of the Area.

24. The fact that some departments at Area are under the direct supervision of the Area General Manager does not in itself confer on those departments a higher status than belongs to those coming under the supervision of the Assistant Area General Manager. At Area, as at all other levels of management, there must be full consultation and close co-operation between all departments.

25. Area General Managers must see that the organization of their Area Headquarters conforms to the pattern laid down in paragraph 23 above, and must ensure that, within each department at Area, the work is properly grouped so that no departmental Head has too many people directly responsible to him. The National Board will issue instructions on the way in which they require Area Headquarters to be organized. Variations from these arrangements in particular Areas will only be permissible when approved by the National Board on the recommendation of the Divisional Board.

26. The Area General Manager may not exercise his powers of appointing staff in such a way as to depart from the authorized pattern of organization for his Area.

GROUP

27. The level of management between Area Headquarters and the collieries is the Group, and the authority in charge at this level is the Group Manager. Each Group must comprise not less than two collieries. Apart from this requirement, it is for Divisional Boards to determine in the light of local circumstances the size of the Groups in each Area and, if they see fit, to change the delimitation of the Groups from time to time.

28. The Group Manager will be accountable to the Area General Manager in all matters which substantially affect the efficient operation of the Group. The Group Manager must be given such staff as are necessary to enable him to do his work. Since the Groups must vary in size and importance and in the management problems which they present, the number and kind of staff which Group Managers should have will also vary. But it is not the Board's intention that there should be at any Group a comprehensive departmental organization such as there must be at the Area Head-quarters.

29. The Area General Manager will delegate to functional Heads at Area powers to issue instructions to Group Managers (see paragraph 8 above) and he may specify matters in which Group Managers are to report to particular functional Heads at Area, though in these as in other matters the Group Managers will remain ultimately accountable to the Area General Manager. Area General Managers may, with the approval of the Divisional Board, exclude from a Group Manager's field of responsibility any matters which do not substantially affect the efficient operation of the collieries in his Group. All matters so excluded must be clearly specified, and the Group Manager must be kept informed of all instructions on such matters issued direct to Colliery Managers (see paragraph 8 above).

COLLIERY

30. The Colliery Manager is accountable to the Group Manager for the efficient management of his colliery, save in those matters which are excluded from the Group Manager's field of responsibility (see paragraph 29). In such matters the Colliery Manager will be accountable to the Area General Manager direct or through such member or members of the Area staff as the Area General Manager may designate.

SUPERVISION AND ACCOUNTABILITY

31. Policy decisions of the Board must be properly and promptly

carried out, and control must be firm; in this all levels of manage-ment must play their part. Policies must be expressed fully, specific-ally, and where necessary, in detail. Each level of management must avoid interfering in the day-to-day work of the level of management below it, but should exercise control by means of modern manage-ment techniques, including the use of approved programmes followed by periodical reports and reviews of progress. The National Board intend that the use of standards and budgets shall be fully developed throughout their organization.

32. The authorities and functional Heads at each level of manage-ment are responsible for ensuring that they obtain the information that is needed for supervising and guiding subordinate levels of management and for holding them to account. They must see that this information is not more than is necessary for efficient manage-ment at their own level and for the needs of the level of management above, and is not required to be supplied more often than is necessary.

21. 'FLECK' CRITICIZED*

The exaltation of authority is the Committee's deliberate solution for what it sees as the main problem of the industry. As a policy it can be criticized on three counts.

First, it does not accord with Labour's philosophy of nationaliza-tion. Socialism has suffered much modification since the time when it was thought that a change to public ownership would inaugurate a free and happy co-operative commonwealth; but socialists have not entirely abandoned the view that public ownership should enable advances towards the 'good society' beyond what is possible in pri-vate enterprise. In this society men would be more free; discipline, if required, would be self-discipline; and some kind of 'industrial democracy' would flourish. Admittedly socialists have not found it easy to demonstrate the exact steps necessary to attain these ends. But, if the Fleck Report is right, the ends are unattainable. Private enter-prise is to set the standard for public undertakings, and, according to the report, the lesson private enterprise has to teach is: more discip-line. This, of course, does not prove the Fleck Report wrong; it only shows what must be abandoned if the report is accepted.

Secondly, the report has little to offer on one of the most serious of the industry's problems, the poor labour relations which exist in

* From H. A. Clegg: 'The Fleck Report', *Public Administration*, Vol. XXXIII, Autumn 1955, pp. 274–5. Reprinted by permission of the author and the editor of *Public Administration*.

some of the coalfields. Apart from the appointment of colliery personnel officers, the reorganization of the staff departments, and welcome advice to the Board not 'to rely as heavily as they have done in the past on the ranks of trade union officials as a source of recruitment into responsible positions' in these departments, they can only recommend consultation with the Unions 'in a further endeavour to find a remedy'. At best the emphasis on authority within management is irrelevant to this problem; at the worst it may spill over into the relations between management and men (where one of the difficulties is that, under full employment, authoritarianism cannot be the final answer) and further exacerbate the problem.

The third criticism is that, even within the terms of the Fleck Committee's philosophy, and within the range of problems to which they directed their attention, their recommendations may not be effective. It is perhaps a natural human reaction to think that shortcomings will be remedied by threats and punishment. The modern world has, however, seen enough examples of disappointing industrial results followed by tightened discipline, and for most of us the outcome has not justified the means. We should not too readily assume that even a mild authoritarianism will necessarily be successful. For the trouble may lie elsewhere. The National Board has complete statutory responsibility for the coal industry. To discharge this responsibility, especially at a time when staff is short, it must be almost entirely dependent on those it appoints to administer the coalfields and the collieries. Discipline is not likely to bring results unless the agents of the Board are already persuaded of the advantages of the course proposed. In these circumstances threats may not be much better than bad-tempered kicking against a wall.

Shortage of manpower will persist in the industry for some time, however energetic the new Board may be in applying remedies. If, following the Fleck proposals, the best men are concentrated in the departments at Headquarters and in the Divisions, the best of policies devised by them may be ill executed in the collieries, not through ill will, nor through indiscipline, but because men of the right calibre are not available. Then more emphasis on discipline would be a useless remedy.

If these suggestions are to the point, another remedy is required. The Fleck Committee is, of course, right to say that 'no organization will work well unless the people who give the instructions and frame the policies are sure that they are carried out'. If the responsibility of the Board is too wide, it must be narrowed to a field in which the Board can effectively ensure that policies are carried out. If reliance on discipline cannot be expected to bring results, then the Board will have to employ other methods, and employ them energetically, for the report has undoubtedly convicted the old Board of lack of drive. The relations between government departments and local authorities may serve as an example, although clearly they are not directly applicable to the coal industry. These relations do not involve insistence on the superiority of civil servants to local officials, nor the standardization of local institutions, nor the flourishing of disciplinary powers; but they have served to raise standards, improve performance, and carry out central policies with success.

The new Coal Board has announced its acceptance of the recommendations of the Fleck Report. Their implementation may well bring some immediate benefit, for a clear policy based on a clear philosophy is to be preferred to muddle. Whether the policy will in the long run provide the best organization for the industry depends upon whether the assumptions of the philosophy are sound. Has the Fleck Committee drawn the correct lessons from the experience of large private undertakings? Can these lessons be applied without qualification to a public undertaking? And do they provide the solutions to the problems of so large an undertaking as the Coal Board? Unless the answer to all these questions is affirmative, the solution is still to be found.

22. A LESSON FROM SCOTLAND?*

Before making comparisons with other nationalized undertakings, it must be made clear that the Board is necessarily different from them. With its 2,000 odd employees it is a pigmy compared with the National Coal Board (750,000) and the Railway Executive (600,000). It is small compared even with most Area Electricity and Gas Boards. Besides this, its region is more scattered and thinly populated than that of any of these Boards. The Railway Executive and the Scottish Gas Board also cover the North of Scotland; but they do not attempt to supply the needs of the many small isolated communities which are already served or will eventually be served by the Hydro-Electric Board. Accordingly, on the one hand, the Board has no need to develop administrative procedures necessary in an organization employing tens or hundreds of thousands of workers; and, on the other, the physical conditions of its region have favoured local autonomy and diversity (which may be equally desirable, but are not so easily attained in more closely-knit undertakings and more popu-

* From H. A. Clegg and T. E. Chester: 'The North of Scotland Hydro-Electric Board', *Public Administration*, Vol. XXI, Autumn 1953, pp. 231–4. Reprinted by permission of the authors and the editor of *Public Administration*.

lous regions with better communications). These considerations must qualify the comparisons presented below, but, in our opinion, they do not destroy their value.

The first comparison is between the North of Scotland Board and the electricity industry in the rest of Britain. The North of Scotland Board controls all generation, transmission and distribution within its territory. In the south the Area Boards deal with distribution alone; transmission and generation are vested in and directly controlled by the British Electricity Authority. At the time of the 1947 Act it seemed only reasonable, perhaps, to leave the Area Boards to deal with distribution alone, since this was the field in which further rationalization was most required; and, since the Central Authority must needs control the national grid, and, therefore, the power stations feeding the grid, to vest transmission and generation in it. The result has been, however, to create throughout the industry local agencies directly administered from London, parallel to the Area administration. The grip of a powerful centralizing body has thus been strengthened, the need for standardized practices increased, and friction and jealousy has been made possible. (For instance, the Secretaries of the Area Boards and the BEA Divisions are on different salary scales.) Before nationalization the arrangement was that the Central Electricity Board maintained, through the grid, technical control over the power stations, which were nevertheless administered by the companies or local authorities to which they happened to belong, and this seemed to work effectively and smoothly. It could clearly have been retained under nationalization by vesting generation as well as distribution in the Area Boards, and leaving the powers of the Central Electricity Board (and the Electricity Commissioners) much as they were. The North of Scotland Board has shown that it is at least possible for generation and distribution to be successfully administered within a single regional organization. Admittedly its conditions are very different from those in the south. It owns and controls its own regional transmission system; its power stations are many and small, and often supply but a single district. Nevertheless its success is an additional reason for questioning the form of organization laid down elsewhere under the Electricity Act, 1947.

The second comparison concerns the composition of the Board. It is the only public corporation composed entirely of part-timers. In other boards at least the Chairman and Deputy-Chairman are full-time appointments, and on the Coal Board and its Divisional Boards, the Transport Commission and most of its Executives, and the British Electricity Authority, full-timers outnumber the part-timers. If it is the function of the Boards to manage the industry, a number of full-time members is essential; but it is at least questionable whether this is the proper function of the national Boards. National management necessarily involves great centralization, and whatever may be the exact distinction between 'policy' and 'detail', clearly full-time Board members, whether or not they have specific departmental responsibilities, are likely to step over the boundary, and concern themselves with detail.[1]

It may also be doubted whether the most competent and qualified men are likely, unless they have an unusual gift of public spirit, to accept the five-year appointments customary for Board members, the more so now that it has become clearly established that appointments are frequently not renewed. A Board composed of men whose main occupation and source of income is outside the industry concerned is likely to be far more widely attractive.

The third comparison concerns the internal organization of nationalized undertakings. The Board has clearly understood its task as that of a development corporation and a holding company. After vesting day great care was taken to change nothing which could well be left alone, and to make such changes as were required, for instance the drawing of Area boundaries, with the greatest possible regard for existing institutions and local requirements. Headquarters then undertook the provision of services which the Areas could not perform for themselves, with the minimum central controls needed to fulfil the duties laid upon the Board by the 1943 and 1947 Acts. Organization on these lines was made all the easier because of the existence of the Board for over four years before vesting day. Continuity was possible at the top as well as the bottom of the new organization.

In comparing this method of building up an organization with that adopted by, say, the BEA and the Area Electricity Boards, or the National Coal Board and its Divisional Boards, it is impossible to use quantitative tests. To the observer, however, the difference is real and important. These larger bodies were created by the nationalization Acts, and therefore did not have the same opportunity to build on existing institutions, but this might have been taken as an additional reason for making use of what was already to hand, and for making such changes as were essential (and it must be remembered that the object of nationalization was to make changes) with as little disturbance as possible. In fact, the grouping of collieries into Sub-Areas and Areas, and of Areas into Divisions, and the arrangement of

---

[1] Compare Mr Lyttelton's defence of the acceptance of private directorships by Lord Reith, Chairman of the Colonial Development Corporation, in answer to a question of Mr Dugdale (House of Commons, July 10, 1953, c. 209–11), and a *Times* editorial on the same subject ('Full-time Chairmen', May 28, 1953).

electricity districts into Sub-Areas under the Area Boards, seems to have been designed to provide local agencies for the Boards, and not to give a headquarters organization to serve the needs of local undertakings. The North of Scotland, on the other hand, did not build from the top downwards, but from the bottom upwards. The very names of the Areas may be read as symbols of the Board's regard for continuity and for local requirements.

Scottish patriotism may explain much of the attitude of the North of Scotland Board and its staff. It reinforces their pride in the independence of their undertaking and their opposition to 'centralization' and 'Londonization' (both complaints frequently diagnosed by employees of other nationalized industries in their own organizations); and it increases their apprehension of the results which might follow from closer connections with the south, still more from amalgamation with the south. Jealousy of independence and resistance to joint action or amalgamation has been one of the main causes of the industrial difficulties which led up to the nationalization programme of 1945. But it was part of the case of those who framed the 1947 Act that the North of Scotland Board was best left on its own. The exclusion was justified. As a result the Board has been able to build an organization which not only is well suited to its region, but also has worthwhile lessons for its bigger but younger relatives in the south, and for those who would reorganize or add to the nationalized industries.

23. A FUNCTIONAL BOARD*

THE PRESENT ARRANGEMENTS

43. The composition of the National Coal Board is governed by statute. There must be a Chairman and not less than eight and not more than eleven other Members. The number of Members, apart from the Chairman, required to render whole-time service is not to exceed eight. One of the Members of the Board must be appointed to act as Deputy Chairman, and a second may be.

44. At present the Board consists of a Chairman, two Deputy Chairmen, four Members who render full-time service and four Members who render part-time service, making a total of eleven, against a possible twelve.

45. When the Board was first constituted under the Coal Industry

* From National Coal Board: *Report of the Advisory Committee on Organization*, February 1955, paras. 43–67. Reprinted by permission of the National Coal Board.

Nationalization Act, 1946, it consisted of nine full-time Members. The Board was 'functional' in that all the Members except the Chairman and Deputy Chairman were responsible for a department. Since then there have been substantial changes. The Coal Industry Act, 1949, enabled the Minister to appoint part-time Members of the Board, and it would now be within the Minister's powers to appoint a Board consisting wholly of part-time Members. Also, it has ceased to be the practice for all full-time Members of the Board other than the Chairman and Deputy Chairman, or Deputy Chairmen, to be responsible for a department. At present, for example, one such full-time Member of the Board has no departmental responsibilities. The four departments which are represented on the Board—by three Board Members—are: Labour Relations, Manpower and Welfare, and Scientific Departments, and the Medical Service. But three of the key departments—Production, Marketing and Finance—are not represented on the Board. This arrangement is unsatisfactory both in theory and practice. Some of our later recommendations, if accepted, would correct it.

46. The Boards that manage large-scale enterprises are usually of two main types. The first type comprises a few full-time executives who usually occupy the positions of Chairman and Deputy Chairman; the other Board Members are mostly people of eminence who spend only a small part of their time on the Board's business. The people on whom the responsibility for day-to-day decisions rests are usually 'General Managers', who do not have a seat on the Board. We do not think that this type of organization is suitable for the coal industry.

47. With the other type of Board, not only the Chairman and Deputy Chairman, or Deputy Chairmen, but also most of the other members are full-time employees of the Company and are often termed 'Executive Directors'. We think that this type of organization, which is found mostly among big industrial and commercial undertakings, is the proper one for the coal industry.

48. So we think that the present way in which the Board is composed mainly of full-time Members is right, and will remain right as far ahead as we can see. At the same time, because of their outside experience and independent viewpoint, part-time Members can make a vital contribution to the Board's work, and we think it important that part-time Members should continue to be appointed.

FULL-TIME BOARD MEMBERS AND THEIR DUTIES

49. It is essential that all Members of the Board should be capable of taking a wide view on all the issues which the Board has to decide.

This quality must not only be present, it must be exercised all the time. Nevertheless, a full-time Board Member can and should be given a field of responsibility and interest, of which he should have greater and more detailed knowledge than the Board as a whole can have. With a Board organized in the way we propose there would always be at least one Member of the Board who, when a particular question arose at the Board table, had a sphere within which that question obviously and naturally lay. This, as we have said in paragraph 33, is one of the essential needs in large industrial undertakings.

50. The Chairman and Deputy Chairman should be free of routine duties, apart from the usual duties of presiding over the Board and Executive Committees of the Board. They would keep a general watch over the work of Headquarters, and over the more important items of the work being done in the field. They would make, subject to the approval of the Board, the senior appointments, and would maintain those contacts with the Government which have to be made at a high level. They would also make it their business to initiate at the Board and its main Committees broad items of policy, or to see that those items were properly initiated.

51. The full-time Board Member should not be regarded as the Head of the department, or departments, concerned with the matters falling within his field of responsibility, in the sense that he would give time to the day-to-day management of the department. Each of the departments should have an executive Head at Headquarters, who would be responsible for its day-to-day management. It would be the Board Member's duty to see that, over the whole field of the department's work, a clear and comprehensive policy was established, and that the policy was reviewed from time to time in the light of changed needs and circumstances. And he would be responsible for ensuring that the department was properly organized and staffed for carrying out its functions, and would watch the department's progress.

52. We have said that the Board can and should run their business generally on the lines adopted by large industrial companies. With this as a working basis it is possible to divide the Board's functions into six main fields as follows:

(1) Production.
(2) Marketing and Purchasing.
(3) Industrial Relations.
(4) Staff.
(5) Finance.
(6) Scientific.

For each of these fields there should be a full-time Board Member.

53. The functions not specifically allocated in paragraph 52, are:

the Medical Service, Carbonization, Opencast, and small ancillaries, such as Bricks. The Board responsibility for these functions could conveniently be divided between two of the Board Members responsible for the activities listed in paragraph 52, as follows:

Medical Service	Scientific Member
Carbonization, Opencast and	
Small Ancillaries	Production Member

54. We do not think it would be appropriate to give to any full-time Board Member a particular responsibility for the Secretary's or Legal Departments. The Head of each of these departments should be responsible to the Board. The Secretary's functional duties—as opposed to the important service which he and his department should provide—are small, and rightly so. He should continue to be departmentally responsible for Public Relations.

55. We feel that if the Board is organized on the lines we have suggested, so that every department is within the responsibility of a full-time Board Member, one Deputy Chairman should be sufficient.

PART-TIME MEMBERS AND THEIR DUTIES

56. The part-time Members of the Board would be men known as having proved themselves outstanding in some phases of industrial leadership, and holding leading positions in the industry of the country. They would be representative of the best industrial thinking and would be men in whose judgment the community could have confidence.

57. The coal industry, both management and trade unions, has always tended to regard itself as different and separate from its fellows, and now that the industry has a monopoly of coal production the increased tendency towards self-centredness should be countered by the presence on the Board of men of wide experience of affairs. If, as we hope, the full-time Board Members were drawn from the younger ranks of the industry, the experience and balanced judgment of the part-time Members would be a source of strength to them.

58. In addition to attending meetings of the National Board, the part-time Members would, as occasion arose, be available to give advice on special problems. We think it would also be advisable for each of them, according to his bent and experience, to endeavour to serve on one of the Board's Committees, so that he could study one particular aspect of the Board's work.

59. In a later paragraph we shall suggest that the part-time Members should have a special function to perform in advising the Minister on the appointment of full-time Board Members. We think

that it should also be recognized that the part-time Members would have the right of access to the Minister—and would be responsible for exercising that right, jointly or severally—if they had any matters of importance affecting the industry to which they wished to draw his attention.

RESULTING COMPOSITION OF THE BOARD

60. In the result the Board would consist of the following:

Field of Responsibility

(1) Chairman	.. .. ⎱	Free of routine duties—see para-
(2) Deputy Chairman	.. ⎰	graph 50.
(3) Board Member	..	Production, Carbonization, Open-cast and Small Ancillaries
(4) Board Member	..	Marketing and Purchasing
(5) Board Member	..	Industrial Relations
(6) Board Member	..	Staff
(7) Board Member	..	Finance
(8) Board Member	..	Scientific and Medical
(9) Board Member	.. ⎫	
(10) Board Member	.. ⎬	Part-time duties—see paragraph 58
(11) Board Member	.. ⎭	
(12) Board Member	..	

An Addendum by Dr Fleck will be found at the end of the Report.

SELECTION OF BOARD MEMBERS

61. Selection of the right persons for membership of the National Coal Board is of dominating importance for the well-being of the industry. We realize that this is a matter which lies wholly in the hands of the Minister and that it imposes a heavy responsibility upon him not only to choose the right people but to satisfy himself that they are likely to work together as a Board. We therefore venture to make suggestions which, without in any way implying interference with the Minister's statutory responsibility or freedom of choice, may help him in this task.

62. As regards the part-time Members, many persons suitable for appointment will be well known by reputation and by their record of achievement in other commercial and industrial spheres. In addition, advice should, we think, be sought from leaders in particular fields, including the President of the Federation of British Industries, the Chairman of the Trades Union Congress, and the President of the British Employers' Confederation, and perhaps one or two others, who will be able to suggest candidates with the qualifications we have described. We recommend therefore that the Minister should appoint

a body of men who would collectively advise him on the appointment of part-time Members of the Board.

63. The part-time Members, by reason of their independent position and the knowledge they acquire of the Board's affairs, can be of special assistance to the Minister in advising him on the appointment of full-time Board Members who, as we later point out, must normally be drawn in future from within the industry itself. We suggest therefore that before appointing a Chairman or a Deputy Chairman of the Board or making new appointments of full-time Board Members, the Minister should consult the part-time Members.

64. We do not think that the suggestions we have made about the selection of Members of the Board would call for fresh legislation, and it would suffice if they were adopted as matters of practice in future.

REORGANIZATION OF THE PRESENT BOARD

65. If our suggestions about the constitution of the Board are adopted, it is clear that a reorganization of the present Board must follow. Several new appointments to the Board, and a reallocation of duties, will be necessary. We are satisfied that the need for this reorganization is urgent and that it should be undertaken without delay.

66. When this reorganization occurs it is important, as we have pointed out in paragraph 61, that all the Members appointed to the Board should have for each other that degree of trust and respect without which a Board cannot work in harmony. However competent individuals may be in their own particular fields, it will be no use appointing them to the Board if their personalities are such that they cannot work together as a team. In this respect the experience of the Board in the past eight years has not been happy. Therefore the necessity of ensuring that the Members of the Board are able to work together is an aspect of the reorganization which will necessarily engage the Minister's special attention.

67. We recommend:

   (a) that the National Coal Board should consist of twelve Members, namely, a Chairman and a Deputy Chairman, six other Members giving the whole of their time to the Board's work and four part-time Members. The division of duties should be as suggested in paragraph 60;

   (b) that the Board should now be reorganized in the way we have proposed and that the reorganization should be carried out as a matter or urgency;

   (c) that in reconstituting the Board, the Minister should give special attention to the necessity of ensuring that the Members of the Board are able to work together as a team;

(d) that in future the Minister, before appointing part-time Members, should seek the advice of a body of leaders in particular fields, as described in paragraph 62;

(e) that the Minister, before appointing a Chairman or a Deputy Chairman of the Board or making new appointments of full-time Board Members, should seek the advice of the part-time Members of the Board;

(f) that it should be recognized that the part-time Members of the Board would have the right of access to the Minister if they had any matters of importance affecting the industry to which they wished to draw his attention, and would be responsible for exercising that right.

24. THE FUNCTIONAL CHANNELS*

90. For the industry to succeed, there must be leadership at all levels, and in particular leadership from the top. This means that the brains and ability concentrated at Headquarters must be of the highest calibre drawn from the most progressive elements in the industry. Only in this way can new ideas and a new outlook be inculcated throughout the Board's organization. Leadership must come in the first place from the National Board themselves. But they cannot effectively lead the industry unless they are supported by a strong, well-organized Headquarters. The Board must be responsible for national policies for the industry and for judging progress in the carrying out of those policies. But the Board cannot form policy without expert advice from people who, each in his own field, can take a view of the industry as a whole. Nor can the Board themselves carry out their own policies or watch the execution of policies in detail. They must rely on their staff at Headquarters to set the execution of policies in motion and to keep track of events. This means that the functional channels connecting the departments at the various levels of management must be used for the great bulk of the work, leaving the central channel, that is the channel connecting the various authorities in the line of command, free for communications on broad policy issues.

91. Accordingly, departments at Headquarters, and in particular

* From National Coal Board: *Report of the Advisory Committee on Organization*, February 1955, paras. 90–101. Reprinted by permission of the National Coal Board.

the executive Heads of departments, must be accorded the open support of the Board. The advice of the Heads of departments on national policies should carry great weight. We are satisfied that in the past the departments at Headquarters have not always or consistently received the support which is their due and without which their task cannot be properly carried out.

92. We find that, in the industry, there are two opposing views on the use of the functional channel, that is the channel of communication and personal contact between a department at one level and the corresponding department at the next level below it. For example, there is doubt about the relationship between Production Department at Headquarters and Production Department at Division; and similarly between Production Department at Division and the Production Manager at Area. On the one hand it is held that the functional channel should be used for exercising direction, management, advice and control. The other view is that, while there must be functional specialists at each of the main levels of management, these specialists must be only advisory and should only be approached by the lower formation when the need for their advice is felt. It is further held that if the advice of specialists at the higher level is sought by the lower level it need not be acted upon. It is important that this confusion in the industry about the use of the functional channels should be brought to an end.

93. In the following paragraphs we give our views on the way in which we think the functional channels should work. Our recommendations are not new or revolutionary, and in the better run Divisions and Areas this method of working has in fact operated smoothly and efficiently since the Board's organization was first set up. Moreover, our views are in conformity with the principle of 'Line and Staff', upon which the Board's organization is, and should continue to be, based. The present division of opinion has, we think, been created in some degree by the provisions of the Board's General Directive on Organization, issued in October 1953, which we shall discuss later, and by the failure of some of the Board's officials, previously employed in small colliery companies, to appreciate the needs of a large organization.

RELATIONSHIPS

94. The functional Head at each level should be of higher calibre and attainments than his functional counterpart at the next level below, and should have a higher status and be better paid. His seniority to the man at the lower level should be officially and openly recognized. For example, the executive Head of a department at

Headquarters should be senior to the corresponding executive Head at Divisional Headquarters, usually a functional Member of the Divisional Board. The views of the senior man on his specialist subject should always be accepted at the next level below him, unless there are compelling reasons to the contrary. It is useless to select, train and pay high grade specialists if their services are only going to be used if and when an officer of a lower calibre and attainments at a lower level decides to use them.

DUTIES AND RESPONSIBILITIES

95. The main task of the functional Head at each level should, in relation to the functional level below him, be:

    (i) to co-ordinate the specialist work of the next level below him;

    (ii) to advise, guide and stimulate his functional counterpart at the next level below him;

    (iii) to keep himself informed about the work of his functional counterpart below him and to satisfy himself that the policy in his field is being carried out punctually and efficiently. If it is not, and he cannot himself put matters right, then the issue must be dealt with by the 'line' authority.

AUTHORITY

96. On matters of established national or Divisional policy the functional Head should be empowered to issue instructions to the next level below him. These instructions should be addressed to the functional Head at that lower level, but a copy must go direct to the 'line' authority to keep him informed. The 'line' authority at each level of management should establish a system under which his functional staff consult with him as necessary before taking action on instructions issued departmentally.

97. The duties and authority which we have described must be interpreted with common sense. The higher level must be satisfied that the work at the lower level is being carried out efficiently. This can and should be achieved without interference in day-to-day management. The routine and day-to-day matters will create few problems, but in any matter of importance or difficulty the position of the 'line' authority must always be borne in mind, so that his responsibility and authority are not undermined.

98. But it must be recognized that in an undertaking which started its life short of experienced staff and which was, on the whole, very backward in terms both of technical and general management, the positive direction and guidance which must emanate from the top must be very much greater than would normally be the case in a

competitive industry whose pattern and traditions of management had been established for a long time. For many years to come, and certainly until the basic patterns of organization have become fully established and until administrative routines and techniques have been standardized, the control at each level over the levels below it will have to be very firm—firmer than it is and has been since nationalization. For the same reasons, national and Divisional policy will have to be expressed fully, specifically and often in detail.

99. We have heard it suggested that Areas sometimes get little help from Divisions and Divisions little help from Headquarters. We find that, in general, this criticism is groundless. Almost all the men that we saw in lower formations expressed the view that they received help and encouragement from their departmental counterparts above them; furthermore, they said that they had no difficulties put in their way which prevented good administration or organization.

100. We recommend: that the functional Heads at each level of the organization should be of better calibre and higher status than their functional counterparts at the next level below. This seniority should be openly acknowledged and reflected in remuneration. The senior man's views in his own field should normally be accepted at the next level below him.

101. We further recommend: that the Board should adopt the description given in paragraphs 95 and 96 above of the duties and responsibilities of functional Heads in relation to the functional level below.

25. AREA BOARD ORGANIZATION IN THE ELECTRICITY SUPPLY INDUSTRY*

276. The Minister has appointed only the Chairman and Deputy Chairman of each Board for full-time duty; the remaining members serve on a part-time basis. The two full-time Board members therefore inevitably hold a controlling and dominating position in the conduct of the Board's day-to-day business, with the part-time members acting as a check on the Board's past activities and assisting in the formulation of future policy when the full Board come together for their regular meetings each month, or in some Areas at more frequent committee meetings dealing with particular branches of the

* From *Report of the Committee of Inquiry into the Electricity Supply Industry*, January 1956, Cmd 9672, paras. 276–83.

Board's activities. This arrangement invites three questions:

1. Do the part-time members provide adequate checks and balances to the power and influence wielded by the Chairman and Deputy Chairman?
2. Does the existence of two full-time members lead to a confusion of responsibility between them?
3. Is the present composition of the Board the best for the proper supervision and encouragement of the Chief Officers, Sub-Area and District Managers, and their staffs?

277. For part-time members, the need is for men of proved ability and varying experience who can bring fresh ideas and uncommitted minds to bear on the problems of electricity supply; men who may not know all the answers but who will ask the right questions; men whose presence will stimulate and exert as needed a healthy discipline on the executive, and secure that any project which may have been ill-considered is rejected. The Area Board Chairmen claim that their present part-time colleagues do in fact exert just such influences upon them. They have spoken most appreciatively of the contributions these members can and do make to the Board discussions, and of their value also as a measure of informed outside opinion against which the full-time members can test ideas and policies generated within the industry. We see no reason to differ from these opinions.

278. We have no doubts of the value of the part which the part-time members of an Area Board can play and we are convinced that the effectiveness of any Board constituted in this way can depend very much on the quality of these members. The power residing in the hands of the Chairman and Deputy Chairman of an Area Board is considerable and we are the more concerned that it should not be exercisable in any arbitrary fashion. We think it important therefore that part-time members of an Area Board should be chosen with the utmost care, and should in all cases be selected not as representatives of any particular interest or section of the community but for their individual and collective ability.

279. It was apparent to us that the different Chairmen regarded their roles in varying lights according to their own personal inclinations, technical experience and individual backgrounds. Some Chairmen are frankly acting as General Managers, some are content to leave their Deputy Chairmen in full managerial control over the entire field and others share the supervision of business with their Deputies. The extent to which Chairmen share responsibility with their Deputies varies from Board to Board. We cannot therefore say we are entirely happy that there is in no case confusion of responsibility between the two full-time members or of the functions proper to the Chairman with those proper to the General Manager or Chief

Executive. In our view the functions of Chairman and Chief Executive should be separated and should vest in two different people. We do not think that, with the best will in the world, an able Chairman— even if he deliberately sets out to play the role of Board Chairman alone and to eschew executive functions—has much chance of succeeding in that aim, if he is appointed for full-time duty, particularly when he is not always able to avoid committing his Board at Central Authority meetings or conferences. His mere presence at Board Headquarters invites approaches from staff and members of the public which will inevitably involve him in day-to-day business matters, and no man worth his salt can be expected to sit back while interesting problems at his elbow continually invite his attention. There is moreover a very real risk under the present system that the influential position of the full-time members and the Board's reliance upon them will lead to their becoming too autocratic. This might leave the Board themselves little scope but to approve schemes which are already cut and dried, and to which the full-time members have already virtually committed them.

280. These are constitutional weaknesses and it is in no spirit of criticism of the present Board members that we say we think it important they should be remedied. To be fully effective, we believe the Board should be so constituted that their controlling position is unassailable. We consider that the Chairman of the Board should be free of executive responsibilities. These should be exercised by a General Manager or Chief Executive who would be appointed by the Board. If the Minister considered that the person appointed as Chief Executive was of Board stature, and in all normal circumstances he ought to be, the Minister should appoint him a member of the Board.

281. We recommend that the Minister should consider appointing the Chairmen of Area Boards for part-time duty only. This would, incidentally, widen the field from which appointments to Board Chairmanship might be made; for we think that more men of high attainments would be attracted by a part-time post offering £3,000 a year than by the present full-time appointment even at the higher salary of £6,000 which we recommend in paragraph 316 as the appropriate rate for such a post. We do not suggest that all Area Board Chairmen's posts could be converted to part-time appointments overnight, but we consider that an early start should be made in one or two Boards as opportunity offers. We would not wish our proposal for the appointment of a Chief Executive to be dependent on the conversion of the Chairman's post to a part-time appointment, and we would hope that the recommended transfer of executive functions to a Chief Executive could be proceeded with in all Areas.

282. We have considered whether the Boards should contain any

full-time members other than the Chief Executive. We think this would be inadvisable, especially as we envisage the business of each Area being run as a number of individual undertakings, managed at the local level rather than controlled in detail from the centre. The establishment of a largely whole-time Board would tend to subordinate local management to functional control and to attract power away from the Districts to the centre—effects which would be opposite to those we wish to bring about.

283. Concurrently with the changes suggested above, we recommend that the office of Deputy Chairman should lapse.

26. THE STRUCTURE OF BRITISH RAILWAYS*

20. British Railways are divided into six Regions; they are the Eastern, London Midland, North Eastern, Scottish, Southern and Western Regions. Considerable differences exist between the Regions, both in size and in the kind of work undertaken. . .

21. Each Region comes under the control of its Area Board. Subject to the limitations placed on them by the Commission, each Area Board manages its railways, improves its facilities and cuts its costs, sees that the needs of transport users are met, and ensures the safety, health and welfare of its employees. They may, subject to a financial limitation of £100,000 (Q. 1581), authorize expenditure on equipment and engineering projects, authorize property transactions and various other matters. They must, amongst other things, submit budgets and forecasts of capital and revenue expenditure to the Commission (Appendix 5).

22. Area Boards (who, for example, in the Southern Region consist of a Chairman and six members) (Q. 1751), are wholly part-time (Q. 1749–50); though their Chairmen, who are all members of the Commission (Q. 239), may be employed on a full-time basis there (Q. 1772). The Boards hold formal monthly meetings and in addition make regular tours of their area (Q. 1751). At times when great changes are taking place in their Area, they are naturally faced with greater problems, and spend more time on their railway work (Q. 1775). The Chairman of one Area Board said he spent about three days a week on railway business (Q. 1768) but was in addition in constant touch with his General Manager (Q. 1751). While it is difficult to quantify time spent in this way, the Chairman of BTC went to some lengths to praise the amount of work put in by these

* From *Report from the Select Committee on Nationalized Industries: British Railways*, July 1960, H.C. 254, paras. 20–2 and 24–42.

men. Their fees, which average about £500 a year, are fixed by the Commission, but the Chairman remarked that the Commission were almost ashamed to be paying them so little for so much (Q. 1595). . .

24. The Commission justified the principle of part-time Area Boards by stressing the experience and distinction that such men were able to bring to railway affairs, and the value of their contacts with other industries (Q. 1776). While there was a General Manager in charge of the management of the railways in the Region, there was no need of a full-time Chairman as well (Q. 1751-2). Another way of doing things would be to give the General Manager the status of a managing director (Q. 1753), and this might even have advantages (Q. 1755); but meanwhile the present system is, in their opinion (Q. 1592) and in that of the Ministry (Q. 60), producing satisfactory results.

25. The Commission set out the fields in which they reserve control of affairs to themselves, rather than delegate them to Regions. It made a formidable list. Starting with general financing control, general commercial policy, labour relations of a major character, dealings with Government and Parliament, higher appointments and research, it then went on to detailed railway matters; the policies and principles to be adopted in railway operations, the overall control and allocation of rolling stock, the design, manufacture, procurement and standards of maintenance of locomotives, rolling stock, permanent way, signalling and various electrical equipments (Appendix 5, para. 8). After a first reading of this catalogue of controls, it seemed hard to form a picture of decentralization.

26. However, as the inquiry proceeded, it became evident that in fact a great field of decision had been devolved upon Area Boards by the Commission, and that there were good reasons for the retention by the Commission of the remaining powers. For example, in railway matters (as to a greater or less extent in problems facing all the nationalized industries) some decisions are taken on grounds which are not strictly commercial, but are believed to be in the public interest. Your Committee comment on the effects of this at various places in this Report, but they are agreed that such decisions should certainly not be taken at regional level (and they discuss later the Commission's relationship to the Minister in this matter).

27. Nearly half of the total of railway traffic is inter-regional, passing the boundary between one Area and the next at some point in its travels (Appendix 50). This illustrates the extent to which the railways form one national unit, and it follows that rolling-stock should in general be able to move anywhere in the system. To ensure this, there must be some standardization of equipment, of stores, of maintenance and training of staff; and this can best be done from the

centre. Regions are consulted on these matters, so that their own individual needs are not overlooked, but the decisions are taken by the Commission, who are satisfied that the result is a more efficient and more economical system (Q. 1238–9).

28. Again, it is clearly more sensible (particularly when the industry is so short of top-grade technical staff) that the work of such staff as they have should be available for the good of the whole system (Q. 1234, 1238). The general dearth of men to fill the top posts in industry to some extent justifies the control kept by the Commission over top appointments throughout British Railways (Q. 1232), especially as the Commission are apparently always ready to take the advice of Area Boards on this matter (Q. 246).

29. These matters and others (such as the allocation of manufacture among the diminishing number of railway workshops) can clearly be best organized from the centre. But on the other hand, in such a vast concern as this, responsibility for operational management must devolve on lower units. The Commission have taken steps to see that the initiative and ability which exists at regional level and below should not be wasted, and the Chairman told Your Committee that new thought generally comes from below towards the top (Q. 1258).

30. Thus, while standards of maintenance must be laid down centrally, the maintenance system itself is left to Regions (Q. 1239–40). Recent changes have given the Regions much more control over purchasing and procurement than before (Q. 1245), and rather more is now done regionally than by the centre (Q. 1251). While coaching stock must conform to standards laid down at the centre, the interior design is left to the choice of the Regions (Q. 1458).

31. The Area Boards have always been allowed a good deal of freedom in fixing the fares they charge for concessional and excursion fares (Q. 1184); under the most recent fares change, they have also now been allowed to fix, within limits, the general level of ordinary fares (Q. 1645). But it is on the freight side that they have been given the greatest opportunities; apart from some major customers who are dealt with on a nation-wide basis by the Commission, anyone can get an individual price quotation for the carriage of his goods, in full load wagons, directly from regional managers (Q. 1184).

32. This freedom is however qualified by the recent creation of a central inspection service (Q. 1221) which keeps headquarters informed of any major or unusual variations of freight practice that may exist in the Regions (Q. 1224). The Commission stress that the purpose of these checks is principally to get information about the attitude of different customers to railway business (Q. 1207, 1211); business throughout the Regions is interlocking (Q. 1210), and comparisons of this kind should be to the advantage of all Regions in the

long run. This inspection system is new and experimental (Q. 1206).

33. The relationship between the Commission and Area Boards can be revealed in the manner in which modernization schemes emanate and are handled. These schemes usually originate with the full-time management staffs of the Region, and go to their Area Board for their approval. While the Board are examining the proposal, there are direct contacts between the regional management and the Commission's central staff on the technical details of the plan (Q. 246). If the Area Board approve the plan, they can set it in motion at once—provided it does not cost more than £100,000. If its cost is greater than that, it must be submitted to the Commission for their decision (Q. 1581).

34. The Commission, in other words, rely in the first place on the recommendation of the experienced Area Boards, particularly in regard to the financial effect of schemes. But they feel that they are better provided than Boards on the technical side, and that therefore their intervention is necessary—first, in the informal talks with regional management, and subsequently in the formal approval of major schemes. They make their final decision on commercial grounds (Q. 1587).

35. The need to send large schemes to the Commission results inevitably in a delay; but an Area Board Chairman said that, for a middling-sized scheme costing £500,000, the delay would be about a month (Q. 1584), and less in urgent cases (Q. 1587); for big schemes, the delay may naturally be quite a lot longer (Q. 1607–8). The Area Boards, who are not themselves technically qualified, say they value the second look at these projects which this machinery allows (Q. 1581–2).

36. The Area Boards are, it seems, on the whole content with the limit of £100,000 put on the schemes which they may authorize; if it went higher, it should go a lot higher, said one Area Board Chairman (Q. 1581). The Chairman of the Southern Area Board said that he himself found that the physical limitation of the work that could be done by his staff was more restricting than the limits placed on his expenditure (Q. 312–14).

37. The nature of a nationalized industry makes it, in one sense, less able to devolve its authority to a subordinate level. The Chairman of the Commission needs to be in constant touch with Ministers of the Crown; many of the Commission's decisions must have important political implications (Q. 275). The Minister of Transport answers something like 200 parliamentary questions a year on matters dealing with BTC, and BTC themselves deal with 120 letters a month from Members of Parliament (Q. 1659). While the answers to these questions make clear, when necessary, that the Area Boards may be

responsible for the matter involved, it must be the Commission which remains responsible in chief for relations between Parliament and the railways (Q. 1603–4). This in itself imposes a limit on the decentralization that is possible within BTC (Q. 1662–3).

38. One of the merits of decentralization is that it enables the particular requirements of a locality to be satisfactorily dealt with, and allows experience of local conditions to be put to good advantage. But the Regions themselves cover large areas, and variations of demand will be met with in a single Region (Q. 1194). It follows that, if the most is to be made of their opportunities, Area Boards must secure a delegation of powers and responsibility within Regions.

39. Decentralization has progressed at different speeds and in different detailed ways in the various Regions. The Eastern Region was the first to produce a scheme of reorganization, under which three Lines, with a number of Districts beneath them, were set up (Appendix 5; Q. 1601). Decentralization within the Southern Region was delayed by special difficulties (Appendix 6). The new pattern of management is still not settled in all respects in the London Midland Region (Q. 1601); and the Western Region, which has Divisions (but not a Line organization) and subordinate Districts, has always been more cohesive than the others (Q. 1494). It is clear from this that there has been no attempt by the Commission to force rigid and unwelcome systems below Area Board level.

40. Changes have been made at regional headquarters, so that the General Manager (who is the Chief Executive of the Region, responsible to the Area Board—Appendix 5) is left much freer, and able thereby to spend more time on planning and exercising general oversight. This has been done by combining the previous operating, commercial and motive power departments into the one traffic department, under an Assistant General Manager. This ensures that the man who sells the traffic is also responsible for seeing that the trains to carry it are available and running well (Q. 239).

41. Commercial policy is laid down by the General Manager (Q. 246). Beneath him, the key man who fills the new post of traffic manager is able to take prompt decisions without requiring the consideration of the General Manager himself (Report, para. 60); he is able both to provide, and to sell services (Appendix 9, para. 41). Something of the same flexibility exists in the realm of passenger services, where for example it may sometimes be left to a stationmaster to fix excursion fares (Q. 1193).

42. From these examples, it can be seen that much of the management of the railways in Regions has been delegated. At the same time as this has gone on, however, there has been a tendency to rationalize the operation of trains within each Region; with fewer workshops

and marshalling yards, the actual dispositions of rolling-stock must be made at regional level, and this must require greater, and not less, control from the centre (Appendix 6).

27. SOURCES OF FRICTION*

NATIONALIZATION AND BUREAUCRATIC NEEDS

The post-war nationalization measures in Britain introduced public ownership in no fewer than five major industries. With only one exception—iron and steel, where the experiment was short-lived—this was accompanied by great changes in the existing management structure; for one of the main objectives of the programme was to introduce the benefits of large scale organization and unified control to industries which for various reasons had tended to ignore them. These changes were not uniform in their impact; in the railways, and in electricity supply, for example, earlier legislation had made attempts to unify and standardize existing services, and here the new boards of management enjoyed the advantage that some steps had been taken towards a more centralized form of organization. The British Transport Commission was able to use the geographical and functional set-up of the old private railway companies as the framework of the nationalized regional organization: while the 'grid' system of inter-connected power stations, developed before 1939, served as the basis of the organization of nationalized electricity supply. Furthermore, in these cases, there was at least a nucleus of trained and experienced staff available for key posts.

But elsewhere, no such advantages existed. The period under wartime control had further underlined the serious shortage of experienced mining engineers and administrators; and most of the government committees appointed to consider the structure of the industries subsequently nationalized, had stressed the problems likely to arise through a shortage of technicians and executives capable of playing a part in the affairs of large-scale organizations.[1] The nationalization programme recognized this deficiency, its advocates claiming that only through public ownership could the need be met. State control, it was argued, would ensure that men of such calibre would be recruited and trained, in contrast to the short-sighted outlook under private ownership. But though the nationalizers recognized the need,

* From J. H. Smith: 'The Rise of a Bureaucracy', *Transactions of the Third World Congress of Sociology*, Vol. II, pp. 56–70. Reprinted by permission of the author.
[1] See Professor Chester's paper.

they also underestimated it. This is to be explained partly by the mood of over-optimism always shown by the supporters of any revolutionary development, but more because estimated requirements were usually based on what was known of the bureaucracies of private industry. Since then it has become clear that the triple demands of large-scale reorganization, of central control, and of accountability to Parliament produced a set of bureaucratic needs unique in the history of industrial administration in Britain.

Bureaucratic systems of control were nothing new in British industry, but nationalization created a new and exacting type. Co-ordination and technical advance were its prime objectives, and to secure them the nationalizers visualized a hierarchy of power arranged, for all functions, as a hierarchy of competence. Accordingly, most territorial levels of administration were designed to carry a full complement of specialists (engineers, planners, personnel officers, accountants), whose competence was to increase at each superior layer. In this way the closest scrutiny could be made of decisions anywhere in the new organization. In intention, therefore, the bureaucratic structures of the nationalized industries came remarkably close to the 'pure' type of bureaucracy distinguished by Max Weber.

The imposition of such structures on industries which had, for the most part, only limited experience of them was bound to produce changes and tensions of great interest to the sociologist. In one case, that of road haulage, bureaucratic systems of control were virtually unknown, and it is with this experience that the present paper is concerned. Attention has been confined to the years 1948–53, before the return to private ownership of certain parts of the public sector.

THE ROAD HAULAGE INDUSTRY BEFORE NATIONALIZATION

The Transport Act of 1947 set up a British Transport Commission to provide 'an efficient, adequate, economical and properly integrated system of public inland transport and port facilities within Great Britain'. The intention was to build the framework for a system of inland transport, in which rail and road would be fruitfully joined through a rational allocation of traffic, and 'unnecessary competition' eliminated. Operation of the system was delegated to agents known as Executives, or boards of management, appointed by the Minister of Transport. Powers to acquire most long-distance haulage by road conferred by the Act were eventually transferred to a Road Haulage Executive, appointed in June 1949. The task confronting this body was a tremendous one, for in three years it was to acquire over 3,500 undertakings and 42,000 vehicles, and create from them a unified national service, with some 80,000 employees, known as British Road Services.

No private haulage company even remotely approached operation on such a scale. A few 'large' firms had established themselves (each with not more than a couple of hundred vehicles), and to one side were to be found well-known undertakings such as Pickfords and Carter Patersons, which had been in road transport for well over a century and which had passed under railway control. But about the rest of the industry it is impossible to generalize. In 1936, 27,000 licences had been issued for the carriage of goods for hire or reward, specifying just over 100,000 vehicles, or an average of 3.75 vehicles to each licence. The small scale nature of the industry is shown still more clearly by the fact that only 300 licensees controlled more than 25 vehicles, and some 3,000 controlled from 5–25; while over 23,000 operators had less than 5 vehicles apiece. At the outbreak of war, the 350 *largest* concerns were found to contain 10,000 vehicles, or an average of 28 vehicles per firm. Apart from the railway-owned companies, no single private haulier controlled as much as 1 per cent of the total fleet.

Among this great mass of small operators, conditions were extremely unstable, firms coming on and off the road almost overnight. Factors such as these make it impossible to speak of this sector of the industry as having any 'administrative structure' at all. Many firms were one-man enterprises, buying vehicles on hire-purchase. The owner would almost certainly have begun as a driver, and would still take out a vehicle when needed. He would have little or no need for specialized staff: drivers would do their own maintenance, and also canvass for traffic. Some would be sent out on 'tramp' runs; picking up a fresh load wherever they could, and eventually arriving back, often after an absence of several weeks.

Record keeping was at a minimum. Records of hours worked were required by law, and for these the drivers themselves were responsible. Apart from this, in view of the small-scale and *ad hoc* nature of the work, scant attention was paid to operating records. Accounts, if kept at all, were kept in the most rudimentary form. (Firms could be classified, it has been said, into those who kept accounts, those who had cash books, and those who used the back of an envelope.)

In view of this, over much of the industry it would have been exceptional to find large numbers of specialized clerical or administrative staff. Most record-keeping and letter-writing would be carried out by the owner himself, or his drivers: when occasion demanded, his family might be called on to help. At this level, control was autocratic; the only formal rules being legal requirements

F

prescribing maximum hours of continuous work—and these were often lightly treated. In the years immediately preceding the last war, over 70 per cent of general haulage workers were employed under such conditions.

However, once a firm became large by the industry's standards, i.e. with more than a handful of vehicles, the need would be felt for the introduction of more systematic procedures, involving specialized clerical work. In a handful of firms, the increase might have been great enough to result in a second level of management, but this was very rare indeed. One clerk, often a driver unfit for the road, helped by a boy, was the common pattern here, dealing with elementary book-keeping, consolidation of records, correspondence, wages, and the simple and unavoidable documentation associated with certain classes of traffic, e.g. parcels and 'smalls'. But whatever the volume of this work, and it plainly assumed sizeable proportions in the 200 largest firms, record-keeping and rule-making remained something of an afterthought. Clerical staff had low status; they were badly paid and unrepresented by trade unions; and they got little sympathy from drivers and other workers, who regarded them as 'the boss's men'. Yet often drivers enjoyed a closer personal relationship with the owner, who had himself begun as 'one of them', and for the most part still behaved like it. Accommodation for clerical workers again showed how little thought had been given to the need for this type of work, though none can doubt the ingenuity subsequently displayed. The less enterprising pressed the front parlour into service, or bricked off a corner of the garage, but others littered their yards with an array of 'offices' which were later to present a formidable problem of replacement. Few of them bothered to build; their clerks were housed in railway arches, worn-out lorries, derelict buses, trams, and even bathing cabins.

Only in the railway-owned sector of the industry had the size of the undertaking and the nature of the traffic led to bureaucratic systems of control. The Pickford and Carter Paterson organization had some 2,100 clerical and administrative employees in 1944; its specialized work such as furniture removal, and parcels traffic carried over a national network, involved much paper work. Here were to be found traffic clerks, accounts clerks, and staff dealing with complaints and claims; at a higher level were the senior office clerks, the commercial representatives (salesmen) and the headquarters staff. Yet even here, staff were not selected because they possessed a specialist qualification—it was not a practice, for example, to recruit qualified accountants—usually men were taken on at an early age and trained, as on the railways, strictly to meet the requirements of work they were likely to do. Nor did it follow that clerical employees in this sector of the industry enjoyed the best wages and conditions; in fact, pay was low even by railway standards. After 1933, when the railways assumed control of the Pickford, Carter Paterson and Hay's Wharf organizations, some progress was made in recruiting clerical workers by the railway clerical union, the Railway Clerks Association. Even so, no agreement governing the wages and conditions of these employees was concluded until 1943, only five years before nationalization. Clerical workers elsewhere in the industry preferred, on the whole, to identify themselves with management, rather than risk disfavour and possibly dismissal because of union activities; moreover, the small-scale and fiercely competitive nature of the industry made contact with fellow workers in other firms extremely difficult. The Transport and General Workers' Union, which was active in recruiting drivers, did succeed in attracting a small proportion of clerical staff, but they remained uncovered by any of the national decisions concerning wages and conditions.

The war brought many changes to the industry. Many services were compulsorily integrated after the assumption of control over long-distance road haulage by the Ministry of War Transport. Control was effected nationally through twelve traffic regions, divided into Districts and sub-Districts. The 390 sub-Districts were the operational units, and were placed under a manager assisted by a traffic officer from the Ministry. The controlled undertakings provided the reporting points for vehicles and office and accounting facilities. New clerical procedures were introduced. Many clerical employees were called up, and temporary workers recruited. But the return of the old conditions in the years immediately following the war indicated that the industry had been little affected by the revolutionary operating systems introduced between 1942 and 1945. This failure to reorganize and to develop services on a bigger and more rational scale provided further ammunition for the advocates of public ownership.

THE GROWTH OF BRITISH ROAD SERVICES, 1948–53

Nationalization of road haulage firms began in 1948. By 1951, British Road Services had virtually acquired full control of long-distance road haulage. Within the space of three years, the structure of this sector of the road transport industry had been changed beyond recognition. Instead of the thousands of tiny units in sharp competition there was now a unified organization, under centralized control, seeking to establish common policies and practices throughout the country. The task before the Road Haulage Executive could be summarized: (*i*) to acquire over 3,500 undertakings, (*ii*) to weld these together into one organization, (*iii*) to introduce new systems of operation and control, (*iv*) to secure the full co-operation of management and men, (*v*) to plan its development under the control of the British Transport Commission, in consultation with the four other transport executives.[1]

Clearly the fate of the experiment depended in the ability of the Executive to devise bureaucratic systems of control which were capable of realizing these objectives, but which would not affect the flexible operation regarded as essential in road transport. What were its assets in this task? As has been shown, its inheritance was very mixed. Only a tiny fraction of its staff had worked in organizations even of moderate size, and thus the fund of experience was low. On the other hand, goodwill and enthusiasm were in fair supply, both from the workers who had long campaigned for nationalization, and from a number of newcomers, attracted by the prospect of a new and constructive enterprise. However, these advantages might quickly be lost if the new organization failed to live up to their high hopes. On top of this, the Executive was subject to continuous hostile propaganda from the still considerable private sector of the industry.

From the beginning, the new enterprise expanded at a phenomenal rate. Total vehicle strength rose from 8,208 in January 1949 to 42,000 by January 1953; total employees in the same period from 23,000 to 70,000. Between 1949 and 1951, the Executive took over 3,000 firms at a cost of £80,000,000; in the summer of 1949, it was acquiring businesses at the rate of 200 a week.

Undertakings acquired were allotted to one of nine Divisions. Eight of these were separate geographical areas; the ninth consisted chiefly of the national network of services built up by Pickfords, known as the Special Traffic (Pickfords) Division. Within each Division were three further levels of management: Districts, of which there were thirty at the end of 1951; Groups, of which there were 227; while the lowest level of management was to be found at the Depots, numbering just over 1,000. Even here the size of the unit was three or four times greater than the commonest form under private ownership.

Within this general framework, the new bureaucratic pattern was quickly established. An examination of the departmental structure gives a clear picture of the growth of new functions and lines of control. At headquarters, with a staff of 250, ten specialist departments were set up, each with its own chief officer reporting direct to the Executive; these were Secretariat and Legal, Organization, Finance and Accounts, Public Relations, Staff and Welfare, Traffic,

[1] At that time the Railway, Docks and Inland Waterways, Hotels, and Road Passenger Executives.

Engineering, Surveying, Stores, Research. At each divisional head-quarters, with a staff of approximately sixty, there were six specialist departments, with chief officers responsible to a Divisional Manager. Each District headquarters had a staff of approximately thirty, with five departmental officers (accounts, staff and welfare, traffic, engineering and stores) responsible to the District Manager. The Group originally had three specialist departments—accounts, traffic and engineering. With the introduction of these new departments, centralized systems of control in specialized and unfamiliar activities were quickly established throughout the industry. Thus the frame-work was provided within which the Executive could set out to realize the unified services and the high technical standards required by Parliament.

THE RECRUITMENT OF STAFF

The recruitment of staff for these new centres of administration and paper work was a major problem. The appointment of the Road Haulage Executive itself was a prerogative of the Minister of Trans-port, who gave it a composition little different from other nationalized Boards. Ex-managing directors sat alongside ex-trade union officials. The Chairman was a soldier formerly in army transport.[1] In doing this, the Minister followed the general requirements of the Transport Act, that he should select members from persons experienced 'in transport, industrial, commercial or financial matters, in administra-tion or in the organization of workers'.

Once appointed, the Executive was responsible for selecting its senior managers—in many ways one of its most difficult tasks. The structure of the industry before the war allowed few men the oppor-tunity to become experienced in the methods and outlook of large organizations, which meant that the Executive often had to go out-side the industry to recruit senior staff. This was particularly the case where specialized functions were being introduced for the first time. To bring the administration in line with modern business practice, qualified accountants were required at each of the main levels of management—Headquarters, District and Group—so that an industry which had previously regarded the keeping of accounts as an annoyance, now numbered its accountants in hundreds and its accounts clerks in thousands. Other examples where new recruits needed to be brought into the industry were in engineering, and in personnel management, both of which had never previously been

---

[1] Contrary to general belief (especially among trade unionists), this was not a common practice. Of the forty-seven full-time national Board members appointed at the time of nationalization, only three had been high-ranking service officers.

recognized as specialized functions. The high rate of acquisition, too, meant a need for staff qualified in estate management.

The new management structure also called for large numbers of senior clerical staff; some of these were recruited from men already in the industry, but many had to be sought elsewhere. Such men would be called upon to exercise initiative and responsibility, and to be suitable for further promotion.

Below this level, the range of clerical jobs was immensely widened, especially in the traffic and accounts departments in which over half the jobs of this type were found. It is difficult to say how far national-ization meant an absolute increase in the numbers of clerical workers in long-distance road haulage: without doubt the numbers of ad-ministrative and senior clerical staff increased, but whether the pro-portion of clerks serving them was appreciably in excess of those in the sector of the industry before nationalization is debatable. Unfortunately, few reliable figures are available, except for data derived from the 1931 Census on the distribution of the labour force of individual industries by function. This lists 6,962 clerical workers out of 168,421 employed in road cartage and haulage, representing 4.7 per cent of the total. Administrative and clerical employees accounted for approximately 20 per cent of British Road Services staff between 1948–53. This fact, and the steady increase in numbers of clerical staff in the early years, was repeatedly held up by political opponents as evidence of red tape, and of an attempt to 'run the industry from Whitehall'. But the figure of 14,900 clerical and ad-ministrative employees in March 1953 does not, however, represent an increased proportion in this type of work compared with 1949. As it was at this time that the Executive was acquiring the larger private firms and their staffs, it is reasonable to assume that the proportion of 20 per cent is similar to that which obtained in the bigger enterprises.

This, however, is a small point when set against the greatly-increased proportion of white-collar workers over the nationalized industry as a whole. In the space of a few years the informal and often unconventional practices of thousands of small firms were swept away: in their place a centralized administrative machine was set up, which put a premium on order, predictability and method. 'Making up the books' was no longer a family ritual, performed once a week in the front parlour: it was a daily process, performed by qualified staff. Every development in this period served to emphasize the loss of individuality on the part of what were once fiercely independent units, from the regular issue of directives from higher levels (includ-ing the 'Management Manual') to the increased use of machines, especially teleprinters, all stressing the interdependence and same-ness of routines all over the country. Such an administrative revolution clearly called for a great increase in the size of the white-collar group. . .

GRADING AND SALARIES

The absence of any hierarchical system of administrative and clerical grades, with a corresponding salary scale, did not long persist in the new bureaucracy. Within two years of nationalization an elaborate grading system had been established, in which status was determined by the nature of the work and the position in the management hierarchy. Districts required more high grade positions than groups, and so on. Personal considerations were firmly excluded. 'It must be stressed,' said the Executive in a statement of policy, 'that *posts*[1] are being classified and that the quality as distinct from the quantity of work arising from the duties of a post will be the determining factor . . . fitness for promotion in the absence of a suitable vacancy will not warrant regrading.' Such practices were in marked contrast to most experiences of private ownership, when a clerk's salary depended wholly on his personal relations with the owner.

Below a salary level of £630 (in 1950) six grades of staff were officially recognized. At the lowest level Class IV, rising to Class I, and above this, two special classes 'A' and 'B'. The Executive distinguished the duties of these various classes as follows: Class IV, clerks performing routine work in all departments; Class III, clerks whose work would still be largely routine in character, but who might be required to take charge 'of a small section of the work of an office', or be entrusted with the supervision of work similar to his own. Much the same criterion applied in Class II, except that responsibilities would be greater, and possibly of a specialized nature, e.g. a cashier. A post in Class I called for responsibility, initiative and supervising ability; its occupant might be directly responsible to a manager at the next level in the hierarchy. The two special classes were to include junior members of management, e.g. superintendents at the smaller depots, and traffic assistants, staff (personnel) assistants and accountants at the smaller groups.

These classifications were subsequently agreed by the two trade unions representing clerical workers, the Transport Salaried Staffs' Association (formerly the Railway Clerks Association) and the Transport and General Workers' Union. The activities of these two unions were given enormous impetus by the requirements of the Transport Act that the industry should set up machinery for the negotiation of wages and salaries, and for consultation between management and workers on safety, health, welfare and efficiency.

[1] Author's italics.

This development naturally strengthened the bargaining position and status of clerical staff, and facilitated the creation of a system of graded posts, as this was in keeping with the desire of the unions for a clearly formulated promotion policy. The collective agreement on grading allowed for promotion to a higher grade, based on suitability, experience and professional qualifications where relevant.

SOME PROBLEMS OF THE NEW BUREAUCRACY

These were some of the highlights of the rapid and far-reaching changes in the road haulage industry between 1948–53. In the space of three years, complex bureaucratic systems of control were imposed on an industry whose economic structure seemed like some relic of an earlier age. Into this time was concentrated a process of development which in most other industries, 'normal' economic forces had achieved only over many decades. The physical patterns of the take-over were formidable enough: but such a process also required tremendous adjustments on the part of those who had known the industry in its former state. The days of fierce cut-throat competition, of buccaneering attitudes, of a disposition to evade the law, were over, and the industry was now under the control of a vast centralized authority, whose *raison d'être* was to substitute the rational order of the large-scale organization for the informal circumstances of the past. Many human problems were created, both for managers and men, by this upheaval.

The problem of the 'diehard' manager to some extent confronted all the nationalized industries, but in road haulage it was especially acute. The small-scale nature of the industry meant that many operators retained by the Executive as managers had been expropriated by none other than their new employer. Thus the Executive was often dealing with a manager who harboured a strong feeling of resentment towards nationalization, and who was little inclined to change his behaviour in response to central directives. And even the manager who welcomed it or who was largely indifferent to the change, found some difficulty in accepting the intervention of specialists in every conceivable subject, backed by the authority of specialists at all levels of the management hierarchy. Previously in matters such as accounts and personnel, he had exercised full control (if only through his freedom to ignore them), and now he was subjected to interference by 'outsiders'.

A major task of the executive, therefore, was to create a corporate spirit among its senior staff, and to secure their support for its policies. Many efforts were made in this direction. From the beginning, considerable authority was delegated to the Division, in order to bring the focus of co-ordination closer to the operating level; Divisional Managers had great independence and were in fact sometimes known as the 'Barons'. In the opinion of many local managers, this independence was inadequately distributed down the line, but attempts were made to enlist their support by regular conferences at the various levels of the management hierarchy. For example, Group Managers would meet regularly at District headquarters to discuss operating results and policy. This managerial consultation was widely used for specialist staff. Divisional specialists regularly attended national level meetings, where proposed policies were recommended and debated. On their return to the Division, divisional officers would hold similar conferences with their subordinates at District level. In this way, a serious attempt was made to secure a full understanding of the nature and purpose of policies before they were put into effect. This machinery was severely tested at such times as the reorganization of groups in 1951, in which the District took over many of the accounting functions previously carried out at group level.

The diehard manager proved to be not the only traditionalist in road haulage. Many of the workers, especially drivers, found the ordered world under public ownership irksome compared with the free-and-easy atmosphere of the past, for rationalization of services put an end to many of the pleasures as well as the hardships under private ownership. In return for the greater security and regular wages offered by British Road Services, the driver often had to forfeit traditional advantages: for example, his complete freedom when out on a job, including the search for a return load, and the extra cash from the boss for a job 'well done' (which often meant illegally done). Under the new system, 'the office' prepared his schedules, at the delivery point 'the office' gave him his return load: while breaking the law meant the risk of dismissal. Controlled timing and new systems of operation such as 'directional services' required men to work in a strange and often irksome manner; routes were broken down into sections, and a vehicle might have several drivers between collection and delivery point. The driver became like the worker on the assembly line, who sees only part of the job, and never the whole. Sometimes the controls broke down; an attempt to extend supervision over the driver on the road by introducing mobile road patrols aroused intense opposition and eventually a serious strike; the scheme was later abandoned. Many of the innovations introduced in this period are not yet accepted.

In seeking the co-operation of workers, the device of consultation was widely used. Committees for joint consultation on questions of welfare and efficiency were required to be set up at all levels. At the

top was a national committee representing headquarters management and union leaders; at the bottom were over 200 local joint
committees (at group level) where the group manager and his
assistants met representatives of the various grades of worker elected
by their fellows. For once a bureaucracy was attempting to secure the
understanding of those whose working lives were shaped by the new
systems of control; and further, to secure their active support by
identifying them with policy-making. But this was not what many
workers had hoped for, a form of workers' control; the lines of
managerial authority were not seriously challenged, for the committees' role was strictly advisory.

This attempt to develop a new relationship between managers and
managed was at once the strongest and yet the weakest element in the
position of the Executive. The foregoing has shown that it had frequently to take decisions which called for great changes in the lives
and attitudes of many of its employees—both for managers and men.
Consultation could soften the blow, and might even make the victim
welcome it, provided that it was properly used. Often this was the
case, especially where reorganization or closure of premises—matters
of immediate practical concern—were involved. But equally often
managers and men refused the opportunity. Diehard managers
resented consultation, regarding it as dictation by the worker.
Similarly, those workers who had looked forward to nationalization
as the end of capitalism, argued that the 'same old gang' were still in
power, and that consultation was just another trick.

Considering the speed of events, it now seems improbable that any
programme of training could have overcome these difficulties. But
it may be questioned whether the Executive was sufficiently conscious
of the human problems of adjustment created. There was undoubtedly
a failure to explain to local managers just what was expected of them
on the consultative committee, and there was, not unnaturally,
marked variation in the conduct and in the effectiveness of local
committees. More serious was the failure to use managers as means
of communicating to workers some idea of the purposes of nationalization. In consequence the task was left to the full-time union official
who could do no more than explain it as he had always done—in the
language of the political platform. Faced with the difference between
this ideal, and the reality of a bureaucratically-administered large-
scale organization, workers were sometimes bewildered and trouble-
some.

It is now clear that the rate of change was so great that many
problems went unnoticed. The physical problems of acquisition,
and of building up new services, dominated management's policy
and on occasion the human element was left to adjust itself as best

it could. This neglect of the human element was, to some extent, the result of a mistaken attitude; the workers wanted nationalization, it was argued, and they would co-operate. But the changes which management made in industrial organization and working methods had social consequences which were not foreseen, and many workers soon forgot their ideology in the face of threats to familiar patterns of life.

CONCLUSION

The change in industrial organization which has been described was of a peculiarly intense and rapid nature. Not only were operating conditions transformed by the advent of a large-scale organization, but for the first time the administrative sector took on a recognizable form. Looking closely at the expansion and developing structure of this group of employees is at times rather like viewing a speeded-up motion picture; the characters jerk on their way at tremendous pace, wheeling and swaying, always seeming to court disaster, yet somehow remaining upright. Indeed, the whole process has an experimental air about it, which makes it of special interest to the sociologist. What light does it throw on the nature of modern industrial bureaucracy?

At this stage, three comments would appear to be relevant to the question. First, at the end of the period 1948–53, the new bureaucracy had become sufficiently sure of itself to be thinking about reorganization and modified systems of control. For the most part, its immediate need for senior staff was satisfied, and it was developing a cadet scheme for training future managers. All this had been achieved in a period of full employment, and of intense competition for staff with other employers, in which the existing salaries paid by nationalized industries were said to be a disadvantage. This in itself is an interesting comment; it shows how quickly an industry, undeveloped managerially, could be brought in line with modern practice.

Second, in explaining the rapid expansion in the size of the bureaucracy, the major factor (apart from the scale of the enterprise), was clearly the introduction of a hierarchical system of management, with groups of specialists at most levels. The size of this group, with its attendant clerical staff, was frequently held up as proof that the industry was highly centralized, but this is questionable. At least part of the increase in administrative and clerical staff was the result of the Executives' attempt to *delegate* authority. One example of this was the original decision to locate a full accounts department, under a Group accountant, at each of the 200 Groups. In fact, it can be argued that decentralization in the large organization often requires an expansion of local bureaucracies, if local management is to be sufficiently served with information (about operations, accounts, personnel, etc.) on which to base the decisions made possible by extended authority. That size alone does not determine the intensity of bureaucratic control is suggested by the considerable variations in the proportions of clerical and administrative staffs in other nationalized industries—coal 5 per cent, railways 16 per cent, electricity generation 12 per cent. The question of how far the control exercised by a bureaucracy depends on its size relative to the numbers in the organization deserves closer study.

Finally, what can be learned from the human reactions observed during these developments? Supporters of nationalization might conclude that managers and men showed a marked capacity to withstand a rapid rate of change; opponents, that the ends of reorganization were only achieved at the cost of the initiative and enthusiasm of the local manager. In the absence of any common standard of judgement, there can be no final answer to these points; it can only be said that evidence can be brought forward to support either of them. It appears, however, that the human problems might have been far more severe if less attention had been paid to consultation both within the management, and between management and workers. Would a slower rate of change ultimately have benefited the organization? On the whole, this is to be doubted. It would have been possible to wait longer to recruit and train senior managers and so raise standards; against this the chances of persuading workers to accept change in small but frequent doses would almost certainly have been far less. The clean break with the past symbolized by the new organization and its methods, with the emotional element for those who had sought nationalization for many years, was under these circumstances far better probably than a policy of gradualism. In any case, it must not be forgotten that the Executive's policy had its origins in a political programme and that it was expected to show results in a relatively short period.

To sum up, the growth of British Road Services between 1948–53 shows that it is possible to implement in a remarkably short space of time a vast programme of industrial change in which all the elements of modern industrial organization are speedily assembled. But it is equally clear that such an assembly is a social process, creating a network of unfamiliar relationships, and new possibilities of tension and antagonism. Weber, in his classic analysis, regarded bureaucracy as 'capable of attaining the highest degree of efficiency and . . . in this sense the most rational known means of carrying out imperative control over human beings'. Examples such as the one studied here remind us that bureaucracies, despite their advantages as administrative organs, are by no means immune from everyday problems

of human relationships and conflict. The fact that we are comparatively ignorant of the precise nature of these problems also reminds us
of one of the central weaknesses of the sociologist's position: that
despite a certain skill in tracing and assessing the significance of
social developments, the complex of human motives and reactions
which lies at the heart of them remains largely an unknown quantity.

A NOTE ON SOURCES

Most of the material for this paper was obtained through interviews with road
haulage employees. There is very little documentary evidence about conditions in
the industry before nationalization, except for official reports such as the Baillie
Committee 1937 (Cmd 5440). Details of the organization of British Road Services,
staff figures, operating results, etc. can be found in the annual reports of the
British Transport Commission. An account of middle management in nationalized road haulage is given in 'Management under Nationalization', a report
prepared for the Acton Society by Professor T. E. Chester and the author of this
paper.

28. A JOINT PLANNING BOARD FOR FUEL
AND POWER*

269. Under present conditions there is in fact some degree of joint
planning between the fuel industries on specific projects. For instance, the National Coal Board and British Electricity Authority
have recently agreed on a scheme for building and operating pit-head
power stations, linked to the grid. The Gas Act, 1948, obliges the
National Coal Board and Area Gas Boards to co-ordinate their
carbonization activities; a national joint body of the two industries
has been established for this purpose. But we believe there is scope
for more co-operation.

270. We have considered various proposals for arrangements to
promote this co-operation: at one extreme is the proposal that a
planning body should be created with powers of control over the
fuel and power industries; and at the other extreme it is suggested
that the present system of collaboration in specific projects as they
arise is sufficient. We set out below what seem to us to be the main
purposes of arrangements for co-ordination in the production and
distribution of fuel and power:

(1) To facilitate joint planning in the supply of fuel and power,
including the development of new techniques.
(2) To collaborate with the Minister of Fuel and Power's Scientific
Advisory Council and other scientific bodies concerned in

* From *Report of the Committee on National Policy for the Use of Fuel and
Power Resources*, 1952, Cmd 8647, paras. 269–72, 274 and 277–8.

promoting research and development involving more than one
of the fuel industries.

(3) To secure routine technical collaboration at all levels.

(4) In the last resort, to ensure collaboration where the interests of
one industry might not coincide with wider interests.

271. It is, perhaps, this last objective that has been most in the
minds of those who advocate a planning authority with executive
powers over the fuel industries; there may be projects requiring combined operation between two or more fuel and power industries which
will harm the interests of one industry whilst benefiting the community as a whole; or there may be large economies possible by
avoiding some duplication of service by two fuel and power industries, each of which is convinced that it can do the service better than
the other and that it will be accepted as better by the consumer. The
problem is how to secure effective co-operation for dealing with
such matters. We have four reasons for thinking that a planning
authority with executive powers is not the answer:

(1) To be effective, such a body would need to wield very great
power over the individual fuel industries. But we regard it as
important for their efficiency that their managerial responsibility should not be reduced.

(2) The Minister of Fuel and Power has a general authority in the
national interest over the policies of the nationalized fuel
industries. As we see it, he could direct a nationalized industry
to act in the national interest, even to its own apparent detriment. In giving such direction, however, the Minister would be
responsible to Parliament. But if large executive powers were
vested in an intermediate authority over the fuel industries,
this Parliamentary control would be weakened, and power
would be diffused between the Minister and the executive
planning authority. This we should regard as an unsatisfactory
state of affairs.

(3) Some degree of overlapping in the services that the different
fuel industries offer is not necessarily uneconomic or undesirable; indeed, it is implied in our recommendation that
competition (in a certain framework) should continue between
the fuel industries.

(4) It would not be practicable to bring the oil companies under the
control of a planning authority with large executive powers,
though oil must have a place in fuel and power co-ordination.

272. Though we reject the idea of a planning body with large powers
over the fuel industries, we are not satisfied that present arrangements
for co-operation on production and distribution problems between
the fuel and power industries are adequate; we see the need for some

new type of joint organization of the industries for this purpose. We recommend that the Minister should establish a Joint Planning Board for fuel and power industries, composed of representatives of the nationalized fuel Boards, including the North of Scotland Hydro-Electric Board. This Planning Board should include also representatives of the Ministry and possibly the Chairman of the Minister's Scientific Advisory Council. There should be an independent Chairman appointed by the Minister. This Board would not itself possess powers to override the authority of the constituent industries. . .

274. The work of the Planning Board would be mainly:

(1) To decide, in the light of the expert knowledge of the different fuel industries as expressed through their representatives on the Board, what projects should be investigated as possible joint enterprises.

(2) To refer the problems selected to the Board's staff for detailed study.

(3) To receive and consider reports from the staff.

(4) To make recommendations to the fuel industries concerned, and perhaps to advise on the establishment of organizations to operate joint projects.

(5) To introduce new projects to the fuel industries. . .

277. The presence of representatives of the Minister of Fuel and Power on the Planning Board would have the advantages of:

(1) Bringing to the attention of the Board projects where the Minister saw advantage from joint action not yet initiated.

(2) Assuring sufficient contact with the oil companies in schemes where their co-operation would be beneficial.

(3) Providing contact where necessary with the Ministry of Transport and the Transport Commission.

278. We think this Board could fulfil the purposes given in paragraph 270—to encourage joint planning, accelerate (in collaboration with the Scientific Advisory Council) the application of the results of research, and secure necessary routine collaboration at all technical levels. In the last resort, the Board would, however, depend on the Minister to ensure collaboration when one industry was unwilling to join in a scheme because its particular interests appeared to be prejudiced.

CHAPTER V

Personnel

As in the last chapter, we here confine ourselves to a consideration of some of the problems specific to *nationalized* industries and make no attempt to deal with those problems of personnel which are common to public and private sectors.

One of the most important and controversial questions in this field is the recruitment and terms of service of the members of the Board. On the correct determination of this question may ultimately depend the success or failure of a nationalized industry. What qualifications should Board members possess? Should they be recruited, predominantly, from within the industry, or from outside it? For what period should they serve, and what causes should justify their removal? Should their remuneration be comparable with that obtainable by persons of similar qualifications and experience employed in the private sector? Apart from the last, these questions also arise in private industry; but in nationalized concerns they have to be resolved as matters of public policy, in so far as appointment and conditions of service are determined partly by statute and partly by the exercise of ministerial discretion.

All the questions catalogued above became the subject of acute party controversy when, on March 15, 1961, the Government announced the appointment of Dr Richard Beeching, a Director of Imperial Chemical Industries Ltd, as Chairman of the British Transport Commission at a salary of £24,000. In *Extract 29* we reproduce passages from speeches by Mr G. R. Strauss, who led for the Opposition, Mr Ernest Marples, the Minister of Transport, and Dr Charles Hill, the Chancellor of the Duchy of Lancaster, in the debate that followed on March 21st.

While these political speeches strongly underline the points at issue, they do not illuminate the subject as clearly as does the pamphlet entitled *The Boards of the Nationalized Industries* by the late Lord Simon of Wythenshawe, who had experience both as a private industrialist and as Chairman of the Board of Governors of the BBC. We accordingly reproduce, as *Extract 30*, a substantial part of this essay, in which the author attempts to apply to the National Coal Board the lessons which he considers can be learnt from private industries of comparable size and complexity.

Lord Simon's views will commend themselves, *in toto*, only to those who believe that commercial, as distinct from social, purposes should predominate in the administration of a nationalized industry, and that the best commercial practices are to be found in the more efficient private sector enterprises. Those who, on the other hand, feel that a nationalized industry should aim at a distinctive 'way of life', different from that prevailing in the private sector, will bring different or at least additional criteria to bear on the problem of the personnel of top management. This is especially so with those who wish to involve the workers, through their elected representatives, in managerial functions, or who consider that representatives of the consumers should play a part in policy-making. An attempt to combine the advantages of an expert, ministerially-appointed Board with those of workers' and consumers' representation was made by the late G. D. H. Cole who, in a pamphlet on the coal industry, proposed that the work of the Board should be subject to review by a Supervisory Council (*Extract 31*). Further material on the subject of workers' and consumers' representation will be found in Chapters 9 and 10.

For the education and training of personnel the nationalized industries have special responsibilities imposed on them by statute. The aim has been to create, within each industry, a career so fully open to talents that any operative with the requisite ability may eventually reach the highest technical or managerial positions. The degree of success in erecting this ladder has varied from industry to industry. Approaches to the problem adopted in the comparatively early days of post-war nationalization by the National Coal Board and the British Transport Commission are described in *Extract 32*.

Training and promotion cannot by themselves produce an adequate number of technical and managerial specialists, and all nationalized industries have looked to the universities and other institutions of higher education as sources of recruits. They have not, however, always succeeded in attracting what might be considered their fair share of the nation's highly-educated manpower. Even the electricity industry, which of all nationalized concerns appears to offer the best prospects, has had its difficulties in this respect, for reasons explained by the 'Herbert' Committee in *Extract 33*.

29. THE BEECHING AFFAIR*

Mr G. R. Strauss (Vauxhall): We should like to know . . . whether the right hon. Gentleman made any serious attempt to find a man

* From *H.C. Deb.* (1960–61), 516, c. 225–31, 233–6, 240–3, 331–2.

with the necessary qualities who was already in the railway service; a man working in a responsible position either on the national or, may be, on the regional level. Plainly, such a man would have had enormous advantages, not the least, perhaps, being the fact that his promotion from within the organization would have stimulated morale among railwaymen instead of depressing it as the Minister has now done. . . .

I should . . . like to quote what was said in the House on January 30th, when we were discussing the Government's White Paper on the reorganization of the Transport Commission. It was then said:

'. . . the ordinary man working on the railway will be glad that at last he will be run by people who care about the railways and who are much more closely in touch with him and his problems than is, unfortunately, now the case.[1]

That was said by the Parliamentary Secretary to the Ministry of Transport. Does the Minister really think that this desirable end will be reached by substituting Dr Beeching for Sir Brian Robertson?

I have made such inquiries as I can among the senior executives of the railway staff to find out their reactions. As far as I am able to judge, they are appalled by what the Minister has done; appalled by a combination of the facts that the head of the new railway set-up will be ignorant of railway affairs, and that his chairmanship will merely be, in the words of the Minister, an interruption of his career with the ICI. They feel—and, I think, rightly—that this is not only the wrong way of appointing a man to this important and difficult post, but that it is an insult to the present management and senior staff.

This feeling has been exacerbated by the Minister's further statement that, at the start, it might be necessary to bring in a few—not one, be it noted, but a few—people at the top. If that means anything, it is that the right hon. Gentleman has overthrown his previously declared intention of encouraging promotion of able management from within, and that he has little confidence in the present senior executives of the railway system.

. . . if he tells us that he looked among the existing railway staff for the right man and failed, did he then look among the large and able staffs of the other nationalized industries? It is difficult to believe that, with such a wide field to choose from, he could not have found the right man. As it is, one cannot escape the feeling that the right hon. Gentleman plumped for a private industry man mainly because of his political prejudice that private industry is in every way superior to public industry. . .

[1] *Official Report*, January 30, 1961, Vol 633, c. 728.

The aspect of this appointment that has so shocked the public is that Dr Beeching's remuneration will be based on an inflated, fancy, prestige salary scale paid to the directors of just a handful of companies in this country; a scale that is wildly out of alignment with the remuneration paid in most other industries, and, even more, with that paid to all who serve their country in high and responsible public positions.

The only acceptable principle on which a Government can properly conduct the nation's affairs is to fix a fair rate for each type of job within their service. Having fixed that fair rate, the Government must stick to it, and not start making a series of spectacular exceptions. If, at any time, the rates are considered too low in relation to comparable work outside, the Government must raise those rates—as, in fact, they have done recently.

But there must be uniformity of reward. Without it there is bound to be administrative chaos and deep dissatisfaction throughout the ranks of the public service. This is a principle of good government which is so obvious that it scarcely needs to be stated. But it is being flagrantly flouted by the terms of Dr Beeching's appointment. . .

Dr Beeching's Himalayan scale of remuneration . . . is bound to have repercussions among the chairmen and other members of the boards of the nationalized industries. Many of them will claim that their experience and ability are as high as those of Dr Beeching and that, in addition, they have an immense and intimate knowledge of the industries which they run. They will claim that it is invidious for them to accept a salary only 40 per cent of Dr Beeching's.

Let me give one example. Sir Christopher Hinton, Chairman of the Central Electricity Generating Board, has an academic and administrative distinction at least as eminent as that of Dr Beeching. To pay one a salary two and a half times greater than the other offends every canon of good administration. . .

A fair analogy is that of a distinguished barrister who is elevated to the bench. He may have been earning £20,000 or £30,000 a year at the Bar, but when he accepts a judgeship he does not ask for or accept a salary equal to his previous earnings. He is prepared to give his services to the nation at the still substantial but much lower figure of £8,000 a year. . .

It is for similar reasons that a Member of Parliament, who may be earning much higher rewards in industry or commerce, is prepared to accept the burdens of ministerial responsibility at a smaller salary. He does so because he believes—a belief which sometimes later proves to be erroneous—that he can thereby use his talents to make a material contribution to the national welfare. It was in the same spirit of service that President Kennedy was able to recruit so many outstanding men to work with him in his Government, all at a personal sacrifice but a sacrifice which they were willing to make in the interests of their country.

Did the Government have any of these broad considerations in mind when they made Dr Beeching's appointment and agreed to his terms, or did they do it blindly without any regard to the repercussions involved? I hope that the Minister will tell us what will happen next. Is there to be a general upward revision of salary scales in the nationalized industries?

I agreed with the comment in *The Times* on this, when it stated:

> 'This is a desirable process, though salary levels need not be pushed quite so far as in some parts of private industry. But it is a long-term process that needs to start at the ground roots. The Government have blithely decided to start in the stratosphere.'

The Minister of Transport (Mr Ernest Marples): The right hon. Gentleman asked me what were Dr Beeching's qualifications for the job. He said that he had read only a little in the newspapers about this and that I had not given his experience at great length when I made my statement to the House. The task is a huge one and it is an immense responsibility for any one man to undertake, but the Government are convinced that the qualities which Dr Beeching is known to possess are those which the situation demands.

This appointment is crucial. Great thought has been given to it. Dr Beeching's career, both in industry and elsewhere, has shown that he has a brilliant mind. He has considerable experience over a wide field of industry and great skill in negotiation. What is probably more important still, he has great qualities of patience, calmness in emergency, resolution and the ability to see the other man's point of view.

Not only did he have a brilliant academic career as a physicist, when he took first-class honours. He has had very varied experience in Government service and in industry. He has been at the Fuel Research Station at Greenwich and at the Ministry of Supply in the design department of armaments at Fort Halstead. He joined ICI in 1948. Five years later, he went to Canada as a vice-president of ICI (Canada) Limited, to start the Terylene organization there and to build a plant at Milhaven, on the shore of Lake Ontario. After two years in Canada, he returned home to be the Chairman of the Metals Division of ICI, which, at the time, was not doing so well. There, incidentally, he managed 18,000 people, which is a fairly high figure for a private industry.

I do not think that anybody in private industry has had to deal with the vast numbers of people that the railways have. Next to the railways in the number of employees is, I believe, the Post Office. At any rate, that was a large number of people for a private industry and Dr Beeching made a great success of it. Then, he was made an executive director of ICI. All those—I repeat, all—who have been associated with him are unanimous in recognizing his abilities.

We in this House must all realize that acceptance of the post of Chairman was not an easy decision for Dr Beeching. He has put himself in a cruelly exposed job, but he has accepted it and he is entering on five years of unremitting work in the national interest. It would be wrong if we in this House were to make his difficult task even more difficult by our statements or our actions. . .

On the question whether the Government should have appointed a railwayman, we must first ask ourselves what will be the most urgent need for the railways when they are standing on their own feet. Clearly, it must be the best possible top management. In Dr Beeching, we have secured a man who has proved himself in top management of one of our most important and most successful industrial concerns. It is for this reason that we believe that he will have a special contribution to make.

The White Paper stated, in paragraph 9, that

'there has been a tendency for technical and operating factors to prevail over others. This has been particularly apparent in financial and commercial matters'.

If, however, the railways are to be put on a sound footing it is essential that there shall be a successful blending of all those factors—technical, operating, financial and commercial. None should be sacrificed to the others. . .

. . . it would, I suggest, be a great mistake to think that only a railwayman could restore health to the railways. Certainly, health and vigour cannot be restored without the help of all the railwaymen, and the White Paper makes it plain that under the new organization there will be greater, not fewer, opportunities for railwaymen to advance to board level. On the other hand, the introduction of new blood from time to time will be of benefit to any large organization, be it nationalized or not. . .

It has been questioned whether it is right to pay Dr Beeching £24,000 a year gross, but let us first ask ourselves what it is that we are aking him to do. We are asking him to leave a job in which he must have high hopes of even further promotion. He is leaving it to come to a job which is even more difficult than his present one in many ways. First, it is an even bigger job, because the railways employ over half a million men and it is probably the largest business in the country. Secondly, Dr Beeching is assuming the responsibility of chairmanship. In his present job he does not have that responsibility. Thirdly, he will not only have to run the railways, but will have to help in a huge reorganization as well. Finally, the industry into which he is coming is still subject to constant political controversy. He will be liable to criticism which is at times merciless and is not always reasonable. . .

It would be a very bold man who would claim that Dr Beeching should accept these heavier responsibilities for a term of five years—which I must emphasize is the normal term for these appointments—and yet, at the same time, accept a cut in salary. Imperial Chemical Industries has undertaken to safeguard Dr Beeching's pension rights during the five years. I think that it has been extremely generous in allowing us to have one of its most brilliant men and in preserving his pension rights. On behalf of the Government, I should like again to thank Imperial Chemical Industries.

We really must get this problem in perspective. The railways are now losing money at the rate of over £300,000 a day. If, as I believe, Dr Beeching's efforts can reduce this loss he will have deserved well of the country. If a man who is paid £24,000 gross can alter that situation I think that it is a very good piece of business for the country.

Discussion has already taken place on the possible repercussions in other nationalized industries of paying £24,000 a year to Dr Beeching. The right hon. Member for Vauxhall raised that point last Wednesday and again today. The position of the railways is exceptional and the salary proposed for Dr Beeching is exceptional. I forecast that a few exceptional appointments might have to be made, first in the White Paper itself and then in my speech on January 30th about the White Paper, when I said:

'The railways must have the best leadership available. There must be opportunities in all parts of the railways for those with ability to get to the top. At the start it may be necessary to bring in a few new people. The task is challenging, and I believe that the time is crucial. The task is not only running one of the biggest industries in the country, if not the biggest; it is the task of transforming its structure, its outlook and its finances. The Government have had to have regard to these special needs in their search for the best available talent and in considering the terms on which it can be obtained.'[1]

I gave the House both in the White Paper and in that speech some idea of the Government's intention at that time. Whether any such other appointments will be required I cannot yet say. It is clear from the remarks which I have quoted that the possibility exists, but it is too early to say, despite what has appeared in various organs of the Press. . .

[1] *Official Report*, January 30, 1961, Vol. 633, c. 618.

The railways are now in an exceptional position. They have exceptional losses, they have a large labour force, and they are in the process of being modified. Therefore, this is an exceptional salary for an exceptional appointment. Consequential changes for the general level of salaries in nationalized industries are not involved. As for the wages of the staff of British Railways, these will continue to be negotiated through the appropriate machinery.

I want to stress two general points. First, our one aim, regardless of all other considerations, is to get the right man, and we believe that we have got him in Dr Beeching. Time will show whether we are right, but we believe that this is a most crucial appointment. Secondly, Dr Beeching personally will be incurring far greater responsibilities and doing far more difficult, and sometimes unappreciated, work for no extra financial reward. The reason why he has accepted the post is the national interest and because the job is a challenge. He has accepted the challenge. The present Chairman, Sir Brian Robertson, and the Transport Commission have promised him wholehearted support, and the restrained and dignified statements from the unions encourage me to believe that they will judge him on his merits. I am sure that they will. We ask no more than that, and I most earnestly ask the House to give him similar support by rejecting this Motion of censure.

The Chancellor of the Duchy of Lancaster (Dr Charles Hill): Can a man who is not a railwayman by training do this job? . . .

Bearing in mind the task which needs to be done, the emphasis which needs to be laid on commercial and financial matters, and the problem of deciding the size of new investment, it would be wrong to assume that only a railwayman could do the job. In any case, it has never been the practice, as the right hon. Member for Vauxhall knows, to limit the field for chairmanship of nationalized industries to inside experts.

I could give many examples. Sir Miles Thomas went to BOAC from the motor industry. Sir Brian Robertson, although he had experience of transport, went from the military and diplomatic fields to the British Transport Commission. As has been mentioned today, Mr Alfred Robens, for all his other considerable experience, could hardly claim an expertise in mining. The Leader of the Opposition, when Minister of Fuel and Power, appointed six chairmen of area gas boards, not one of whom came from within the gas industry. One came from the Indian Civil Service, another from an engineering company, another from the board of the Co-operative Wholesale Society, another was a town clerk, another came from British South African Airways, and another was chairman or managing director or both of Coal Wharves Limited. I make no complaint of that, but let us not sustain the pretence that it is not reasonable and proper to bring to the chairmanship of a nationalized industry a person from outside.

30. HOW TO CONSTITUTE A BOARD*

PRIVATE ENTERPRISE

It is often assumed that since the public owns the nationalized industries, they will be managed solely in the public interest, whereas private companies will be managed for the profit of the shareholders. This was largely true of most private enterprise a hundred years ago; the typical cotton king of those days was a rich and powerful individual who believed that his whole duty to himself and to the community was to make a good profit. In accordance with the economic theories of the time he did not feel he had any responsibility for the welfare of the workers beyond the necessary wages to secure efficiency: such action would only pauperize them. He was single-minded in the pursuit of profit; if he succeeded, his conscience was satisfied. There were, of course, exceptions, but this was the general rule. Even fifty years ago, the industrialist normally built his factory without any regard to amenity, external appearance or surroundings, either for the benefit of his staff or for the public. Trafford Park in Manchester is a shocking example: the factories are ugly; they are crowded together, there is hardly a blade of grass or a tree to be seen. In this matter, practice has been revolutionized in the last generation; very few industrialists would dream of building under Trafford Park conditions today. Firms vie with one another in getting good architects and laying out their factories on good town planning lines, to provide pleasant and healthy conditions for the staff, and to make the factory an ornament to the neighbourhood. The climate of opinion on this matter has changed steadily and rapidly, especially during the last generation. The boards of most good private enterprise concerns today, especially perhaps some of the largest, have a very deep sense of accountability not only to their shareholders but also to their employees, to their customers, and to the community. In general, the board members, at least of the largest private enterprise concerns, are not owners but professional managers, and there seems little reason to think that their attitude either to efficiency or to public service is different from that of the board members of a nationalized concern.

* From Lord Simon of Wythenshawe: *The Boards of Nationalized Industries*, Longmans, Green, 1957, pp. 13–33. Reprinted by permission of Lady Simon and the publishers.

But, of course, the test of success in private industry is profit; in fact, the necessity to make profit provides competitive private industry with an automatic and invaluable measure of success. This is the very foundation of the capitalist system, as proved by its tremendous success in raising standards of living in Western Europe, and even more in the USA where competition for profit is much keener than in Europe.

No doubt there are firms which are out for the largest profit with little regard to other considerations except to keeping within the law. This is hardly true of the larger well-established firms, but admittedly many companies may take advantage of monopoly conditions or of their own efficiency to make profits which might be regarded as excessive.

Nationalized industry has no such automatic tests of efficiency. Where there is little or no competition, as in the case of coal, it is exceedingly difficult to determine the efficiency of different parts of the National Coal Board's vast organization, or to find weak spots with the speed and certainty with which such weaknesses are discovered in competitive private industry.

It is of interest to note that in those fields in which the National Coal Board works in competition with private industry and others, namely, in its ancillaries: Coke-ovens, Brickworks, Farms, Houses, Briquetting Plants, Manufactured Fuel Plants and Secondary By-Product Plants; the profit has risen from £1½ million in 1947 to £4 million in 1956.[1]

The Boards of Private Enterprise Companies

I have inquired from eight of the largest and most successful private enterprise concerns for certain particulars as to their boards and they have been good enough to give me the facts contained in Table I.

The core of every board consists of a number of whole-time directors, often called executive directors even when the board may be wholly or mainly a policy board. The number of whole-time directors ranges from five in the case of Dunlop (Dunlop is a holding company; they have 100 whole-time executive directors on their subsidiaries) to twenty-four in the case of Unilever. An interesting point is that the three largest companies each have about twenty whole-time directors, between two and three times as many as the Transport Commission or the Coal Board, though the latter are very much larger concerns. Why?

All the companies take great care in the selection of entrants, both from schools and from universities; all have training schemes,

[1] Annual Report and accounts for 1947 and 1956 respectively, Schedule IX.

TABLE I

THE BOARDS OF EIGHT PRIVATE ENTERPRISE COMPANIES

Company	Full-time Executive Directors					Total Number of Part-time Directors	Size of Company as shown by 1954/5 Assets[1]
	Total No.	Average Service with Company before appointment as Director	Average Service with Company since appointment as Director	Retiring Age	No. of Graduates		
		years	years	years			
Imperial Chemical Industries Ltd	19	25	5.5	62[2]	18	5	437.9
Unilever Ltd	24	20.5	9	65	16	0	246.1
Imperial Tobacco Company Ltd	21	21	11	60/65	9	11[3]	170.5
Courtaulds Ltd	13	11	14	65[4]	7	3	127.8
Dunlop Rubber Company Ltd	5	22	8	—[5]	3	5	88.6
Associated Electrical Industries Ltd	6	27	5.6	65[6]	5	10	62.8
General Electric Company Ltd	11	26.6	14.8	65	2	3	59.6
Associated Portland Cement Manufacturers Ltd	7	13.5	6.0	65	NA[7]	7	40.8

[1] Total net assets. The figures are from *A Classified List of Large Companies engaged in British Industry* (NIESR) 1955.
[2] Retiring age of chairman and deputy-chairman is indeterminate.
[3] Eight of these are directors who have now retired from active service.
[4] Not regularly enforced.
[5] No rule.
[6] No retiring age laid down for the chairman.
[7] Not available.

including special training of selected candidates for top management. The table shows that there are a considerable number of graduates on the boards, which means that graduates must have been appointed on a large scale thirty years ago. Is this one reason why these companies are so successful?

Whole-time board members are almost invariably appointed from within the company. It will be seen from the table that they have usually had more than twenty years' service with the company before appointment.

All boards regard the selection of new directors as one of their most vitally important tasks. The lead is usually taken by the chairman and deputy-chairman, and great stress is always laid on acceptability of new directors to the whole board.

It will be seen from the table that the retiring age in the different companies varies between 60 and 65. Once a director is appointed, it is the almost invariable rule that he continues in that position until he reaches the retiring age.

Salaries, pensions, and other conditions of employment are not known, but they are always such that it shall be the ambition of every member of the staff to join the board, and that the directors shall be satisfied with their conditions of work. It is, so far as we are aware, unknown for an executive to refuse appointment to the board of his company. Contrast the Coal Board, where high executives have in recent years refused promotion because the attractions of a position on the central board have been insufficient.

The following would appear to be the chief common characteristics of the boards of good large private enterprise concerns:

(1) There are always substantial numbers of whole-time directors who form the core of the board. It would, I think, be generally agreed that the whole-time directors in these firms normally have:

(*a*) The usual qualities that make a good administrator and director of policy: integrity, ability, tact, drive, loyalty to their colleagues and to their concern, power to select and train good staff and keep them keen and happy, and so on.

(*b*) Long experience in the industry so as to have acquired instinctive powers of judgment as to its problems.

(*c*) Confidence in the security of their jobs and satisfaction with the financial and other conditions of their service.

(*d*) The feeling that they are doing a worthwhile job.

(2) *Part-time directors.* It is almost universal practice both in private enterprise and in the nationalized industries to appoint a number of men of distinction and wide experience in different fields of industry, finance and public affairs as part-time directors. The number of such directors in the eight firms in Table I varies from none in one case up to eleven, and probably averages six or seven. They generally give enough time to

have a good understanding of the affairs of the company and can often give advice, ask questions and bring in fresh ideas from the outside world.

(3) The chairman almost always devotes the whole or nearly the whole of his time to his work. He is usually selected from among the whole-time directors by the vote of the whole board, though in a few cases a distinguished outsider with wide experience of men and affairs has been appointed. In some instances there may be one or more deputy-chairmen, and there is often (perhaps always in the case of larger boards) an inner group of the chairman and one or two others who are freed from routine duties and are responsible for the general supervision of the affairs of the whole company.

(4) *The board as a whole*

    (*a*) The members of the board are normally on personally friendly terms and co-operate wholeheartedly as a team in the interests of the concern as a whole.

    (*b*) Changes in the board are slow. Continuity is of the first importance to build up good traditions, wise policy and high efficiency.

    (*c*) The board as a whole have complete freedom and responsibility and are self-perpetuating so long as they are successful in their conduct of the business and retain the confidence of the shareholders. . .

THE COAL BOARD

The First Coal Board—January 1947–51

(Chairman: Lord Hyndley)

The original Coal Board consisted of a Chairman, a Deputy-Chairman and seven other whole-time members. Apart from the Chairman and the Deputy-Chairman, all members had functional responsibilities. The Board members were appointed for five years and even during that short period there were several changes; one or two of the new members were appointed on a part-time basis. Among these was Sir Robert Burrows, who headed a committee of investigation into the organization of the industry. One of their recommendations (which was partly accepted) was that full-time members should cease to be in charge of functional departments.

The Second Board—1951–55
(Chairman: Sir Hubert Houldsworth)

The Coal Industry Act of 1949 increased the maximum size of the Board to twelve members instead of nine, provided that not more than eight should be full-time. The second Board consisted of the Chairman, two Deputy-Chairmen, four full-time members, who, in accordance with the recommendations of the Burrows Report had no functional responsibilities, and five part-time members: a total of twelve. The whole-time members of the second Board were again appointed for five years; again there were several changes in membership during that period.

The Fleck Report

Within two years of the appointment of the second Board many people felt that things were not going well, and the Board, under pressure from the Minister, appointed in 1953 the Fleck Committee (of which Sir Alexander Fleck, Chairman of ICI, was Chairman) to report once again on the organization of the industry. The Committee was a strong one.

The main recommendations of the Fleck Committee as regards the constitution of the Board are as follows:

(*a*) In principle, it is right that the Board should consist essentially of a limited number of whole-time members, and that this Board should be given complete authority over the industry as is the case in private enterprise.

(*b*) There should always be 'at least one member of the Board who, when a particular question arises, has a sphere within which that question obviously and naturally lies'. They recommend for this purpose six whole-time functional members in addition to the Chairman and Deputy-Chairman, who should be free to cover the whole field. But the full-time Board member should not be regarded as the head of the department for which he is responsible; there should be under him an executive head at headquarters responsible for day-to-day management.

(*c*) There should be four part-time members of wide industrial experience who, apart from advising the Board, would advise the Minister on the selection of whole-time Board members.

(*d*) The Board, therefore, would consist of:
   a Chairman and Deputy-Chairman;
   6 whole-time Board members;
   4 part-time Board members.
   Total: 12.

(e) Every effort should be made to recruit the whole-time Board members from within the industry. All appointments should be 'career appointments' which an efficient Board member can expect to hold until the normal age of retirement.

(f) Salaries of Board members should be raised so as to make it possible to pay executive heads of big departments at head-quarters a salary of about £7,500.

(g) The Minister should give special attention to the necessity of ensuring that the members of the Board are able to work together as a team. (The report points out that this has by no means been the case in the past.)

After receiving the Fleck Report the Minister took drastic action. All the full-time Board members offered their resignations to the Minister. He accepted those of the two Deputy-Chairmen and one other whole-time member; another whole-time member had resigned just previously and two of the part-time members resigned. This amounted to something approaching a clean sweep of the Board. The reasons for such drastic action were not publicly explained. Clearly, it must have had an unfortunate effect in shaking the confidence of members of nationalized boards in the security of their positions.

The Third Coal Board
(Chairman: Sir James Bowman)

The third Board was appointed in February 1955 in accordance with the recommendations of the Fleck Report, consisting of eight full-time members: the Chairman and Deputy-Chairman with general responsibilities, and six other members each of whom was given responsibility for one or more departments. There are also four part-time members, so that the total Board still numbers twelve. Shortly afterwards the Chairman died and was replaced by Sir James Bowman.

In recent months two of the whole-time members have been transferred to high executive posts in the divisions and have been replaced by two new Board members.

It is obvious from the above summary of the history of the first three Coal Boards, covering a period of under eleven years, that the changes in membership of the Board have been very frequent.

There have been twenty-four full-time members of the three Boards, though the number at any one time has never exceeded nine. The average length of service of those who have left has been 3.6 years; none of the present members has served for as long as three years.

Such insecurity of tenure is clearly unfortunate and must have made continuity of policy exceedingly difficult.

The Future

'The most important single factor is to obtain stability on the Boards so as to ensure continuity of direction and policy.'

Three months after the National Coal Board was formed, I said in the House of Lords:

> The Coal Board has already appointed 1,000 managements for different pits, forty-eight Area Boards, eight Divisional Boards. . . . I believe this is the most gigantic task of organization that has ever been laid upon the shoulder of a Board in the history of industry in this or any other country. I am sure Noble Lords on all sides of the House will congratulate the nine courageous men who have taken on this grave responsibility, and will extend to them their thanks and good wishes.

Unfortunately, the results have not yet been what was hoped. I have already indicated the main difficulties; above all, the Board has changed far too frequently, both in personnel and in functions, nor have appointments always been wise; this is perhaps partly due to the fact that the Ministers have also changed frequently, as shown by the following list:

The Rt. Hon. Emmanuel Shinwell:	July	1946–47
The Rt. Hon. Hugh Gaitskell:	Oct.	1947–50
The Rt. Hon. Philip Noel-Baker:		1950–51
The Rt. Hon. Geoffrey Lloyd:	Oct.	1951–55
The Rt. Hon. Aubrey Jones:	Dec.	1955–57
The Rt. Hon. Lord Mills:	Jan.	1957–

Ministers have served on the average just over two years; it has been said that new Ministers usually come in ignorant and dangerous, but improve rapidly with experience; unfortunately, they have not been given much time to improve.

There is reason to hope that the third Board may be much more stable than the earlier ones. It is also encouraging that the members of the present Board have, on the average, a good deal more experience of the industry than the average of the first two Boards, and that they appear to be developing into a friendly and co-operative team. The Board is likely to prove to be a stronger one than the industry has known in the past, and the relations between the Chairman and other members of the Board and the Minister are, it is believed, excellent.

But certain actions by Parliament, by the Minister and by the Board are urgently required to ensure both a high degree of effi-

ciency and proper conformity to national policies. Let us consider
what needs to be done.

Efficiency

Improved efficiency, so far as the Minister and the Board are concerned, depends mainly, I believe, on the way in which the following
matters are dealt with.

Status of the Coal Board. There is one general point which may be regarded as important. The coal industry unfortunately has low prestige;
it has for many years been the plaything of party politics; the parties
are only now learning to discuss its affairs objectively. The prestige of
the industry must depend primarily on the success of the Coal Board
and the public respect and recognition which always result from success. But there are certain things the Government can do. The first and
most important is to ensure the right appointments and continuity in
the Board. One wise and important step which the present Government has taken has been to show its respect for the power industries
by putting the Minister into the Cabinet; another has been to increase
the very inadequate salaries of Board members. And, having regard
to the heavy responsibilities of the public work of the senior staff of
the coal industry and to their remuneration, which is still relatively
low, the Government might well, instead of almost ignoring the coal
industry as in the past, distribute a reasonable number of honours
among those members of the staff who have rendered specially
conspicuous service.

Selection of Graduates. ICI last year took in more than 500 university
graduates; the National Coal Board took in over 200. Graduates are
in a position today to choose their jobs, and they tend to go to industries or firms which have prestige. Owing to the low prestige of the
coal industry, the Board finds it hard to get enough good graduate
entrants. Contrast the Ruhr coalfield; it has only half as many employees as the Coal Board, yet the annual entry of graduates is double
that of the Coal Board. The prestige of mining in the Ruhr is very
high, and it is often the first choice of graduates, which is far from
being the case here. The National Coal Board is doing its best in this
matter, but it will not be fully successful until the prestige of the
industry has been built up.

Training. Deliberate training for management has been adopted by a
few progressive firms for a considerable time; it is only in the last
few years that it has been seriously studied on a wide scale. The Coal

Board has begun to tackle this matter with energy; among other things it has founded a staff college, for the training of senior administrators, which has made an excellent start. But it is understood that the Board fully realizes that there is still a long way to go, and that it cannot hope to have a steady and adequate stream of first-class candidates for Board vacancies for another ten or twenty years.

Appointment of Members of Coal Board. Clearly, the Minister must have the final responsibility for appointing and, if necessary, discharging Board members. Coal is a monopoly of overwhelming importance. There are no shareholders; there is no other authority except the Minister who can intervene to make sure that the industry is being conducted in the national interest, and in accord with the policy of the Government.

The Minister's responsibility in appointing (and controlling) the Board is dual:

In the first place, he must try to appoint a Board which will make the industry as efficient (in the broadest sense) as the best private enterprise.

Apart from efficiency, there are certain matters of national policy which must be determined by Parliament and by the Government, and the Minister must endeavour to appoint a Board which will willingly accept ministerial directions on policy and loyally do its very best to implement them.

If the Minister is to make wise appointments, it is essential that he should, with the help of his advisers, know rather intimately the personalities and the problems of the Board. It is understood that the practice has grown up in the Ministry of Power that the Minister and his senior officials keep in close touch with the Chairman and leading members of the Coal Board, not only by formal meetings when necessary, but also by a good deal of informal contact.

In appointing a whole-time Board member, the Minister should ask the existing Board for advice, no doubt through the Chairman. If he finds that the whole Board—Chairman, executive and part-time—are unanimously in favour of a certain nomination, then, so long as he has confidence in the Board, he would naturally accept that nomination. I would add that till the Minister does get such confidence in the Board, the relations between the Minister and the Board cannot be satisfactory. In any case it is vital that no Minister should ever appoint a new Board member without satisfying himself as to the views of all the existing members of the Board, whether whole-time or part-time.

The Fleck Report recommends that in making new appointments

G

of full-time Board members, the Minister should consult the part-time members (para. 63). It also recommends that the part-time members 'should have the right of access to the Minister if they have any matters of importance affecting the industry to which they wish to draw his attention'. This recommendation has been much criticized; it is suggested that part-time members should be loyal members of the Board; that if they have these responsibilities they would in a sense be spies and would undermine the authority of the Chairman and the full-time Board members.

One serious difficulty has arisen in the past and may perhaps arise again: if a member proves unfit for his position, his colleagues on the Board, even though they realize this, are unlikely, out of personal friendship, to inform the Minister. On the other hand, it is important that the services of an unfit member should be dispensed with; in such a case, only a strong Chairman, or the part-time members who are not an intimate part of the family, are likely to inform the Minister. The best chance of the Minister getting the facts in such a case is through personal and close contacts with the Chairman, and when doubts arise probably through consulting the part-time members and possibly some of the whole-time members privately. It is not possible to lay down a definite procedure which would be best in all circumstances. A good Minister would, by formal and informal talks personally and through his senior officials, get to know a great deal about the principal personalities and problems of the Coal Board; the best method of dealing with the varied problems that will arise can only be left in the hands of the Minister, subject to one overriding consideration—that he should never make an appointment until he is satisfied that it is acceptable to the Board as a whole.

There is one other matter of great importance as regards whole-time Board appointments; it will be generally agreed that all, or very nearly all, Board appointments should be of men who have been trained and gained their experience within the industry. This is almost universal custom in good private enterprise firms.

The Chairman is, in this matter, in a special position. It has sometimes been felt, both in the nationalized industries and in leading private enterprise firms, that a distinguished outsider with wide experience of the management of men and affairs may make a better Chairman than anybody available from within the industry. It is not possible to lay down any general rule in this matter; but one important consideration is that it will certainly not improve the morale of the coal industry if the ablest men in it have no confidence that the top posts will be available to men from within the industry.

Career Appointments. All good private enterprise concerns in this or any other industrial country make an almost invariable rule that when a man has been appointed a director, he continues his service till the retiring age. In most companies the directors retire in rotation, often at three-yearly intervals, and have to be re-elected at the annual meeting by the shareholders; in Unilever all the directors have to be re-elected every year; in some cases managing directors have long-term agreements. But, whatever the arrangements may be, in actual practice, unless things go badly wrong, any man appointed to the board of a good company knows that, subject to accidents, he will stay there till retiring age; he feels almost completely secure.

As regards the nationalized industries, an extraordinary custom has arisen of appointing whole-time Board members for a period of five years. In some of the industries renewal is frequent; in others, and especially coal, it has been very rare. This seems a wholly deplorable custom and nobody seems to know how it grew up. The two essentials are that any competent person appointed as a Board member should feel secure up to retiring age, and, on the other hand, that the Minister should, if things go wrong, have the right to terminate the appointment at any time. But, as the Chairman of one of our leading private enterprise concerns recently remarked: 'If a board member fails, it is the fault of the chairman or of the board for appointing him, and the least they can do is to give him ample compensation.' This applies with equal force to appointments made by Ministers. It may be hoped that such cases of dismissal will be exceedingly rare in the future.

There can be no doubt that security of tenure is by far the most important step to secure continuity and efficiency in the Coal Board.

Salaries and Pensions. What is the right salary level for the Chairman and members of the Coal Board? Some people hold that they ought to be comparable with similar salaries in private enterprise. Others suggest that in view of the honour of serving the public in so distinguished a capacity as Chairman of the National Coal Board, able and public-spirited citizens should be prepared to accept a lower salary than they would from private industry. For instance, it is pointed out that the Chairmen of Regional Hospital Boards, the Chairman of the London County Council Education Committee, and many others often do something like whole-time jobs and receive no salary and no expenses. Further, it is the case that some of the part-time members of, for instance, the National Coal Board or the British Transport Commission, often industrialists earning top salaries, give up to two days a week to their part-time membership for a derisory salary of £500 a year. This is an encouraging aspect of British democracy.

But experience has now amply proved that in the industrial world, where salaries are recognized as a measure of the importance of a job, this self-sacrificing habit of mind does not apply. It is notorious that great difficulties have been caused in nationalized industries owing to the inadequacy of salaries in securing and retaining the services of first-rate men in top jobs, whether as Board members or as leading executives.

In July last the Prime Minister announced increases in the salary scales of the Boards of nationalized industries. The effect in the case of the Chairman of the Coal Board is as follows. In 1947 the first Chairman received £8,500 which, after deduction of tax, amounted to £3,500 net. The new salary of £10,000 for the Chairman will, after deduction of tax, amount to £4,400 net: owing to rising prices the purchasing power is equivalent to an income of £2,600 in 1947. The purchasing power of the salary of the present Chairman after the new increase is accordingly 25 per cent less than the salary of the Chairman in 1947.

The salaries of the Board members have been increased from £5,000 to £7,500.

The Government's action in this matter is a substantial step in the right direction though it is feared that even now the salaries are by no means fully adequate to secure the best possible persons both as Board members and as top executives.

It is understood that pensions and other conditions of service in the Coal Board, both for Board members and for others, are reasonably satisfactory.

31. QUIS CUSTODIET?*

What I suggest is that the *administration* of each socialized industry should be put in the hands of a non-representative full-time body, constituted on the same lines as have been followed in setting up the NCB, but that there should be in addition a second body, a Supervisory Council or Commission, consisting of the members of the Board *plus* a number of representative members chosen by the Trade Unions and professional bodies connected with the industry and by other interested parties, such as the principal groups of consumers and closely related industries. This Supervisory Council would have nothing to do with the day-to-day administration, which

* From G. D. H. Cole: *The National Coal Board: its Tasks, its Organization, and its Prospects*, Fabian Society, Research Series No. 129, Revised edition, January 1949, pp. 38–9. Reprinted by permission of the publishers.

would be left in the hands of the full-time Board; but it would be much more than a mere Advisory Council. It would be empowered to review the activities of the administrative Board, and to make recommendations on matters of policy to the appropriate Minister, who, if he approved, would direct the Board to take action upon them. It would have the right to call for an account of the Board's doings in any specific connection, and for relevant papers and statistics, and would be consulted by the Minister in respect of nominations to fill vacancies on the Board. Its members would not receive salaries, but only expenses, and would retain their connections with the bodies appointing them. Finally, the appropriate Minister would appoint the Chairman of the Council, but would himself preside over its meetings on special occasions, and would bring before it any matters to which he wished consideration to be given.

The purpose of this arrangement is both to introduce a representative element into the control of nationalized industries, without involving the representatives in the responsibilities of administration, and to give the Minister an agency through which he can bring well-informed criticism to bear on the Board's proceedings, without fettering his final discretion in matters of policy. In the event of a difference of opinion between the Board and the Council it would be for the Minister, acting on the Government's behalf, to pronounce judgment, and to instruct the Board about the policy to be followed.

I believe that some arrangement along these lines would have great advantages. It would make it much easier for the Minister to prevent the Board from following a policy inconsistent with the maintenance of good relations; and it would associate the NUM and other bodies representing the various sections of the industry with the control without making them responsible for policy. It would also make easier and less open to objection a subsequent transformation of the administrative Board into a body representing, not the Trade Unions and Professional Associations, which would be represented on the Council, but the actual working personnel of the industry, in such a way as to make the reconstituted Board the apex of a structure of self-government built up from the bottom, within the productive system and not imposed on it from outside.

SOME OBJECTIONS ANSWERED

I know that objection will be riased to this proposal on a number of grounds. It will be urged that a Council of the kind proposed, being without direct responsibility for the running of the industry, will be a fifth wheel to the coach, and will advance all manner of impracticable suggestions and comments. It will be said that its existence will take away power from the Minister, by interposing a buffer between him and the Board responsible for the administration. It will be contended that the Council will be impotent unless it is given a full-time staff of its own, and that such a staff will involve duplicating the staff of the Ministry of Fuel and Power, or of the Board itself. It will be said that the Board, having been appointed to do the job of running the industry, ought to be allowed to get on with it with the least possible interference from anyone else.

These criticisms seem to me to rest on a wrong attitude. I do not agree that the proposed Council will be too inexpert and irresponsible to be trusted to offer valuable advice and comment on the Board's proceedings. I do not believe that any Board of experts, technical or administrative, should be left to get on with its job without being subject to regular scrutiny. I agree that the Council would need to have a small full-time staff of its own, and power, when it thought fit, to employ its own consultants; but I can see no objection to this, except that which comes from rival claimants to the influence the Council is meant to exercise. If the equipping of the Council with a small staff meant that fewer Civil Servants would be needed at the Ministry of Fuel and Power to oversee the Board's doings, I should think the change all to the good; for I want to keep down as far as possible the amount of Civil Service control and supervision and regard such a Council as I have proposed as a preferable agency for many aspects of supervision in the public interest. Finally, I deny that the Council would in any way lessen the powers of the Minister. What it would do would be to make the Minister rely more on the Council's advice, in matters falling within its scope, and less on that of his regular Civil Servants. I can quite understand Civil Servants not liking the plan. I remain unmoved because, in common I think with most of the human race, I do not like Civil Servants—at all events, when they seek to apply to industry methods which may be right for the administration of ordinary Government Departments, but are quite at variance with what is needed in the conduct of business affairs.

32. FIRST STEPS IN COAL AND TRANSPORT *

THE NATIONAL COAL BOARD

On the nationalization of the coal industry, the Coal Board found

* From R. W. Bell: 'The Relation of Promotion and Training to Higher Management in British Nationalized Industries', *Public Administration*, Vol. XXIX, Autumn 1951, pp. 207–12. Reprinted by permission of the author and the editor of *Public Administration*.

themselves heir to a very large number of private companies greatly differing in size, and many of them having an exceptional range of ancillary activities. Although valuable work had been done by the Mining Association of Great Britain on the technical side of the industry, there was no central staff plan nor conception within the industry of membership of a single service. Moreover, recruitment to the coal-mining industry at all levels was patchy, and for anyone contemplating a career in it the course of promotion was problematical.

To meet the first need for a flow of promising recruits to the medium levels of the industry, the Coal Board have produced a scheme to which they have given the name of 'The Ladder Plan'. The essence of this scheme is that, for all new entrants to the industry undergoing preliminary training, there should be available a definite ladder of promotion to higher ranks; and further that, as the individual progresses upwards, the available ladders should increase in number as they diminish in width, so that the best use of varying talents can be made. Present juvenile recruitment to the coal industry runs at the rate of about fifteen thousand a year, and the ladder plan provides that about 20 per cent of each year's entrants get on to the main ladder right away.

Progress up the training ladders will lead to the acquisition of various certificates—the General Certificate leading either, on the one hand, to qualification as a certified tradesman or as the holder of a Statutory Certificate eligible for employment as a deputy; or, on the other, through the acquisition successively of the Ordinary National Certificate and the Higher National Certificate, to eligibility for employment as under-manager, mechanical or electrical technician, or surveyor. In speaking of the scheme at the beginning of 1950, Sir Geoffrey Vickers, VC, the Manpower and Welfare Member of the National Coal Board, said: 'These certificates will not by themselves constitute a qualification for any job in the pit. They will supply only the formal part of the qualifications. Those who are to be tradesmen will have to complete a five years' apprenticeship, taking a General or Ordinary National Certificate before being qualified in any skilled job in their trade at the pit. Men selected for training as deputies must have practical experience and must undergo practical and oral test, whether they have a certificate or not, though those who have a certificate will be entitled to practise as deputies, and subsequently as overmen, earlier than they otherwise would. ... The importance of the scheme lies in ensuring that men who have it in them to fill responsible posts may not be held back later through having failed to pursue their general and technical education sufficiently in their first years after leaving school.'

The value of a scheme of this scale and variety in giving effect to the aspirations which, as mentioned at the outset of this article, were encouraged by nationalization, needs no emphasis. The Board record[1] that in preparing it they drew on much work done in the past by the Mining Association of Great Britain and other bodies, and that the plan brings together the projects and ideas of many people over many years. The scheme is, indeed, the foundation-stone upon which the National Coal Board seek to fulfil their basic promotion policy for their technical staff on the production side. 'It is the Board's policy to fill most of the senior posts on their staff from among people already employed in the industry. In future many of those who achieve promotion to the higher ranks will have entered the collieries as mineworkers, and by means of the courses of study and experience provided under the Ladder Plan will have joined the ranks of management. Others will be men and women who have been recruited into clerical, administrative or specialist posts straight from school or from the University. Whatever their educational origins, all will have opportunities for learning their job thoroughly and, as time goes on, of broadening their experience. In this way the best will be able to fit themselves for promotion.'[2]

When we come to the level of colliery manager, the Board have instituted important training arrangements. Sir Geoffrey Vickers, VC, has said, 'All colliery managers have to take a statutory qualification for which a university degree or the Institution of Mining Engineers' professional examination may in future be accepted partly or wholly in substitution. In addition, they will receive three years' directed practical training in accordance with a syllabus prepared by the Institution. The men who enter on this training may be men from within the coal industry who have taken or are about to take the appropriate examination by part-time study. For these the Higher National Certificate is expected to be of substantial assistance. Equally they may be men from within the industry who have graduated in mining through a whole-time degree course. Finally, they may be mining graduates who have not previously worked in the Industry. To stimulate the flow of mining graduates both from within and outside the industry, the Board in 1948 and again in 1949 awarded 100 scholarships, tenable at any University, and it has decided to award a similar number of scholarships for 1950.'

The scholarship and directed practical training schemes to which reference is made above are a novel experiment within an industry. The training will last for the individual up to three or four years, depending on previous experience, and is supervised by senior

[1] National Coal Board Report, 1949, paragraph 289.
[2] National Coal Board Report, 1949, paragraph 391.

members of the National Coal Board's staff in the coal fields. Among other things it provides for sending prospective colliery managers to residential courses of a fortnight's duration, at which they study their future responsibilities. At the earliest of these residential courses, which were held in the Mining Departments of six Universities, the syllabus was arranged under three main heads:

(1) The status, duties and responsibilities of a colliery manager;
(2) The place of the colliery manager in the organization of the National Coal Board;
(3) The relation of the colliery manager to the labour force.

The study took the form of group discussions, organized on the basis of 'briefs' in which problems were set out, and persons of wide practical experience in the subject attended the courses in order to guide the discussions and give lectures based on their own knowledge.

Under the first heading mentioned above the prospective colliery manager studied all the duties and responsibilities that would fall to him within the colliery under his own control, and emphasis was laid on the standing which he must keep in the eyes and minds of all working in that colliery. Under the second heading he was invited to look outwards and to survey and understand the wider organization of the National Coal Board and the responsibilities which he would bear both to the higher levels of the Board at Area, Division and Headquarters, and laterally to other parts of the organization with which he must be linked for various purposes. It was under this head, too, that the students particularly studied their relationship to technical specialists and others whose assistance and advice would be available to them in their task. Under the third heading was conducted what amounted to a specialized study of the handling of trade union relationships and the process of joint consultation.

This directed practical training has been too recently instituted to assess results, but there is no doubt that, apart from any other benefits, it will be specially valuable in enabling the colliery managers of the future to rub shoulders with each other, instead of attempting to develop quite separately as individuals. It will have, too, a secondary advantage to the Board in fostering a sense of membership of a united service. The training is available every year to 200 men selected by the Divisional Boards.

The Coal Board have already held four very successful summer schools, at each of which some 400 or more attended from all grades in the service of the Board, including mineworkers. At these schools a most useful mixing of the different levels of employee takes place, and the summer schools play as important a part in ensuring vertical contact as do the other arrangements in providing it laterally.

It is only right to record, however, that the National Coal Board regard the schemes only as the first and important steps to meet training needs on the productive side of the industry. They are by no means comprehensive, as they do not provide for the whole range of the Board's employees.

THE BRITISH TRANSPORT COMMISSION

As has already been mentioned, the British Transport Commission have delegated the duties of training and education laid upon them by the Transport Act, 1947, to the Executives set up under the Commission, namely, the Railway Executive, the London Transport Executive, the Docks and Inland Waterways Executive, the Hotels Executive, the Road Haulage Executive and the Road Passenger Executive. The Commission retains, however, co-ordinative power and, indeed, is bound to submit to the Minister of Transport a programme to which the Executives are to work. In their first annual report the Commission were able to declare that they had made a survey of the existing training and educational facilities of the Executives and, as a result, had formulated proposals to widen and improve them. These proposals were designed to secure the following objectives as circumstances might permit:

(*a*) To equip staff as quickly, as thoroughly and as economically as possible to perform their tasks with the maximum of efficiency and safety and personal satisfaction in their calling;

(*b*) To interest staff in their work, and give them a sense of pride in the job to be done, without which technical proficiency loses much of its value;

(*c*) To interest staff in the work and aims of the organization as a whole, and by fostering their 'sense of belonging' enlist their interest in the success of the undertaking;

(*d*) To maintain efficiency, alertness and interest in the work by providing refresher courses in up-to-date ideas, methods and developments;

(*e*) To provide opportunity to acquire the necessary knowledge and skill for promotion;

(*f*) To provide trained staff from whom higher posts can be filled.

The proposals were thus intended by the Commission to provide for vocational training, background training, voluntary training and further education.[1]

The Commission have also established a Standing Training and Education Committee, comprising members and officers of the Commission and the Executives, to advise on major problems concerning

[1] British Transport Commission Report, 1948, paragraph 57.

training and education. The purpose of this Committee is, of course, to ensure co-ordination of policy between the Executives.

In the following year the Commission were able further to report that the programme for staff training and education, drawn up on the above lines, had been approved by the Minister of Transport, who had given authority to the Commission to proceed. Since then the Executives have been preparing their schemes under the programme in close co-operation with each other and with the Ministry of Education in England and Wales and the Scottish Education Department in Scotland. They have also kept close touch with local education authorities through directors of education.

These schemes are, of course, in the early stages, and it would be premature to attempt a detailed description. It may, however, be well to give some account of the position of the Railway Executive who, by reason of antecedent events, in that the railways had already been grouped some years before nationalization into four large companies, inherited a more coherent situation than the non-railway Executives (other than the London Transport Executive).

Within the activities covered by the Railway Executive special problems had to be faced at the outset. The Executive took over four large companies created under the Railway Act of 1921, namely, the Great Western; London, Midland and Scottish; London and North-Eastern; and Southern Railways. There was no very marked divergence between the general staff policies pursued in each of these large units, but there were strong traditions in each of them which went back before 1921 to the days of the original railway companies. The railway system of Great Britain has always been haunted by the ghost of George Hudson, MP, the nineteenth-century 'Railway King' whose lavish promotion of railway lines, especially in the Midlands, set so many problems for posterity. The nature and amount of railway equipment and property make the physical side of the railways a fact which legislation cannot suddenly change. The railways must be administered as they are, however strong the desire to unify the system may be. All schemes, therefore, for the organization and day-to-day running of British railways are conditioned and limited by the physical layout and operational peculiarities of the lines.

Before the Transport Act, 1947, there was little movement of staff between one railway group and another. Today, up to the salary level of £750 a year, it remains the normal practice to advertise posts only within each railway region. These regions are the London Midland, Southern, Western, Eastern, North-Eastern and Scottish Regions. Above the salary level of £750 a year vacancies are advertised in all regions. The actual power to make the appointment rests, below the £750 a year salary level, with the Chief Regional Officer of the region concerned; above that level and up to the £1,000 a year level the same officer can make the appointment with the approval of the Railway Executive. Numerous transfers between regions result in this upper level from these circumstances, though there are signs, perhaps not unnaturally, that Chief Regional Officers, when other things are equal, prefer to appoint to a vacancy a man from their own region of origin, trained in the tradition with which they are familiar.

Above the £1,000 a year salary level all appointments are made by Railway Executive Headquarters, a board being suitably composed, according to the nature of the appointment, of chief officers from headquarters and the region concerned. In case of disagreement the decision is by a majority of the board.

The Railway Executive were fortunate in finding that, in general, the policies of the groups which they took over had not given rise to any notable mal-distribution of age groups, and difficulties arising from blocks of individuals with inadequate outlets for promotion are not found to be unduly hard to solve.

One of the hopes of some advocates of nationalization has always been the reduction of staff and saving of manpower which could be brought about by unifying services and amalgamating duties so that overlapping would be avoided. The possibilities of savings of this kind on the operational side of the railways have been slight. The working of trains being a through operation, little can be done by mere amalgamation of posts to make savings of staff, and some types of apparent duplication of officials cannot be avoided. For example, Birmingham is served by the lines of the old Great Western Railway, London and North-Western Railway and Midland Railway, and there were, and still are, three railway superintendents overseeing the operation of these distinct sections. What appears here to be a mere duplication of effort is, in fact, the coincidence at the same place of three operational units engaged on different tasks. The physical methods of working these old lines differed—for example, Great Western locomotives have always been right-hand driven, London and North-Western and Midland locomotives were some right-hand and some left-hand driven, and the later London, Midland and Scottish locomotives are all left-hand driven; signals and other apparatus vary accordingly, and even the systems of logging trains on the three lines are quite distinct. For such circumstances the only present solution is to continue to operate the three units as before, and this is further justified by the fact that, in any event, the volume of work involved would require the three superintendents and their staffs, however the duties were rearranged. It is, of course, the aim of the Railway Executive to unify the railway system of the country in time, but it needs no emphasis that any project of that kind can only be carried out slowly over a very long period.

On the commercial side of railways, on the other hand, it has been found possible to do a great deal of amalgamation of posts, and the Railway Executive has had to face the problem of staff rendered redundant by these reorganizations. Here again, the transfer of individuals from one region to another is obviously much easier, and the opportunities for unifying procedures far greater. Greater flexibility, too, can be incorporated in staff transfer and training arrangements.

Within the Railway Executive there is no 'Ladder Plan' comparable to that of the National Coal Board, but the long-established railway apprentice scheme provides opportunity for advancement to talented young men in the service. Before nationalization some of the main line railway companies had set up internal staff colleges, that established by the London, Midland and Scottish company at Derby being a prominent example. The future use of these colleges and the possibility of their expanding to serve wider needs is now under examination. The present concentration by the Executive is on the production of an adequate supply of teachers, and two residential training colleges at Darlington have been combined for training in teaching method. The resultant supply of teachers will be the foundation of the Executive's educational programme.

33. RECRUITMENT AND PROMOTION OF STAFF*

321. It is most desirable that everyone in the industry should feel that the highest posts are open to him. Although the industry does and will benefit from the knowledge and experience of men appointed from outside, and it is necessary to infuse new blood from time to time, it is obvious that the majority of senior and top management posts will need to be filled from within the industry. How the industry is ensuring that it will in fact throw up its future leaders, now that the generation of men with management experience acquired before nationalization is passing out of the industry, is a matter we consider to be of vital importance. We have therefore given close attention to the Authority and Boards' policy on recruitment and promotion which bears directly on this question. Although the highest technical and management posts in the industry are and should be open to all workers, the industry undoubtedly looks chiefly to the entrants under the graduate training scheme for the men who in later life will provide the nucleus from which the senior appointments can be made. We have therefore been seriously disturbed to

* From *Report of the Committee of Inquiry into the Electricity Supply Industry*, January 1956, Cmd 9672, paras. 321–8.

find that the numbers of men recruited under the graduate training scheme have fallen off at an alarming rate in recent years. The table at paragraph 163 shows that there were only 93 graduate trainees recruited in 1954–55, compared with the peak intake of 401 in 1949–50; and of these 93 entrants only eight were university graduates with engineering degrees, compared with 104 in 1949–50. We recognize that there is severe competition from many quarters for young men who are qualified and show promise. It may well be that the electricity supply industry, with its organization into Divisions, Sub-Areas and Districts, and with its inflexibility of grading and inadequate incentives, may be less attractive to the more vigorous and imaginative of the young men of today than, say, the aircraft, chemical and electrical manufacturing industries. If this is so, and we think that it is so, the electricity supply industry must undertake an urgent and fundamental review of the conditions which are causing qualified men with the calibre of potential leaders to turn away from electricity supply as a career to other more attractive and apparently more exciting industries.

322. We have endeavoured to see the industry through the eyes of a keen, intelligent young man, with a good engineering degree. Even if the starting salary is low, he might be attracted to the industry if the nature of the work on which he will be engaged retains his interest and if advancement to the more senior posts may be expected at a reasonable age. In this connection, the Authority's recent assumption of responsibility for the construction and operation of nuclear power stations provides them with a great opportunity to use the potential attraction of this new and exciting field in order to bring the best type of recruits into the industry. We have been told that the graduate entrant on completion of his training will specialize on generation or transmission with the Central Authority or on electricity distribution with an Area Board. If he is appointed to a post on the Area Board side it is unlikely that he will reach a four-figure salary much before his middle thirties and his prospects after then are uncertain. The lowest managerial unit on the Area Board side is the District Manager. We have seen little evidence of this post being considered as a training ground or stepping stone for the younger men to fit them for more senior positions later on. On the generation side of the industry the prospects are brighter but there is still a long haul in front of the young man before he reaches a senior post.

323. As we have already shown, before nationalization there were some 540 supply undertakings varying considerably in size and importance and in the majority of cases covering both generation and distribution. A young man would get his experience by working his way up a smaller organization acquiring managerial experience as he

went and moving, as a regular feature of his career, from one undertaking to another. The present top management of the industry under nationalization largely consists of men who acquired their experience before nationalization and in a variety of fields and undertakings. The problem now confronting the industry is how to ensure that its future leaders will be forthcoming from within the industry and with at least the same degree of skill in management as their predecessors. We consider this problem to be as important as any in this report and we propose to discuss what we think to be the matters at issue.

324. The first difficulty is the starting salary offered to graduate trainees. We have been informed that until recently a graduate entrant of age twenty-two was paid only £400. The salary has now been increased to £475 but this figure, in our opinion, is still inadequate to attract the high-quality graduates which the industry simply must have if it is to be a technically progressive industry. It is possible that the Authority and the Boards find themselves unable to make any significant advance in salaries at the lowest levels because of consequential repercussions on salaries to technical staff. We would hope that the recommendations we have made elsewhere in this report will provide the industry with more elbow room in the determination of salary scales and differentials. In any event the decline in the recruitment of graduate trainees is too serious a matter to be allowed to continue and the Boards must not fail to undertake any improvement in conditions or terms of service which have a material bearing on recruitment.

325. The second matter which disturbs us is the attitude of the Central Authority towards the advancement of graduate trainees, and their policy on the training of potential top managers. We have described in paragraphs 169–71 the promotion policy of the Authority and we have set out in Appendix K the established promotion procedure. Under present arrangements the graduate entrant after initial appointment following training can only achieve promotion by applying for vacancies that arise from time to time for which he considers himself suitable. He competes for these posts with possibly older men from inside the industry with greater experience, who may therefore be more suited for that particular post although they are not of the calibre for advancement to top posts in the industry. In those circumstances there is no certain prospect of the graduate being given the planned training and experience in various posts on the generation and distribution sides which we consider to be essential for eventual leadership of the industry.

326. Management courses and conferences are valuable and what the Authority and some Boards are doing in this field is highly commendable, but it is no substitute for a deliberate scheme under which

men are carefully selected, trained and advanced in particular posts so that they emerge in their middle life as potential leaders of the industry. The best possible training for potential top managers is the practical one of doing jobs for themselves at successive levels of difficulty and status. We do not believe in the conception of an industrial Officers Training Corps. We do consider however that the leaders of the industry should deliberately select (without the knowledge of the young men concerned) those whom they consider to be potential leaders, and should ensure by a system of knight's moves across the board, as it were, that they are given the opportunity to hold down particular posts and demonstrate whether they have the quality of leadership.

327. But the Authority have told us that they do not believe in the earmarking of individuals for particular jobs as 'this would be invidious in a great national undertaking and contrary to the best industrial practice'. We have approached major industrial organizations on this question and we believe that the Authority are misinformed if they consider that selective training and posting of staff is contrary to the best industrial practice. The Authority are clearly hoping that, through selection by competitive interview for particular posts on the one hand and extensive facilities for education and training on the other, a pool of trained and experienced staff will be continually available from which the managers of the future will be recruited. We think that the Authority's confidence that under the present arrangements future leaders will automatically be forthcoming is ill-founded. We are seriously disturbed about this whole matter, to which we attach the greatest importance. We would like to see the starting salary for graduates with good degrees improved; and we would favour a scheme under which unseen tabs would be put on the bright young men so that they could be posted to particular jobs even though their apparent qualifications for those jobs were less than those of other personnel. We would like to see more extensive cross-posting of such men between the generation and transmission and distribution sides of the industry and we would hope the new Central Authority would encourage this.

328. We fully understand the Authority's preoccupation with the need in a public industry to avoid charges of favouritism, but this particular nettle must be firmly grasped as the industry depends for its efficiency and progress on the quality of its leadership. Unless deliberate steps are taken on the lines we have indicated above for selective training and posting, we do not consider the industry will be able to provide a future top management of the requisite calibre from within its own ranks, and the Minister and the industry will be impelled continually to make appointments from outside.

CHAPTER VI

Finance

Under this heading, we concentrate on the two problems that have provoked most discussion, viz. price policy and investment. We begin (*Extract 34*) with Mr D. N. Chester's attempt to elucidate the price policies indicated in the Nationalization Acts themselves. This is followed by an article by Mr Francis Cassell, in which he presents, in a manner fully intelligible to the non-specialist, views about price policy which are widely accepted among economists (*Extract 35*). The same article deals with the inseparable problem of determining the correct level of self-financing.

The relationship between cost, price, demand and investment is also the theme of much of the Report of the 'Herbert' Committee, which was anxious to ensure, by relating unit prices more closely to unit costs, that a very capital-intensive industry should use its expensive equipment as efficiently as possible and thus limit its demand for capital funds to an economically-justifiable level. *Extract 36* explains why the statutory requirement that the electricity boards should 'promote the simplification and standardization of methods of charge' is incompatible with the correct allocation of costs as between different types of consumer. *Extract 37* provides a lucid explanation of the 'load factor' problem, describes how the Boards are attempting to solve it, and suggests that they could bring more information and vigour to the task.

That prices should reflect costs, and that any subsidization of particular classes of consumers, if considered desirable, should be deliberate and unconcealed are generally-agreed propositions. But how are costs to be calculated? We are here confronted with the unsettled argument, referred to by Mr Cassell (*Extract 35*), between 'marginal costs' and 'average costs'. This divided the 'Ridley' Committee, which presented in its Report an excellent summary of the arguments on both sides (*Extract 38*).

Both determination of prices and calculation of capital requirements are part of the process of planning. In respect of capital requirements, the machinery adopted by the electricity supply industry is described in *Extract 39* by Professor R. S. Edwards, now Chairman of the Electricity Council.

New capital may be provided (*a*) by the issue of fixed-interest stock, with or without Treasury guarantee, (*b*) from 'below the line' budgetary funds or (*c*) from the ploughed-back 'surpluses' of the industry concerned. 'Correct' policy in this field, as in the field of pricing, has been the subject of much controversy. In 1956 the Government decided that, for the time being, all external capital financing should be 'below the line'. This method of provision was considered by the 'Radcliffe' Committee on the Working of the Monetary System, which reported on it favourably (*Extract 40*). In this it differed from the 'Herbert' Committee which, reporting three years earlier, had expressed the view that nationalized industries should 'go to the market' and there attempt to raise their requirements in equal competition with other businesses.

On self-financing, which involves the question of whether the pricing of a nationalized industry should merely enable it to break even or permit it to accumulate a surplus, the 'Herbert' Committee was equally forthright in its views (*Extract 41*). These were widely criticized as involving the piling up of excessive debt and the sacrifice of the financial viability of the public sector to the supposed needs of the private sector. This opinion is given trenchant expression by Mr John Hughes, lecturer in economics and industrial relations at Ruskin College, in his Fabian Tract (*Extract 42*). In its White Paper, *The Financial and Economic Obligations of the Nationalized Industries*, the Government accepted the need for a measure of self-financing and attempted, *inter alia*, to define both the possibilities and the limitations of this practice (*Extract 43*).

The last of the controversial matters here dealt with is the adequacy of Ministerial and Treasury control over the demands of the nationalized industries for fresh supplies of capital. This has been very much the concern of the Select Committee on Nationalized Industries, which took up the question in its Report on the National Coal Board (*H.C.* 187–I of 1957–58) and returned to it with greater vigour in its Report on British Railways. Its sharply critical remarks on the quality of the 'vetting' by the Ministry of Transport and the Treasury of large proposed investments under the Railway Modernization Plan are reproduced in *Extract 44*.

34. PRICING: THE STATUTORY REQUIREMENTS*

So much has been written by economists about the theoretical considerations which should govern the price policy to be followed by the

* From D. N. Chester: 'Note on the Price Policy Indicated by the Nationalization Acts', *Oxford Economic Papers*, January 1950, pp. 69–74. Reprinted by permission of the author and the editor of the *Oxford Economic Papers*.

managements of the various nationalized industries that it will at least be a change to look at the actual legislation and see what is contemplated in practice.

Each of the Acts usually lays upon the Board which is to manage the particular industry the duty of supplying the commodity or service in a manner variously described as 'efficient', 'economical', 'adequate' (the Transport Act uses all these three), and 'co-ordinated' (or 'properly integrated' for Transport). The National Coal Board, for example, has among its duties 'making supplies of coal available, of such qualities and sizes, in such quantities and at such prices, as may seem to them best calculated to further the public interest in all respects, including the avoidance of any undue or unreasonable preference or advantage'. This is a very large umbrella capable of covering many different schools of thought, for all are concerned with furthering the public interest in all respects, though those who wish to take special advantage of different elasticities of demand may be a little chilled by the last eleven words. There is thus not much guidance here.

During the discussions on the various Bills it emerged that everybody was concerned with securing greater supplies at much lower prices—more and cheaper was clearly the slogan. But there was little or no discussion on what was meant by the various adjectives. In the Committee stage of the Gas Bill Mr Hugh Gaitskell (Minister of Fuel and Power) had an entertaining exchange with a member of the Opposition on the meaning of efficient and cheap when resisting an amendment to replace the reference to co-ordinated, efficient, and economical gas supplies by the simpler words 'To provide a cheap and abundant supply of gas'. One member pointed out that a Rolls Royce was efficient but not cheap, at which no doubt the Minister remembered his days as a teacher of economics. As for the phrase 'furthering the public interest' Mr Shinwell (on the Coal Bill) was good enough to say 'It means exactly what it says', but went on to explain for the benefit of lesser minds: 'Furthering the public interest depends on the circumstances. It may be appropriate, in certain circumstances, in order to further the public interest, not to export coal, but to utilize coal in such a fashion as will enable us to export other commodities. On the other hand, there may be such a super-abundance of coal in given circumstances as would enable us to supply, more than adequately, the needs of coal consumers overseas.'[1]

In the same discussion Mr Shinwell made the important statement that 'everybody here with the most elementary knowledge of economics knows that one is bound to relate price levels to the cost of

[1] Standing Committee C, February 12, 1946, col. 1004.

production'.[1] But he was tantalizing enough not to say what he meant by 'cost of production'. The Acts, however, appear to lean heavily in favour of the supporters of average costs. The Government's general policy is to be found in Section 36 (1) of the Electricity Act, 1947, the important words being: 'It shall be the duty of the [British Electricity Authority] so to exercise and perform their functions . . . as to secure that the combined revenues . . . are not less than sufficient to meet their combined outgoings properly chargeable to revenue account taking one year with another.' Other Acts vary the wording somewhat. For example, though it is now usual to use the phrase 'taking one year with another' the Coal Act uses the phrase 'on an average of good and bad years'. But the general purpose is always the same: the boards need not cover[2] their outgoings on revenue account every year but they must do so over some not very well-defined period.[3]

The first important point to notice is that the wording applies to the whole of each board's affairs, whether viewed geographically or functionally. In the first instance, with the same kind of economic interests, e.g. producing coal, the board may make a loss year after year in some areas providing it covers its total outgoings over a period. There is nothing in this section which would prevent the National Coal Board running the South Wales coalfield permanently at a loss providing other coalfields offset this loss in the national accounts.[4] A similar policy could be followed by the boards operating electricity and transport and by the proposed Iron and Steel Board. In the case of iron and steel it is proposed that though most of the existing companies should continue under their own name, as publicly owned companies, the individual concerns will be under no statutory obligation to cover their total costs so long as the Iron and Steel Corporation balances its accounts over all its companies, 'taking one year with another'. The only exception is found in the Gas Act, for here each of the twelve Area Gas Boards are treated as separate financial and management entities and the general rule applied to each of these boards. The Regional Coal Boards are, of course, purely administrative and not statutory bodies, and though the Area Electricity Boards are statutory they have little or no measure of financial independence and the rule in this case is applied to

[1] Col. 1028.

[2] The rule is that revenue shall not be *less* than (not merely equal to) outgoings, i.e. continuous profits are legal but not continuous losses.

[3] The Coal Act contains the limiting phrase 'consistently with the proper discharge of their duties under sub-section (1)', i.e. of making supplies of coal available, etc. and of securing the efficient development of the industry.

[4] It may be argued that such action would be incompatible with the board's statutory duty of 'securing the efficient development of the coal-mining industry'.

the total accounts of the British Electricity Authority.

In the second instance the general law implies that where a board supplies several kinds of product the rule about covering outgoings applies to the total of these products and not to each form of product.[1] Thus the National Coal Board besides the production and sale of coal also produces and sells bricks, coke, motor benzol, and certain other products. There is nothing in the Act to prevent the board selling all or any of such products below their average cost providing the loss can be made up on coal sales or on other activities. A more significant example is transport. Here, though each of the main forms of transport (including hotels) are managed by different executives appointed by the Minister (and not by the board), the rule about revenue being not less than outgoings applies to the total of all the executives' accounts and not to the accounts of each executive. Thus, providing the British Transport Commission could recoup its losses from the operations of one or both of the two Road Executives, there is nothing to prevent the Railway Executive following a price policy which led to its accounts showing a large loss. Again, whereas previously the London Passenger Transport Board had to cover its own costs the executive which replaced it has no such statutory obligation. It is the total financial effect, not the effect of any particular activity of the Transport Commission, which is governed by the rule.

I am here concerned only with the words of the various Acts. How the boards will act within the limits of their discretion is a different question. It should be noticed that the accounts which have to be published by the various boards must show the financial results of the different activities. The normal rule here is again to be found in the Coal Industry Nationalization Act. The Accounts of the National Coal Board 'shall conform with the best commercial standards and . . . shall distinguish the colliery activities and each of the main ancillary activities of the Board'. In the case of electricity the accounts of the central authority and of each area board must be shown separately and separate information must be given for generation, distribution, and for each of any other main activities, e.g. selling appliances. For iron and steel it is proposed that the publicly-owned companies should continue to be subject to the provisions of the Company Acts as regards accounts and that in addition the proposed corporation (or holding company) should publish a statement of accounts of each company.

The Minister of Transport (Mr Barnes) drew a distinction between

---

[1] The Gas Act, 1948, is a partial exception in that the manufacture of plant and gas or coke fittings (taken together) are treated separately from the other activities of the board.

the keeping of separate accounts and the separation of the individual activities for purposes of financial and price policy. He said: 'This Bill (i.e. the Transport Bill) is to integrate all forms of inland transport in this country, and if we were to proceed on the physical break-up of each section . . . we should defeat the aim in view. If (the) whole case rests upon the need for publication of the accounts so that public opinion can see . . . the contribution to the general pool which each section has to make, that is another matter . . . (which) will undoubtedly be met.'[1] A minute or two later he went on to say 'the whole purpose of this Bill is . . . to unify the services, so that the average cost of transport will be economic and will be efficient', but I do not hazard an opinion as to what is implied by this statement. The fact that the accounts of the various activities must be shown separately is bound to encourage boards to treat such activities separately for the purpose of the receipts-outgoings rule. There are other interesting aspects of the rule that revenue must not be less than outgoings taking the board's activities as a whole. For one thing, the range of activities covered by the rule in each case is partly a matter of chance, partly a matter of choice. Because some colliery companies owned brickworks and coke ovens the National Coal Board can merge the costs of these with the costs of producing coal. Had the Government decided to have a National Fuel and Power Board and had treated the coal, gas, and electricity in the same way as the Minister of Transport has treated railways, road transport, and canals (i.e. as executives subordinated to the one board), the rule would have enabled the board to offset losses on one kind of fuel by gains on another. I am not arguing that one or other system is right, but only pointing out that the application of the rule to the 'firm' and not to the 'product' has certain possibly accidental consequences. Incidentally, on the different treatment of fuel and transport some words of the Minister of Fuel and Power (Mr Hugh Gaitskell) have a special interest. On the Second Reading of the Gas Bill he said:

'It is not our view—let me make it perfectly plain—that we should dictate to consumers what fuel they should use. To do this and to ignore consumers' preferences would not in our view give the best results, and freedom for consumers to choose is something which, as a long-term proposition, I regard as an essential part of civilized society. . . . Nor should we overlook the value of retaining competition between electricity and gas. It has been a stimulant in the past and it can bring benefits to the community in the future, provided it is subject to certain safeguards; but this does not mean that there should be no co-ordination whatever in this field . . . while the consumers should be free their choice should

[1] Standing Committee B, February 19, 1947, col. 1441/2.

be influenced by reference to costs . . . charges for different fuels should reflect the true cost of production and distribution to the community. . . . The principle must be that charges can and should correspond to real costs.'[1]

A different question may arise where the board has a complete monopoly for one part of its activities but is in competition with either private firms or with another nationalized board for the other part. The fear that a board might subsidize its competitive activity at the expense of its monopoly activity was expressed several times by the Opposition during the discussion of the various Bills. Mostly it tended to get mixed up with a rather different but still substantial fear that a board might give preferential terms to a Government department or to the board of another nationalized industry at the expense of its private customers.[2] For that reason words are usually included by which a board is usually required to avoid undue or unreasonable preference (the wording varies from Act to Act). But undue preference has never been an easy phrase to interpret and in any case it has no application to one activity being subsidized by another.

The point about discrimination came up very prominently in the discussions on the Iron and Steel Bill and these are worth reading. During its passage through the Commons various amendments were made to meet the Opposition's fears on this point.[3] These rather vague words 'to satisfy the public interest' were changed to 'to satisfy the reasonable demands of the persons who use these products for manufacturing purposes and to further the public interest in all respects'. Also a new sub-clause was added preventing unfair or undue discrimination, 'but without prejudice to such variations in the terms and conditions on which those products are supplied as may arise from ordinary commercial consideration or from the public interest'.

Further amendments were made to this clause in the House of Lords, of which one was rejected by the Commons. The Lords cut out the last five words in the sub-clause just quoted. The Commons gave as their reason for disagreeing with the Lords on this point 'the words to be left out are necessary to furtherance of the export trade and to give a margin of discretion in meeting the demands of the home market'.

Two other points need touching upon briefly—the meaning of

[1] *H.C. Deb.*, February 10, 1948, Vol. 447, cols. 237–8.
[2] Cf. Mr Shinwell's reply to this. 'There is no reason at all why a National Coal Board should discriminate unfairly in favour of one customer against another', but then he went on to say that discrimination might be required in favour of the export trade. Standing Committee C, February 13, 1946, col. 1068.
[3] See *H.C. Deb.*, April 27, 1949, Vol. 464, cols. 187–234.

'outgoings' and of 'taking one year with another'. In some of the Acts the items chargeable to revenue are specifically prescribed. Thus Section 93 of the Transport Act, 1947, reads: 'The Commission shall charge to revenue in every year all charges which are proper to be made to revenue, including in particular proper allocations to general reserve, proper provision for depreciation or renewal of assets and proper provision for redemption of capital. . . .' Similar obligations are placed on the boards' management in the coal, gas, and electricity industries. Only the Iron and Steel Bill makes no reference to the redemption of capital. In other words, the boards mentioned are required to charge prices which will enable them not only to cover ordinary operating costs, depreciation, and interest on capital but also actually to pay off part of their capital each year.

There is little or no guide to the meaning of 'taking one year with another'. None of the Acts contains any interpretation of the phrase. The general impression gained from reading the discussions, however, is that some comparatively short period is intended and indeed the main stress is on the accounts being balanced annually. Mr Hugh Gaitskell, who, as might be expected, is usually clearer and more explicit on many of these points than some of his fellow Ministers, in dealing with the particular point, said:

> 'We say that over a period of years the accounts must balance. . . . There may be circumstances which may involve them for a time in loss. . . . Private companies make losses and recoup them later. There might even be occasions when the Government might feel, if there was a heavy slump and a lot of unemployment, that it might be desirable on the whole not to insist on costs being covered. I agree that may be a rather remote contingency, but it is the kind of thing referred to in the Coalition White Paper on Employment Policy, and we have, therefore, provided for it here. I would emphasize that I attach a great deal of importance to the principle that normally we should expect area boards to cover their costs each year.'[1]

35. THE PRICING POLICIES OF THE NATIONALIZED INDUSTRIES*

THE REQUIREMENTS OF THE ACTS

The pricing policies of the nationalized industries are of concern not only to consumers of the industries' products but to the entire com-

[1] Standing Committee D, April 29, 1948, col. 1145.

* From Francis Cassell: 'The Pricing Policies of the Nationalized Industries', *Lloyds Bank Review*, October 1956, pp. 2–18. Reprinted by permission of the author and the editors of the *Review*.

munity. As a determinant of the inflationary gap they are second only to the Budget itself; and they exert enormous influence on both the gilt-edged market and the general credit situation. Yet the principles on which these policies should be based and the standards by which they should be judged have received very little detailed consideration.

Many advocates of nationalization have indeed argued that the great advantage of public ownership would be the freeing of the industries from the tyranny of the profit and loss account; the profit motive would be replaced by dedication to the welfare of the community. Some of these Utopian sentiments pervade the Nationalization Bills, particularly the clauses which require the Corporations to promote the 'national interest'. The National Coal Board, for instance, is required to make supplies of coal available 'of such qualities and sizes, in such quantities and at such prices, *as may seem to them* best calculated to further the public interest in all respects'. (My italics.) Similarly, the duty of the Gas Boards is to 'develop and maintain an efficient, co-ordinated and economical system of gas supply for their area and to satisfy, so far as it is economical to do so, all reasonable demands for gas within their area'. The duties of the Transport Commission in the 1947 Act are set out in rather more detail: 'To provide, or secure or promote the provision of, an efficient, adequate, economical and properly integrated system of public inland transport and port facilities within Great Britain for passengers and goods with due regard for safety of operation.'

The national interest itself, however, is never explicitly defined. Adequacy, efficiency, economy and co-ordination are cited as highly commendable virtues which are decidedly in the national interest, but no attempt is made to indicate which actions in particular are likely to be 'adequate', 'efficient', 'economical' or 'co-ordinated'. The width of the interest is embodied in the requirement that in dealing with particular consumers the Corporations shall avoid any 'undue or unreasonable preference or advantage'—a requirement which is sometimes linked with an additional direction that the Corporations' tariffs be as simple and standardized as possible. There is a general, rather hopeful, implication that prices should be kept as low as possible, but this is subject to the overriding requirement that they must produce a revenue, as the Electricity Act phrases it, 'not less than sufficient to meet [the Corporation's] combined outgoings properly chargeable to revenue account taking one year with another'.

The establishing statutes have never had sufficient substance to serve as a definite guide to practical policy. There is therefore no basis for asserting that the four industries have in any way infringed the Acts by earning net revenues which are totally insufficient by commercial standards. The Acts nowhere state that revenues should be sufficient to provide funds for new investment. Indeed, the hope that prices will be kept as low as is consistent with the covering of *current* costs implies that the drafters did not favour this form of finance. The gas and electricity industries have certainly fulfilled the requirements of the Acts. Whether the Transport Commission has failed to do so depends entirely upon the interpretation of 'taking one year with another', and similarly for the National Coal Board upon the interpretation of 'on an average of good and bad years'. In serving the national interest, however, the spirit of the law is surely as important as its letter. Whatever the strict legalistic interpretation of 'taking one year with another' may be, it is clear from the debates that the drafters of the Nationalization Bills had a short, well-defined period in mind. Mr Gaitskell, who as Minister of Fuel and Power was responsible for drafting one of the major Bills, left the House of Commons in no doubt of his intention:

> There may be circumstances which may involve (the area boards) for a time in loss. There is nothing peculiar about that. Private companies make losses and recoup them later. There might even be occasions when the Government might feel, if there was a heavy slump and a lot of unemployment, that it might be desirable on the whole not to insist on costs being covered. I agree that might be a rather remote contingency, but it is the kind of thing referred to in the Coalition White Paper on Employment Policy, and we have therefore provided for it here. I would emphasize that I attach a good deal of importance to the principle that normally we should expect area boards to cover their costs each year. Normally, that should be the case, although we are not actually imposing that obligation on them legally, and I will expect them to arrange their affairs accordingly.[1]

Such *obiter dicta* show that the clause permitting a deficit in any particular year was included primarily to assist employment in times of depression. It was never intended as an escape clause in more prosperous times and it is surely ironical that it should now be invoked to justify deficit financing as part of a campaign against over-full employment.

CALCULATING THE COST

The Acts are more explicit on the composition of the costs 'properly chargeable to revenue account', but before recalling their directions it may be useful to glance briefly at the general problem of costs which confronts every public utility, whether owned by the State or not.

[1] Gas Bill: Standing Committee D Official Report: Session 1947–48: Volume 2, Column 1145.

Everyday running costs—labour, materials, fuel, etc.—present no difficulty in principle. They represent a demand for current resources which bears a reasonably stable relationship to output and must clearly be covered in full. This assumes, however, that the money cost of the resources to the industry accurately reflects their true social cost—their value in other uses. If one of the resources used by the industry is underpriced—coal is an obvious example—the mere covering of money costs by the industry will not promote the best distribution of resources. It may in fact exaggerate the maldistribution caused by the initial mispricing of the material. The fault, however, lies wholly in the pricing of the material and should be remedied by its suppliers; the industry using the material should surely not be required to compensate for defects of pricing elsewhere.

The allocation of overhead costs, those associated with the fixed capital of the industry, is more difficult as these stem from an investment of resources in the past. A common characteristic of the four industries under consideration is the large capital investment needed to produce even the smallest output. In the gas, electricity and transport industries especially, the assets involved are often indivisible, in the sense that the size of installation required bears no close relation to the output it is intended to produce—a railway track cannot have less than two rails and a certain number of sleepers because only one train a day will use it. These overhead, capital, costs would still be incurred if production ceased entirely, but on the other hand they remain constant over wide ranges of output, and unit production costs may decrease as output rises.

The problems arising from this disproportion between high overheads and low running costs have perplexed economists and engineers for over two centuries. Basically, the problem is that capital represents resources already used and, once resources have been embodied in a power station, railway track or other asset with no alternative use, that asset may as well be employed to capacity so long as running costs—the cost of current resources which could be used elsewhere—are covered. But if all output is priced merely on the cost of current resources, how are overhead costs to be met? A few economists—one fancies a rapidly declining number—argue that such industries can legitimately claim a subsidy, but this argument bristles with difficulties too complex even for the modern welfare theorist, let alone the practical commercial manager confronted by the cold facts of a profit and loss account. The general opinion—and certainly the intention of the drafters of the nationalization statutes—is that the full costs of the overheads must be recouped in one way or another from the consumers of the industry's products.

Overhead costs consist of two principal items: the interest on the borrowed capital invested in the assets and the amortization of those assets to provide for their renewal at the end of their working life.[1]

The payment of interest on past investments needs no defence. Interest is merely a method of charging a past cost against a present benefit or of capitalizing a future benefit into a present cost. Even a socialist society which prohibited all income from property could not dispense with the notional test which it provides of the prospective profitability of an investment. One qualification is required: to avoid burdening present management with the mistakes of its predecessors the interest should ideally be based upon the current value of the capital and not upon its historic value. That is, of course, the case if capital is raised in equity form. But the nationalized Corporations rely wholly upon fixed interest capital. It is perhaps possible that if the railways had remained in private hands their capital would have been drastically written down in the past ten years. Nationalization rules out such capital reorganization, as the Government accepts obligations which it cannot afterwards repudiate merely because circumstances have changed. However, as most companies were taken over at their current Stock Exchange valuation there is no reason to believe that at their inception the Corporations were saddled with an unfair burden.

Nor can the need to provide for depreciation be queried. Obviously, some provision for the replacement of assets must be made out of current earnings if the continuation of the business is to be assured. The basis on which that provision should be decided is far more contentious. The traditional accounting method of writing down the original cost of the asset over the whole of its working life has been severely criticized of late on the grounds that in times of inflation it fails to provide a fund sufficient to replace the asset at the new higher level of cost. Depreciation, it is argued, should be based not upon historic cost but upon the current, replacement, cost of the asset concerned. The controversy still rages but the current value school seems to be winning the day. The Herbert Committee which recently reported on the electricity supply industry were unanimously in favour of replacement cost depreciation:

> In the case of a State-owned monopoly . . . on which competitive forces do not operate strongly, prices must be determined by a process of calculated assessment. It seems to us that a proper element in arriving at these prices is the cost of the resources used up in the process of manufacturing and delivering the product. . . . It also seems to us that

[1] This treats depreciation strictly as a function of time; where the life of an asset depends also upon wear and tear such depreciation through use ('user cost') is a current cost and should be charged accordingly.

this cost should reflect current price levels rather than those ruling at the time when the plant was originally installed.

The establishing statues indicated no preference as between historic and replacement depreciation but the Herbert Committee imply that, although the Corporations have so far chosen historic cost, a change to replacement cost would not conflict with the Acts. The inadequacy of the present method of calculating depreciation is revealed in the latest National Income Blue Book, which shows that in the years 1951–55 the Corporations' depreciation provisions— £779 million—covered little more than half of their actual consumption of capital—£1,389 million.

Among the overhead costs chargeable to revenue account, the Statutes include 'proper provision for redemption of capital' which they seemingly regard as something distinct from 'proper provision for depreciation of assets'. Interpreted literally, this requires the Corporations' earnings to be sufficient not only to maintain physical capital intact but to repay the borrowed capital over the life of the asset. The Transport Commission still puts aside an annual sum for the redemption of its stock but the Gas and Electricity Boards have decided to subsume this provision under the general depreciation heading, regarding the two as alternatives (as they logically are) and the Government appears to have readily accepted this interpretation.

TARIFF POLICY

The tariff policies to be employed in raising a revenue sufficient to cover these costs are not specified. The general requirements of the Acts—overall balance, simplicity and uniformity of treatment— could be most easily satisfied by a straight flat-rate pricing, charging all consumers a price based on average costs of production (including overhead costs). This is the method of charging adopted by the Post Office, the most successful of all the nationalized undertakings, for its inland mail service. Its great public appeal is that it does not discriminate among consumers in any way. But economically such a tariff has grave defects. Its failure to discriminate means that consumers are charged the same price irrespective of the costs involved in supplying them. The costs of serving different consumers vary very little in the handling of mail and the Post Office is justified in neglecting them; but in other industries they vary considerably and unless they are taken into account in fixing individual charges they can cause a serious maldistribution of resources.

Hence differential charging is not necessarily 'discriminatory': to charge one consumer more than another because the costs of supplying him are higher is a totally different matter from charging him more because, through greater urgency or necessity, his demand is less elastic. The second would be rank exploitation, rightly eschewed by Corporations dedicated to the national interest. The first is merely charging the consumer the full costs of meeting his demand. There is nothing inherently equitable in flat-rate charging: rather it means subsidizing extravagance and taxing economy.

Average-cost pricing is particularly inappropriate for gas, electricity and transport. It is not only a poor way of allocating the heavy overheads among consumers; it also neglects the considerable excess capacity and low marginal costs in those industries at certain times and the consequent desirability of concentrating consumption on those times. Marginal-cost pricing ensures that consumers are not, on the other hand, supplied with additional goods at less than the cost of the resources needed to produce them. Marginal-cost pricing, in a word, promotes the best distribution of resources. But, owing to the heavy overheads in the industries, the disparity between average and marginal costs is very large and strict marginal-cost pricing is precluded by the need to cover these overheads. However, a sophisticated tariff structure can combine the covering of overheads with the advantages of marginal pricing and we now turn to see how individual Corporations have tackled these problems.

THE ELECTRICITY INDUSTRY

The problem of heavy overheads occurs in its most acute form in electricity generation. Electricity cannot be stored and the amount of generating plant required therefore depends upon the peak demand expected to be made upon it. At off-peak hours, considerable excess capacity exists and the cost of generating additional units of electricity is very low.[1] From its earliest days the industry has tried to make its tariffs reflect the different capital costs involved in supplying different consumers.

Originally, the tariffs were based upon some form of two-part charging, the consumer paying a fixed standing charge related to his maximum demand to cover overheads, and a low variable charge related to his actual consumption over a period to cover running costs. In recent years, the block tariff has tended to replace the strict two-part tariff, though for most consumers the change in the basis of charging is a mere formality. The block tariff charges the first, say,

---

[1] The coming of nuclear-generated electricity is likely to increase the disparity between high overheads and low running costs. The latest estimates suggest that the capital cost of a nuclear power station will be about £100 per kW of capacity, against £60 per kW in the latest conventional station, while running costs will be appreciably below those of a conventional station.

50 units of electricity supplied per quarter at a relatively high rate, to recoup overheads, and then offers subsequent units at a lower rate. The marginal rate may in fact fall several times as consumption increases.

In the domestic tariff, the number of units charged at the primary rate (or the standing charge in the case of a two-part tariff) is related to the size of the house—floor space, number of rooms, etc.—although it is recognized that this can give only the roughest of indications of the maximum load that the consumer is likely to put on the system at any one moment. For larger consumers, more accurate measurement is possible and the number of primary units can be more closely related to maximum demand. As most consumers will use far more than the number of primary units, the high cost block is in effect a standing charge and the tariff becomes merely a variant of two-part charging. But from the supplier's point of view strict two-part charging has one important advantage: overheads are covered even if the consumer uses no electricity whatever in the period.

The tariff for the largest industrial and commercial consumers is much more scientific. Consumers are charged for each kilowatt of maximum demand (measured by a demand meter) and for each unit of electricity consumed (as recorded on an ordinary type meter), the marginal charge per unit often falling as consumption rises. A 'coal clause' allows any increases in coal prices in the Area to be passed on to consumers. Clearly, this tariff conforms much more closely to the costs of supplying individual consumers and it seems highly desirable that, by improved metering and the introduction of a coal clause, the domestic tariff should be adapted to the industrial. The Herbert Committee hoped for progress along these lines and recorded their 'impression' that 'domestic consumers as a class are not contributing as much as they ought towards the cost of their supplies'. Since the Committee reported, any disparity must have increased, as industrial tariffs were raised following the increase in coal prices while domestic tariffs were frozen. The Committee also detected a conflict between cost and simplicity in pricing and came down heavily on the side of cost, recommending that householders be offered tariffs which reflect more closely the individual loads they put upon the system.

Unfortunately, a measure of individual maximum demand is not an accurate measure of the overhead costs involved in supplying the consumer. The crucial point is the time of day at which his peak demand occurs. A consumer with a maximum demand of 10 kWs but who uses current only in off-peak hours imposes far less strain on the system than a consumer whose demand never exceeds 1 kW but remains constant throughout the day. The marginal cost of generating electricity at the peak is many times the cost at off-peak hours. This is so not merely because additional generating capacity must be installed to meet the peak demand but because the generators called in at the peak are usually the highest cost generators still in commission. Continual technical progress usually means that a new power station has lower running costs than its predecessors and it is therefore used to meet the base load. As demand rises during the day, high cost generators are brought into operation until the peak is reached. The difference in running costs is quite startling. In 1954–55, the most efficient stations were producing current at less than $\frac{1}{2}$d a unit, while the cost at the least efficient was more than $1\frac{1}{2}$d.

Is there not here a very strong case for differential charging at peak and off-peak hours? Peak consumers should surely pay a price which reflects the higher running costs of the low-efficiency generating stations retained in commission to serve their particular need. Moreover if the peak is very pronounced—as it appears to be—there are good grounds for arguing that 'load spreading' should be encouraged by making peak consumers cover the industry's overheads in full. This could be achieved by basing the standing charge (or number of primary units) on the consumer's maximum demand between, say, 7 a.m. and 6 p.m., thus giving him a powerful incentive to curb his demand in peak periods. Such differential pricing is not exploiting the 'essential' consumer; it is simply charging him the full cost of the resources needed to supply him. The standard charge for electricity irrespective of time of day militates against the most effective utilization of the industry's capital equipment.[1] Nor is the waste confined to existing capacity: valuable resources are devoted to building new generators although there is no certainty that such vast expenditure is economically justified.

The bulk tariff of the Central Electricity Authority—which supplies the Area Boards with their current—is more realistic in these respects. The CEA makes the usual distinction, charging a fixed sum (£5 for 1956–57) per kW of maximum demand to cover capital costs, and a running charge (at present $\frac{1}{2}$d. per kW-hour), which varies slightly with the average cost of fuel used at power stations in the Area, to cover running costs. But the fixed charge is now based entirely upon the peak demand between 7 a.m. and 7 p.m. on weekdays, and the Area Boards have therefore been given an incentive to increase their demand for current at night and at weekends. The Boards, however, have been slow in adapting their own tariffs correspondingly and still do not discriminate between peak and off-peak demand or even generally between winter and summer demand.

---

[1] Britain's 46.8 per cent load factor in 1954–55 compares with about 60 per cent in the United States. The fuller utilization in America is due mainly to the greater prevalence of shift working; and while admittedly electricity costs can play only a minor part in the encouragement of shift working, they must have some effect.

THE GAS BOARDS

The gas industry faces a similar problem of fluctuating demand, with marginal cost well below average cost at off-peak hours. The peak, however, is less of a problem, as gas can be stored and production maintained at a fairly even rate, although consumption varies considerably from hour to hour. Gasholders permit the industry to meet daily and weekly peak demands without extending capacity but their costs are high and it would be uneconomic to use them to even out production between summer and winter. The peak presents a distribution rather than a production problem, as the elaborate system of mains and pipes distributing the gas must be capable of meeting the peak consumers' demand.

In the earliest days of the industry, consumers were charged according to the number of lights installed, but the introduction of the gas meter in 1830 changed the method of charge to a flat-rate consumption basis, and such average-cost charging persisted for over a century, although a thermal estimate of consumption later replaced the volumetric. An important amendment of gas legislation in 1934 allowed gas companies to introduce two-part charging similar to that adopted by electricity and telephone undertakings, and in the years before the war many companies took advantage of this new freedom.

Nationalization brought a great simplification and standardization of tariffs and at the moment there are four main tariffs in use. A flat-rate tariff at a standard price per therm is still operated by some Boards, though its defects must by now be obvious. A slightly more sophisticated tariff is the so-called step-rate, by which the price of gas is related to the consumer's expected consumption. Like the block and two-part tariffs, the step-rate charges the smaller consumer a higher rate per therm but it does not attempt to encourage additional consumption by offering lower marginal rates. Two-part tariffs are still favoured by some Boards as the neatest way of covering the heavy overhead costs, but, as in electricity, the most general tariff is the block tariff.

The two-part tariff has considerable advantages over the block tariff in the gas industry, where overhead costs are more closely attributable to individual peak demands. There has been a tendency recently for Gas Boards to move back towards two-part charging, even if the new tariff still retains the block form. The most interesting tariff is that introduced a year ago by the East Midlands Gas Board. This is in form a block tariff but the number of primary units is so low that for virtually all consumers the primary block becomes a standing charge. The Board's General Purposes tariff charges all consumers 30.25d per therm[1] for the first 10 therms consumed per

[1] The charges vary slightly from zone to zone within the Area.

H

quarter and 17.3d for the following 4,990 therms. Thereafter, the marginal rate falls away in seven more steps until it reaches 10.3d for more than 2 million therms per quarter. The merits of this tariff are obvious: the Board recovers the bulk of the cost of overheads in the high charge for primary units and thereafter the marginal price falls in quite dramatic steps. The tariff is not perfect. The number of primary units should, I feel, take more account of the costs of supplying individual consumers. But it is nevertheless a great advance on the previous tariffs and it is to be hoped that other Boards will experiment along the same lines.

The major defect of the Area Boards' tariffs is probably their excessive standardization. The Boards are generally very reluctant to depart from the standard prices and the result is the usual averaging of surpluses and deficits. The costs of supplying a consumer vary considerably with topography and the degree of urbanization and it is very doubtful if the Boards are sufficiently discriminating in their charging. It is no victimization for the out-of-town consumer to pay more for gas than the consumer living next to the gas works. He has, after all, compensating advantages.

The Gas Boards on the whole are far less sinners in these respects than the Electricity Boards. Unlike the Electricity Boards, many Gas Boards reduce their standard prices for the summer quarters and there is more attempt to reflect local costs in local prices.

RAIL TRANSPORT

Rail transport resembles gas and electricity in that a strongly defined peak demand determines overheads and results in considerable unused capacity, and hence low marginal costs, at off-peak times. The overheads stem from the vast capital expenditure—on track, signalling, terminals, rolling stock—required to meet the peak demand, which in large urban areas is usually determined by the daily rush of commuters. Freight traffic can be spread more evenly throughout the day (and night). There is therefore a strong case for making peak-hour passengers bear a high proportion of overheads. To some extent, this is accomplished by offering cheap excursions at off-peak times, but standard fares are usually the same throughout the day and in so far as season ticket holders and 'workmen' constitute the main rush hour demand it may be said that the average price charged at the rush hour is below the standard price. Public opinion, as expressed for over a century in Parliament, seems firmly convinced that people who travel at rush hours do so from necessity and that to charge them a higher rate would be gross exploitation.

Similarly, the public seems wedded to a flat-rate mileage charge.

Such views ignore relative costs; and rational pricing must surely be guided by costs and not sentiment. Flat-rate mileage charging is hopelessly uneconomic. Three years ago the British Transport Commission calculated that the costs of carriage per passenger mile varied from $\frac{1}{3}$d by main line express to 1s 2d by stopping train and 2s 1d on branch line services. Yet the standard rate per mile is the same for all three services. The long-distance traveller is forced to pay nearly six times the real cost of his transport in order to subsidize the operation of local train services which would otherwise be unable to compete with road passenger transport.

A study of freight costs would probably reveal a similar pattern. In the past, freight rates have been even more arbitrary than passenger fares. They have been based not upon costs or even distance but upon the expedient of charging what the traffic will bear—i.e. according to its value. As some of the most valuable consignments are also the cheapest to carry, it is obvious that in any war between road and rail transport the road hauliers would be likely to cream the business and leave the railways with only unattractive consignments, uneconomic to carry, which could not be refused owing to the railways' obligations as a common carrier. Fortunately, the Government were aware of this difficulty and the Transport Act of 1953, which ended the State monopoly of long-distance road haulage, also allowed what may justifiably be termed a revolution in rail freight charging. It relieved the railways of their obligations as a common carrier and allowed them to draw up a schedule of maximum charges alone, leaving them free to fix whatever charge they thought fit below that limit. The usual delays ensued. It was not until last July that the Commission's proposed maximum charges were approved by the Transport Tribunal and it will probably be several more months before the new rates come into operation.

The outstanding merit of the new charges scheme is that it is based primarily upon the costs of carrying individual consignments. The rate for each consignment depends upon its weight and 'loadability'. As a contribution towards overheads the new rates comprise a charge per ton for the first ten miles, a 'standing charge' which should discourage uneconomic short hauls, and a running charge per ton-mile thereafter. The success of the scheme will depend largely upon the enterprise of district commercial managers, but unless the charges become outdated by inflation the new flexibility should produce a notable advance in rail freight charging.

THE PRICE OF COAL

The correct pricing of coal is indispensable for the correct pricing of electricity, gas and transport, in whose production costs it is a major element. If the price of coal is too low, the prices charged by the other industries will be too low and their output will tend to be over-expanded—especially where two-part or block tariffs, with marginal prices sufficient only to cover running costs, are operated. The persistence of rationing indicates the the current price of coal is below its economic equilibrium price, and the conditions of inelastic supply and demand confronting the industry suggest that the difference may be great.

Coal differs significantly from the three industries considered so far. There is no marked 'peak' problem and marginal cost is generally well above average cost. Moreover coal is not, as is electricity, gas and to some extent transport, a homogeneous product. The problem of price structure thus relates to the differentials between grades of coal and not to a differential between similar coal supplies at different times. The National Coal Board has gone a long way towards restoring the price differentials between grades of coal which, as Mr S. R. Dennison explained in an article in this *Review* four years ago, had been whittled down by a series of uniform increases.

The Coal Board's price structure, however, continues to be marred by its insistence upon delivered, and not pithead, prices as the basis for charging domestic consumers. The Board still has 'under consideration' the introduction of zone-delivered prices for industrial coal. Uniform delivered prices throughout a zone, of course, mean that transport costs—which are a high proportion of the final cost of coal—are averaged among all consumers in the zone.

Nor is the averaging principle, with all its drawbacks, confined to transport costs. The pithead price itself is determined by averaging costs over a whole coalfield, which may comprise as many as a hundred pits, each with its own particular cost conditions. The result, as ever, is that inefficient pits are kept working and the development of new pits is hindered. The Coal Board's average-cost pricing has come under heavy fire from economists, who claim that marginal costs should determine prices, which in this case means that prices should be set by the highest cost pit in the field.

This controversy caused a deep cleavage of opinion among the members of the (Ridley) Committee on Fuel and Power Resources in 1952. The Committee were unanimous that 'price should not be less than cost' but they divided equally on whether the relevant cost was average or marginal. The arguments of the marginalists are surely more convincing; indeed the case of the four members supporting the Coal Board's averaging policy seems in the end to rest upon the rather specious proposition that:

. . . the overriding principle is that coal is so important to the economy that it should be sold at the lowest price which is consistent with the

National Coal Board's covering its costs. Indeed . . . one advantage of the nationalization of coal is to realize this principle.

In particular they pointed out that the marginalists' proposal that prices should be raised by £1 a ton to equate them with long-run marginal cost would give the Coal Board an annual surplus of £200 million and that 'to charge coal consumers £200 million more than the total cost of production would be quite unjustifiable'. The marginalists in reply argued that the surplus in fact represented the royalty charge for superior pits and corresponded to the economic rent of agricultural land.

In my view, the marginalists' case is far the better one. From the Coal Board's own point of view—the question of 'national interest' will be discussed later—it was surely bad business to sell coal at home for 34s a ton less than could be obtained for it abroad, or, more recently, to sell coal at home for £2 a ton less than was being paid for it abroad. Two recent substantial price increases have provided an appreciable margin of price over average cost (though price is still well below marginal cost) and this may enable the Board to earn a surplus large enough to eliminate the whole of its £37 million accumulated deficit. The need for a substantial surplus is underlined by the Coal Board's revised *Plan for Coal*, which envisages an expenditure of £1,000 million between 1955 and 1965. The Plan stresses the extremely heavy rate of depreciation in the pits, for mines are notoriously wasting assets and without heavy investment their output capacity would shrink by four or five million tons a year. The right policy would seem to be to set aside substantial sums for amortization out of a large annual revenue surplus and there are signs that the National Coal Board has some such proposal in mind.

HOW BIG A SURPLUS?

The cardinal error of the Corporations, on this analysis, has been their excessive neglect of individual costs, which has shown itself in the application of standard charges to groups of widely differing consumers. The remedy is as obvious as the defect; but the adoption or tariffs more closely aligned to the underlying structure of costs—including the full cost of depreciation—would still leave unsolved one enormous problem: that of obtaining the resources needed to implement the Corporations' investment programmes. Ideally, the resources should be made available by the voluntary savings of the community, but in present circumstances the savings are simply not there. If the investment is to be financed without inflationary consequences, the necessary funds must be exacted from consumers by prices pitched well above costs. This is admittedly hard on the consumers and the Herbert Committee stated bluntly that 'to make present consumers subsidize . . . the capital requirements of future consumers would be inequitable'. But would it be as inequitable as finance by inflation?

Private industry, as a whole, has always found the funds for investment out of trading profits. Indeed, in recent years it has been a heavy net lender to other sectors. The latest National Income Blue Book's estimates of capital consumption at last give us some idea of net investment by the various sectors of the economy. In the years 1951–55, net fixed investment of £969 million by the Public Corporations was accompanied by net *dis-saving* of £520 million. This means that the Corporations borrowed on average nearly £300 million a year, a third of which was required not for new investment but merely to keep existing capital intact. By contrast, net fixed investment by private industry—£1,398 million—was covered more than two-and-a-half times by net savings.[1]

Such facts assort ill with the price freeze and it seems a strange conflict of policy that the Corporations should be asked to budget for a larger 'gap' at the very time that the Chancellor is extolling the virtues of an overall surplus on the Government's own accounts. The nationalized industries face a problem similar to that of the great oil companies, and they may in the end be forced to solve it in the same way: by making profits far in excess of those indicated by a strict alignment of costs and prices. The 1955 Report of the Central Electricity Authority puts the case plainly:

> In present economic circumstances it is quite clear that if the industry's financial stability is to be assured, it will be necessary to earn larger annual surpluses, in order to provide for a greater degree of self-financing of future capital programmes.

PROMOTING THE PUBLIC INTEREST

The larger surpluses, however, were not forthcoming. In June last, the Central Electricity Authority stated that increased costs had prevented the industry from achieving its aim in 1955–56. And, on the prospects for the current year the Authority said:

> The latest increase in coal prices would . . . in the normal course have necessitated an advance in tariffs generally in order to preserve at its present modest level the surplus hitherto achieved by the industry.
>
> Nevertheless, having regard to the national situation, the Authority consider that the Area Boards should for the present avoid increases in their tariffs . . .

[1] The inclusion of changes in the value of stocks, capital transfers and switches from taxation and dividend reserves complicates the full picture but does not alter the marked contrast between the two sectors.

The other major nationalized industries similarly agreed to forgo in the interests of stability the many acknowledged advantages which would result from changes in both the level and the structure of their tariffs.

Those decisions exemplify the view that the industries are responsible for more than their own affairs, that they are in fact supposed to promote the national interest, which in this instance is seen as stable prices. That view was expressed in just this context four years ago by the members of the Ridley Committee who objected to the marginalists' proposed higher coal price on the grounds that it would 'provoke an inflationary series of wage demands out of all relation to the actual increase in the cost of living due to the higher price of coal'. The appropriate answer has now been given by the Herbert Committee:

> We state our view without any qualification that the governing factor in the minds of those running the Boards should be that it is their duty to run them as economic concerns and to make them pay.
> If it is thought in the national interest that some course other than a purely economic course should be followed, it is in our opinion the responsibility of the Minister on behalf of the Government to require that course to be adopted. . . . It is not for the persons running the industry to undertake uneconomic schemes of expansion, whether in rural or urban areas, in the supposed national interest, if the effect is to subsidize one particular body of consumers out of the pockets of others.

The first concern of the managers, in other words, should be to make the operations of their industries profitable. Far from that profitability being inimical to the 'national interest' it is, in present circumstances, essential to it. The 'national situation' surely calls in reality for *higher* prices from the nationalized industries, prices which reflect the true costs of their operations and provide funds for financing their investment.

It would be unreasonable to expect too rapid strides, not merely because of administrative difficulties but because any sudden change in the basis of pricing would be unfair to existing consumers who— through no fault of their own—have entered into commitments in the belief that the existing terms of supply will continue. One would certainly not suggest that anomalies and inequities of pricing which have existed for over a century should be rectified overnight. But the rate of progress since nationalization has in my submission been far too slow and the present price freeze is a disturbingly retrograde step. More realistic prices are urgently needed. They would at least enable the Corporations to judge whether all their investment plans were warranted. Resources are too strained to allow us the luxury of gigantic shots in the dark.

36. RETAIL TARIFFS*

384. Under the Act the Electricity Boards are required to 'promote the simplification and standardization of methods of charge for such supplies'. The Electricity Boards have by now introduced a considerable degree of uniformity of tariff structures throughout the country. Certainly in each Area there has been effected a substantial standardization of tariffs for each of the main classes of consumer. The present position is that eight Boards have introduced standard tariffs for industrial supplies, nine Boards for commercial supplies, ten for farm supplies and eleven for domestic supplies. The one Board which has not yet introduced a standard domestic tariff is to do so on April 1, 1956. We have been informed that the Electricity Boards, through the Retail Tariffs Committee which the Boards set up in 1948 to consider the standardization of tariffs, have agreed to conform to a common set of principles which they would use in the determination of their standard tariffs. These tariff principles were submitted by the industry to the then Minister of Fuel and Power in 1951 and received his general approval. Since then many standardized tariffs have been in operation for some years, and in the light of experience of their working the Retail Tariffs Committee are now undertaking at the request of the Minister a comprehensive review in order to remove any anomalies which may have been caused and to consider whether the original principles need modifying.

385. Apart from this statutory obligation on the Electricity Boards to simplify and standardize their methods of charge, which has inevitably meant a certain averaging of charges between consumers, we have also had regard to the acceptance by the Government of one of the principal recommendations of the Ridley Committee on Fuel and Power Resources,[1] whereby electricity tariffs should reflect the costs of supply. The Ridley Committee felt that the best pattern of fuel use would be secured by maintaining the consumers' freedom of choice between competing fuels, provided the charge for each fuel reflected the cost of supply. We feel that the statutory requirement under the Electricity Act that methods of charge should be both standardized and simplified is to some extent inconsistent with this recommendation by the Ridley Committee that charges should reflect cost. The demands made by electricity consumers vary considerably as between groups of consumers and as between individual consumers within the groups. The simpler and the more standardized

* From *Report of the Committee of Inquiry into the Electricity Supply Industry*, January 1956, Cmd 9672, paras. 384–8 and 395–8.
[1] Cmd. 8647 (September 1952), Report of the Committee appointed by the Minister of Fuel and Power in July 1951 under the chairmanship of Viscount Ridley to advise on national policy for the use of fuel and power resources.

the tariffs are made, the greater the degree of averaging and the greater, inevitably, the divergence between the cost of supplying a particular consumer and the charge made to that consumer.

386. We have drawn attention in earlier paragraphs to questions involving the economics of electricity supply in order to explain the background to the representations made to us on tariffs by representative consumer associations and the reasons for our subsequent recommendations. There are two aspects of tariff-making particularly to be considered:

(i) the appropriate method of charge for each class of consumer;
(ii) whether the tariff results in the appropriate charge for individual consumers within each class.

387. Standardization of tariffs by the Electricity Boards has been introduced for each main class of consumer, industrial, commercial, farm and domestic. Reduction of tariffs to only four classes of consumers inevitably means that averaging is widespread and consumers within each group may feel that they are not charged according to the costs of their supply, particularly in relation to the charges made to other consumers within their class. At the same time, consumers of one class may feel that they are having to pay much more than is warranted by reference to consumers with similar characteristics of demand in a different class.

388. This question of the correct cost-relationship between the various classes of consumer has been brought to our attention particularly by the complaint that industry is required to pay much more for its electricity than domestic consumers who may have similar individual load characteristics. In justification of this complaint it is alleged that the average price per unit of electricity for domestic consumers has risen only slightly since 1938, whereas the average price of electricity for industrial consumers has risen by 77 per cent during the same period. It is a fact that there is a marked difference between the methods of charging for industrial and domestic supplies, in that, firstly, the actual electrical demand of industrial consumers is measured by a demand meter in addition to a consumption meter and, secondly, industrial tariffs contain a fuel clause whereby increased cost of fuel to power stations in the area of supply is automatically passed on to the industrial consumer. On the other hand the development of the five-day week and shorter working hours has meant that industrial firms working one shift per day tend to concentrate their electrical demand during about eight hours on each of five days a week. We think there should be further research into the relationship between the cost of supplying the different classes of consumers and the charges made to those classes of consumers...

395. We think that most of the complaints we have heard about

tariffs would be avoided if it were demonstrably clear to all consumers that the charges made were related as closely as practicable to the costs of supply. The word 'practicable' in this context is intended to recognize two facts, first that joint costs involve a certain amount of arbitrary allocation and second that the process of ascertaining the costs of supply must not be carried beyond the point at which the expense outweighs the advantage of measurement. We think that the Electricity Boards by and large have made considerable improvements in tariff structures, subject to the statutory requirement of simplification and standardization. The developments, especially in off-peak tariffs, deserve to be better known than they are. Whilst recording our satisfaction with the progress made, we think there is still much more work to be done in applying the principle of charging according to costs.

396. The industrial tariff has gone furthest towards this ideal. On the other hand, we are not satisfied that the commercial, domestic and farm tariffs have been so designed as to reflect as closely as practicable the costs of supplying electricity to those classes of consumers and to the individuals within those classes. There should be further inquiry into the electrical characteristics of those consumers who have been charged under the commercial tariff to see whether more valid bases can be chosen to measure the costs of supplying them. We have noticed that certain Boards have in fact introduced a two-part tariff with maximum demand metering for commercial consumers with demands as low as 5 kilowatts. We consider that this is a development in the right direction and that this type of tariff should be more widely available to commercial and farm consumers. We would hope that there would be further research into the possibility of designing suitable and cheap meters to enable the smaller commercial and farm consumers, with demands of even less than 5 kilowatts, to be offered a maximum demand type of tariff. As for the domestic consumers, although the Electricity Boards unanimously favour the promotion of this load, the bulk of which is said to fall outside the period of peak demands made by other classes of consumers, we are left with the impression, in the absence of any significant supporting data, that domestic consumers as a class are not contributing as much as they ought towards the cost of their supplies. There should be investigation into the possibility of applying a coal clause to the domestic tariffs as long as it remains necessary for the electricity supply industry to apply such a clause to industrial and large commercial consumers. We understand that in Northern Ireland the coal clause applies to domestic consumers equally with other consumers, and we would regard the introduction of a simple price variation allied to coal prices as being entirely in accordance with the objective that

charges should reflect costs. We do not suggest that the present coal clause applicable to industrial tariffs is appropriate, and we recognize (for the reasons set out in paragraphs 380–1) that the form of the present coal variation may need to be modified. In addition to such investigations as are needed to ensure that domestic consumers as a class are meeting their proper share of the costs, we believe that there is room for much more research and experimentation with tariffs, and the necessary metering, to enable at least the larger domestic consumers to be offered tariffs that would reflect the individual loads they put upon the system.

397. We recognize that the closer tariffs conform to the 'cost principle' which has been accepted by the Government and the electricity supply industry, the greater may be the departure from simplicity. We have no hesitation, however, in advocating that the statutory requirement to simplify tariffs should not permit or require Electricity Boards to deviate from the 'cost principle'. We think that the standardized tariffs have been made simpler than they would have been but for this statutory requirement. We would, therefore, recommend that the Electricity Boards be relieved of their obligations to simplify their tariffs.

398. We appreciate the difficulties confronting Electricity Boards in framing methods of charge. Before introducing or modifying their tariffs they submit their proposals to the Electricity Consultative Councils. They also have to face criticism from the public who, in general, are averse to any change in electricity tariffs, unless of course it is to their benefit. In addition, the Electricity Boards have to conform not only with the statutory requirement for simplification and standardization of methods of charge, but with the further requirement to avoid showing undue preference and discrimination in the application of these charges. There must be present a temptation to propose what may be administratively or politically convenient rather than what is strictly justifiable on economic grounds. We do not in any way suggest that Boards are consciously actuated by such a consideration, but we feel that it should be recognized, not only by the electricity supply industry but also by the public, that the first principle in tariff-making should be to secure that charges reflect costs.

37. THE LOAD FACTOR PROBLEM*

375. Many electricity consumers do not appreciate that electricity is produced for instantaneous use; that unlike gas or coal it cannot be

* From *Report of the Committee of Inquiry into the Electricity Supply Industry*, January 1956, Cmd 9672, paras. 375–7, 399–403 and 407–8.

stored (at least on a large scale). Every time a switch is turned on its effect is felt in the generating station. This means that the electricity supply industry has to install and keep in readiness generating capacity capable of supplying any demand for power at any second of the day and night. If the demand for power were constant throughout the twenty-four hours a much smaller amount of generating capacity would be needed to supply the same number of units than under present conditions when demand is concentrated at relatively short periods during the day. Most industrial and commercial consumers make their demands for power between 7 a.m. and 7 p.m., during which time most domestic consumers also require electricity. The load on the power stations, therefore, begins to rise at the beginning of the day, reaching its maximum in winter between 8 a.m.–12 noon and 4 p.m.–5.30 p.m., after which time it begins to tail off. This shape of the load curve gives rise to one of the major problems of the electricity supply industry—how to provide for sufficient capacity to meet peak demands and how to charge consumers according to the demand they place on the system. This problem of the peaks also requires the electricity supply industry to have continually before it the improvement in load factor that would result if consumers transferred part of the demands they made at peak times to 'off-peak' periods when demand is much lower and spare generating capacity is available.

376. Other industries are confronted with this inconvenient habit of consumers to want satisfaction of their requirements at the same time. In certain industries such as the transport industry, this particular problem is brought home physically to the public when they compete together for existing capacity—the phenomenon of rush-hour travel. In the case of the electricity supply industry, however, the electric switch is available to all and generating capacity must, therefore, be provided to satisfy the instantaneous demand which consumers may make. Consumers, however, although not so conscious as in the case of transport of the way in which their demand is creating difficulties, will nevertheless be required to pay the cost of calling into existence and operation capacity to meet their peak requirements which at other times will remain idle. There are two major elements in the cost of making electricity which are relevant— the cost of providing the generating plant and mains capacity which is required to meet the potential demand, and the cost, mainly fuel, of actually running the power stations. The plant in power stations consists of machinery such as boilers, turbo-alternators, condensers, valves, etc., which must be manufactured to operate under certain conditions of heat and pressure and within definite limits of safety. This plant is expensive and must be paid for out of the revenues of the

electricity supply industry, no matter how little call is actually made upon it by electricity consumers. If a consumer takes the bulk of his electricity during a certain relatively short period during the day-time, the electricity supply industry has to provide for that consumer a greater amount of generating capacity than would be the case if he spread his requirements over a longer period.

377. The problem of estimating the cost of electricity supply at different times of the day and year is extremely complicated. Only the general nature of the problem can be indicated here, as follows. When a new station is brought into commission it will have a lower running cost per unit than most of its predecessors. In consequence it normally takes on part of the job of meeting the base load, i.e. it operates twenty-four hours a day throughout the year, except for periods of maintenance. Some part of the plant which had formerly operated twenty-four hours a day and which has higher running costs is now operated for parts only of the day and year; plant which has higher costs still is run for even shorter periods and so on until at the bottom of the efficiency table, so to speak, a plant with the highest operating costs falls out of operation altogether unless demand is expanding as fast as the new capacity is created. During 1954–55 the average running cost of the units generated by the more efficient plant, supplying 87 per cent of the total output, was $\frac{1}{2}$d per unit; whilst the running cost of the units generated by the least efficient and generally the oldest plant brought into operation to meet the 'peak', which supplied only 4 per cent of the total output, averaged about $1\frac{1}{2}$d per unit. The cost of providing an extra kilowatt therefore involves a complicated computation which must take into account the general trend of demand, because this affects the total volume of additional capacity needed, and the consequential effect on utilization of all the plant as new and more efficient capacity is brought in. It is not our intention to discuss the computations needed, but it should be clear that the cost of providing power is lower per unit at night than it is during the day and lower in the summer than it is in the winter, since the higher the demand the higher the proportion of high-cost plant that is running. . .

399. The present system load factor of the British electricity system (1954–55) is 46.8 per cent. At this level, not only is there an ample margin of spare plant for the Central Authority to fit in their main-tenance programme, especially during the summer, but the plant capacity as a whole is much under-employed. In the United States, system load factors of about 60 per cent are experienced in various regions but apart from the difference in the method of calculation there are real differences in climate and social habits between the two countries which make an exact comparison of load factors impossible.

It can be said, however, that the industrial load factor in America is generally higher than in this country owing to the greater prevalence of two- and three-shift working in the United States. On the commercial and domestic sides there is a very much lower use of electricity for winter space heating in the United States, but a considerable summer demand for refrigeration and air conditioning purposes. American habits therefore tend to improve their system load factor. The Authority have stated that they envisage a general load factor improvement from 44.4 per cent in 1953–54 to 48.2 per cent in 1959–60, and we have seen that the system load factor for 1954–55 was 46.8 pre cent. The extent of the prospective further improvement in load factor is important in assessing whether any reduction in average costs may be expected over these next few years. The higher the load factor (certainly up to the range of 60–70 per cent) the more effectively employed will be the generating plant. We have, therefore, reviewed closely the means by which the Electricity Boards hope to secure the improvement in load factor they expect.

400. The greatest single contribution that could be made to improve the British load factor would be the introduction of extended shift working in industry. This would even out the industrial demand and would also affect the commercial and domestic demand through the alteration in domestic and leisure habits of workers. The only way that the Electricity Boards can influence industry in this direction is through the offer of reduced charges for supplies taken during off-peak periods. The difficulty here is that electricity charges are in many instances only a small fraction of the total production costs of firms, so that the prospect of lower electricity costs is not in itself sufficient inducement to extended shift working, with its attendant management and staff problems. Despite this, many Electricity Boards are offering standard off-peak or restricted hour tariffs, or special terms to attract those industries which can suitably use electricity off-peak or for processes which create a steady demand for electricity throughout the twenty-four hours. The Boards do not expect, however, that these measures can, in fact, produce any substantial improvement in the industrial load factor unless two- or three-shift working becomes more common. The Electricity Boards further consider that the general structure of their tariffs provides automatic encouragement to industry and larger commercial users to use more electricity over longer periods. The nature of the maximum demand and unit two-part tariffs, they contend, is a powerful incentive to the improvement of load factor.

401. In the commercial field, the scope for off-peak electrical use is also somewhat limited, although the increased use of floor warming and storage heat appliances will provide some benefit. As regards

domestic consumers, the Electricity Boards consider that, apart from the operation of the two-part tariff which induces consumers to use more electricity, the greatest scope for improvement in the domestic load factor lies in the extended use of electrical equipment of all kinds, in particular the extension of those appliances which have good load characteristics such as the immersion heater and electrical storage water heater. The Boards contend that the more varied and widespread the use of electrical appliances, such as cookers, water heaters and refrigerators in the home, the greater the proportion of consumption which would tend to fall outside peak hours.

402. The Electricity Boards are thus tackling the problem of load factor in the following ways:

(*a*) through the promotional character of their normal tariffs;
(*b*) by offering special off-peak or restricted hour tariffs;
(*c*) by promoting the sale of all kinds of electrical apparatus;
(*d*) through the development of particular appliances with good load characteristics.

It would appear, therefore, that in their hope to secure an improvement in the overall system load factor the Electricity Boards are relying mainly upon an extension of domestic use and on the expectation that its major demands will fall more off-peak than on-peak.

403. We do not quarrel with any of the four ways in which the Electricity Boards are seeking an improvement in load factor. We have, however, some important qualifications to make. Firstly, the Committee wishes to press in this context, as in other contexts, for a more vigorous effort to discover the facts. More needs to be known about the load characteristics of appliances and the nature of demands made by various classes and types of consumers. We are left with an uneasy feeling that policy in a number of directions is determined more by personal impressions, e.g. about the load characteristics of electric fires, than by scientific investigation. We therefore recommend that the Authority should undertake as a matter of urgency a thorough investigation into the problem of load factor improvement. . .

407. If charges more clearly reflect the difference in cost of supply at different periods, consumers will be given the opportunity of deciding for themselves whether it is worth their while to alter their habits in relation to a pattern of charges that make off-peak electricity cheaper and on-peak electricity dearer. We think it important that off-peak concessions should be available wherever possible over the whole range of electrical use, since this may create a demand for suitable appliances which will induce manufacturers to develop and promote apparatus with off-peak characteristics, e.g. the heat pump, thermal storage heaters, floorwarming and other devices.

408. Despite the progress made in introducing off-peak tariffs, we do not think that every individual Area Board is pushing as enthusiastically as it should the development of off-peak loads. Most Boards still do not offer off-peak tariffs to the larger domestic consumer, and some Boards are less progressive than others in the scope of their off-peak tariffs to industrial and commercial consumers. We are also concerned with the attitude of Boards towards the 'selling' of off-peak tariffs. It is, in our opinion, not enough that these tariffs should be on offer. What is required is a more forceful and vigorous attitude by the Boards. They should go out and sell these tariffs, particularly to those consumers who would benefit most by them. Consumer habits tend to be deeply entrenched but we regard the selling of off-peak units as a challenge to the Boards.

38. MARGINAL COSTS VERSUS AVERAGE COSTS*

54. We have not been able to agree what principle should determine the general price level for coal. The Committee are divided equally on this subject: half of us consider that the price of coal should be raised so as to cover its *marginal* cost of production; the other half consider that the price of coal should as at present correspond to the *average* cost of production.

55. We now set out in some detail the arguments on both sides of this controversy, both because the matter is somewhat complicated, and also because the division between us is likely to be reflected amongst other people. Before setting out the opposing views, however, we first give a short theoretical statement of the economic approach to pricing in general, since one cannot decide what price level is appropriate for coal without considering rather fundamentally the effect of price on the use of a commodity, and of cost on price.

GENERAL PRINCIPLES OF PRICE POLICY

56. A useful commodity has a price because it is scarce, whatever the cost of production. A commodity would have a price even if it had no cost of production, so long as it was wanted but limited in supply; on the other hand, no commodity could be sold at any price if no one wanted it, however much it might cost to produce. Coal is not freely available where it is wanted in the quantities and qualities

* From *Report of the Committee on National Policy for the Use of Fuel and Power Resources*, 1952, Cmd 8647, paras. 54–74.

required. It would therefore have a price even if it cost nothing to produce.

57. The effect of pricing is to restrict supplies of a commodity to those buyers who are most willing to pay for it. In theory, this is the same as restricting it to its most urgent uses; in practice, since income is not evenly divided throughout the community, this equation is not exact, but special account is taken of this by redistributive taxation designed to prevent those with higher incomes from bidding away more than their fair share of scarce commodities.

58. In the special context of coal, the existence of a price promotes economies in several ways:

(a) It checks waste of coal, both by discouraging people from using coal for inferior purposes (e.g. as ballast) and by stimulating users to burn coal efficiently.

(b) It shows how far spending money on labour or equipment is worthwhile for the purpose of increasing the thermal efficiency with which coal is used. The lower the price of coal, the less the stimulus to spend money on increasing thermal efficiency.

(c) As a result of (b), the manufacturers of fuel-using equipment are stimulated to improve its thermal efficiency. The lower the price of coal, the less the effort made, in designing and producing fuel-using equipment, to improve fuel efficiency.

(d) The fact that it has to be paid for releases for export some coal which would otherwise be used at home. To the nation a ton of coal is worth at least the amount of foreign exchange which could be obtained if this ton could be sold overseas. If the home price of coal is very substantially below the export price, it seems most probable—unless it is 'rationed'—that some coal will be used inside the country which could more profitably have been exported.

59. Although the dominant fact in determining that coal should have a price is its scarcity, coal does cost something to produce. Cost of production sets the upper limit to price, since at any price above the cost of production it always pays to increase output—assuming output can be increased—to meet demand; it sets the lower limit because at any lower price production no longer pays. This lower limit is important for the best employment of the country's productive resources. The cost of producing a commodity is simply the cost of the resources which could have been used in producing something else. The labour, machinery, and other resources used in producing coal could be employed alternatively in expanding (say) the output of agriculture, or the building of houses, and one reason for charging a price for coal is so to limit demand as not to use in mining

coal any men, materials and capital resources better employed else-where. On this ground, from the community's standpoint, price should not be less than cost. From the standpoint of the National Coal Board, under statutory obligation to pay their way, the case is equally strong.

60. The Committee accept this conclusion unanimously; they divide on the question of what the relevant cost is. Professor Haw-thorne, Professor Lewis, Mrs McIntosh and Miss Schofield think it is *marginal* cost; Lord Ridley, Mr Lincoln Evans, Mr Gardiner and Sir Claude Gibb think it is *average* cost. In the following paragraphs these opposing views are explained.

MARGINAL COST PRICING

61. Those members of the Committee who think price should be based on marginal cost argue that, in comparing the value of resources used in one industry with the value of the same resources to some other industry, it is necessary to think only in terms of the little more or the little less. The practical problem is whether some part of the resources should be shifted from one industry to another, and the value of this marginal part only is relevant; the price of coal should correspond not to the average cost of producing all the coal mined, but to the cost of producing additional supplies. The demarcation of marginal output is in practice somewhat arbitrary: a smaller or larger tonnage might be taken. We have been told by the National Coal Board that 7 million tons of their annual output is produced at a loss of 15s or more a ton. For practical purposes this may be taken as the relevant marginal output; since at present the coal price level is based on average cost, the marginal cost on this inter-pretation is at least 15s higher. Hence, these members conclude that the present price of coal in this country is in general *at least* 15s a ton too low.

62. It would, however, in the present condition of acute coal shortage, be possible to take the marginal cost pricing argument much further. Supply is at present so far below demand, not only at current prices, but probably also at considerably higher prices, that, if coal were not 'rationed' and price-controlled, it would sell at very much higher prices than those now charged in this country. On a strict interpretation of marginal cost pricing, there would in present con-ditions have to be a very sharp increase in the price of coal—say £3 a ton at the pithead—to equate 'unrationed' demand with available supply. But the marginal cost is expected to fall as new pits are developed, though not so fast as average cost. This interpretation of marginal cost pricing would therefore mean a very steep initial coal price increase, followed by a fall as supplies improved.

63. Those members who advocate marginal cost pricing would not push the argument so far as to relate price to short-run marginal costs in the present coal shortage. They agree with the other half of the Committee that wide fluctuations should be avoided, and that 'rationing' and allocation of coal must be continued until supplies are much nearer to demand. But they believe that this position would be reached the sooner if prices were raised to close the gap they expect to persist between average and marginal costs. They think that this persistent gap may tend to widen to something like £1 a ton as coal production is increased. The more output is pressed up, the wider the gap. These members therefore advocate raising the average price of coal to a level of about £1 a ton above average costs in any year.

64. Such an increase would involve an extra charge on coal consumers of more than £200 million a year, which this half of the Committee think perfectly justified. Their argument goes back to the proposition that a commodity has a price because it is scarce, and not because it has (or may have) a cost of production. Some coal is easily won, and some costs a great deal to produce. Easily-won coal is scarce, in the sense that there is not enough of it to supply all the demand. The community must save easily-won coal just as much as it must save coal which is expensive to mine, and this is why the real value of easily-won coal is neither the cost of winning it, which is low, nor some average cost, but the cost of winning the marginal coal which would not have to be dug if the more easily-mined coal were efficiently used.

65. These members say that in this respect coal mining is just like agriculture or like any other industry which uses resources that differ widely in fertility or efficiency. In agriculture, some land is much more fertile than other land, but agricultural produce tends to be sold at a price equal to the cost of production on the least fertile land on which it is grown. As a result, land of different fertility attracts different levels of rent. In relation to coal, the State is like a land-owner with lands of widely differing fertility, and should charge mine rents which vary according to the ease of winning coal in them. The surplus which would appear if the National Coal Board were to sell coal at its marginal cost is not really a profit; it represents a rent, or royalty, springing from the difference between high cost and low cost mines. If the Board were to include in the price of coal an adequate royalty charge (to be paid to the State), the gap between marginal and average costs would be bridged, and the coal consumer would be paying an economic price for the scarce resources used to supply him.

AVERAGE COST PRICING

66. The other half of the Committee do not accept this argument. They consider that price should be equal to average cost. This means that some coal is sold at more and some at less than its actual cost of production to the Board. Some buyers are subsidized, but it is impossible to distinguish which. This half of the Committee do not dispute that it may be theoretically wrong to use scarce resources to meet those demands which would not be made if the prices charged were raised to cover the marginal cost—if it were possible to define marginal cost in practice. They consider, however, that although a price increase would normally balance the supply of a scarce commodity with demand by increasing supply as well as by reducing demand, in the case of coal an increase of £1 a ton is unlikely to call forward any increased quantities of coal in the near future. This would force the full burden of adjustment on to the consumers of coal and this half of the Committee do not consider this to be acceptable or necessary: in their opinion the overriding principle is that coal is so important to the economy that it should be sold at the lowest price which is consistent with the National Coal Board's covering its costs. Indeed they assume that one advantage of the nationalization of coal is to realize this principle, and that to charge coal consumers £200 million more than the total cost of production would be quite unjustifiable.

67. These members see also the following difficulties in raising prices to the level of marginal costs:

(a) If the National Coal Board were greatly to increase their apparent profits, there are two possible effects which would mean constantly increasing costs—both marginal and average:
  (i) mine managers might become less conscious of the importance of keeping down costs, and
  (ii) the miners would consider that these apparent profits justified corresponding wage increases;

(b) An increase in price would raise the general price level, and this might reduce exports, to the detriment of the country's foreign balance of payments.

(c) The rise in prices of coal and, consequently, of manufactured goods, might set off demands for higher wages, and accelerate the inflationary spiral.

68. The members of the Committee who think that the price of coal should be raised to its marginal cost recognize that there is some force in these considerations, but attach less importance to them.

69. On (a) (i) those in favour of average cost pricing hold that the staff of an industry, at all levels, work best when the industry is barely able to cover its costs, so that maximum effort is required

from all if it is to succeed; if profits were easily made, effort would slacken. The other half of the Committee are suspicious of this argument, but, in so far as it is valid, they would meet it by bringing the price increase into effect by levying an excise duty upon coal. (They call it 'excise duty' for convenience—in effect it is a royalty payment for the use of a valuable and wasting national resource.) The Board would then still have the same stimulus of having to cover costs. The whole Committee agree that if there were such an increase in price, it would be better in the form of an excise duty or royalty.

70. On (*a*) (ii) the argument is that if there were these large proceeds, the miners would feel entitled to higher wages whether the proceeds were retained by the Board as profit, or paid to the State as an excise duty. Those members who favour marginal cost pricing are not impressed by this argument. First, because excise and purchase taxes are levied upon many industries, without their giving rise to higher wages in taxed than in untaxed industries. And second, because they think there may be a case for paying higher wages in order to attract more men to jobs which are exceptionally arduous and particularly valuable to the community. The other members of the Committee agree that there may be a case for increasing miners' wages in a period of coal shortage, but they do not think this excise duty would be an appropriate justification because it would not necessarily be related to the need for wage increases to increase output or to meet advances in the cost of living.

71. Argument (*b*) is that an increase in the price of coal would raise the general price level and so affect the prices of UK exports. Those opposed to increasing the price of coal above average costs of production consider that it would reduce the country's foreign exchange earnings because UK goods would be less competitive. Customs drawback would be difficult to work because of problems of assessing the varying coal content of different exports. The opposite view, however, is that coal costs form only a small proportion of the total costs of most manufactured articles, so that even a large increase in coal prices would not greatly affect the competitive strength of exports; where, however, coal costs are a significant part of total costs it is by no means clear that any loss of trade would not be offset by the increased earnings from the higher prices charged for the exports that still found a market; some people indeed think that many UK exports with a high coal content are in any event being sold at prices below their true market worth.

72. Argument (*c*) is that an increase in the price of coal would directly affect the cost of domestic fuel and power services to the consumer and would increase the costs of other goods. Those opposed

to increasing the price of coal believe that this increase in the cost of living would provoke an inflationary series of wage demands out of all relation to the actual increase in the cost of living due to the higher price of coal. On the other hand those who support marginal cost pricing believe that it is dangerous to the economic system, at a time when world prices are rising, to hold down arbitrarily some prices which happen to be easy to control, while allowing others to take their course. This is itself an inflationary act, since it diverts purchasing power to the uncontrolled commodities, and makes their prices rise even more. It also distorts the economy; the price mechanism gives misleading indications to demand and to supply; and important commodities become even scarcer, while the shops are full of things that people do not wish to buy. They point out further that even if the increase in the price of coal were allowed to enter fully into the cost of living, a £1 per ton increase would raise the cost of living only by 1 or 2 per cent and this is a small increase compared with what has taken place over the last three years. In any case to a considerable extent the higher cost to the consumer can be offset by the Chancellor's use of the proceeds of the coal excise tax. He could reduce taxes all round, or he could also take some more direct action to offset the increased cost of living by subsidizing some other goods out of part of the receipts of the excise duty on coal. Where the increased price of coal might cause particular hardship—for example, to old age pensioners, or to large families—the Chancellor might increase old age pensions or family allowances.

THE EFFECT OF HIGHER COAL PRICES ON COAL CONSUMPTION

73. We differ on the theory of average and marginal cost pricing and on the practical weight to be given to the points mentioned in paragraph 67. But we also differ about how much an increase in the price of coal would stimulate greater fuel efficiency. Those who oppose an increase in price think that in many industries coal costs form such a small proportion of total costs that even an increase of £1 in coal prices would not have any significant effect on fuel efficiency; and that in many industries where coal costs are a large proportion of total costs (as in iron and steel production) the present level of coal prices is already high enough to give a strong incentive to fuel efficiency and where in such cases efficiency is not achieved, other means apart from increasing the price of coal must be sought. For domestic consumption they believe that since, as the whole Committee agree, house coal 'rationing' must continue for some time, a duty of £1 a ton would give little stimulus to economy, and that the other measures discussed in Chapter V will be more effective.

74. Those who favour a coal price increase think that a sharp increase in the price of coal will give a salutary shock to all coal consumers and compel attention to fuel economy. In industry, under conditions of increasing competition, even relatively small additions to total costs will affect the firm's attitude towards fuel economy; firms whose fuel costs form a large proportion of their total costs will be forced to reassess the economic gains from fuel saving against the cost of making that saving. Part of the proceeds of the coal excise duty could be used to subsidize fuel efficiency measures for industry. For domestic consumption they believe that the increase in gas and electricity prices due to the increased price of coal will have the desirable effect of emphasizing the coal costs in these commodities. They further believe that the duty of £1 a ton will accelerate improvement in domestic fuel efficiency and enable 'rationing' to be dispensed with at an earlier date. This half of the Committee accordingly think that an increase in the price of coal of £1 a ton would bring a substantial reduction in demand and accelerate the improvement of fuel efficiency.

39. CAPITAL PLANNING IN THE ELECTRICITY SUPPLY INDUSTRY*

The finance of the public sector of British industry is quite properly a matter of general concern. Its pricing policies affect practically every citizen. Its capital investments are a significant part of the total for the whole of industry.

The Electricity Boards in England and Wales—with which this essay is concerned—command net assets of a written-down value of £2,000 million. They invest in plant and other fixed assets some £300 million a year, receive in electricity revenue well over £500 million a year, and run retail trading businesses with an aggregate turnover of £70 million a year. Figures of this order raise questions of the first magnitude. Do the prices charged for electricity cover the full costs? Is a sufficiently large proportion of the required capital secured by 'self-financing'? Are the budgets, both short and long, competently prepared and adequately scrutinized? Can electricity investment be adjusted upwards and downwards in a counter-cyclical manner? Is the problem of the peak load being vigorously tackled?

The recent publication of the annual reports of the Electricity

* From R. S. Edwards: 'The Finance of Electricity Supply', *Lloyds Bank Review*, October 1960, pp. 14–30. Reprinted by permission of the author and the editors of the *Review*.

Boards and the Electricity Council makes this a suitable occasion to consider briefly some of the issues raised by these questions. On two important matters I shall have nothing to say. On the financial aspects of nuclear energy I could add nothing to the paper given by Sir Christopher Hinton, Mr Brown and Mr Rotherham at the Madrid meeting of the World Power Conference[1] and the recent government White Paper.[2] On whether nationalized industries should be allowed or required to go to the capital market I could say little that would not be highly speculative, since the question is so closely bound up with wide issues of economic and fiscal policy.

The opinions expressed here are personal and are not necessarily shared by all my colleagues on the Electricity Council.

REVENUE AND COSTS

The Electricity Boards are *each* required by statute to ensure that their revenues are not less than sufficient, taking one year with another, to meet outgoings properly chargeable to revenue. The statute refers to 'proper' provision for the depreciation or renewal of assets, 'proper' provision for the redemption of capital and 'proper' allocations to reserve funds which each Board is bound by statute to set up.

In practice, the Boards have interpreted their statutory obligations concerning accounting in a normal commercial manner. Thus they provide fully for depreciation and deem this, so far as charges to revenue are concerned, to cover proper provision for capital redemption. If Boards provided for capital redemption in excess of depreciation, consumers would be paying not only for the assets they used up but would in effect be buying out the stockholders and the Treasury. The Boards make allocations respectively to Generating and to Area Reserve Funds, but in the consolidated statement of accounts these are shown as an appropriation of surplus—again in line with normal practice in industry.

Depreciation

Since the war many, perhaps most, businesses have followed the practice of providing above the line for depreciation on an historical cost basis, while setting aside part of the profit to meet the difference between this provision and the likely cost of replacement at post-inflation prices. A few bold spirits have engaged in major revaluations.

The electricity supply industry follows the historical cost basis,

---

[1] Hinton, Brown and Rotherham: *The Economics of Nuclear Power in Great Britain.*

[2] The Nuclear Power Programme (Cmd 1083, June 1960).

some of the Boards making supplementary 'below-the-line' reserves. Does this mean that current electricity costs fail to cover real capital consumption in current value terms? The question is of great importance in so capital-intensive an industry. I believe the answer to the question is 'no': real costs are fully covered.

In the first place the book lives used by the Boards are, on the basis of experience, conservatively short. Where technological advance suggests that lives should be reduced or depreciation be accelerated this is done. In 1958–59 the Generating Board shortened the book lives of important classes of assets and thus added nearly £6 million to the depreciation bill for that year. In 1959–60 the Board extended to power stations the practice, already followed for other assets, of computing depreciation from the beginning of the construction period rather than from the date of commissioning. This, together with small changes made by certain of the Area Boards, added a further £6 million to the depreciation provision.

Not only are the lives of the assets conservatively assessed, but it is the general practice in the industry to write off, on the straight-line basis, the whole of the original cost. There is, however, commonly some scrap or residual value when assets actually reach the end of their lives and, moreover, consumers make in some cases contributions to capital expenditure which reduce the net cost to the Boards. Thus, in judging the adequacy of the aggregate depreciation provisions of £82 million in 1958–59 and £95 million in 1959–60, account must be taken of the fact that in these two years the industry received £7 million and £9 million from the two sources just mentioned.

The third, and most important, factor concerns the replacement cost of assets. The cost per unit of capacity that the industry needs to create in order to make good the 'consumption' of its assets has not been rising proportionately to the general price level. For important classes of equipment, it has actually been falling. This for two reasons: the integration and growth of the supply system enables units of small capacity to be replaced by larger units which secure greater economies of scale; and the advance of manufacturing technology reduces the cost of plant of a given capacity. The Central Electricity Generating Board have made calculations to show that, for example, the capital cost per kilowatt of a generating unit decreases exponentially with the increase in capacity, giving a reduction of 20 per cent in cost per kilowatt for a 100 per cent increase in capacity. Further, given price stability, improvements in manufacturing technology can be expected to result in real costs reducing exponentially at the rate of $2\frac{1}{2}$ per cent per annum.[1] The effect of these and other factors is shown in the dramatic fall in the cost of conventional

[1] See Hinton, Brown and Rotherham: *op. cit.*, p. 3.

generating plant: 30 MW sets have resulted in capital cost for a complete station of £67 per kW, whereas a 550 MW set to be commissioned in 1963 will, at tender prices, result in capital cost of a complete station of £39 per kW.

The allowances to be made for these various factors are matters of judgment. It is more realistic to think of a range of acceptable figures for depreciation, rather than of one figure that is right, all others being wrong. At the lower end the figure would be scarcely adequate and at the upper end unreasonably high. Although they must be kept regularly under review, the total annual provisions now being made are at present comfortably inside these limits.

Interest on Borrowing

At present the Electricity Council undertakes all borrowing, both long and short, on behalf of the industry in England and Wales. The long-term debt of the Electricity Council is about £1,800 million, of which nearly £1,200 million is for stock issues guaranteed by the Treasury, and nearly £600 million for advances made by the Minister of Power (Exchequer Advances). Since the Chancellor in 1956 decided to make the Treasury directly responsible for the supply of capital to all the nationalized industries, these advances, which are repayable by equal annual instalments over twenty-five years, have become the sole source of long-term finance. Bank advances (at present limited to £55 million) are the only other important source of borrowing.

Interest is a very large item of cost: £60 million in 1958–59 and £68 million in 1959–60. The bill is rising because (a) net indebtedness is increasing and (b) the rate of interest is rising. While the average rate of interest payable on all outstanding borrowings in 1959–60 was $4\frac{1}{4}$ per cent, the current rate on Exchequer Advances is $6\frac{1}{4}$ per cent. It is worth mentioning that all interest is charged straight to revenue, despite the fact that some of it is attributable to borrowings which finance power stations and other works during the period of construction.

As Exchequer Advances come from the Government, and part of the Government's below-the-line expenditure is financed from the budget surplus, the electricity industry is sometimes loosely accused of being subsidized from public funds. More sophisticated criticism is directed to the fact that the rate of interest paid by the industry would be higher but for (a) the compulsory saving which is imposed by the Government through the budget surplus, and (b) the passing on of Government credit terms in the rates of interest charged by the Treasury to the industry.

Certainly, the finance of below-the-line Government expenditure from taxation eases the burden on the capital market; if there were no compulsory saving, the capital market would be a much tougher place for borrowers. This, however, would affect not only the electricity industry, nor only the public sector as a whole; it would affect all borrowers and, for that matter, the whole economy through a smaller supply of capital and higher interest rates.

If there were no budget surplus or if the surplus were used for debt repayment, and the electricity industry was told to fend for itself and given freedom to choose how best to do this, it could make a good showing on the capital market. If, however, it were restricted to normal forms of fixed interest borrowing, the industry, with others similarly placed, would suffer from the effect of the present dislike by investors of stocks which provide nothing for growth or as a hedge against inflation. Even so, the credit-worthiness of so strong a borrower would not be much below that of the Government itself. This is not to be taken as advocating any major change in the present method of financing—which I have already said will not be discussed—but merely to deal with the criticism referred to earlier. Since the industry fully covers its costs and makes a surplus it is scarcely reasonable to accuse it of being subsidized. In the financial framework within which it is asked to live it pays its way. It could do so in any other.

The Surplus

After providing realistically for depreciation and meeting interest charges, the industry's aggregate surplus in 1959–60 was £27 million, nearly 1.5 per cent of net assets. The surplus earned by each Board is automatically ploughed back into the business of that Board.

How large should the surplus be? The statutes give little guide to the industry in this matter. The Boards have a duty to develop and maintain efficient, co-ordinated and *economical* systems. They must 'have regard to' the desirability of preserving natural beauty. They must 'secure so far as practicable' the development, extension to rural areas and cheapening of supplies. Having decided how best these and other duties can be reconciled, each Board must then bear in mind the injunctions to make proper allocations to a Reserve Fund and to ensure that revenue, taking one year with another, is 'not less than' costs.

THE PROBLEM OF SELF-FINANCING

The Herbert Committee considered that the industry should carry sufficient reserves to cushion it against short-run changes in demand and costs, and to avoid the need for violent or frequent alteration of tariffs. It suggested that the industry should aim to earn (after providing for full depreciation and interest) say 1 per cent on the capital employed. It did not, for reasons which were explained at length, believe that present consumers should 'subsidize' the capital requirements of future consumers. Sir Roy Harrod, on the other hand, has expressed the view '. . . that the nationalized industries be told that in future they will have to find all their capital requirements by internal finance . . .'.[1] For electricity supply, doubling in size every decade, to generate the whole of its capital requirements through prices would mean that revenues from consumers would have to be increased by more than 25 per cent. How much more would depend on consequential tax liabilities and on the elasticity of demand for electricity. The Radcliffe Committee came to the conclusion that it would not be realistic to look for a solution of the problem of capital supply along these lines. The Committee thought that, in the case of electricity, opportunity might be taken to find some additional capital by refraining from price reduction as costs fall. 'But we are aware that, when it comes to hard figures, opportunities of this kind are likely to be small in relation to the total new capital needed by these industries.'[2]

He would be a bold man who would argue that in this matter there is one clear principle that ought to override all other considerations; he would be equally bold to argue that the conflicting considerations, when weighed, would lead to only one defensible decision so far as the earning and retention of surplus revenue is concerned.

The Long-Term Investment Programme

Soon after its formation the Electricity Council had to face as a practical and urgent issue the problem that the industry was coming to the end of its statutory borrowing powers and had, through the Minister, to ask Parliament to increase them. Estimates were prepared for the seven years to March 1965, showing that the industry would need to incur £2,130 million of capital expenditure (gross). In considering what proportion of this should be financed from internal resources the Council recognized, on the one hand, the duty of the Boards to do justice as between present and future consumers and, on the other, the burden which would be imposed on the supply of capital. It felt that there should be no major change in policy and in particular no change which would jeopardize the industry's competitive position against the other publicly-owned fuel industries. But it hoped, subject to these conditions, to finance more of its capital requirements from internal resources than hitherto.

[1] *Policy Against Inflation*, Macmillan, 1958, p. 238.
[2] Report of the Committee on the Working of the Monetary System, p. 219, para. 592.

Power for the Future (published by the Council in December 1958 in support of the industry's application for increased borrowing powers) stated that the industry expected to finance from internal resources 48 per cent of the industry's gross capital requirements during the seven years to March 31, 1965, as compared with 42 per cent over the previous decade. This meant that £1,030 million would have to come from consumers for depreciation and surplus and by way of capital contributions.

The capital programmes were fully discussed with the Ministry of Power and debated in Parliament. Mr Maudling's summing up on self-financing was as follows: 'This is a matter on which it is impossible to be dogmatic. All one can do is to put the principles on which the industry is working and suggest that in the view of the Government, by and large, those are sound principles.'[1]

The Electricity (Borrowing Powers) Act, 1959, raised the industry's borrowing limit (for sums borrowed up to March 31, 1965) to £1,800 million or such greater sum, not exceeding £2,300 million, as the Minister of Power may by Order specify. Any such Order would require approval by resolution of the House of Commons. It is estimated that the lower limit will be reached early in 1962. The pattern of the first two years has been as follows:

	1958/9	1959/60
	£m.	£m.
Capital requirements	250	305
Depreciation, etc.	91	106
	159	199
Surplus	27	27
Net borrowing	132	172

The percentage of capital requirements financed from internal resources was 47.4 in 1958–59 and 43.6 in 1959/60. There was nothing untoward in this reduction. Given large year to year variations in capital expenditure there are bound to be material differences in the self-financing ratio, since it would be wrong to attempt to vary tariffs on a short-period basis to maintain a stable self-financing ratio. The industry's expectations in this matter are based on the longer term. The combined figures for depreciation and surplus for the two years are broadly in line with expectations. As the business of the Boards expands, there will need to be reasonable increases in surpluses.

[1] *Hansard*, January 20, 1959, col. 55.

The Growth of Efficiency

The consolidated statements of accounts have shown some solid savings in costs, of which the most striking have derived from increased thermal efficiency and the economies that flow from the growing concentration of generation in the cheaper coal areas. In 1959–60, the savings in coal costs as compared with what they would have been but for these economies amounted to £13 million. In addition, there have been many other illustrations of the steady drive for economy. The 1959–60 report of the Council shows that on the Area Board side there has been a reduction in the cost per unit for distribution, consumer service, meter reading and billing, administration and general expenses. These savings were, however, offset by increased interest charges, increased payments for local rates (it is worth pointing out that the electricity industry paid in rates some £24 million, as compared with about £68 million paid by the whole of private industry), by salary and wage awards, and by higher figures for depreciation which have already been mentioned. Nevertheless, the overall result shows that total costs per unit sold fell from 1.507d to 1.472d.

Why, then, was the surplus for 1959–60 not higher, especially when it is remembered that an *extra* £3 million profit was made in the business of contracting and sale of fittings? The answer lies in the characteristics of the tariffs. In the case of most industrial tariffs, reductions (or increases) in the cost of fuel are passed directly through to the consumers by the coal price variation clause. Since most domestic and other small consumers are on a two-part or block tariff, an increase in the average consumption per consumer results in a fall in the average price per unit received by the Boards, since the additional units are sold at the 'marginal' unit rate. In 1959–60 the average revenue received per unit sold by the industry as a whole was 0.048d less than in 1958–59, equivalent to a 3 per cent reduction in average price.

Before leaving this aspect of our subject it is necessary to emphasize that the Boards are *individually* responsible for their financial results. It is convenient to refer to the 'industry' in discussing the overall achievements and problems, but the Board by Board responsibility is a reality. The annual reports show that the financial out-turn varies very much from Area Board to Area Board, mainly as a consequence of the timing of retail tariff adjustments but partly as a result of the incidence and scale of the winter peak demands. If the surpluses necessary to achieve the 1958–65 self-financing programme are to be earned, individual Boards will require to increase tariffs to the extent that cost increases cannot be met from even greater advances in efficiency.

It is in a way unfortunate that the expression 'surplus' is used to describe the difference between the revenues of the Electricity Boards and their costs. Surplus connotes something left over and, by inference, available for distribution. The surpluses of the electricity industry are not available for distribution. To the extent that they are not required to cushion the Boards against short-term financial changes, they are in effect planned as a small contribution from consumers towards the development of the Boards' undertakings. Like the depreciation provisions, surpluses go straight into the purchase of assets. Nothing is 'left over' in the colloquial sense.

CAPITAL PROGRAMMES

The process of capital planning starts with the forecasting of future demand. For certain purposes very long-term estimates are needed. For reasons of space these paragraphs will be limited to a discussion of the industry's five to seven year planning.

Forecasting Demand

If the winter peak demands on the Central Electricity Generating Board (adjusted to 'average cold-spell' conditions) from 1948–49 to 1959–60 are plotted on a semi-logarithmic scale, they show a fairly close stright-line fit to an annual growth rate of 7 per cent. The industry has, each year, to make up its mind whether this steady load growth will continue at the same rate, whether it will accelerate, or whether it will slow down over the following five to seven years—the period needed to plan, design, manufacture and install new generating capacity.

Each Area Board makes a sales forecast in the light of its local knowledge of developments in industry, housing and so on, and according to certain agreed general assumptions. These Area estimates are then aggregated and compared with national estimates (both of consumption and of maximum demand) made by the Generating Board and the Electricity Council.

The long-term load forecasts, assuming 'average cold-spell' conditions, when adopted by the industry, enable the Generating Board to determine three programmes of generating capacity: a firm programme for the fifth year ahead, a provisional programme for the sixth year and a tentative programme for the seventh year. In determining these programmes, estimates are made of (i) the very old plant which will still be serviceable and economic, (ii) the total plant in existence which will be available at time of system peak, and (iii) the allowance to be made for abnormally cold weather. Load forecasts must similarly be translated into requirements of transmission capacity and Area Board networks.

Inevitably, there is scope for error in these forecasts. A study of past forecasts shows that the tendency has been to underestimate demand rather than to overestimate it, but the shortfall in generating capacity has been bridged by the improved availability of plant. So much of this improvement is, however, now embodied in the forecasts of capacity expected to be available that future under-estimating of demand would have more serious consequences.

The primary purpose served by the annual long-term national forecasts of future consumption and load is to give an early indication of changes in trend. If the estimates were to show a movement away from the past trend, they would be a signal to those concerned to identify the forces at work. Today, practically the whole of industry and commerce, 95 per cent of the homes and over 80 per cent of the farms are already using the public electricity supply. The rate at which new consumers are connected must soon begin to decline. Therefore, although overall demand is at present rising as briskly as ever, the industry is working to a generating programme slightly below the trend line, on the assumption that any consistent departure from it is likely to be downwards rather than upwards. Whether it is prudent or not to assume this slight drop in the rate of demand increase, time alone will tell. It can, however, be said with assurance that the forecasts on which new plant commissioning is based err, if at all, on the low side.

Suppose, however, that despite the indications, the long-term demand forecasts turned out to be over-estimates. What would be the cost? More plant would have been installed and would have become available than was needed in the year of commissioning. This over-provisioning would, of course, be rectified by a lower provisioning for the following years, but for the year concerned the over-provisioning would be equivalent to a replacement of the oldest plant still in service. The new plant would come into immediate base load operation, since it would be the most efficient; the plant rendered idle would be the least efficient. All plant in between would move down the order of merit which determines which plant is brought into use as load increases. It follows, therefore, that the over-provision of *additional* plant would be uneconomic only to the extent that *replacement* of the very oldest plant was uneconomic.

Hitherto, practically the whole of the new plant has been installed to provide additional kilowatts. Only the smallest of the most inefficient and in some cases unserviceable generating units have been taken right out of commission. The Generating Board have recently made a study (as did the Central Electricity Authority before them) of whether plant replacement on a more significant scale would be economically justified. The exercises showed that, if the tranche of old plant under consideration were scrapped, there would be only a slight loss on the transaction after meeting capital charges.

Capital Programmes

Revised forecasts of future load are made in the spring and summer, after each winter's peak experience. Capital budgeting, however, must follow the accounting year of the industry: namely, the year to the end of March.

Each Board is under statutory obligation to consult with the Electricity Council (in effect the central forum for the industry) about its programme, after which the Minister's approval has to be secured. The process is as follows. Each Board prepares in December–January forecasts of capital expenditure, internal resources and borrowing requirements for each of the six years beginning on the following April 1st. The procedures for doing this are broadly the same as in other large industrial undertakings, so there is no point in elaborating them here.

The Boards' forecasts are forwarded to the Electricity Council in mid-January. Copies of the Boards' estimates are sent by the Council immediately to the Ministry, so that the process of consultation and approval may be concentrated into as short a period as is consonant with efficiency. Consultation between Boards and Council headquarters takes place in the next ensuing two months and the capital estimates are reviewed by the Finance Committee of the Council and then by the Council itself. By the time this process of consultation is approaching completion, the Boards will have experienced one more winter's weather, and in the light of this later knowledge of peak demands the Boards and Council may modify their forecasts and estimates.

When the Council has completed its review, it submits to the Minister of Power a consolidated statement of programmes for the industry as a whole. Having made his own review, the Minister gives approval, in July or August, to the Boards' programmes and to the incurring of capital expenditure of a certain amount (which may, of course, be less than was proposed) during the succeeding year, and provisional approval for the year beyond that. And so the process goes one step forward each year, the provisional figures being finally approved or varied, and a new set of provisional figures being adopted for the next ensuing year.

Although no formal decision is taken about the projected expenditure in the years beyond the first two, the industry must inevitably

I

commit itself to such expenditure, since much of its equipment takes longer than two years to order, build and install. While the aggregate figures for the more distant years necessarily contain an increasing element of conjecture, these long-term estimates are an essential part of the industry's planning and, in view of their size, are necessary to the Government's consideration of major financial and economic policy.

In between the annual reviews, all the Boards supply the Council quarterly with revised estimates of their capital expenditure, their borrowing requirements and their forecast trading results for the current and two following years. Furthermore, they inform the Council each month of their capital expenditure incurred and the probable actual expenditure for the year against the current year's approved capital budget.

These monthly and quarterly returns are designed to ensure that the Council receives early warning of any variation from the adopted forecasts. It must be appreciated that quite large variations are possible for reasons beyond the control of the industry itself.

The timing and rate of completion of work, however carefully planned and progressed by the engineers—and much attention is being paid to this—is subject to the hazards of weather, illness, technical setbacks and strikes. Some deviation between the time pattern of actual expenditure and the pattern assumed in the estimates made more than a year earlier is inevitable. With entirely new engineering projects, such as the large nuclear power stations, the difficulty is even greater, since there is so little experience to serve as a guide. All in all, with contracts of £500 million on hand, a difference in time pattern can easily throw £10 million to £20 million from one year to another. What really matters is to get the money spent on construction in such a way that none of it is unnecessarily idle.

On the Area Board side, there are other difficulties in capital forecasting. The Boards' forecasts are based on their estimates of the demands which they are likely to have to meet for supplies to existing consumers and for the connection of new consumers, and these demands are liable to material variation at short notice. It cannot be emphasized too often that the Boards are bound by statutory and near-statutory obligations. They have to furnish new and additional supplies, they have to meet the increasing demands of existing consumers, and at the same time maintain supplies within stated limits of the declared voltage. These demands are largely outside the Boards' control. The Boards estimate, as accurately as they can, the demands which they are likely to have to meet within a given period. If, however, there is an unexpected acceleration in house-building or factory construction, or if the load from existing consumers increases more rapidly than forecast, the Boards have no option but to meet these increased demands at the earlier date, if necessary seeking increased authorization to cover the additional capital expenditure involved.

If Area Board networks were easily capable of carrying existing loads, the cost of an unexpectedly large upsurge of new connections could be met without serious embarrassment by decreasing the capital work on reinforcement. Unfortunately, shortage of capital over the years has left the Boards with networks which in many places are seriously inadequate even for present loads. In these conditions Boards cannot carry unexpected increases of demand without extra capital unless security of supplies is to deteriorate still further. It was, in fact, necessary this spring to ask the Minister to increase the capital authorization for 1960–61, which he made in August 1959, since experience over the last autumn and winter has shown a recovery in the economy, and hence a demand for electricity, greater than had been forecast.

COUNTER-CYCLICAL BUDGETING

When the pressure on the total resources of the community is too high there is, rightly or wrongly, growing criticism of the level of government expenditure. This criticism rarely distinguishes investment expenditure from the rest. It seems a little hard to those involved that, while increasing investment programmes in the private sector are regarded as meritorious, public sector investment, however productive, is regarded by some as though its sole purpose was to make life difficult!

The investment programmes for electricity supply are designed to meet the customers' demands. They cannot be turned on and off just as happens to suit other considerations. The capital projects are large and inter-connected in a complex manner. Once contracts are let they must run their course. The Generating Board is a big ship: it cannot alter direction like a corvette. The Area Boards, though less tied by long contracts, do a considerable amount of their own capital work, and cannot increase and decrease the size of their constructional teams rapidly and extensively without serious loss of efficiency.

It is therefore easy to over-estimate the extent to which the electricity supply industry, without serious loss of efficiency and higher cost, can help to counter changes in the pressure of total demands on total resources. Nevertheless, something is possible and in this connection a lesson can be learnt from recent experience.

In the autumn of 1958 the Area Boards were given authority to increase expenditure. They were also permitted to bring forward work into 1959–60, in the quite correct expectation that, overall,

1959–60 would be an easy year and 1960–61 a difficult year from the standpoint of pressure on resources.

Although the figures involved were not large, they were significant; they helped the economy through the stimulus given to employment and helped the industry to make good a little of its backlog of capital works. What we did not fully allow for, however, was this: although capital expenditure on the electricity system can help the pump-priming exercise, electricity is one of the first industries to feel the effect of pump-priming. As the economy revives, more new houses and more new factories and shops need connecting, and existing consumers demand more power through the networks. Therefore, an increase in electricity capital expenditure can be succeeded by a reduction (or reduced rate of increase) only if there is distribution capacity in being to meet the demands resulting from the pump-priming itself. The upsurge of demand in 1960–61 could not be accepted on the systems without capital expenditure exceeding the original estimates. In short, if the electricity supply industry is to play a part in counter-cyclical operations, some fat must be put on the systems first. At present the bones of the distribution networks are almost showing through the skin.

THE LOAD FACTOR

The capacity of the electricity supply industry is more fully used than most capital assets in British industry. Nevertheless the large capital requirements of the industry demand that strict attention should be paid to the problem of the peak.

The problem is being tackled in three ways. First, in the field of generation, the development of the super-grid enables the fullest use to be made of capacity and therefore reduces the spare plant that must be available for peak use. In addition, special projects are in hand. A pumped storage scheme of 300 MW is being constructed at Blaenau Ffestiniog, where electricity will be generated at hours of peak demand from water previously pumped up to a high-level reservoir by electricity produced at the most economic stations in off-peak hours. A cross-Channel link with Electricité de France has been arranged, enabling 160 MW to be transferred in either direction with considerable saving, because of the difference in peak hours in the two countries.

Secondly, the industry is seeking to stimulate (*a*) existing uses, such as refrigeration and water heating, which offer long hour use or have a high diversity between individual consumers or, best of all, generally fall off-peak, (*b*) new developments in load improvement, e.g. user equipment with thermal storage characteristics such as floor warming and block storage heaters, and (*c*) new techniques in industry, such as batch annealing of steels, which offer possibilities of load reduction at peak times.

Thirdly, the industry seeks through its tariffs to relate prices to costs. The Generating Board have so framed the bulk supply tariff as to recover their fixed costs fully in the charge paid by each Area Board per kilowatt of maximum demand put on the system by that Board; only the bare running charges are recovered in the rate per unit consumed. In 1960–61, there was introduced a new feature of the bulk supply tariff, namely special terms for loads which can be restricted by not less than 25 MW by the Generating Board during short peak periods. A rebate of £3 19s 0d on the normal annual kilowatt charge of £7 2s 0d will be allowed to Area Boards for such loads. Area Boards all offer industrial and commercial consumers tariffs made up of components proportional to the maximum demand and to the units purchased, with reduction in the unit charge related to higher load factors. Special inducements are offered to industrialists who can curtail their demand during peak periods and take extra supplies at other times. Low rates are offered to all classes of consumer for supplies made available only during specified off-peak periods: for instance, at nights and week-ends. In 1959–60, 30 per cent more units were sold than in the previous year on restricted-hour and other off-peak tariffs.

It is important, despite the enthusiasm for low unit charges in retail tariffs, to ensure that they are kept slightly above marginal costs. It is necessary to avoid slipping into the position where increasing volume of business results in lower rather than higher surpluses.

COST AWARENESS

The electricity supply industry is strongly expanding and, in certain fields, subject to little competition. The classical pressure of inter-firm rivalry which is important in many industries is partially, though not wholly, absent from the sale of electricity. Nevertheless, the Boards are cost-conscious and fully alive to the need for economy and improvements. Many examples could be given were the space available. The research programme is increasing rapidly, revenue expenditure having risen from £900,000 in 1958–59 to £1,400,000 in 1959–60, with big laboratory extensions in hand and a good deal of development work not covered by the research figures. There has been a long and intensive drive to secure maximum scale and location economies, with generating sets on order up to 550 MW and stations being developed for as much as 2000 MW on cheap-coal sites. The super-grid is being pressed forward and distribution systems developed (within the limits of capital available) to ensure that plant is run in merit order so as to secure the lowest overall costs. The period between initiating and completing capital projects is being shortened. Standardization of equipment and purchasing arrangements are constantly under review. Boards have achieved significant reductions in the levels of their stocks of equipment. Economic appraisals are being used not only at senior levels but also down the line. Modern computing and programming devices are being employed in order to operate local and national systems at high efficiency. Management and staff training schemes are a feature of the industry and are constantly being developed.

There is a risk that this article will have sounded either defensive or complacent. It is intended to be neither: the industry is proud of its achievements but well aware how much remains to be done.

40. 'BELOW THE LINE'*

84. The nationalized industries all have large capital programmes, for which they have to raise money by borrowing in so far as finance is not available for this purpose from their commercial earnings. Some of these industries have also incurred losses on current account, which have also had to be financed by borrowing. We consider later how far these corporations are affected in framing their investment decisions by monetary measures. Here we note that the main capital spenders in this group emerged from the war with large arrears of ordinary maintenance and renewal of capital assets (including repair or replacement of assets damaged or destroyed by enemy action) which had accumulated not only during the war but in some cases over a period of years before the war.

85. This would in any case have dictated a sustained programme of heavy capital spending after the war, to which had to be added, as circumstances offered, modernization to take account of technical developments. Particularly in the early years of the period after the war, the limitation on the size of the capital programme of these industries was that of resources of manpower and of materials. The general level of their investment programmes has continued to be determined by agreement with the Government in the light of, and to accord with, the Government's assessment of their due share of total investment; and on occasion, particularly since 1955, their capital spending programmes have been deliberately reduced at the request

* From *Committee on Working of the Monetary System*: *Report*, August 1959, Cmnd 827, paras. 84–9 and 591–5.

of the Government as part of the effort to restrict the pressure of investment demand. Throughout the period these industries have not suffered from any shortage of economic projects to be undertaken; nor have their capital spending programmes been geared to, or hampered by, their ability to get money, or the price which they had had to pay for the money they borrowed.

86. The nationalized electricity, gas and transport industries were authorized, by the statutes which incorporated them, to borrow by the issue of stock guaranteed as to capital and interest by the Treasury. The stocks issued by these industries were all fixed-interest and fixed-term stocks. These stocks were managed and regarded as gilt-edged securities, in that they were formally 'issued' by prospectus in stated amounts. Some issues were made directly to the National Debt Commissioners (NDC) in which case the effect was to diminish the amount which the NDC could lend to the Exchequer, so that the Exchequer had to borrow an equivalent sum for its own purposes from the market, and was therefore in effect borrowing to finance the nationalized industry concerned. Most issues were however made to the market, in which case amounts not subscribed by the public at the time of issue were taken into the portfolio of the Issue Department of the Bank of England, and subsequently sold through the Government broker as opportunity offered at market prices. In proportion as unsold stock was taken up by the Issue Department, the Issue Department was obliged to reduce its lending to the Exchequer, and the Exchequer was forced to borrow more from the market by the issue of Treasury Bills; in effect the authorities were obliged to increase the total of Treasury Bills in order to finance the nationalized industries until such time as the Issue Department had sold the stock which it took up at the time of issue. In so far as the additional Treasury Bills were taken up by the banking system, they replaced the nationalized industries' bank borrowing; thus the 'funding' of these bank advances made the banks more rather than less liquid.

87. In 1955 the authorities experienced increasing difficulty in selling nationalized industries' stocks to the public, and a succession of such issues had to be taken up almost entirely by the Issue Department. Not only did the Bank of England become alarmed lest the Issue Department might become 'cluttered up with a lot of unsaleable stock', but the effect upon the liquidity of the banking system was directly contrary to the Government's declared aims of restricting credit and, for that purpose, keeping the liquidity of the banks as near to the conventional minimum as possible. It was therefore decided to suspend issues of nationalized industry stocks and finance the industries from the Exchequer; the Finance Act 1956 gave power

for the Treasury to make advances of long-term capital to these industries, as it had done from the outset for the National Coal Board and other public corporations, and authorized the Treasury to borrow for the purpose of so doing. This system of financing has remained in force since that time.

88. The National Coal Board has from its inception been financed wholly by Exchequer advances (it has power to borrow short-term from the banks, to which it has only resorted once in its history). The capital expenditure of the Post Office is also financed by the Exchequer (until 1954 the sums issued by the Exchequer for this purpose were borrowed from the National Debt Commissioners; since then Exchequer borrowing for this purpose has not been distinguished in this way from other borrowing by the Exchequer). Certain other public corporations (e.g. the Colonial Development Corporation and

TABLE 4

CAPITAL ACCOUNT OF NATIONALIZED INDUSTRIES AND OTHER PUBLIC CORPORATIONS, 1951–1958

£mn.

	1951	1952	1953	1954	1955	1956	1957	1958
Receipts								
Undistributed income before providing for depreciation and stock appreciation	142	146	176	209	180	197	173	175
Additions to tax and interest reserves and capital transfers (net receipts)	34	43	24	−1	−5	24	8	2
Loans from Central Government (net)	61	73	38	100	142	267	604	573
Stock issued for cash *less* stock redeemed	135	228	219	205	367	21	−2	−1
Increase in bank loans and overdrafts outstanding	72	12	−55	70	−96	81	−36	2
Total receipts	444	502	402	583	588	590	747	751
Payments								
Gross fixed capital formation at home	360	409	481	522	564	588	662	689
Increase in value of stocks and work in progress	84	45	−31	−62	39	24	68	37
Net acquisition of other financial assets and net investment abroad	—	48	−48	123	−15	−22	17	25
Total payments	444	502	402	583	588	590	747	751

the New Towns Corporations) also raise their capital finance by borrowing from the Exchequer.

89. Over the period 1951–58 the capital requirements of the nationalized industries and other public corporations were met as in table on opposite page. . .

591. Given the general structure of market facilities, and the relevance of the public sector's debt operations in relation to the Government's economic policy, we have to consider how the financial requirements of the nationalized industries should be provided. As we have noted in Chapter III the first plan of allowing some of these corporations to make their own issues was abandoned, in effect because it tied the hands of the authorities in making new issues by prospectus. At present the funds these industries need, other than purely temporary finance, are provided by the Exchequer, which is thereby left with the task of finding the money by methods of the authorities' own choice and in markets uncluttered by directly competitive issues. The task is, however, a very large one; it has been the largest single factor in making the Government for the first time an habitual net borrower in peacetime, and we have therefore thought it necessary to explore other possibilities.

592. Contrary to general impression, the nationalized industries are required by statute, not 'to break even' (i.e. to make neither loss nor profit) taking one year with another, but to attract sufficient revenue to enable them at least to break even (i.e. at least not to make a loss) taking one year with another. They are thus free in law to include in the prices of their products, as the general run of private industries do, some margin to allow for addition to as well as replacement of their capital equipment. But it would not be realistic to look for a solution in this direction: at present the nationalized industries are in total getting no net return on capital employed, and no rise in prices would increase the receipts of the railways or the coal industry enough to allow a margin for all their capital development. There may be room for some further margin in the electricity industry; at least opportunity might be taken to find some additional capital by refraining from price reduction as costs fall. But we are aware that, when it comes to hard figures, opportunities of this kind are likely to be small in relation to the total new capital needed by these industries, and we have to look therefore for the best way of raising the very large sums that will certainly be required from outside the industries' own revenues.

593. Various proposals have been made for the issue of some kind of equity by the nationalized industries, but none of these proposals seem to us to be either appropriate or feasible. It is in the very nature

of the nationalized industry that it cannot offer a share of the ownership of the business to private investors, and that the benefits of the
success and development of the business accrue not to private shareholders but to the nation. It is therefore appropriate that these
industries should raise such new capital as they require on fixed
interest obligations. Moreover, if a nationalized industry did issue
equity shares, they would presumably not carry a Government
guarantee either of principal or interest; it does not seem likely that a
nationalized industry equity with a fluctuating yield (and perhaps
in some years no yield at all) and without a Government guarantee
would attract much money. Professor E. V. Morgan made a proposal which would overcome some of these objections; his suggestion
was for the issue of a modified form of equity in some of the
nationalized industries. Dividends would be linked not to profits but
to sales, subject to a guaranteed minimum; and there could be no
voting rights. Professor Morgan suggests that:

> 'The shareholder would have the advantage, compared with the holder
> of fixed interest stock, of a fairly good hedge against inflation and a
> prospect of sharing in an increase in the sales-capital ratio resulting
> from increasing efficiency.'

Securities of this kind would in fact have some of the advantages of
index bonds without entailing the confession of failure we find so
repugnant. We doubt however whether in the event they would be
found attractive in any except the electricity industry, and resort to
them in this industry would inevitably reduce the scope for accumulating some capital out of current revenue.

594. Professor Morgan also suggests, as have others, that all the
stocks of the nationalized industries should be issued directly in the
market, as many of them were until 1956. The advantage he sees in
this system is that it might enable these issues to be underwritten in
the market as the new issues of public companies are. The stock
issues of the nationalized industries were not commercially underwritten in this way before 1956, but treated just like issues of Government stock, any unissued balance of a new issue going into the Issue
Department of the Bank of England. It is very doubtful whether it
would be possible to get such large issues underwritten at all; even if
it were possible to need to ensure that they could be so underwritten
might affect the terms of issue. There are also the problems of timing.
If the nationalized industries are to make their own issues, either they
must time them according to the level of their bank borrowing (the
practice until 1956), or they must time them at their own discretion,
or they must be subject to Treasury discretion. Either the first or the
second would be liable to lead to just the same kind of difficulty as

before 1956, and we should prefer that, as long as the securities are equivalent (as most of them must remain) to Government bonds, the monetary authorities should have unfettered discretion in their issue.

595. In the absence of any satisfactory alternative method of raising capital we therefore recommend that the nationalized industries should continue to look to the Treasury to cover all their permanent requirements. For purely temporary needs it may be convenient for them to continue using ordinary bank advances. As these advances in effect have the security of the State behind them it is reasonable that they should be obtainable from the banks at a lower rate than that charged to any private borrower. But their amounts vary at the convenience of the nationalized industries; for meeting this convenience the banks can reasonably look for a rather higher yield than that obtainable on Treasury Bills. We see no advantage in the issue by these industries of their own bills or short bonds: in so far as their financial requirements are fixed for periods fitting these instruments they should borrow through the Treasury, leaving to the monetary authorities the freest possible hand in market management.

41. FINANCING EXPANSION*

342. In private industry many of the most successful concerns have been largely built up from profits ploughed back. . . We have to ask whether a publicly-owned industry ought similarly to finance itself substantially out of its own income, i.e. out of the prices paid by its customers.

343. In our opinion publicly-owned electricity undertakings should not go beyond the limits described in paragraph 341 (i.e. *to make sufficient revenue to cover its costs, maintain its capacity and to contribute appropriate sums to reserves*). If a private undertaking manages in active competition or against potential competition to win large profits these profits are, so to speak, the prize of success. They belong to the undertaking and it is for those to whom the undertaking in turn belongs to decide, with the aid of their advisers, how they shall use their prize. If they decide to use it to expand the undertaking the decision is an entirely proper one. In practice, of course, those who own as shareholders the great undertaking of this country do not take the decision; it is taken for them by the directors and the decision may not always lead to the best use of the capital. Nevertheless the principle is clear enough, the profits have been won in com-

* From *Report of the Committee of Inquiry into the Electricity Supply Industry*, January 1956, Cmd 9672, paras. 342–5.

petition and their disposition is not a matter with which the customers have any concern. Any profit ploughed back because the directors consider it prudent to withhold a portion as capital for future expansion is virtually a compulsory investment of the shareholders' money. It is not a compulsory provision of future capital requirements by the consumers.

344. The electricity supply industry, however, is neither privately owned nor operating in a fully competitive market. The demand for electric power is strong and rising and there is no rivalry over the same territory between competing undertakings. Electricity price-making is an act of policy which we shall discuss in the next chapter. For our present purpose it is necessary to note only these facts. It would be quite possible to raise prices to an extent that would enable a good proportion of the capital needed for expansion to be internally generated. These prices would not, however, have been fixed in open competition and the surpluses accruing would not have been won as the price of efficient rivalry. Further, the policies adopted by the management of the electricity supply industry are not subject to the ultimate sanction which can be exercised by shareholders of a private undertaking.

345. In such circumstances, to use prices charged to the consumers as a device for raising capital for expansion is to impose compulsory saving on electricity users; to make them pay, so to speak, a tax in proportion to their electricity consumption so that the community may build up the electricity industry for the benefit of future consumers. To make present consumers subsidize in this way the capital requirements of future consumers would in our judgment be quite inequitable. But also, we believe it would lead to inefficiency. In our opinion the electricity supply industry should wherever practicable have to face the same kind of problems that other industries face, and in particular it ought to have to fight for its capital by going to the market. To enable it to short-circuit the market by taxing its customers will, we believe, encourage the attitude that capital is easy to come by. If this attitude is allowed to develop capital will undoubtedly be wasted. Neither on grounds of equity nor efficiency do we think it proper for the electricity supply industry to go beyond the limits of self-financing that we have suggested above.

42. THE EXPLOITATION OF THE
PUBLIC SECTOR*

REPLACING ASSETS FROM REVENUE

It is not merely that the nationalized industries have failed to secure out of revenue any contribution to *net* capital formation. Revenue has fallen far short of what was required even to cover depreciation *on a replacement cost basis*. The National Income Blue Book provides for public corporations, as a sector, estimates of capital consumption (i.e. depreciation of capital assets estimated on a current replacement cost basis).[1] Using these, it transpires that *in the decade 1949–58 the public corporations failed even to provide for capital consumption, and revenue fell £1,295 million short of what would have been needed to do so.* Moreover, the deficits tended to grow. Between 1949 and 1953, revenue fell £491 million short of what was needed to provide for capital consumption; between 1954 and 1958 it fell short by £804 million. Only £115 million of the ten-year total was financed by capital transfers, the rest (£1,180 million) had to be financed by borrowing and represented, in a strict sense, so much dead-weight debt burdening these industries. In consequence, the public corporations not merely had to borrow to finance all their net capital formation and all their stockbuilding, but also two-fifths of their estimated capital consumption in the last decade.

Of course, any estimate of depreciation is an arbitrary one, and this is as true of the National Income estimates of capital consumption as of any others. However, there is not much doubt as to the general magnitudes involved. What is even more instructive is to compare the overall financial position of the public corporations with that of the company sector. I attempt to indicate this comparison in the Table overleaf which shows the position of the company sector and of the public corporations in 1949 (as a convenient year soon after nationalization begins) and 1958.

The contrast between the two sectors is extreme. The public corporations had a large deficit after allowing for depreciation, calculated at replacement cost, and a much larger one after allowing for

---

* From John Hughes: *Nationalized Industries in the Mixed Economy*, Fabian Tract 328, October 1960, pp. 8–11. Reprinted by permission of the author and the publishers.

[1] All my data in this paragraph are taken from the Blue Book *National Income and Expenditure*, 1959. Public corporations as a group incorporate some other bodies besides the nationalized industries, but the latter constitute the bulk of this sector. The method of estimating capital consumption, and the distinction between this and depreciation based on 'historical cost', is explained in detail on pages 76-8 of the Blue Book.

PUBLIC CORPORATIONS AND COMPANY SECTOR: CURRENT INCOME AND INCOME AVAILABLE FOR CAPITAL CONSUMPTION AND NET CAPITAL FORMATION (£ MILLIONS)

	Company Sector		Public Corporations	
	1949	1948	1949	1958
Total income	2,360	4,016	177	405
less (−)				
Dividend and Interest	−610	−1,162	−86	−221
Taxes (and remit. abroad)	−885	−1,180	− 2	− 16
Available Income	865	1,674	89	168
Provision for (−)				
Stock Appreciation	−170	+ 22	Nil	+ 5
Capital Consumption	−300	−753	−176	−379
A. *Surplus* (+) *or Deficit* (−)	+395	+943	− 87	−206
B. Net Domestic Capital Formation:				
Fixed	290	606	88	317
Stocks	49	− 5	33	40
Finance available (+) or required (−) after providing for investment (A−B)	+ 56	+342	−208	−563
Capital Transfers	+ 55	+ 13	+ 42	+ 9
Acquisition of Financial Assets (+) or Borrowing (−)[1]	+111	+355	−166	−554

Source: National Income Blue Book, 1959.

[1] This final item includes investment abroad, i.e. companies may be increasing overseas investment rather than accumulating financial assets.

net investment. By 1958 this involved them in borrowing over £500 million p.a. The company sector not only had a large surplus (A. in the Table), after allowing for depreciation, *but even after financing all their net investment in Britain*. The company sector could finance its total investment programme out of current earnings and emerge with a surplus (additional financial assets). Perhaps we should call this the mixed-up economy from now on. For these two sectors buy from and sell to each other.

DEFICITS AND DEBTS

Having indicated the extent to which public corporation revenue falls short of costs of production (and capital consumption), e.g. by £206 million in 1958, the implications now concern us. Firstly, note that this represents an annual subsidy to industrial and commercial users of nationalized industry products. National Income information indicates that about 20 per cent of total sales by public corporations are in fact sales to public corporations, and approximately 25 per cent are sales to individual consumers; thus sales to industrial and commercial users account for more than half the total and are at least twice as big as sales to individual consumers. This is equivalent to an annual subsidy to such industrial users, therefore, of well over £100 million a year (that is, well over half the true deficit of the public corporations on their current costs of production). But it should not be concluded that higher nationalized industry prices would by themselves, *in the absence of price controls within the company sector*, significantly reduce company profits and redistribute income. The conception of an alternative policy has to take into account the complexity of the problem of securing a markedly changed relationship, and distribution of income, as between the two sectors.

Secondly, these deficits represent an increased debt burden for these industries and this does not correspond to any increase in tangible assets. In the case of electricity this problem is least acute since technical advances (especially those arising from economies of scale in power stations) keep down capital costs per kilowatt on new plant; even so, the Herbert Report (Chapter 15) estimated that in 1954–55 the accounting rules followed understated the provision needed for depreciation by £17 million. The problem is most acute in the case of coal and transport. In coal, the annual exhaustion of capacity (which has to be made good if output is to be sustained in the long run) is estimated to be about four million tons a year, costing some £40 million to replace,[1] but very little of this has been covered by coal prices.

THE GROWING BURDEN

The debt burden on the nationalized industries mounts swiftly, and in coal and transport has to be carried upon a shrinking capacity. The capital liabilities of the major nationalized industries (NCB, BTC, electricity, and gas) were about £2,100 million when they were first nationalized. By 1958 they were nearly £5,000 million, and are now well above that as borrowing mounts by over £500 million a year. Already, by 1958, their interest repayments per annum were *over three times* the interest payments due to the initial compensation. In 1949 the interest payments of the public corporations as a whole were £91 million p.a.; by 1958 they had risen to £221 million p.a.; by now the rentier income extracted from the public corporations each year is over £250 million. In the last five years alone the interest charges borne by the public corporations must total £1,000 million. On present trends, we should expect the annual burden

[1] Cf. *NCB—The First Ten Years*, article by Schumacher.

to be about £350 million by the mid-1960s, and interest payments in the next five years to be about £1,500 million.

Thus, instead of a redistribution of income beneficial to the community, nationalized industry pricing has contributed to a rapidly swelling 'prior charge' of payments to rentiers. The surplus income of the companies and property owners in the 'private' sector is lent, under state guarantee, to the industries the state has imposed its price policies upon, and becomes a vast debt burden dragging them down.[1]

In coal the capital charges per ton produced have doubled since 1956. For transport the capital burden is now openly recognized as intolerable, but not before the finances of the BTC had acquired a lunatic appearance. With the capitalization of their deficits, they were even advanced money to pay the interest on the money borrowed to pay the interest on compensation stock and other debt. And *on that* they will have to pay interest. (If the railways *had* succeeded in paying it all out of current revenue, they would have been pursuing a price policy economically damaging to the community and wasteful, as we shall see.) Moreover, the consumer who 'benefits' from low prices will bear the burden of higher prices in the future. Supposing that the community's increased demand for power requires a net investment of £200 million per annum. If this is financed out of current prices, the annual investment charge to the community is not more than that in the long run. Suppose such a programme to be financed by borrowing over a twenty-year period at $5\frac{1}{2}$ per cent or more p.a., as at present, then the long run annual investment charge becomes astronomically high. This is where the Labour movement's crude equation of 'public service' and the 'break-even' rule leads it. In addition, some of the burden may be carried by the workers in the nationalized industries. Rentier, unearned, income has become a 'first charge' on these industries before earned incomes. This is economically damaging to them in those nationalized industries that face substitutes in the private sector. It is politically damaging to the Labour movement, in that the press can argue a direct conflict of interest between wage earners in the nationalized industries and all other wage or salary earners *qua* consumers. The growing transfers to rentiers go uncommented upon. The system is therefore politically conservative in its implications.

---

[1] Keynes had thought that the euthanasia of the rentier was a necessity if full employment was to be sustained; with this kind of economic policy, nationalization give parasitism a new lease of life.

43. THE FINANCIAL AND ECONOMIC
OBLIGATIONS*

A NEW FINANCIAL FRAMEWORK

17. In the Government's view there would be no advantage in altering the basic financial and economic principles which the nationalized undertakings are by their statutes required to observe. If, however, these principles are to provide a satisfactory basis for their operation in the public interest they need to be interpreted more precisely in the form of financial objectives for the nationalized undertakings generally.

18. The main heads under which clarification or restatement of the obligations and relationships envisaged in the nationalizing Acts is needed are as follows:

> Revenue Account
> Capital Account
> Prices and Costs.

REVENUE ACCOUNT

19. The Government consider that the financial objectives of the nationalized undertakings under their Statutes should now in general be interpreted on the following lines:

(a) Surpluses on Revenue Account should be at least sufficient to cover deficits on Revenue Account *over a five-year period*: in arriving at the surpluses and deficits for each year there should be charged against revenue the items normally so chargeable (including interest, and depreciation on the historic cost basis).

(b) Provision should also be made from revenue for:
  (i) such an amount as may be necessary to cover the excess of depreciation calculated on replacement cost basis over depreciation calculated on historic cost as in (a) above.[1]
  (ii) adequate allocations to general reserves which will be available *inter alia* as a contribution towards their capital development and as a safeguard against premature obsolescence and similar contingencies.

20. It is the Government's view that in general anything more than

* From *The Financial and Economic Obligations of the Nationalized Industries*, April 1961, Cmnd 1337, paras. 17–33.

[1] The undertakings would not be required specifically to make good now any under-provision (i.e. on account of the difference between the historic cost basis and the replacement cost basis), which has already occurred in years prior to the operation of these new arrangements.

a five-year period as the balancing period for the formula in paragraph 19 would be too long for effectiveness. They propose, in consultation with each board which has financial autonomy under the Acts, to agree a framework on the above lines for the next five years as an experimental period, but the operation will be subject to review each year in the light of events inside and outside the industry. This procedure will be applied in all the major nationalized industries,[1] including the Post Office.

21. The wide differences in the economic conditions of the various nationalized undertakings have been emphasized earlier in this paper. Their earning power, total depreciation provision and reserve requirements will vary according to their prospective commercial, technological and financial development. The criteria in paragraph 19 would be consistent with the general run of the existing statutory obligations, but they cannot be expressed as one standard formula to be applied to all nationalized undertakings alike.

22. Experience has shown, however, a general need for nationalized industries—even those which were at one time reckoned to be relatively free from commercial risk—to build up adequate reserves to deal with contingencies which may affect their capital as well as their revenue accounts. Moreover, there are powerful grounds in the national interest for requiring these undertakings to make a substantial contribution towards the cost of their capital development out of their own earnings, and so reduce their claims upon the nation's savings and the burden on the Exchequer: this is particularly so for those undertakings which are expanding fast and which have relatively large capital needs. In normal circumstances, the desirable level of reserves should be related to the amount of capital employed in the business.

23. It follows from all these considerations that the State, as owner or guarantor of the capital of the nationalized industries (which are investing over £800 million a year, more than half of which comes from the Exchequer), would expect capital employed in this kind of business to earn a higher rate of return than the cost of the money to the Exchequer. The objective for each undertaking will be determined in the light of its own circumstances, needs and capabilities in relation to the criteria in paragraph 19. For some, the objectives may be expressed in terms of progress towards an appropriate level of self-financing of their capital expenditure, concurrently with the provision of suitable contributions to reserve. For others, the objective may be in terms of a specified rate of return on capital employed.

[1] Separate proposals have been made (Cmnd 1248 of December 1960) for some of the nationalized transport undertakings, including the railways.

CAPITAL ACCOUNT

24. The existing procedures for discussion and authorization of matters concerning investment and borrowing will be continued and can be codified as follows:

   (i) The Government will each year discuss with the undertaking and approve the general lines of its plans for development and capital expenditure for the next five years ahead and be ready to agree to long-term commitments as appropriate.

   (ii) In the light of (i) the Government will each year fix an upper limit on the amounts to be spent on investment by the undertaking during the two years ahead.

   (iii) The Government will approve proposed borrowings on the basis of an annual reasoned estimate submitted by the undertaking.

   (iv) The Government will require to be kept informed of the extent to which the undertaking is proposing to invest new capital in projects which are expected to yield a relatively low return.

25. These requirements flow from the Government's responsibility to keep public sector investment generally within the nation's resources, as well as from the Government's role as provider of public capital. It would be the Government's task to satisfy themselves that the procedure within each organization for scrutinizing and approving capital expenditure was effective.

26. The existing arrangements under which capital expenditure in excess of the approved ceiling, or borrowing in excess of the estimates, are subject to investigation and discussion between the undertakings and the Departments would continue. These procedures fit in with the recent arrangements under which Parliament has been given more detailed information about the estimates of investment and borrowing from the Exchequer and the Government's undertaking to inform Parliament of the reasons for any marked variation between the estimate and the out-turn.

27. While the proposed arrangements are adapted to the present system, under which the industries resort to the Exchequer for their long-term capital requirements, the proposed clarification of financial obligations and the improvement in financial performance would be necessary and desirable in any event. The reasons which caused the Government to discontinue in 1956 the procedure of borrowing from the market, with the support of a Government guarantee, and to withdraw the financing of the transport, gas and electricity industries from the market into the Exchequer are still valid. While the

Government recognize the force of the arguments in favour of requiring nationalized bodies to raise money from the market on their own credit, they see no possibilities of an early move in this direction. They accept the view of the Committee under the chairmanship of Lord Radcliffe on the Working of the Monetary System (Cmnd 827, paragraph 595) that such unguaranteed borrowing is not a realistic alternative, at least for the present. The amounts of money needed are much too large to be raised in the open market without Government support and the industries are, of necessity, closely associated in the public mind with the Government, so that it would be difficult for the market to regard them as independent financial concerns. Whatever may be the possibilities for the future, an improvement in the financial record as contemplated under the present proposals would be a prerequisite.

28. The procedures in paragraphs 20 to 26 would be applicable as long as the financial performance and prospects of the undertaking were satisfactory in terms of the new financial framework. In other cases the Government would be bound to take a closer interest. Thus inability or prospective inability to meet the requirements in paragraph 19 (*a*) would be regarded as falling so far short of the objectives that the undertaking would be required to propose specific measures for righting the situation: it would naturally consult the Minister about these and the Minister would expect to be satisfied on various issues, including the financial justification for major investment proposals. Even if the undertaking were fulfilling the requirement in paragraph 19 (*a*), inability to achieve the objective set for it under paragraph 23, would be regarded as inadequate performance. In this case, the undertaking would be under an obligation to inform the Minister of the general plans for preventing the situation from deteriorating further and for making up the leeway.

PRICES AND COSTS

29. A clear definition of each Board's financial obligations inevitably raises the question of the extent to which the Boards should have freedom in their pricing policies. Although the Government possess no formal power to fix prices in the nationalized industries, nationalized undertakings have, in fixing their prices, given great weight to considerations of the national interest brought to their attention.

30. Increased prices would not be the only way in which nationalized undertakings could carry out the prescribed financial obligations. For a variety of reasons, such as fructification of investment and reduction of unprofitable activities, combined with continuing im-

provements in commercial efficiency, some of the industries will be capable of increased productivity, part of which should be available to improve their financial results. The aim of the industries generally will naturally be to secure the necessary additions to their net revenue as far as possible by reductions in costs. The Government recognize, however, that the industries must have freedom to make upward price adjustments especially where their prices are artificially low.

31. While recognizing the case for greater freedom and flexibility in the pricing policies of nationalized industries the Government must interest themselves in the prices of these goods and services which are basic to the life of the community and some of which contain a monopolistic element. In addition to the formal arrangements for the representation of consumers' views through Consultative Councils in the various industries and for the regulation of fares and charges in certain cases, the existing informal arrangements are that the Chairmen of the Boards ascertain in advance the views of the appropriate Ministers when they prepare to make substantial changes in the level of their prices. In the Government's view these arrangements should continue. If a Board decided to modify their own proposals by reason of views expressed by the Minister it would be open to them to require a written statement of those views, which could be published by the Minister or the Board, and to propose an appropriate adjustment of their financial objectives where, in their opinion, this modification would significantly impair their ability to meet them.

32. Financial performance is affected not only by the level of prices but by the level of costs. Costs may in turn be significantly affected by the amount of commercially unprofitable activities carried on by individual undertakings. These activities will, so far as practicable, have been taken into account in fixing the financial standard for each undertaking. To the extent that commercially unprofitable activities are subsequently imposed from outside, a Board would be entitled to ask for an adjustment of its financial objectives.

CONCLUSION

33. The nationalized industries are from their size and nature bound to play a major role in the economic life of the country. They cannot, however, be regarded only as very large commercial concerns which may be judged mainly on their commercial results: all have, although in varying degrees, wider obligations than commercial concerns in the private sector. The object of these proposals is to find for each industry or Board a reasonable balance between these two concepts. The Government believe that the closer definition now proposed for the financial and economic obligations of the industries

should help improve their performance and morale. It should also reduce the occasion and need for outside intervention in the affairs of the industries and enable them to make the maximum contribution towards their own development and the well-being of the community as a whole.

44. CALCULATING FINANCIAL RETURNS*

THE TESTS

384. Both in view of the importance of deciding for the future what should be the size and shape of the railways and because of the very large sums of money involved, it might have been expected that, in the first place, fairly precise calculations would have been made by the Commission—

    (i) of the additional net return to be secured by each proposal, and

    (ii) of the overall profitability—after that proposal had been carried out—of the service affected by it;

and that, secondly, these calculations would have been critically examined by the Minister of Transport and the Treasury before approval was given to the necessary borrowing.

385. The evidence shows that the Commission duly calculated the additional net return on each scheme ((i) above), but that they did not and, under their existing accounting arrangements, could not make the other calculation—that is, the estimate of profitability that would result. As to the critical examination by departments, this has only recently been undertaken—that is, more than five years after the Modernization Plan began.

386. Thus the financial test has not been fully applied. Your Committee do not overlook the number of examples they were given of how modernized equipment had led to improvements in net revenue even greater than anticipated; nor the point that a grand total of expected betterments in net revenue which exceeds the Commission's deficit at the start of the Plan would appear to secure a future profit. But the fact remains that large expenditures have been undertaken on modernizing parts of the undertaking, without any precise calculation of what the profitability of those parts will be on completion.

387. Your Committee are surprised that the Ministry of Transport and the Treasury have not until recently examined the returns to be secured from the schemes for which they were lending public money. In their report on the National Coal Board, the Select Committee

* From *Report from the Select Committee on Nationalized Industries: British Railways*, July 1960, H.C. 254, paras. 384–90.

on Nationalized Industries (Reports and Accounts) said in April 1958:

> 'Great sums of public money are involved here . . . The Board . . . must find themselves frequently taking decisions on projects of border-line profitability. There would seem to be a strong case that the Ministry, who are the judges of 'where the public interest lies', should as a matter of course be judges in these cases; and there can be no doubt that they should be told of the projects of border-line profitability for which they are being asked to lend money, so that they can apply some financial test. As stated above, there is no case for them applying a further *technical* test—for schemes are amply tested in that way by the Board's experts—but the Ministry should at least make a greater financial check on the anticipated return on money they lend than they do at present . . . Your Committee therefore recommend that a change should be made, and that the Board should present the Ministry each year, not only with the average yield expected from the total investment, but also an account of the major schemes estimated to give the lowest yield, and the reasons why those schemes are put forward. This would help the Board and would not involve the Ministry in detailed consideration of the technical aspects of the major schemes, or of any consideration of a large number of small schemes.'[1]

This recommendation was accepted by the Government at the time.[2]

388. Your Committee are not saying that the financial tests mentioned above (paragraph 384) are the only tests that should properly be applied; but they are the first that should be applied. The Ministry of Transport and the Treasury, who stand in their relation to the Commission as bankers and financial advisers, should behave as such in the first place.

389. Thereafter, other considerations of a national economic or social character may rightly be applied by the Ministry, and these may rightly persuade them to approve borrowings for schemes which are not expected to yield much more than enough to cover the borrowing rate of interest, and which are far below normal industrial returns.

THE YIELD

390. In Part I of the Report (paragraph 221), your Committee comment on the lack of agreement between Commission and Ministry about how to reckon the rate of return on any one large investment. They do not express any view on what the yield should be for new railway schemes. They wish however to make two points in this connection. First, it must not be forgotten that the Commis-

[1] H.C. 187 of 1957–8, paras. 31, 33.
[2] *H.C. Deb.*, 591, col. 845.

sion reckon that half of the modernization plan is replacement, and this may well affect the decision as to what is the right yield on the cost of such schemes; and secondly, that a scheme to be justified solely on financial grounds should normally aim, after providing for all overheads and depreciation and the share of central charges, to give a return of more than the interest on the relevant loan capital.

CHAPTER VII

The Minister and the Enterprise

The statutory powers of the responsible minister *vis-à-vis* the enterprise and the manner of their exercise have frequently been described and analysed; but the possibilities and limitations of ministerial action have probably never been so realistically defined as by Mr Frank Milligan, in the article from which *Extract 45* is taken.

Lack of ease about the prevalent informal or 'old boy' relationships between Minister and Board and about the consequent difficulty of assigning clear responsibility for policy decisions has been frequently expressed ever since the early days of post-war nationalization, when the 'general direction' clauses were under debate. One of the clearest expressions of opinion on this issue, providing the starting point for much subsequent discussion, came from the 'Herbert' Committee, which considered that questions of 'public interest', which were the Minister's business, could and should be sharply distinguished from those of 'commercial policy', which were the Board's (*Extract 46*). This distinction, however, rested on particular views about the nature of the Board's responsibilities which by no means won general acceptance (see, for instance, Chapter VI of Professor W. A. Robson's *Nationalised Industry and Public Ownership*).

The same 'demarcation' issue has been frequently taken up by the Select Committee on Nationalized Industries which, as a parliamentary body, is naturally anxious that Members of the House should know precisely who is responsible for what. Its first animadversions on this subject are contained in the Report on the Coal Board (H. of C. Paper 187–I of 1957–8). It returned to the charge in the Report on the Air Corporations (*Extract 47*). In its Report on British Railways it provided a most useful analysis of the actual relationship between the Minister of Transport and the British Transport Commission and envisaged a relationship between the two not dissimilar from that prescribed for the electricity supply industry by the 'Herbert' Report (*Extracts 48 and 49*).

It cannot be said that this issue has been clearly decided one way or the other. Moreover, it would seem that the projected reorganization of the responsibilities of the British Transport Commission may represent a move away from, rather than towards, the type of Minister-Board relationship which the 'Herbert' Committee and the Select Committee have held to be desirable (see Chapter III, *Extract 14*). The question therefore arises whether the original concept of the public corporation will undergo substantial modification. That circumstances should confront us with this question lends interest to the 'dissident' views of Professor H. R. G. Greaves which were expressed on the eve of the post-war spate of nationalizations (*Extract 50*).

45. THE LIMITS OF MINISTERIAL ACTION*

In a sense there are no limits, at either extremity, to the range of control open to a Minister. To the extent that it rests with him to decide, he might on the one hand be content merely to appoint a governing board and give them absolute powers over the nationalized industry, with virtually automatic reappointment. In such a situation he could effectively divest himself of all control, and his statutory functions would become the mere formalities of a *roi fainéant*. At the other extreme, a Minister might decide to direct the actual operations himself, using his control of the board's composition to ensure its complete tractability.

The two cases are, of course, equally unreal; but they deserve mention nevertheless, to emphasize that having regard to the law alone, a Minister may choose to be anything from a cipher to an absolute autocrat. In this, as in so many other aspects of their government, the British have chosen a legal framework permitting the maximum flexibility, and have left the determination of actual working arrangements to the persons concerned, always with the unspoken premise that the force of convention is more powerful than the caprice of the individual. All would agree that it is virtually inconceivable that a Minister should be free in practice to choose either of the roles suggested above. The very forces in the community which gave rise to nationalization and determined the form it was to take, will continue to exert pressure on the Minister through Parliament, party, and the other organs of public experession, and more immediately through his colleagues in the Government; and any Minister following either course would soon find his political career cut short.

* From Frank Milligan: 'Ministerial Control of the British Nationalized Industries', *Canadian Journal of Economics and Political Science*, Vol. XVII, May 1951, pp. 179–83. Reprinted by permission of the author and the editors of the *Journal*.

Within the limits imposed by these forces there is still a significant range of possibilities. Even within this range, however, the Minister's freedom to determine his role is qualified by factors which, if not entirely beyond his control, at least owe more to his situation than to his personal predilections. The immediate task, then, becomes the modest one of considering some of these aspects of the Minister's situation which will condition the control exercised by him, within the broader limits imposed by the main stream of British politics.

In the first place, control over a nationalized industry will be limited in much the same way as control of a large Government department by certain basic characteristics of ministerial appointments. In relation to the activities of the corporation concerned, the Minister is a layman; the career which has led to his appointment has been in the business of politics and not in the business of the industry. He may indeed have been associated with the industry during some period in his past, but it is highly unlikely that that association will have been so intimate, so long, so recent, and at such high levels that he can hope to compete with the board and its officers in expert knowledge of their operations. Moreover, not only is he a layman, he is also something of a transient, brought to office by a particular combination of circumstances quite unrelated to the affairs of the industry and likely to be replaced at almost any time by a different combination of circumstances. In these respects, then, much of the analysis of relations between Ministers and their departments, such as that found in Jennings's *Cabinet Government* or Laski's *Parliamentary Government in England*, is scarcely less pertinent to the question of the Ministers' relations with public boards.

The similarities between the two relationships are all too often overlooked. Fears are expressed that instability and confusion will beset the nationalized industries as a result of the wilfulness (or, it may be, enthusiasm) and ignorance of the all-powerful Ministers. But critics who express such fears make two errors which could have been avoided by studying the relations between Ministers and their departmental officers: they underestimate the influence of the permanent officials, and they overestimate the foolhardiness of the Ministers. It is true that Ministers have on occasion acted precipitously and even foolishly, in disregard of the counsel of their advisers, but few have survived such an action for long. . .

At the other extreme, one encounters the notion that, because the Minister is inexpert and transient, he can wield little effective control. On the face of it, there is much to be said in support of the contention. The affairs of the nationalized industries are vast and complex. It is obvious that no Minister, however assiduously he applies himself, can ever hope to appreciate all the factors that must be considered in coming to a decision on the industry's activities. Mr Gaitskell's action in compelling adoption of the winter surcharge on electricity actually lends weight to this argument; the Electricity Authority was able to demonstrate that its opposition had been justified and the surcharges were dropped. One or two instances of this nature, it might be thought, and any Minister would be so chastened as to become very chary of intervening.

Or again, one might point to the fact, already indicated, that in arriving at any decision concerning a board's activities, the Minister is dependent almost entirely on information and advice from the board itself and its officers. He may indeed, as Mr Gaitskell did, seek independent advice, based perhaps on a special inquiry, but even such advice is likely to prove inferior to the judgment of 'the men who make the power'. And if in the case of the ordinary department of government this freedom to consult independent advice can be considered wise, as Lloyd George once wrote, only ' . . . if that liberty is tactfully and judiciously exercised by the Minister and wisely acquiesced in by the service,'[1] how much more sparingly should it be used by a Minister in relation to a nationalized industry. Senior civil servants may grow up in a tradition of 'my Minister, right or wrong', but heads of the nationalized industries, bearing a large measure of the responsibility for the success or failure of their enterprises, are likely to be far more jealous of their authority.

Once again, many of the arguments have been put forward in the context of a Minister's relations with his departmental officials. And in so far as the situations are similar, the rebuttal made by Professor Laski[2] is equally valid in connection with the Minister's relations with a public board. It should not be necessary to repeat this rebuttal, but it may be useful to call to mind one of the central themes in the argument: that Ministers need not possess expert knowledge of their departments (or nationalized industries) in order to control them effectively; that, on the contrary, 'the best type of Cabinet Minister is a really intelligent man of the world who can think rapidly and in an orderly way upon the multifarious questions he has to decide. His first quality is common sense; his second, the art of judging men'. Then follows the crux of Laski's argument: 'The very nature of the competition for political place assures us that most Cabinet Ministers will have these qualities.'

The situations are not, however, completely similar. In his relations with a public board a Minister is not called upon to sit in judgment constantly on the affairs of the industry, forming the apex of a tightly-

---

[1] *War Memoirs*, III, 1172, quoted by W. I. Jennings in *Cabinet Government* (Cambridge, 1946), 96.
[2] *Parliamentary Government in England* (London, 1938), 280–308.

knit hierarchy through which there is a steady flow of memoranda upwards and decisions downwards. It was, in fact, in order to avoid this situation that the public corporation was evolved, wherein the board becomes the apex, and the Minister is given an external role, as a sort of *deus ex machina* who intervenes at the crucial moment in the name of interests beyond the comprehension of a rather single-minded board.

However, too much weight should not be given to this idea. Both the Minister and the members of the board will normally be anxious to establish and maintain close liaison. Exponents of this argument, in fact, misconceive the basic relationship existing between the Ministers and their boards. They assume a dichotomy of outlook which will not ordinarily exist, given that degree of mutual confidence between the political head and the directors of the industry which it is reasonable to expect. What is more likely, and what is indicated by experience to date, is a situation in which (as Mr Eden remarked, but with a rather different intention), 'there is no clear line of demarcation . . . between the Board and the Minister'. There may well be a difference in outlook, but one of degree rather than of kind. After all, the men who become Ministers and the men they appoint to public boards are not so very dissimilar in experience and in qualities of mind. And just as the Minister will normally recognize and respect the board's more intimate knowledge of the industry's capacities and limitations, so the board members will recognize and welcome the special contribution to the direction of their undertaking which the Minister's experience and position enable and entitle him to make.

It is the nature of this special contribution which finally determines, if not the full scope of the Minister's intervention, at least its irreducible minimum. He may do more. His interest in and influence on the operations of the industry may go far beyond what is dictated by his role of trustee for interests beyond the board's comprehension. It depends on the Minister himself, and on the relations he establishes with his board. In any event he will discharge this basic trusteeship unless he is an exceptionally poor sort of Minister. Nationalization was, to some extent at least, a declaration that the public had interests in these undertakings which could not be expressed effectively within the restricted limits of the market, or the courts of law. These interests may have concerned their investment or employment policies, or the effects of their activities on health and public welfare, or strategic questions involving outputs, capacities, and services. Each Minister must evaluate such considerations, consciously or unconsciously, before he can arrive at a clear idea of how far the public interest requires his intervention. Intervention, then, is simply a question of where the line should be drawn, and the general principle remains that for each Minister there will be a line, indicating the minimum degree of control that he can permit himself to exercise. Beyond that, it is possible for him to push his interest to the point where it fails to meet with a receptive response from his board, the point of diminishing returns in this relationship.

46. THE POWERS AND DUTIES OF THE MINISTER*

492. Our terms of reference are to inquire into the organization and efficiency of the electricity supply industry. We feel that we cannot completely discharge this task without some reference to the relations between the Minister and the industry.

493. The industry belongs to the nation. The Central Electricity Authority, the Generation Board, and the Area Boards envisaged in our proposals are the chosen instruments for the purpose of operating the industry and they must be responsible to the Minister, who in turn is responsible to Parliament, for an account of their stewardship.

494. In our opinion the most important task falling to the Minister is the appointment of Authority and Board members. No task surpasses this in importance, for unless the best appointments are made the industry's efficiency must suffer. In this industry the task is peculiarly difficult. The industry is a monopoly with a strongly rising tide of demand. It could carry for long periods, without any very obvious symptoms of inefficiency, men of mediocre talents. The greatest care and skill are therefore needed in making the key appointments. We are well aware of the heavy load of responsibility and work that falls on the Minister and his principal advisers, but we venture to say that few tasks could justifiably claim more of their time and attention than this one of choosing men.

495. What other tasks must fall to the Minister depends very much on the framework in which the industry is to operate. If our conception of the industry as a strictly commercial undertaking is accepted then many questions answer themselves. If prices are to be related to costs and the industry is to go to the market for its capital in competition with other industries the Minister will be involved in few policy questions. He will from time to time have to adjudicate where there are differences of opinion inside the industry. He will, in the last resort, have to decide whether to authorize the issue of a direction by the Authority.

* From *Report of the Committee of Inquiry into the Electricity Supply Industry*, January 1956, Cmd 9672, paras. 492–9.

496. The further our conception is departed from, the more policy questions will the Minister have to decide. If the fuel industries are to continue to pledge the national credit through the medium of the Treasury guarantee, the scale of investment in the industry is no longer fully subject to the market test. The volume of investment is then a political matter for which the Minister must take responsibility. Similarly, if some class of consumer, such as the rural consumer, is to be subsidized in one way or another, this too is a political decision to be made by Ministers, approved by Parliament, and conveyed by the Minister of Fuel and Power.

497. We have expressed the view that the less the principle of commercial operation is invaded the better it will be for the efficiency of the industry. Taking the long view we believe this to be of the greatest importance to the success of nationalization. But it must be recognized that unless Parliament and the Government are prepared to deny themselves the power, always and in every particular, to require the industry to act on other than purely economic considerations, the Minister must be armed with the necessary authority. We would however, urge that the lines of demarcation between the industry and the Minister should be clear. There should be no doubt as to where the responsibility lies when the industry is acting on other than purely economic considerations.

498. Against this background, we see the principal duties of the Minister as follows:

(a) to make the appointments to the Central Authority and the Boards;

(b) to satisfy himself through the reports of the Central Authority and the individual Boards that the industry is being run efficiently as a commercial concern, or, to the extent that it is not run as a commercial concern, in accordance with the directions issued by him;

(c) to authorize the amount of capital to be raised and the terms of issue;

(d) to give the industry precise instructions if and when it is required to act in some way different from what would be dictated by purely economic considerations;

(e) to decide whether or not to give consent to the issue of directions by the Central Authority in the rare cases in which this is likely to be required.

499. It follows from the foregoing that the Minister must retain the general powers given to him in the Electricity Act, 1947, to issue directions.

47. A FORMIDABLE COLLECTION*

215. The extent of the Minister's statutory powers over the Corporations was set out in a memorandum put before Your Committee ...; but, as the memorandum explained, in practice the relationship is closer than the statutes actually require. There is a constant exchange of information, and frequent discussions between the sides. The closest co-operation is inevitable, say the Ministry, not only because the activities of the airlines may have an impact on matters of national policy, but also because the Minister has to answer for the Corporations in Parliament. The result is a relationship of 'complete frankness and goodwill' (Q. 76). The Ministry stress the paternal interest they take in the airlines' troubles (Q. 2030).

216. That the relationship is both warm and mutual was shown by the tributes paid by the Corporations to the department (Q. 1204, 1220; 563–4). The atmosphere of trust is exemplified by the fact that the Ministry, in discussing with the airlines such things as their fares or their maintenance, are content to rely to a large extent on information and advice obtained from the airlines themselves (Q. 2185). But the strongest evidence of the co-operation existing between the two sides is given by the extent to which the Corporations tacitly allow powers to the Minister which the statutes do not.

217. These unofficial powers comprise a formidable collection. Thus, although the Minister has no express statutory control over the Corporations' capital expenditure, they always seek his approval (and that of the Treasury) for orders of aircraft, and these amount to 80 per cent. of their total capital expenditure. They have agreed not to open new routes without the Minister's consent. They fly on various routes, domestic and international, because he asks them to, and they lose money in the process. They seek his approval for all fares and rates on non-international routes. They refrain, at his wish, from keeping aircraft specially available for charter work (page 11). They come to him for permission before creating or investing in a subsidiary company (Q. 213), and, in effect, get his authority before they dispose of such an investment (Q. 1956).

218. In discussing some of these points individually in this Report, Your Committee have noted the powerful arguments adduced in favour of the Minister's use of these non-statutory powers. It is significant, as noted above, that the Corporations have accepted the assumption of these powers by the Minister, generally without protest.

* From *Report from the Select Committee on Nationalized Industries: The Air Corporations*, May 1959, H.C. 213, paras. 215–18.

Relations between Ministry and Corporations are clearly good, and the last thing Your Committee want to do is to disturb such a relationship. But, faced with the total extent of the Minister's non-statutory powers, they are bound to ask if these do not add up to a degree of control far in excess of that envisaged by the statutes under which BOAC and BEA were created, and so lead to an undesirable diminution in the authority of the Chairmen and Boards of the Corporations, and in their feeling of responsibility. Your Committee consider it essential to the efficient running on commercial lines of the Air Corporations that there should be a clear-cut division of responsibility between the Chairmen on the one hand and the Minister on the other. When the Minister wishes, on grounds of national interest, to override the commercial judgment of a Chairman, he should do so by a directive, which should be published.

48. MINISTER AND COMMISSION*

61. The Minister's statutory position, *vis-à-vis* the Commission, is set out in a memorandum that was laid before Your Committee (Appendix I). His powers are similar to those exercised over other nationalized Boards (Q. 212). They include the appointment of members of the Commission, the right to approve of the general lines along which any major reorganization is to take place, the power to issue general directions to the Commission on matters affecting the public interest, an extensive control over the Commission's finances, and the right to obtain full information from the Commission about any of their activities. The organization within the Ministry that exists to carry out these functions was also delineated (Appendix 1).

62. It is axiomatic that the Minister requires to work in very close contact with a nationalized industry, and *vice versa*; the activities of such an industry so frequently have political implications that there must be a constant exchange of information and advice between the two sides (Q. 275). One aspect of the relationship is that the Minister of Transport has to answer about 200 parliamentary questions every year touching on the activities of the British Transport Commission, and many of these are framed in a way that is critical of the Commission. The Commission, being unable to defend themselves in the House, can only turn to the Minister to do this for them; but he has not got the statutory responsibility, and may not have the

* From *Report from the Select Committee on Nationalized Industries: British Railways*, July 1960, H.C. 254, paras. 61–83.

K

wish, to do so. This is clearly an uneasy situation, and some criticisms are bound to go undefended (Q. 1659).

63. The Minister's responsibilities are, of course, much wider than a concern only with the operations of BTC; they take in the functioning of the transport system throughout the country as a whole. The Ministry, with the Treasury, are concerned to consider the future of transport conditions in the country; although it is left to the Commission to make their own assessment, through market research, of what their traffics are likely to be in the years ahead, this assessment would be checked at the Ministry (Q. 37–9, 43). There are, it seems, some misgivings at the Ministry itself about whether they are at present strongly enough equipped to deal with research on this score (Q. 44). It would appear that the increase in motor-car travel in recent years has been underestimated by both Commission and Ministry (Q. 1929–30), as has perhaps been the increase of road traffic in general that was to be expected as a result of recent expenditure on new roads (Q. 1935–6).

64. The Minister is responsible for transport nationally; it follows that, in the case of nationalized transport it should be he who defines what is best for the national interest (and it is on that ground that he can, if necessary, give directions of a general nature to the Commission). The Commission have set out their view of how this problem affects them. On the one hand, they have, they say, 'to act like a normal commercial undertaking and . . . base their decision on business considerations. . . . On the other hand, the Commission's services are often expected to be guided primarily by the public interest. . . . These two approaches, the commercial and the often unprofitable public service, frequently conflict' (Cmnd 813, para. 62). This conflict involves decisions on matters of national economic and social policy; elements of strategy, of what is needed for national defence, have not come into it, because the existing railway system is considered quite adequate for this purpose in its present form (Q. 65, 162). (Under the 1953 Act, power is reserved to the Minister to direct the Commission to engage in activities in the interests of national defence—Annex I to Appendix 1—but this power has never been used—Q. 208.) In this conflict between business considerations and wider interests, the Commission have from time to time themselves decided, without consulting the Minister, what it is that the public needs; their statutory duty includes having a due regard 'to the needs of the public, agriculture, commerce and industry' (1 & 2 Eliz. 2, C. 13, s. 25 (1)); and they have provided services to meet those needs, even though this may have run counter to their duty to act as a commercial concern (Q. 253–5; Q. 1904).

65. The Ministry's view is different. They believe that no conflict

should exist for the Commission, because it should not be for them to have to decide where the public interest lies. If for example some of the capital schemes that comprise the Modernization Plan cannot be justified on strict commercial grounds, as offering a good return on the money to be invested, then it should be for the Ministry, and not for the Commission, to say that they can be justified on social grounds (for example, because they offer a service that is necessary for the people in the area) or for other reasons (Q. 119, 123-7, 158). When questions of reductions of the Commission's services arise, it would in the first place be for a statutory body, the Transport Users Consultative Committee, to consider them (Q. 184). It is the Ministry's belief that, so far as the Modernization Plan is concerned, the Commission have in fact based some of their decisions in the past on social grounds, without seeking or getting the advice of the Ministry as arbiters of the public interest (Q. 1904, 1931).

66. The Ministry thus impinge on the activities of the Commission for two reasons; first, because their statutory function requires it of them, and secondly because they have a broader duty of seeing that the decisions of the Commission conform to the public good. The way the Ministry involve themselves in the Commission's affairs must now be considered. It can be looked at under three headings: the manner in which the Ministry control the capital finance of the Commission, the influence they exert over fares and charges, and their impact on the Commission's general managerial functions.

CONTROL OVER CAPITAL

67. The Ministry believe that, in conjunction with the Treasury, they have the large responsibility of making sure that public funds are being advanced on a reasonable basis (Q. 157). This responsibility stems from two different sources. First, under Section 4 (2) of the 1947 Act, the Minister's approval must be given from time to time to the Commission's general lines of reorganization and development involving substantial capital outlay. Secondly, under Section 88 of the 1947 Act, the Minister's consent and that of the Treasury must be given to the Commission's proposed borrowings.

68. Under the first head, the Ministry see that the annual investment in the Commission conforms to the national plans for investment as a whole (Q. 4); the Commission's plans may have to suffer for this reason. An instance of this is the way in which sharp, sudden cuts can be imposed on the Commission's capital plans whenever Government policy so requires. Thus in September 1957 the Commission were informed that they would have to restrict their total spending for 1958 to £170 million, and for 1959 to £175 million—these figures

being respectively £15 million and £19 million less than the sums that had been provisionally agreed earlier (Q. 823, 836). The effect of this was that at least one major scheme had to be cut back—causing the loss of the direct penalties paid to the contractors, a slowing down of work in their own shops in order to avoid paying compensation in other jobs, and the wasting of a considerable amount of planning work that had been done (Q. 824–6); the total cost of this action was impossible to identify, but it might have been considerable (Q. 829–30).

69. Another way in which the Ministry's powers over the Commission's investment can be illustrated is by considering the actions taken in recent times. Both the original Modernization Plan in 1954 and the Reappraisal of 1958–59, being 'programmes of reorganization or development involving substantial outlay', were submitted to the Government and received their general blessing (Q. 34): and the Commission found their schemes within the Plan getting a general approval (Q. 841–2). But when recently the department began to believe that the future of the Plan as a whole was 'less rosy', they were able to impose a very considerable degree of new control over investment plans (Q. 5, 105, 118); all schemes costing more than £250,000 now have to go to the Ministry before they can be authorized (Q. 1863), and they are examined with considerably more stringency than before (Q. 48–9).

70. The second point at which the Minister can control the Commission's capital plans is by the use of his powers over their borrowing. The Ministry act, as was said, as the Commission's bankers (Q. 1888). In doing so, they would not be able to check the technical aspects of the plans for which they are asked to provide money, because they have not themselves got a technical staff (Q. 160, 174–5); they could only ask intelligent questions on the basis of the financial information given to them by the Commission themselves (Q. 122), and, if necessary, query the conclusions which the Commission have drawn from that information (Q. 167, 173). But, in the early days of modernization at least, the Commission's experience was that the schemes and budgets that they put forward to the Ministry were not altered very much (Q. 841–2).

71. Yet, here again, the Ministry have been able to vary the degree of their control as and when they have required, and the extent of this has increased as the Commission's financial position has deteriorated (Q. 848).

72. Another aspect of the Ministry's powers over borrowing is the way in which the Commission's forward planning is held on a very close rein by the department. The Ministry say that at present the Commission are able to plan on a three-year basis; the sum to be

allowed for the coming year is fixed definitely, and amounts for the two succeeding years are also provisionally agreed. This, they say, should be sufficient to allow forward plans to be made on a reasonably firm basis (Q. 117). The Commission's view of things is rather different. They point out that, if they are to be making the long-term contracts which their present schemes demand, they need much more assurance about future supplies of capital; they would like to know what their capital position will be in five years' time. They think this is a reasonable suggestion, one that has had the support of the Federation of British Industries, and they ask that 'quiet consideration' be given to it (Q. 814). Furthermore, the present three-year allotment is not, they say, as firm as is necessary for making future plans; the past cancellation of a contract in progress imposes undue caution on them in the present (Q. 839). Even the allocation for the oncoming year is made at a time that is inconveniently late (Q. 814–5). When Your Committee suggested that the present situation was unsatisfactory, the Ministry witnesses agreed, and said they would be willing to hear the Commission's representations on this point (Q. 1998–9).

73. To sum up: it is clear that, even at the time when the Commission were finding that their annual capital budgets were being readily agreed to by the Ministry, the Ministry retained a considerable tactical hold over them. When, as in recent years, the Commission's finances have been a subject of general concern, the department's control has come right out into the open. It amounts today to a situation where the Minister can, if he so wishes, exercise a control over the Commission's capital plans for the railways that is similar to the control which he exercises statutorily over the country's roads programme (Q. 1902). But although the Ministry have been able to exercise power of this kind when they believed it to be needed, the lesson of the early years of modernization is that more control might well have been exercised then (see paragraphs 221 to 224).

CONTROL OVER FARES AND CHARGES

74. Elsewhere in this Report, consideration is given to the revenue that the Commission have been deriving from their passenger and freight traffics. The practical effects of Ministerial action are mentioned there (paragraphs 94 to 95), but this is a subject which deserves a rather closer look. It was the only point which modified the Commission's satisfaction at the way they had been treated by the department (Q. 275).

75. There are two occasions on which the Minister has formally intervened in the Commission's intentions to charge higher fares and rates. The first occasion was in 1952, when the Minister issued a

direction which forbade an increase that had been authorized by the Transport Tribunal; this interdiction remained in force for six months, and was then withdrawn (Appendix 4; Q. 195–6). The Ministry's own estimate is that this caused a loss of revenue to the Commission amounting to £6½ million (Q. 195–6).

76. In 1956, the Commission applied to the Minister under Section 80 (2) of the 1947 Act for permission to raise their freight charges. The Minister consulted the Transport Tribunal, and then, as he was statutorily entitled to, authorized the Commission to increase their rates by a lesser sum—a sum that was in fact half of what had been asked for. At the same time as they had applied for the increase in freight rates, the Commission had mentioned their intention of going to the Transport Tribunal to ask for an increase in passenger fares; because of the general situation then of the railways, and because of the reassessment of the Modernization Plan that was in progress, the Minister asked the Commission to delay their action for a while. Both the delay, and the reduced freight charge increases, were to last only for six months. The Minister's actions in this case—as, of course, was his formal direction in 1952—were publicly announced at the time (Q. 98). The loss of revenue caused by the 1956 case was, according to the Ministry, £8.4 million (Q. 197), and, according to the Commission, £17 million (1956 Report, paragraph 217) (see paragraph 408 below).

77. The Ministry say that, apart from these cases in 1952 and 1956, there has been no intervention in the Commission's requests for increases; nor has the Minister persuaded the Commission not to proceed with increases which were in their opinion desirable. In the case of the 1959 Passenger Charges Scheme, there were however discussions about the date on which the fares increase should be introduced, and the Commission decided that this should not be until after the holiday season (Appendix 4).

78. But, in addition to these precise and definite interventions, it can be said that there are prolonged and continuous discussions between Ministry and Commission on broad points of fares policy (Q. 83, 89). Private discussions between Minister and Chairman are not in evidence; but in view of the overriding power which the Minister has, it would seem unlikely that, as a result of these informal discussions, the Commission's formal proposals about fares should vary in any great degree from what the Minister thought best.

CONTROL OVER GENERAL MANAGEMENT

79. Apart from the duties which are laid on them by statute, the Ministry say they consult the Commission on many subjects. 'If the

Commission and the Minister are to fulfil their respective roles and responsibilities in a spirit of mutual trust and confidence, it is necessary that they should know a good deal about each other's thinking and policy in matters of common concern,' said the Ministry (Appendix 2). This is the justification of a system in which the Commission are open to the influence of the Minister over a greater area than the statutes lay down.

80. There are a number of matters which touch on public policy and on which, accordingly, the Minister has the duty to express an opinion. The extent to which the Commission rely on their own workshops (rather than going to private industry) for the construction of locomotives, for instance, raises issues which affect the country's export trade. For this reason, the Minister has in the past expressed his view on this subject to the Commission (Appendix 2). But, while the Commission doubtless pay due regard to what they hear, they are in no way bound to be affected by it; the decisions taken would be their own (Q. 209, 219).

81. Similarly, the more general problem of how many workshops the Commission should retain in operation has a considerable impact on employment conditions in a number of places (Q. 206). Here, again, though, after discussion with the Minister, the final decisions will be those of the Commission, and it is doubtful whether the Minister has the legal power to give a direction which could change the specific closures which BTC had decided upon (Q. 217–8).

82. But an example of how the department can impinge upon the Commission's handling of its affairs can be seen in the way in which the Minister, at a time when the railway's finances were deteriorating, was able to call on the Chairman to make substantial economies, amounting in the first place to £20 million in a full year (Q. 146–8). In so doing, he did not interfere in management to the extent of specifying how the economies should be made (Q. 146, 278); he asked for certain results, and left it to the Commission to decide how they should be attained. The Chairman of the Commission considered such a request quite natural in the circumstances (Q. 278).

83. This incident exemplifies the influence which the department can exercise over the Commission. When the public interest so requires, the Ministry can call for action from BTC whether or not the statute specifically allows. But there is never any desire to interfere with the actual process of management; that can be left to the Commission (Q. 62, 1920).

49. PROFITABILITY, NATIONAL ECONOMY
AND SOCIAL NEEDS*

420. What size and shape should British Railways be? The first consideration must be financial; the size and shape must be such as can enable the Commission to carry out their statutory task of balancing their accounts, taking one year with another. But if the Commission are to know which of their services are justifiable on grounds of direct financial return, they must first have some form of accounts by which the profitability of Regions and services can be judged.

421. However, the consideration of direct profitability is not the only one which applies in this case. Because of the cost of the roads, and of the congestion on them, the national interest may require railway services which do not in fact directly pay for themselves, but which may cost the nation less than the alternatives.

422. In some cases, there may be a third and different consideration—one of social need. A service may be justified on other than economic grounds, because for example the less populous parts of Britain might otherwise be left without a railway service. Account may, in other words, need to be taken of social considerations.

423. The consideration of profitability, mentioned above, should be left to the Commission. But if decisions are to be taken on grounds of the national economy or of social needs, then they must be taken by the Minister, and submitted by him for the approval of Parliament.

424. Furthermore, if Parliament is to specify that certain services should be undertaken, despite the fact that the Commission cannot profitably undertake them, then the additional cost of them should be provided, in advance, out of public funds.

425. If subsidies of this kind are to be paid to the Commission, then they should be paid for specific purposes, and they should be paid openly. They should not be disguised as, for instance, a payment of the track costs (which are an integral part of railway operations), nor as the writing-off of the burden of interest; and they should not be hidden away in the Commission's accounts.

426. This need for clarity in the accounts is important. Your Committee have suggested, at various points in this Report, that payments should be made to the Commission of appropriate sums from public funds. Provided that these payments relate to specific services dictated by the Minister, or are compensation for specific losses incurred by his actions, the Commission would be able to

* From *Report from the Select Committee on Nationalized Industries: British Railways*, July 1960, H.C. 254, paras. 420–7.

publish accounts for British Railways which would reflect only the matters within their control.

427. If this were done, there would be one important consequential advantage—the advantage that both the Commission and the Minister would become much more clearly accountable to Parliament for their separate railway responsibilities.

50. THE HETERODOXY OF PROFESSOR GREAVES*

I

Despite apologists of this 'discovery' of the inter-war years, there is nothing new about the independent board to administer a national service. Between 1832 and 1914, from the Poor Law Commission and Board of Health to Mr Lloyd George's Road Board, the only noteworthy fact about them is that they failed and were absorbed by State departments under ministerial responsibility. With the sole exception of quasi-judicial bodies like the Civil Service Commission, the whole tendency of the period was for the subordination of such functions under Treasury control to the direct and embracing supervision of Parliament. Old and new autonomous bodies suffered the same fate. The liberal State of the nineteenth century succeeded in subjecting administration generally and for the first time in history to effective control by elected representatives in Parliament. In the main it was successful also in unifying by the adoption of common principles the recruitment and general treatment of the staff of such services. The MacDonnell Commission, by its condemnation of the use of boards for the administration of Scotland which led to their termination, put the finishing touches to this work. The attitude was endorsed not only by the Haldane report of 1918 but by the response of the Bridgeman Committee of 1931–32 to the proposal that the Post Office should be placed under an independent board.

Nevertheless a reversal of this tendency took place in the lean inter-war years. It was due primarily to the enhanced power of business interests. The conservative business man was distrustful of the State unless he could convert it to his own service. He was suspicious of politicians, by which he meant those politicians whom he could no longer rely on as sharing the same political background and political ideas with himself. He disliked the prospect of such popular representatives having the power to question his activities. And yet

* From H. R. G. Greaves: 'Public Boards and Corporations', *The Political Quarterly*, Vol. XVI, No. 1, January-March 1945, pp. 69–77. Reprinted by permission of the author and the editor of *The Political Quarterly*.

he was forced to admit the need, in some cases where it was obviously even to his own advantage, to bring order into competitive chaos. Having admitted that need, he naturally preferred a statutory authority to fulfil it, which he rather than the politician or the civil servant might control. For Labour also suspicion and distrust lay at the root of acceptance of the independent board. Doubt of the loyalty and ability and working class sympathy of the civil servant; fear of the successful pressure of powerful interests; a certain unwillingness to entrust the running of a socialized service to anti-socialist successors who might see advantage in proving it unworkable; perhaps too, a lack of self-confidence owing to the weakness of its political position which led it to pay exaggerated attention to hostile criticism and to be unduly nervous lest tendentious opposition might unfairly stress deficiencies in any particular socialized service and so damage the cause of socialism; these are enough to explain why Labour was misled into welcoming this apparent solution. To them must be added the possibility offered by the board for direct trade union representation on the governing body. Thus for both sides there was a distrust of politics in relation to management, politics meaning of course the other man's politics. When to these mutual distrusts is joined the natural preference of the Minister and the official for avoiding the tiresomeness of Parliamentary questions, the explanation is complete.

But not only has this effort to escape from responsibility shown itself in relation to new services of an economic kind. An unsuccessful attempt was made in regard to an old service, the Post Office, and a successful effort in relation to a social service, the administration of unemployment assistance. Nowhere, indeed, is the intention more evident than in the establishment of the Unemployment Assistance Board. It was hoped to shift the onus of making recommendations on to a board which could not be criticized in Parliament, but in this case the House of Commons asserted its authority to the extent of forcing the Minister to take and admit responsibility for the Board's regulations. Here, however, the case for independence is not influenced by the considerations which relate to the productive service. There is no call for those qualities of enterprise which are claimed to justify autonomy in a body managing an economic service but which are not needed for the administration of relief.

If the independent board represented a compromise between mutual antagonisms its justification was sought in more substantial argument. The very fact of its being a compromise between complete freedom of enterprise and complete submission to public authority seemed to commend it. Both these have proved in the past to be workable methods, but whether this hybrid makes the best or the worst of them needs examination.

The advantages claimed for it correspond to the alleged defects in the alternative, the responsible department. These relate to the three principal characteristics of the department, its detailed subordination to Parliament, its ministerial direction, and its organization as part of the civil service. Too much can be made of the trouble, and the administrative complications, involved in the answering of Parliamentary questions; but scarcely too much can be made of their value as a corrective to unjustifiable action, Since the Bridgeman Committee reported that the argument about the 'supposed results of Parliamentary intervention in matters of detail is somewhat unduly stressed and that, in the long run, the advantages of the power of Parliamentary intervention outweigh its disadvantages', less has been heard of this aspect of the case, and it needs little attention. If House of Commons criticism is ill-informed then it is not the most difficult to meet; if it is concerned with principles then it should be met, if with detail not raising matters of principle then it is unlikely to cause excitement or embarrassment. The pressure of interests may be exerted through the House, but such pressure will be exerted in any case and it is much better in the open, where it can be resisted by being shown up as interested pressure, than when it is pushed into backstairs intrigues carried on in the obscurity of institutions that need give no account to the public of any specific decision. True, the fear of criticism may discourage initiative, but the House is not the only source of such criticism. Moreover, Parliament provides the best possible platform for defence against criticism; the need and opportunity to impress it with an account of solid achievement are indeed positive encouragements to initiative.

Attack on ministerial control further betrays the anti-democratic connotation of each such 'step towards a corporative State'. If we entrust to ministers the lives of millions and the making of war and peace, we can scarcely deny them the capacity to supervise the use of a particular part of public property. It is said that the Minister has too little time for dealing with the affairs of such services or that he is too frequently changed to secure continuity of policy. But continuity is provided by the permanent experts and administrators who run the service under him, and who are no less competent to do so because he is there than when they are called the members of a board. Besides he is not there to run the service in its details but to act as a two-way channel between it and the public, to see that its operations are carried out in conformity with the wider considerations of public policy, and to act as its spokesman bringing the support of public authority to its legitimate activities. Indeed, the real case for ministerial control is that the very independence and initiative which are admitted needs can best be secured by it, for they are the consequences of strong leadership, not of attempted and necessarily ineffectual insulation from public criticism. Secrecy, irresponsibility and the lack of a strong advocate at the centres of power lead to frustration, not enterprise.

But a department is part of the civil service structure and a public utility service is not. This is not quite true, for the civil service includes the Post Office and a number of dockyards and industrial establishments. It includes not only the administrative grade with its subordinate executive and clerical grades but the much larger and increasingly important body of professionals and specialists as well as much industrial labour. These last groups correspond closely to the servants of public boards. Many reforms are called for, especially with regard to the relations between the specialist and the administrator, the opportunities of promotion and training, and the operation of Treasury control, but the essential fact remains that within the civil service proper in peace-time—and still more in war-time—appear all the types of public servant required by public utility boards. The dichotomy established between them has no basis in administrative need or difference of function. There is greater similarity between the duties and qualifications of many civil servants and their counterparts in the service of public boards than there is among the whole body of civil servants themselves. That similarity offers a basis for co-ordination that would both freshen the old civil service, widening its field of opportunity, and ensure the application of publicly accepted standards to these more recent employees of public authority. The prevalence of too unimaginative and narrowly financial an attitude in the Treasury was an argument against giving it responsibilities in relation to these newer public enterprises, but reform now overdue must remove that argument and the corollary is a closer integration of the public services as a whole under more enterprising direction. In the way stands the principle of independence and the practice of staffs established in watertight compartments.

II

So far independence has been used as though it were a simple term. This is justified because the idea of independence has been the distinctive aim when these new authorities were being established. But the form given to it has varied with each case. It is worth while looking at the meaning of independence and its consequences in regard to the main aspects of organization.

The staffing of such Government agencies shows the greatest uniformity. In all cases except the Forestry Commission, which is under general Treasury control, it is the exclusive responsibility of the governing body. No regulations are laid down as to recruitment, grading, pay, promotion, retirement, pensions, dismissal or staff representation. None of the safeguards operative in the civil service are enforced, although strong criticism of the methods adopted by the BBC led the Postmaster-General to undertake that it would advertise vacancies and use an appointment board which should contain a civil service commissioner for chief appointments. Although this was resisted by the BBC as an interference with its autonomy it had to be accepted. The responsibility, however, still remains where it was, and the change may be more apparent than real. A similar practice has been adopted in some other cases, the Electricity Commission being an example, and for some kinds of employment; but the general system is one of patronage modified only by the need in many cases for professional qualifications. True there is a general desire to live up to accepted standards of public morality, but there is no guarantee that this is always achieved; nor is there any appeal on evidence that recruitment or promotion has not been properly determined. The only real safeguard exists where, as in the case of the London Transport and Central Electricity Boards, strong trade union organization exists. Whitley Council procedure is not the practice, except in the Port of London Authority. Policy conforms with that of private industry and not of public authority. It is not surprising therefore that where trade unions are not strong complaints are heard of arbitrary action, favouritism and prejudice. It is one of the costs of independence in these closed corporations that no effective means of investigation or of ensuring that just practices prevail is available. There can be no doubt that needless inefficiencies result and may be expected to grow.

As to appointment to the governing bodies themselves, this is normally the responsibility of a Minister. LPTB is one exception; the PLA is another in that besides the three ministerial appointees there are eighteen elected members and seven representatives of local authorities. The Executive Committee of the British Council, in which its powers are vested, has about half its members ministerial nominees and half other persons, presumably co-opted, but its Chairman and Secretary-General although elected by it must first by approved by the Secretary of State for Foreign Affairs. In most cases there are some conditions as to qualification for at any rate the technical members of boards. Pay often differs considerably from civil service standards. When the second in command of one board receives a salary nearly three times that of the head of the civil service and more than that of the Prime Minister a wholly undesirable contrast is created.

Something called self-contained finance is another feature of independence. Autonomy as to sources of revenue means that the majority of these boards cannot be discussed on a ministry vote. The LPTB, BBC, CEB, and PLA have such independent sources. It is true that they are apt to be regulated in some fashion by outside authority, such as a Minister laying down maximum charges or determining the amount of licence revenue to go to the Treasury, the Railway Rates Tribunal fixing fares, or the Electricity Commission deciding rates to be levied by the CEB, but with the exception of the allocation of licence revenue which is now made in principle as a permanent policy these are quasi-judicial rather than administrative decisions, and all provide for essentially settled revenues. The same principle of fore-ordained revenues was the original intention for the Forestry Commission, though it has in fact been chopped and changed by Treasury action. The grant to the British Council has grown steadily in amount, but it is supplemented by earnings from fees, publications and donations, as is the BBC's income from its highly remunerative publications. It would seem that in nearly all these cases expenditure falls outside the supervision of the Comptroller and Auditor-General. Thus, although they are essentially public monies, the normal check on the spending department of state is not operative. The raising of loans may require ministerial approval or Treasury sanction, although even this is not always necessary; and there may be provision by statute for the meeting of prior charges as with LPTB. But on the whole the principle of self-contained finance applies.

Policy and development, again, are matters falling within the board's independent competence. The belief that there is any general principle that day-to-day operation is for the board's discretion and wider policy for the Minister is quite unrelated to the facts. The Minister of Transport would appear to have no such overriding control over the CEB, PLA or LPTB. Although he lays down the terms of general operation in the grant of its operating licence and has certain powers of enforcement, this is not a proper description of the Postmaster-General's relation to the BBC. It may perhaps be truer of the Foreign Secretary's connection with the British Council, but that does not seem yet to have been clearly determined. An even greater doubt prevails where the prospective relations between the Air Minister and the British Overseas Airways Corporation are concerned.

The connection with Parliament shows that the aim of independence has been pretty fully achieved. Financial autonomy, as has been said, removes the principal opportunities for debate. The operations of a board may be discussed on adjournment, but in the absence of a responsible Minister to answer for the board this is not likely to be very fertile in results. The fact that in war-time, either under emergency powers or because new services are under ministerial responsibility, such willingness to reply for a board is more in evidence should not be allowed to obscure the position. The Minister of Information is responsible for the foreign services of the BBC and it may be for this reason only that he has cast his cloak more completely than the Postmaster-General ever did in the past over its general activities. But the fact remains that hitherto it was always almost impossible to ask a question in the Commons on the BBC. Similarly it has been complained that 'there is no machinery in existence whereby a Member of this House can approach the LPTB'. The practice favoured by some Ministers of admitting a willingness to answer 'about' and not 'for' a board introduces an undesirable combination of irresponsibility and what must be a measure of real influence upon a board. It is safe to assume that in such a case the apparent independence of the board will be effectually modified by its need to limit itself by what the Minister is prepared to defend. Where exactly effective decision lies will then be even more difficult to determine. That extremely dangerous position has already shown a tendency to develop. When it is possible for a Member, as has now more than once happened, to preface a criticism by the remark 'I do not know whom I am attacking but it must be someone,' then it is more than an administrative anomaly that is revealed, it is a situation fraught with the prospects of constitutional conflict. As it is, with the London Transport and Electricity Boards, Parliament has no effective opportunities for general debate. With the BBC its chance comes once in ten years when the charter is renewed. There can be no doubt that such sporadic intervention is inadequate.

The relations between the board and the general public, or its own consumers, show a tendency to recognize the need for developing the channels of public influence. There is indeed a sensitiveness to criticism which indicates nothing so much as the natural anxiety of the public servant to gain the approval of his masters. Some danger lies, however, in the irresponsibility of the connection. It has its value but it is not conducive to leadership and strong direction. That can come only at a higher level than that of complaint and suggestion about detail. On the whole it must be said that we are confronted rather by a strongly developed state capitalism mitigated sometimes by a willingness to listen to and take advantage of the statement of grievances. We have not the active consciousness on the part of the public that they own a service and are sharing, through their democratically elected leaders, in guiding its policy and development. Not independence but responsibility is the instrument for achieving that necessary objective.

Co-ordination of these services in the light of generally determined policy, economic and social, is the need. That will become increasingly the case as they grow in number and importance. Hitherto they have been created as the need arose and in forms which the conflict of interests permitted. They have tended to stabilize a status quo and the form given to them has been dictated by the necessity for compensating and assuaging hostile interests. They must be regarded instead as functions of a single society with an interest overriding 'interests', and as instruments of its centrally determined policy. That implies the need not for independence but for the building of the means of integration. For the old Treasury control exercised as a check upon the extravagance of spending departments there must be substituted an economic and social control, in a responsible Ministry of Production and Development, which is directed on the basis of information, social, statistical and economic, and which can draw up its plans in the knowledge that public services are there to carry them out. A static society may aim at avoiding political interference. A dynamic society requires that its functions shall be enlivened and integrated by the directive of political purpose. The one may be content with corporative independence, the other is obliged to seek for common and conjoint responsibility in the organs of society as a whole.

CHAPTER VIII

Parliament and the Enterprise

The extent and quality of parliamentary supervision of nationalized industries will depend on a number of factors, including (a) the powers statutorily assigned to the responsible Minister and his manner of exercising them, (b) the time made available by Government and Opposition for debating matters relevant to the public sector, (c) the degree of satisfaction or dissatisfaction felt by Members with the performance of particular industries, and (d) the amount of information that the House has at its disposal.

In the early days of post-war nationalization, there was much controversy about the allowability of Questions which appeared to trespass on matters of 'day-to-day' administration, for which the Board was held solely responsible, as distinct from those of 'general policy', which could attract ministerial intervention. Eventually the problem of Questions was referred to a Select Committee, whose Report is reproduced as *Extract 51*. Since the Speaker's ruling of June 7, 1948, referred to in this Report, there have been no major changes in the rules and conventions on the admissibility of Questions. The last ministerial statement on the subject was by Mr R. A. Butler on February 25, 1960 (see *H.C. Deb.*, Vol. 618, cols. 577–83).

The controversy about Questions reflected uneasiness about the Board-Minister-Parliament relationship. Many Members were dissatisfied not merely with the ambiguity of the whole situation but with the insufficiency of their information about nationalized industries and with the poor quality of their debates on the subject. This dissatisfaction was responsible for the decision to set up a Select Committee on Nationalized Industries, now annually reappointed. The original impetus came from the Conservative side, and the first reasoned case for such a Committee was advanced by Mr Hugh Molson in an article in *The Times* (*Extract 52*). When the Conservatives took office in 1951 the proposal was itself referred to the Select Committee whose first Report, on the Parliamentary Question, has already been mentioned. In its Second Report (*Extract 53*) this Committee, despite the hostile evidence it had received from several of the Board Chairmen, gave its support to the 'Molson' proposal.

The first Select Committee on Nationalized Industries (Reports and Accounts) to be set up failed—according to its own account—as a result of the restrictiveness of its terms of reference. Subsequent Committees have not suffered from this disadvantage and have performed their duties to the general and freely-expressed satisfaction of Members on both sides of the House. (For examples of their work, see Chapter IV, *Extracts 16 and 26*, Chapter VI, *Extract 44*, Chapter VII, *Extracts 47, 48 and 49*, and Chapter XI, *Extract 66*). A valuable account of the work of the Select Committee up to the autumn of 1961 is provided by its former Chairman, Sir Toby Low, in *Extract 54*, which reproduces a lecture given by him in the Royal Institute of Public Administration's series entitled *Recent Administrative Developments*.

The effectiveness of parliamentary supervision, whether through Question, Debate or Select Committee investigation, will largely depend on the quality of the Annual Reports which Parliament receives from the nationalized industries. The improvement of these is the subject of an article by Mr Raymond Nottage, Director of the Royal Institute of Public Administration, from which *Extract 55* is taken.

51. WHAT QUESTIONS SHALL BE ALLOWED?*

6. In general, Questions must be confined to matters for which the appropriate Minister is responsible. In the case of the Nationalized Industries, a large amount of responsibility has been vested by statute in the Board. The list of duties for which the Minister is still responsible, and on which he may therefore by the practice of the House be questioned, is usually set out in a definite Section in each statute. The duties vary slightly from one industry to another, but very roughly may be classified as:

(*a*) giving to the Board directions of a general character as to the exercise and performance by the Board of their functions in relation to matters appearing to the Minister to affect the national interest;

(*b*) procuring information on any point from the Board;

(*c*) a number of specific duties in connection with the appointments, salaries and conditions of service of members of Boards; programmes of research and development, and of education and training; borrowing by Boards; forms of accounts and audits; annual reports; pensions schemes and compensation

* From *Report from the Select Committee on Nationalized Industries*, 1952, H.C. 332-1, paras. 6-17.

for displacement; and the appointment of Consumer's Councils, their organization and operation.

7. Opportunities for asking Questions under heading (*a*) above are limited by the words of the statute. Directions must be 'of a general character', and must be 'required by the national interest'. This has been interpreted as implying a major matter of policy, or action required by crisis conditions, as contrasted with day-to-day working. But it will be obvious that there is a wide range of possible divergence of opinion as to the application of both these criteria to individual cases. Where neither criterion is held to apply, the proposed Question would fail as coming under the general rule of Questions (Rule 22 of May, p. 345) which prohibits raising matters under the control of bodies or persons not responsible to the Government and matters in which the Government have no power to intervene. Where Members press Questions which have been ruled by the Table not to come under this heading, the Question must be submitted to Mr Speaker for his decision.

8. In the case of Questions coming under heading (*b*) above, which would normally be allowed by the rules of Questions, the application of the rules has been made more severe by the express policy of Government. The principal statement of this policy was made on December 4, 1947, by Mr Herbert Morrison (Hansard 445 c. 566):

'*Mr H. Morrison:* In the light of experience so far gained, the Government have reviewed the question of replies to Parliamentary inquiries about the work of socialized industries. During the war the Government exercised direct control over certain industries, since actually socialized or to be socialized, notably the railways. The Ministers were directly responsible for the running of such services and, therefore, answered detailed questions on matters of day-to-day administration. This situation was, however, exceptional.

'Under recent legislation, boards have been set up to run socialized industries on business lines on behalf of the community; and Ministers are not responsible for their day-to-day administration. A large degree of independence for the boards in matters of current administration is vital to their efficiency as commercial undertakings. A Minister is responsible to Parliament for action which he may take in relation to a board, or action coming within his statutory powers which he has not taken. This is the principle that determines generally the matters on which a question may be put down for answer by a Minister in the House of Commons. Thus, the Minister would be answerable for any directions he gave in the national interest, and for the action which he took on proposals which a board was required by Statute to lay before him.

'It would be contrary to this principle, and to the clearly expressed intention of Parliament, in the governing legislation, if Ministers were to give, in replies in Parliament or in letters, information about day-to-day matters. Undue intervention by the Minister would tend to impair the board's commercial freedom of action. The boards of socialized industries are under an obligation to submit annual reports and accounts which are to be laid before Parliament. In the Government's view, it is right that Parliament should from time to time review the work of the boards, on the basis of the reports and accounts presented to Parliament.'

Although Mr Herbert Morrison was only purporting to say what Questions the Government would answer, and not what Questions should go on the Paper (which was a matter for the Speaker), Mr Speaker Clifton-Brown, in answer to a supplementary, made it clear that a refusal to answer a Question would by normal practice prevent such a Question being put on the Paper a second time (cols. 567–71). Mr Speaker also, in a subsequent statement (June 7, 1948), said:

'I propose to leave the Rule which excludes Questions on matters outside Ministerial responsibility unchanged. But I am prepared if it is generally approved, to exercise my discretion to direct the acceptance of questions asking for a statement to be made on matters about which information has been previously refused, provided that in my opinion the matters are of sufficient public importance to justify this concession. "Public importance" is one of the tests for Motions for the Adjournment of the House under Standing Order No. 8 and in my experience it is not an unduly difficult test to apply.'

9. It is in respect of the limitation expressed in Mr Herbert Morrison's statement that the importance of Rule 26 in May, mentioned in paragraph 3 above, becomes particularly apparent. The present practice of the House is that when a Question has been refused no similar Question is accepted by the Clerks at the Table or the Table Office. The result, in the case of Questions bearing upon Nationalized Industries, has been that when an answer has been refused by a Minister, the Clerks at the Table and the Table Office have been obliged to close to Questions a section of the affairs of the Nationalized Industry, and no Question coming within its limits can be printed on the Order Paper. Thus, for instance, Mr Gordon, the Second Clerk Assistant, in evidence before Your Committee gave the example of Questions on the subject of dirty coal. He said: 'The previous Minister of Fuel and Power answered on the subject of dirty coal on which there was a large number of complaints. We now have many fewer complaints about that, and the last answer we had to a similar Question which we put down, because the previous Minister regularly answered such Questions, was that the new Minister replied: "This is a matter for the Coal Board." Consequently, that shuts out, as

far as we are concerned, the subject of dirty coal. If it is a matter for the Coal Board we can no longer put those Questions down because the Minister is no longer willing to answer them. That is a Question of a type now fully answered for this Session.'

The Minister can always indicate to the Table that he is willing to answer a class of Questions which are temporarily the subject of particular public interest. On the other hand, the rule by which the Table refuses Questions which a Minister has stated that he will not answer applies only for each Session. It is open to Members to put the same questions down at the beginning of the subsequent Session.

10. Your Committee have considered whether the matters mentioned by Mr Herbert Morrison should in future retain their immunity to parliamentary questioning. This immunity is principally the result of two factors, (i) the establishment by statute of the public corporations as separate legal entities having full responsibility for day-to-day administration, and (ii) the policy of Government referred to in paragraph 8 hereof. Because of the first factor, Ministerial responsibility in that field is clearly excluded. It follows that any attempt to remove the immunity must lead to an alteration of the terms of the Statutes under which the public corporations are constituted. Your Committee are not empowered to recommend amending legislation. The arguments in favour of the retention of the immunity on the basis of the first factor appear to the Committee to be conclusive. It would be possible within the terms of the existing Acts for the Minister to obtain information on any point from the Board but this power should not be used so as to make it difficult for the public corporations in their present form to carry out their statutory responsibilities.

11. In the statement of policy referred to in Paragraph 8 it is stated that 'a large degree of independence for the boards in matters of current administration is vital to their efficiency as commercial undertakings'. Your Committee have examined the Chairmen of three great Nationalized Industries as to whether the removal of the immunity would seriously hamper the work of the industry.

12. They replied, in effect, that in any case the responsibility for supplying a Minister with detailed information about the day-to-day running of the Boards in order to answer Questions of this kind would mean an increase in their staff in order to collect the information and formulate considered answers. It would mean that the executives of the industry would be hampered by a constant necessity to have regard to the possibility of Parliamentary Questions on their activities, and that they would be, to use a common expression, constantly 'looking over their shoulders' in the course of their work, a process which in their view was inconsistent with managerial efficiency. In

such matters they felt Questions to Ministers were an inappropriate procedure of eliciting information. If Ministers became responsible for answering questions on detailed administration, they would find themselves interfering in the affairs of the corporations. The Chairmen all welcomed, on the other hand, letters of enquiry from Members of Parliament, which they found both useful in individual cases, and helpful in establishing an atmosphere of understanding and co-operation.

13. Your Committee also examined Sir Thomas Gardiner, who was formerly Director-General of the Post Office, upon which Questions can be freely asked, without any of the restrictions which apply to the Nationalized Industries. Sir Thomas was asked if he had found that the obligation to prepare answers to Parliamentary Questions on all the details of the work of his department constituted an embarrassment in the efficient work of the staff. He replied that Questions constituted an irksome addition to work, but that apart from that they could not be said materially to have increased the difficulties of his own work. He thought that for Civil Servants working under modern conditions they might cause more difficulties, and that for great nationalized industries they were perhaps unsuitable.

14. Your Committee are aware of a strong desire in some quarters to make the Nationalized Industries as generally subject to Parliamentary Questions as the Post Office and all the other Civil Departments. Certain points, however, must be borne in mind in considering the advantages and disadvantages of such a policy.

15. The public corporations which control the Nationalized Industries were constituted on different lines from the usual civil departments. The public corporations were established as independent entities, with statutory obligations to meet their expenditure by their own revenue. Their activities involve commercial transactions on a large scale, and it is desirable that they should not be unduly hampered by external interference. On the other hand, it is urged that the nation has become the owners of the enormous assets involved in those industries, and it is widely felt that there should be means of enquiry and criticism.

16. There are various other means of criticism and enquiry open to Members of Parliament, such as debates on the annual reports and statements of accounts of the various corporations. Your Committee intend if reconstituted in the next session to consider whether additional machinery ought to be established to meet this problem.

17. The basic feature of the Parliamentary Question is that it is answered by the Minister ultimately responsible for the decisions about which he is questioned. Under their existing constitution, the Nationalized Industries are not subject to any direct control by

Ministers in individual matters of detail. Your Committee therefore feel that without altering the terms of the statutes under which the public corporations are constituted, which they are not empowered to recommend, Questions on matters of detail in the Nationalized Industries are inappropriate.

52. MR MOLSON TAKES THE INITIATIVE*

It is known to be the intention of the Government to provide time in the autumn for the House of Commons to discuss the policy and administration of the boards responsible for certain of the nationalized industries. This new form of inquiry by Parliament leads into un-explored fields and it is of the utmost importance that Parliamentary procedure shall be so used, adapted or amended as to enable Par-liament and people to obtain a clear view of how the basic industries, such as coal, electricity, gas, and transport, which they have recently bought, are now being managed.

For better or for worse, various industries are nationalized, and the Conservative Party has officially stated that it will never seek to return some of them to private ownership. It is, therefore, important that their administration should be scrutinized in Parliament solely with a view to obtaining the best results from the nation's investments, and that they should not become involved in party controversy. Indeed, it clearly would not suit either party to be obliged to accept responsibility for the administration of the boards simply because it was at the moment in office. To do so would also make the life of the boards too carefree, for they would be assured of the unfailing support of the Government of the day, and therefore of its majority in the House of Commons.

THE PRICE SYSTEM

It is perhaps worth while, first, to consider what changes in theory and practice have taken place and what kind of supervision, there-fore, it is now necessary for Parliament to exercise. So long as coal mines, for example, were in private hands, the price system and competition were deemed to provide the automatic control needed. If a colliery company produced coal, it was making a profit or it expected to do so. The wish to pay dividends tended to keep down

* From Hugh Molson: 'Nationalized Industries: Select Committee to Secure Parliamentary Control'. © The Times Publishing Company Limited. All rights reserved. Reprinted, by permission, from *The Times* of September 8, 1949.

costs, whether labour costs or overheads, the smallness of the unit tended to establish a relation between efficiency and the financial outcome, and competition tended to bring all units of production up to the standard of the best. These factors may not have produced satisfactory results, but at any rate they worked after a fashion.

Nationalization has integrated industries like coal into a single unit. Internally, though not, of course, in international markets, competition between units of production has been abolished and, in fact, the efficient producers may be required to carry the inefficient ones. All accounts are merged in those of the nation-wide industry; and as there are no shareholders to complain that high costs or low receipts have resulted in profits being too low, careful analysis is needed to ascertain what the financial position of any coalfield or colliery really is.

When the old 'automatic' and local controls, based upon the price system and competition, have been swept away by nationalization, it is important that scrutiny, both general and detailed, should replace them. To take again the coal industry as an example, it will be necessary to assess its place in the economy of the nation. Is its labour cost in line with that of other industries or has the political and economic power of those particular workers obtained for them wages, welfare schemes, industrial injuries payments, etc., which take a disproportionate share of the national income? Should its export policy be competitive—thus providing the only impartial check on efficiency for the benefit of home as well as foreign consumers—or should markets be divided with foreign competitors? These are broad and crucial issues of policy, and from them it must also be possible for Parliament to come down to small matters of detailed administration, for inefficiency at the periphery is the chief defect of over-centralization and can become a fatal disease.

DEBATE AFTER SCRUTINY

The proposals of this article are that every two or three years there should be a long and full debate in the House of Commons upon each nationalized industry; that this should be kept outside the party dog-fight; and that the salient issues must first have been elucidated by an investigation by a Select Committee, equipped with an adequate staff.

The control which the House of Commons obtained over the Executive Government was established by means of the right to refuse supply or to demand explanation before the money was voted. The House constitutes itself into the two great committees of Ways and Means for raising money and Supply for spending it. The twenty-six days devoted each session to the Committee of Supply are among the most useful that Parliament spends, for they enable the Opposition to discuss all matters of policy and administration and the Ministers concerned to offer explanation and defence. It has, however, long been clear that no detailed criticism of expenditure or of administration can usefully take place in so large a committee and without machinery for investigation and inquiry.

It was the need for much closer scrutiny that led to the setting up of the Committee on Estimates to consider 'what, if any, economies consistent with the policy implied in those Estimates should be effected therein'. This is now a committee of some thirty-seven members, which sits in six sub-committees, selects each year certain estimates for scrutiny, and requires officials of the appropriate departments to explain and justify the expenditure, In suitable cases it inspects the work being done and has even visited colonies in Africa.

During the two wars estimates were not issued, and consequently the Estimates Committee was replaced by a Committee on National Expenditure. During the last war this committee, which took a broader view of its powers than the pre-war Estimates Committee, considered many branches of the administration and reported on such wide topics as payment by piece rates of munition workers and British tank design. Although some Ministers complained that it presumed to deal with matter of policy, the House of Commons as a whole was of the opinion that it did valuable work in exposing blunders, inefficiency, and waste. Because it had no detailed estimates to consider it affords the closest precedent for the proposed Select Committee on nationalized industries.

It would be a mistake for the Estimates Committee to undertake this work of investigating the nationalized industries. It already has enough work to do, and, moreover, it would almost inevitably apply the methods used in the case of Government departments to the boards, thereby destroying the flexibility of the board method of administration. Both the Public Accounts and Estimates committees should, in fact, keep clear of the nationalized industries.

Another important effect of a Select Committee should be to elucidate the principal issues and direct attention to them. It is a familiar defect of House of Commons debates on wide topics that the speeches deal with diverse matters, and there is often no thread of continuity nor even a meeting of minds. One speaker may discuss export difficulties, the next may expatiate upon some new safety device in the industry which he thinks should be compulsory, the next may ask about the industry's long-term development pro-gramme, the next may criticize disparities between wage rates. A general discussion of a nationalized industry could easily degenerate into one of these rambling and discursive debates, with many speeches delivered primarily for constituency consumption.

Usually the House is at its best in debating a Bill or other document which specifies a limited number of issues upon which Parliament has to pronounce. The simplest way to obtain the same precision would be to base the debate upon the matter contained in the Select Committee's report. Parliament has learnt by experience that in order to supervise administration and expenditure it is necessary to appoint a small committee with power to send for persons and papers—a procedure which would enable the whole matter to be investigated by calling witnesses and cross-examining them.

It is likely that the report of the Select Committee will usually be somewhat critical of the administration of the board and of the explanations it will have provided in its annual reports. There is a danger that the Opposition will seize upon the Select Committee's report as ammunition to attack the board and that the Government of the day will be betrayed into the position of automatically defending the board right or wrong—as recently happened when the Parliamentary Secretary to the Ministry of Transport was put up in Parliament to defend, against general criticism, the Railway Executive for introducing buffet-cars embellished and adorned in mock-Tudor style.

SUPPLY DAYS

This is the main reason why the debate on a nationalized industry should not take place on one of the twenty-six Supply days. It is the privilege of the Opposition to put down any vote and naturally it usually chooses those on which it can most effectively criticize the Government. If there was a change of Government, the errors of a board would be liable to recoil upon the new Opposition, in which case there would probably be no debate on the issue, however great the need to expose blunders and abuses.

Subsidiary reasons against taking a Supply Day are, first, that it would be wrong to reduce still further the opportunities for discussing the administration of Government departments, and, secondly, that a rule of procedure would exclude any proposal requiring new legislation. This objection applies equally to a debate on the adjournment. It would probably be best therefore, for the debates to be on some substantive motion which would enable the real issues to be discussed.

It is a curious fact about House of Commons procedure that no such motion at present exists, but an improvement on the adjournment motion could and should be devised.

The relation between a board and the sponsoring Minister is defined in the Coal Industry Nationalization Act, 1946, Section 3, thus: 'The Minister may, after consultation with the Board, give to the Board directions of a general character as to the exercise and performance by the Board of their functions in relation to matters appearing to the Minister to affect the national interest, and the Board shall give effect to any such directions.'

This has now become almost common form. It is intended to bring the general policy of the boards under the Government's control, while leaving them free from political interference in their day-to-day administration. It is upon this principle that Ministers decline to answer Parliamentary questions relating to details of administration in the nationalized industries.

The rule of procedure which makes this principle effective is stated in Erskine May as follows: 'Questions addressed to Ministers should relate to the public affairs with which they are officially connected . . . or to matters of administration for which they are responsible. . . . The following types of question may be enumerated as being out of order, viz.: (22) raising matters under the control of bodies or persons not responsible to the Government.'

A NEW PROBLEM

It can hardly be doubted that this exclusion of Parliamentary questions is wise. It applied before the epoch of nationalization to such bodies as the British Broadcasting Corporation, the Central Electricity Board, and the various Agricultural Marketing Boards. The immediate effect of changing the rule would be to centralize all authority in the Minister. If he were made answerable for everything, he would have to control everything. It may be inevitable in the case of the Army that the Secretary of State should answer in the House for details of administration in the smallest and remotest unit, but it results in red-tape, rigidity and centralization; and in fact no industry could be successfully run on such lines.

Parliament is, therefore, faced with a new problem: how to control the strategy of nationalized industries and apply a periodical efficiency audit without going as far as that detailed interference which would cause a paralysing centralization. The past experience of the House of Commons suggests the machinery and the spirit through which this result can be obtained. A Select Committee, served by an appropriate staff, must inquire by sending for persons and papers into the industry, and its report should focus attention upon the most important issues. In the light of this report it should be possible for the House of Commons to discuss with knowledge and relevance at reasonable intervals the state of each nationalized industry and its proper relation to the national economy as a whole.

53. THE 1953 PROPOSALS*

THE ARGUMENTS FOR A COMMITTEE

7. The arguments in favour of the proposal to set up a Committee were briefly summarized in the evidence given by Mr Molson, speaking for himself, as he was careful to point out, and not for the Government, in the following words:

'In the past the House of Commons has always found it convenient when confronted with a special problem, to appoint a committee. I think the reasons for that are threefold. First, in order that a few Members of Parliament may give intensive study to the problem; secondly, that there may be interrogation of witnesses and investigation of papers and maps; thirdly, in order that in the seclusion of a committee room there may be comparative freedom from political prejudices. . . . I believe that the committee which I am advocating should elucidate what I might call deep problems of policy. I am sure it is important to avoid day-to-day interference with detail, but there is I think a great need that from time to time Parliament should have an opportunity of taking stock.'

8. The possibility of setting up a Committee was put to Lord Hurcomb and Sir Edward Bridges, and additional arguments for the proposal were given by them. Their support was perhaps more measured, and influenced by the knowledge that we were considering the proposal, and by their own experience as civil servants of the analogous work of the Committee of Public Accounts. Lord Hurcomb said, 'The sort of Committee that it seems to me would do much to satisfy the very legitimate demand of Parliament for a greater knowledge than can be got in debate about the affairs of one of these great corporations, would be something in the nature of a standing committee, so that there would be continuity of *personnel*— a group of members who took a special and continuing interest in a particular activity, not merely because it was nationalized, but more from the actual interest that the Committee has in the subject.' He went on to say that 'a Committee of this sort would, or ought to mean, on that aspect, as these matters get further away from the highly controversial, that a large number of Members of Parliament would have an opportunity of satisfying themselves and conveying,

* From *Report from the Select Committee on Nationalized Industries*, 1953, H.C. 235, paras. 7–27.

not by way of attack and of public speech, but by way of suggestion to the organization, the points where they thought something might be going wrong, or, at any rate, would be worth looking into. That would be of great value'.

THE ARGUMENTS AGAINST A COMMITTEE

9. It was strongly represented to us that the proposal to set up a permanent Committee of Enquiry into the Nationalized Industries was not only contrary to the spirit and intention of the Acts under which the industries were nationalized, but an innovation in and hostile to the general pattern of the British constitution. As Lord Reith said, 'I should have thought the appointment of a select committee, *ad hoc*, on a Nationalized Industry was in effect a negation of what Parliament deliberately did in setting it up. Parliament passed a sort of self-denying ordinance taking from itself the right of direct interference, as with Government Departments. Unless there is to be a revision of attitude, I would have thought it was contrary to the principle of what was done that you should set up a committee whether of one House or both. . . . It would seem a sort of institution-alization of the Parliamentary Question, the very thing Parliament denied itself.' The argument expounded by Lord Reith would appear to apply even more strongly to a permanent Select Committee.

10. The same argument was enlarged by Mr Herbert Morrison. Later, in the course of his evidence, he adduced a more fundamental objection. When he was asked 'Really your objection to the Select Committee is not only to its possible ineffectiveness, but also that it is not perhaps the function of Parliament to intervene on the efficiency side to the extent which is envisaged by a select committee going into it?' he answered, 'I would die for Parliament—I have an enormous admiration for it—but I do not think it is the kind of body to which you could entrust this to the point of alteration of the actual management of a complex industrial concern.'

11. Another argument against the proposal was that a Committee would raise the whole question of the responsibility for managing and directing the operations of the public corporations. If a Select Committee were constantly enquiring into the policy and operations of the corporation, it would necessarily cause uncertainty in the industry as to where the ultimate decisions lay; and this might possibly make accountability less rather than more secure. As Lord Reith said, when the proposal was put to him, 'For whom would the public corporation be working, putting it quite straightly?' And he indicated that a select committee which might start as a friendly communicative body might end by investigating and controlling.

12. The main argument, however, which has been advanced against the proposal is that it would impede the working of the Nationalized Industries and destroy initiative in them. Mr Herbert Morrison said, 'The . . . point that I am apprehensive about is that it would create a rather un-nerving prospect for these ordinary business men who are running in the main, the publicly-owned industries. It might un-nerve them and tend to develop in them a rather red-tapeish, unadventurous and conventionally Civil Service frame of mind, which is all right in the case of Government Departments but is wrong in the case of public corporations, and that is why Parliament decided on public corporations in part.' Witnesses were apprehensive of a committee if its functions included enquiries into wide decisions of policy. Sir Geoffrey Heyworth, the Chairman of Unilever Limited, and a part-time member of the Coal Board, was asked, 'Do you think that Parliament could possibly be better-informed if the chairman and board of members were to meet a Committee of Parliament purely to answer questions on their annual report and accounts and on their policy?' He replied, 'Well, I can see some point in that. I do not believe it might work too well because I cannot help feeling you would have to ask them questions such as "Did that thing turn out as well as you thought it would?' and they would have to say no or yes, whichever was the truth. "What hopes have you got for this particular new idea you are now pursuing?" In this imperfect world things do not turn out as they should be, and then someone turns up next time and says you did not do so well with that.' Witnesses expressed themselves even more strongly over the possibility that the Committee might investigate the detailed management of the industries. Lord Reith even spoke of it as a terrifying prospect.

13. We were told by Sir Geoffrey Heyworth that the great public corporations had not yet had time to settle down as integrated bodies, and that in due course they, like Unilever and other great commercial undertakings, would develop their own internal controls and their own adequate relationships with the outside public. A natural development of this was, as Sir Geoffrey said, 'The more you make this into autonomous units, I think the better chance there is for success.' He indicated that the process of integration in the case of the Coal Board, for instance, might take a very long time.

THE DETERMINATION OF THE ARGUMENT

14. The basic argument for the establishment of a Committee to be a liaison between the nationalized industries and Parliament and elicit such information as is necessary on behalf of the House of Commons is that such a Committee is the only practical means of

performing those functions. Last session we investigated the possibility of extending the sphere of the Parliamentary Question, and reported that it was inadvisable. Apart from this the number of ways by which the House of Commons can, on its own initiative, obtain information is limited. There is debate, the various forms of which we have already set out, but which has not fully satisfied members and sometimes has not occurred sufficiently frequently or sufficiently soon after the issue of Reports; there is the procedure of moving for returns, which is not frequently used or altogether appropriate. There remains only the Committee, a body appointed by the House to obtain information for it.

15. We have, therefore, decided that we must either accept the objections and thus abandon all possibility of dealing with the present situation; or, despite the difficulties, make—with due safeguards—provision for such an enlargement of the field of parliamentary accountability as will provide the House of Commons with the information which it rightly requires without, in obtaining that information, interfering with or jeopardizing the efficiency of the Nationalized Industries. A Committee appears to be the most appropriate means by which this can be done. It is essential that the Committee which we are recommending will, when appointed, set up a tradition of conduct which will result in its being regarded by the Board not as an enemy, or a critic, but as a confidant, and a protection against irresponsible pressure, as well as a guardian of the public interest. In our opinion, the terms of reference of the proposed Committee can be so drafted as to avoid the graver of the objections alleged against it.

THE NATURE AND WORK OF THE COMMITTEE

16. The question next considered was whether the proposed Committee should be a Committee of this House only, or a Joint Committee of both Houses. The advantages of a Joint Committee were urged by some of the witnesses, particularly Captain Crookshank and Lord Hurcomb. The arguments in favour of a Joint Committee, which appeal strongly to some of us, are that the House of Lords has a great number of members with business and executive experience available for the work; that in general the peers are less encumbered with the pressing distractions of everyday work; that the members of the other House are less dedicated to party allegiance; that their membership of their House would give the committee the element of continuity which it would need; and that if a Committee were appointed of one House alone, the other House might possibly set up another Committee with unfortunate results.

17. We feel, however, that some of the work of the proposed committee must be of a financial nature, and would be more fittingly done by a Committee of the House of Commons. Nationalization arose as an act of policy and, for certain industries and services, has been carried into law on the initiative of the representatives of the people in the House of Commons. It can be said that the general public are now the owneıs of the Nationalized Industries. It seems entirely appropriate to us, therefore, that any Parliamentary Committee set up to examine, and obtain information about, these industries at this stage of their development should be an exclusively House of Commons Committee. We are confident that a tradition of public service could be built up in a Commons Committee not inferior to that of the Committee of Public Accounts. On balance therefore we decided with some regrets against the proposal of a Joint Committee.

18. We then considered the nature and methods of work of the proposed Committee. In the first place, it should, we considered, take over the right which the Committee of Public Accounts at present has to examine the accounts of the Nationalized Industries, and which that Committee is unable at present fully to exercise. The proposed new Committee should consider all the published accounts and auditors' reports of the public corporations, and make representations about such matters as seem to require consideration by the Boards or debate in the House.

19. In examining this problem, we have confined our attention to Nationalized Industries which are conducted on a commercial basis, and whose annual receipts are derived from services rendered or the goods they supply. Other public corporations such as the New Towns Corporations do not appear to us to fall into this category and should in our view be left within the field of responsibility of the Committee of Public Accounts.

20. In the second place, the Committee should, in our opinion, be empowered to extend its enquiries more widely than those which the Committee of Public Accounts makes into the Government Departments. It should have a regard, not merely to present and past financial probity and stability, but to future plans and programmes.

21. In the third place, we consider that the Committee should have power to get information as to the policy of the corporations. It would have no need to investigate any decision which is the result of a direction from the responsible Minister, and for which he is accountable to Parliament. Again, any matters which are normally decided by collective bargaining arrangements should be avoided.

22. The Committee should, in the first instance, examine and deal with the Chairmen and Boards of the Nationalized Industries and we hope that the Boards will come to regard the Committee, not as a

criticizing body but one which they can approach to explain their policies and their difficulties. We feel, therefore, that the emphasis of the work of the Committee should be not only upon finance but also upon general lines of policy. In view of the overwhelming evidence we have received, we feel strongly that the Committee should avoid the investigation of matters which fall into the category of detailed administration.

23. We were impressed by the suggestion of Sir Frank Tribe that it would be of great value to the Committee if the great public corporations should be encouraged to prepare statements of their anticipated revenue and expenditure. This would enable it to satisfy itself that the corporation was genuinely trying to comply with its statutory requirements of breaking even, taking one year with another, and it would give it a means of comparing what had been expected at the beginning with the actual out-turn. We commend this suggestion to the attention of the new Committee.

24. We recognize that the proposed Committee may not have time each year to conduct a detailed examination of each of the Nationalized Industries. We therefore suggest that for the information of Parliament as a whole, and having particular regard to the duty of the House of Commons to safeguard the interests of consumers, each Corporation should publish with its annual report to Parliament the best estimate it can make of the percentage increase or decrease since the date of its establishment in the average cost to the consumer of its products or services, taken as a whole. This figure should accompany the annual accounts and reference to it should be included in the auditors' reports. This would enable the Committee to form some opinion, though not a conclusive one, on the efficiency of the industry, as it could be compared with the general cost of living index.

25. Although the range of the Nationalized Industries is too vast to be adequately examined by one Committee sitting as a single body, we were advised by the Leader of the House that it would be inexpedient, owing to the increasing calls upon Members' available time, to set up more than one such Committee. We consider that it should have power to set up sub-committees.

26. It has been suggested that the proposed Committee should have the task of directing the debates which are held in the House on the Nationalized Industries, and of suggesting the allocation of time to each subject of debate. We feel, however, that such direction of the work of the House might not appeal to the House and that it conflicts in some degree with the principle of free debate which has so far prevailed in the House of Commons. We consider that the proposed Committee should determine its own programme and rate of progress.

L

27. The Standing Order under which the Committee shall be set up should, in our opinion, run as follows:

'There shall be a select committee, to be designated the Committee on Nationalized Industries, for examining the Reports and Accounts of, and for obtaining further information as to the general policy and practice of the Nationalized Industries established by Statute whose controlling Boards are wholly appointed by Ministers of the Crown and whose annual receipts are not wholly or mainly derived from moneys provided by Parliament or advanced from the Exchequer. The Committee shall consist of not more than twenty-one members, who shall be nominated at the commemcement of every session and of whom seven shall be a quorum. The Committee shall have power to appoint sub-committees from its own members. The Committee and any such sub-committee shall have power to send for persons, papers and records, and to report from time to time.'

54. THE SELECT COMMITTEE ON NATIONALIZED INDUSTRIES*

The Select Committee on Nationalized Industries is a committee of thirteen members of the House of Commons drawn from all parties in approximate proportion to their numbers in the House, its present composition being 7 Conservatives, 5 Labour and 1 Liberal. The task of the Committee is to examine the Reports and Accounts of the nationalized industries.

To understand how the Committee has worked it is necessary to have some knowledge of its historical background.

HISTORICAL BACKGROUND

The Select Committee, described in *The Times* recently as 'one of the most important *ad hoc* functional bodies serving the Commons', has not always been so honourable blessed. It owes its origin to the desire, widely felt amongst Members of Parliament, to secure some form of closer relationship between Parliament and the industries nation-alized between 1945 and 1950. This is, I think, what is meant by the phrase 'greater Parliamentary accountability'. Members wanted to find a method by which they could best inform themselves about the activities of the nationalized industries without acquiring responsi-

* From Sir Toby Low: 'The Select Committee on Nationalized Industries', *Public Administration*, Vol. 40, Spring 1962, pp. 1–15. Reprinted by permission of the author and the Editor of *Public Administration*.

bilities which properly belong to Ministers or encroaching on the independence of these commercial enterprises.

Ministerial Responsibility

In the post-war nationalization Acts, the powers and duties of Ministers were carefully limited and spelt out. For these powers and duties the Ministers would be responsible to Parliament and Parliament would have such control as it wanted in the ordinary way by questioning Ministers and debating with the threat of withholding supply. These ministerial powers and duties, though they did not extend to day-to-day operations, were more extensive than those given in the 1920s and 1930s to Ministers over public corporations created then—such as the BBC, the London Passenger Transport Board and the Central Electricity Board. Chief amongst the powers given to Ministers by the post-war nationalization Acts were the appointment of members of the Boards; the power to give general directions on matters affecting the national interest; and important controls over the finances of the Boards. Of these powers, the influence of that of the appointment of Chairmen and members of the Boards has probably been underestimated and that of the general direction has probably been overestimated. The power and the duty in regard to finance seems to have been under-used until recently—as will appear later on.

Over the rest of the activities of these nationalized undertakings, the Acts provided for no ministerial responsibility, but in practice Ministers have extended their influence and interest over much of this sphere also.

Parliamentary Accountability

Each Board has to make an annual report to Parliament covering its activities and disclosing its accounts. But, as one of the chief architects of these Acts later wrote, 'the precise character of the accountability of these Boards [had] to be worked out in the light of experience'.[1] By 1951, however, there had been insufficient experience and certainly no progress towards a solution in that regard. The House of Commons concerned itself with the nationalized industries through Parliamentary Questions and debates. In fact, it was not until 1956 that the House established a Select Committee on Nationalized Industries with terms of reference that would enable it to make an effective inquiry into each industry.

[1] Mr Herbert Morrison (now Lord Morrison of Lambeth) in his *Government and Parliament* (1954), p. 251.

Earlier Select Committees

The first Select Committee on Nationalized Industries was appointed on December 4, 1951, 'to consider the present method by which the House of Commons is informed of the affairs of the nationalized industries and to report what changes, having regard to the provisions laid down by Parliament in the relevant statutes, may be desirable in these methods'. The Chairman was Mr Ralph Assheton, now Lord Clitheroe.

The Committee's first report[1] dealt with the rules about Parliamentary Questions. In their second[1] they proposed that a House of Commons Committee be set up to examine the nationalized industries. 'The object of the Committee should be that of informing Parliament about the aims, activities and problems of the Corporations and not of controlling their work.' They also recommended that the Committee's staff should include an officer of the status of the Comptroller and Auditor-General who should be an officer of the House of Commons with high administrative experience, and at least one professional accountant and such other staff as might be required.

Some of the comments on this report were not very friendly. *The Times*, whose distinguished Editor I know takes a personal interest in the problem of Parliamentary accountability of public corporations, made three important points:

(1) The real problem is to discover how Parliament can make better use of the information it already gets, rather than to devise ways and means for it to acquire more. (In my opinion the problem is how to understand what the industry is doing and how. This does need periodically more information.)

(2) If Parliament is going to preserve the relative independence of the industries it must not devise new instruments which are really the creatures of distrust. (I agree with this. There must not be an atmosphere of distrust between Parliament and these industries.)

(3) The pursuit of pure efficiency in this way is a will of the wisp. Real efficiency will be got neither by nagging nor by exhortation. It will be secured by the Minister appointing the best Boards and the organization being allowed to get on with the job. If things go wrong, they will not remain hidden for long. (I don't disagree with these statements, but an outside inquiry, carried out with mutual confidence, can help efficiency. *The Times* did not sufficiently comprehend the importance in this

---

[1] H.C. 332 (1951–52) and 235 (1952–53) surveyed in the Spring and Autumn 1953 issues of *Public Administration*.

respect of ministerial functions, nor indeed did many others.)
These are all serious points and I shall deal with them later. But
now I must continue with the history.

Despite the thunderings of *The Times*, a new Select Committee was
set up in 1955, but its terms of reference were such that, as the Committee itself reported[1] on November 14, 1955, they were left with
'insufficient scope to make inquiries or to obtain further information
regarding the Nationalized Industries which would be of any real
use to the House'. Over a year elapsed, partly because of the pressure
of other Parliamentary business and partly because of fresh consideration of various alternative proposals before the House of
Commons debated a motion to establish a fresh Select Committee
without restrictive terms of reference.

The Terms of Reference

The 1955 Committee had been specifically excluded from four types
of matters:

(1) Those which concerned Ministerial responsibility.
(2) Wages and conditions of employment.
(3) Day-to-day administration.
(4) Those which were to be considered through formal machinery
established by Statute, e.g. the Transport Tribunal.

The Chairman of that Committee, Sir Patrick Spens (now Lord
Spens), explained in the debate that after learning from the departments of those matters that came under the first category of ministerial responsibility, they came to the conclusion that it would have
been a waste of their time and of the House for them to continue in
such limited spheres.

The terms of the Motion under debate on November 29, 1956, provided for the appointment of a Select Committee 'to examine the Report and Accounts of the Nationalized Industries . . .' Objection was
taken by the Opposition that these were too wide and would allow
the Select Committee, for example, to make an inquiry into wages and
conditions of service or to examine railway fares in detail—the duty
of the Transport Tribunal. It was generally agreed that the Committee should keep away from these matters. Other objections were
taken to the Motion that amounted to a rejection of the idea of a
Select Committee. It was argued that the Committee would interfere
with the proper chain of responsibility; would create a new bureaucracy; would make the executives running the industry look over
their shoulders; and would expose the commercial activities of these
commercial enterprises to their competitors.

[1] H.C. 120 (1955–56).

Mr R. A. Butler, as Leader of the House, in introducing the Motion, gave a lead on the guidance that the House wished to give to the Committee about its terms of reference. 'The Reports and Accounts reveal a wide range of subject matter all affecting the finances and efficiency and scope of the industries which the Committee can usefully consider. But at its two extremes—namely where the issues involved are purely matters of day-to-day administration at the one extreme, and at the other where they are matters of major Government, as distinct from commercial, policy—it is surely right that the Committee should not seek to trespass upon the authority of these bodies respectively responsible, namely, in the one case the Corporations themselves, and in the other, the Ministers of the Crown.'[1]

It was left to the Chairman and the Committee, however, to establish 'case law' what should and should not be investigated and for the Committee to use their discretion and avoid the pitfalls to which I have referred. The House wanted a body to screen the information available, comment on the issues and criticize where criticism was due, but in a constructive spirit so that it could use such time as it has available for discussion of the nationalized industries affairs to discuss the major issues. Though the terms of reference were wide, the House had told the Committee throughout the debate of the spirit in which they should be interpreted.

THE WORK OF THE COMMITTEE

I now pass on to describe how, in fact, the Committee has worked in these last five years. During that time the Committee has been responsible for five major reports. The first report was on the Scottish Electricity Boards; the second on coal; the third on the two air corporations, namely BOAC and BEA; the fourth on British Railways and the fifth on gas.

The First Report

I was a member of the Committee, most ably chaired by Sir Patrick Spens, which produced the report on the Scottish Electricity Boards. Because it was the first report, it included a very valuable description of the part the Treasury played in the control of the finances of the nationalized industries. Also since it was a first report, the Committee did not go deeply into a number of subjects which it would now investigate. It was very much feeling its way and I am quite

[1] *H.C. Deb.* (1956–57), Vol. 561. Col. 596.

certain that Sir Patrick Spens was right in the careful leadership which he gave.

The Times' leading article about the first report was headed 'A Brave Attempt'. A fair summary of this leading article would be that it praised the report with faint damns. It praised the Chairman without any damns at all. It ended with these words: 'But everything will depend on the Chairman of the Select Committee always being as wise as Sir Patrick Spens. The evidence contains plenty of hints of the dangers there could be if the Committee should ever fall into less able hands.' It was with those words smarting in my eyes that I took on the Chairmanship which I held for four years.

The Measure of Efficiency

Each of these four inquiries was fairly wide ranging and I must admit exhausting. The main object of each inquiry was to find out whether that particular industry or corporation was efficiently managed. This involved asking additional questions, such as why are its financial results not better? What are the important problems? What are the future plans? Is the enormous expenditure on capital account wise and necessary and properly controlled? But the big question was— how did one judge the efficiency of a nationalized corporation? Was it possible, for example, to compare the performance of the Coal Board in 1957 with the performance of the Coal Board itself in earlier years, or with the performance of other coal mines, whether nationalized or not, in other parts of the world?

We quickly found that in the case of coal there was no yardstick by which we could easily judge the performance of the Coal Board. Comparisons made with the coal industry before nationalization or with foreign coal mines were of no value. When we came the following year to consider the performance of the nationalized air corporations, we found that it was possible to make certain useful comparisons with the performance of other airlines. But even then we had to be very careful; we had to make certain that we were comparing like with like. We found, for example, some useful figures in the Pan American aircraft maintenance costs to compare with BOAC's maintenance costs. It was also useful to compare operating costs by capacity ton mile of similar airlines. When we came to British Railways we tried to find some useful statistics of continental and other railways which might help us to decide whether the British Railways could be more efficient, and if so, in what fields. But we quickly found here too that there was a danger of trying to compare like with unlike. Even the figures we mentioned of the time of wagon turnround are not wholly meaningful because of the different practices on the continent. However, some of these comparisons did help to point the finger at sensitive spots.

A more useful comparison has been to compare the performance of these nationalized corporations in one year with their performances in previous years. But there is a limit even to the value of this type of comparison as a real test of efficiency. At the best it is a test of relative efficiency.

What other tests are available to the investigator? Obviously one should look at the profitability of the corporation's operations as a whole, and if possible of parts of those operations. But in taking this look we very quickly came up against the vital snag that in most nationalized industries the prices were controlled in one way or another and tended to be artificial. We found, for example, that the coal prices had been kept artificially low and indeed below the price which properly covered depreciation; that fares in British Railways had been kept low, partly by the Transport Tribunal (and on previous occasions by Government persuasion), but in recent years by the Commission's own policy. On the other hand we found that BEA had been prevented from lowering their fares on at least one route; and that the profit figures of the gas industry had been seriously threatened when the Government persuaded certain Boards not to raise their gas tariffs. And so the profit figures—and the financial results—do not by themselves give a real guide, even comparing one year with another, of the efficiency of these corporations.

We were driven to look right across the Board at all the factors that go to make up efficiency in management. This meant looking at a mass of information, and trying to digest it ourselves so that we could write a summary of the facts which would be both accurate and useful to the House of Commons as a whole. But we had another duty too: when taking oral evidence, we had to try to elucidate the points of real importance and, by a process of discussion with the people in charge of the industry, to clear our minds and draw the right conclusions.

Thirteen Members of Parliament may seem an odd kind of Committee to charge with the investigation into the activities of widely differing industries, many of them with highly technical activities. But in fact this Committee of thirteen has worked very well. Each one of us had varying experience and came with a different approach to the problems we were considering. It is important, I think, that some members of such a Committee should themselves have had experience of management, of the financial and technical side of industry, and that some should have a good understanding of general economic and financial questions.

Inevitably it falls upon the Chairman of this Committee to take the lead in choosing what are to be the most important points and in cross-examining the witnesses. In this he is greatly helped by the two Clerks who are allotted to the Select Committee—we used to have only one. It is not generally appreciated how high is the intellectual standard of the Clerks of the House of Commons, or how broad their ability. The Committees of the House of Commons depend to a very large extent on their Clerks; but of no committee is this more true than the Select Committee on Nationalized Industries. These Clerks are not trained economists; they are not trained accountants. But they do have highly trained minds; and they know and really understand good House of Commons procedure. They have one other advantage—at least my Clerks had—they write good, bright, enjoyable English.

It might be thought that with a Committee of thirteen laymen, instructed to examine the reports and accounts of complicated technical industries, there must be a real need for some technical staff, expert in financial accounts and in understanding particular technical problems of the industry under examination. I did myself, at one time, feel the lack of a professional accountant at my elbow. I have never felt the need for special technical advice, for it is always possible to seek a technical explanation from a witness from the nationalized industry itself, formally or informally, or to find an explanation from an outside source. But in fact it is not the Committee's duty to reach a judgment on technical decisions.

The other need I felt from time to time was for a trained economist to put my nose on the right scent so that the Committee would not waste their time in running along false trails. It was largely because of these thoughts that, at the end of the Session 1958–59, we decided to give special consideration to the question whether we might achieve more if we were provided with additional assistance. At that time we had only one Clerk to help us, who was very heavily over-worked.

The special report[1] we issued in July, 1959, is still, I think, of interest. I will not weary you with a repetition of all the points we made. We rejected the proposal that there should be a comptroller and auditor general of nationalized industries. We did not want to get involved with anything that looked like a grand inquisition by officials acting on behalf of Parliament; nor did we wish to build our own bureaucracy. We rejected too the idea that had been put to us by the Government that we should make more use of the Treasury liaison officer. We had found in our reports that we had some telling criticisms of the Treasury, and we really did not think it would help us to make these criticisms, or make for a very happy Treasury official if he and we

[1] H.C. 276 (1958–59). See *Public Administration*, Winter 1959, pp. 406–8 for summary.

came too closely together. Furthermore, the Treasury has a distinct part to play in the nationalized industries, and we did not think that it should confuse that part by getting involved in rather wider spheres of activity which were ours. We gave some thought to the advisability of getting assistance from outside the House either in the form of an economist or an accountant, but we did not pursue that idea very energetically. We decided we wanted our staff to be the servants of Parliament and nowhere else. We wanted to make quite certain that our staff and the Committee itself continued to enjoy the confidence and the respect of the nationalized industries with whom we were dealing. We stated three general principles:

(1) Any staff working for us should be and should be seen to be the servant of Parliament and not of the executive.

(2) Any alteration in the staff provided for our Committee should not alter the general lines on which we had been working and should, in particular, not lead to interference in the working of the nationalized industries. The sole object of any additional staff is to aid the Committee in their work and not to introduce a new piece of machinery between Parliament and the nationalized industries.

(3) It was important that the nationalized industries should have full confidence in the Committee's staff.

In the end we made a positive recommendation that we should have an additional Clerk and that our Senior Clerk should have had experience with us for a number of years. This was accepted and has been implemented. We left it to the House of Commons to decide whether we should also have power to appoint an assessor to our staff from outside. They did not so decide; but I have no doubt that if future committees make a case for more assistance they will find the House of Commons sympathetic in trying to help them to get it.

Since that report in July 1959 I had experience, as had my colleagues, on the Committee, of two reports—one very long and important on the railways and one fairly long and almost as important on the gas industry, both of which were compiled with the help of two excellent Clerks. I did not during either of these inquiries feel the need for expert staff assistance. There was a moment during the inquiry into railways when we got involved in a heady discussion on what were the proper criteria to apply to the proposed investment of £160 million (even that was a moving figure) in the London |Midland Region electrification scheme. I am bound to say, without appearing over-conceited, that I thought the minds of the House of Commons Committee were far clearer than those of some of the witnesses of British Railways; that is, far clearer on the essentials of the criteria.

Although we lacked expert staff assistance, it was always possible for a Chairman of a House of Commons Committee, or indeed any member of the Committee, to get access to expert advice as background; and this can be done quite easily without breaching any security or privilege. I made it a point in recent inquiries to meet and have a discussion with economists, professors or otherwise, who had studied the industry under review, and where appropriate to have a talk with an expert consultant. This was done on a friendly basis. I wanted to be helped to grasp the essentials of the problems. This kind of informal briefing of the chairman is certainly a useful thing which I commend to others. If, of course, it was to influence the Committee's decision rather than give background thought, it would have to be done formally and the advice published.

THE OBJECT OF THE COMMITTEE

The kind of staff one wants for a Committee like this is, of course, related to the object of the Committee. I have found it necessary to explain from time to time to people who have not had experience of this Committee, that it was not our duty to try and administer any of these nationalized industries; it was not our duty to go into their day-to-day activities; it was not our duty to make an efficiency or financial audit; neither was it our duty to check in detail the rightness or wrongness of technical decisions, and so on. We were there to try and understand what they were doing, and make our comments on the points that mattered to the big question whether circumstances within and without their control were such that they had a full chance of running the industry efficiently—and whether they were doing so. We found that there was not any very great mystery in working out what were the essentials in each of these industries. The same kind of point arose in most of them; but there were, of course, special points in each.

On the general points I think the most important were these:
(1) The attitude of mind of the Chairman and the Board in charge on the question of whether they were carrying out a public service or doing a commercial job.
(2) The degree of ministerial interference; the direct effect of this upon the financial accounts and results; and the indirect effect through blurring the lines of responsibility.
(3) Which really follows from 1 and 2, the provision of and continuance of uneconomic services.
(4) The control of capital investment.

It is the delving into the facts on these points and the elucidation and discussion of the arguments, that in my opinion is the chief value of the Select Committee's work. I have called this the twilight area between the Ministers and the corporations. We were not encroaching specifically on ministerial responsibility. We were examining how the whole system works. On other matters peculiar to each industry, I think the Committee performs a very useful function in clearing away misunderstandings and in concentrating the attention of Members of Parliament and the public on the particular important points in the industry for the time being. And we rightly inquired into work study methods, training and research and so on. But in my view, the chief value of the Committee's work lies in those four more general questions rather than in the particular. That does not mean that I underestimate in any way the value of the careful work that is done in screening the mass of information that is given to the Committee and in explaining in simple language what it is that the industry is doing. This takes much of the time of the Committee and is an absolute essential to its work, but it is not in the end going to be the most important. I would now like to say a word about the four headings I have mentioned.

PUBLIC SERVICE OR COMMERCIAL UNDERTAKING

There is always some danger in simplification but I think it would be fair to describe the position of four of the nationalized industries in this way. The National Coal Board told us in 1957 that they found themselves in a kind of half world in which they were neither wholly a public service nor wholly a commercial undertaking. I think it changed after 1956. It changed because of market conditions and because of new thoughts by the Chairman and the Minister.

The Air Corporations were in rather a different position. We accepted that most airlines in the world are to a greater or lesser extent intentionally or unwittingly the instruments of national prestige. Both BEA and BOAC had to meet the competition from overseas that comes from small nations being ready to lose money to keep their national airlines on the world's routes. It seemed to be accepted by those who run these corporations that they were carrying out their duties as a public service by the way in which they sought efficiently to meet this kind of world competition. But we were also told about the duties they performed which they would not have done as commercial concerns. In the case of BEA this applied to the services to the Highlands and Islands. In the case of BOAC there seemed to be little doubt that if they had been a purely commercial undertaking, some at least of their operations in the West Indies and the Middle East—operations of their subsidiaries—would have been terminated.

The most striking case of the conflict between the interpretation of the duty of public service and the requirements of good economics and commerce, was found in the British Railways. As we said in our report the Commission had been guided in a number of decisions by what seemed to them to be social needs as well as by what was economically wise. It is in this way they have considered proposals for new modernization schemes without asking the Minister for his views on the subject. Of course the operation of railways in these days is a public service whether it is performed by a nationalized corporation or by privately-owned companies. But in their report, the Select Committee entertained no doubt that the confusion in judging between what is economically right and what is socially desirable had played an important part in leading to the situation in which the Commission found themselves in 1960.

In the gas industry the conflict did not seem to arise, perhaps because the industry has had a long and happy experience as a public utility.

It was not, of course, the Select Committee's business to approve or to criticize Government policy in this matter. That is left to the House of Commons as a whole. But it was part of our business to point out the results to the nationalized industries of present policies. And we have interpreted it as part of our business to add recommendations as to how, in the interests of the efficiency of the nationalized industries, present policies might be altered. Before I comment on that, I would like to say a few words on the second of the two headings—the degree of Ministerial interference.

MINISTERIAL INTERFERENCE

I have already mentioned the important points at which Ministers have powers and duties. But in each of the inquiries we did we were greatly impressed by the additional influence which Ministers had over the policy of the nationalized industries by their frequent and informal discussions with the Chairmen of the Boards. I say without fear of contradiction or need to produce specific evidence in support, that in these last ten years and before, the Chairmen of nationalized Boards have done things simply in order to please Ministers which they would not have done otherwise. The Select Committee's attitude to this problem has been to recommend that when Ministers do interfere, then they should do so openly by some kind of written direction. The feeling of Ministers on this point is that the less they interfere formally, the happier their relations with the nationalized industries will be and the better for the national interests. But the trouble about this attitude, which to be fair follows the spirit of the nationalization statutes and the debates which gave rise to them, is that the responsibility for the important decisions that settle whether the industries should be conducted efficiently or not, is in danger of becoming blurred.

To get real efficient administration—and I am sure the Royal Institute would agree with this—it is absolutely vital to have clear-cut lines of responsibility. The Chairman should know exactly for what he is responsible. If he does not know that he cannot decentralize. It has been sad to note in recent years how many of those who have advocated greater decentralization in the nationalized industries have almost in their next breath been advocating greater control by Ministers over the Chairmen of those nationalized industries. You cannot have your cake and eat it. That brings me on to the question of uneconomic services.

UNECONOMIC SERVICES

These are important to the economy of the country for two main reasons. Firstly, they upset the results of the nationalized industries and may destroy the value of the accounts as any test of efficiency. Secondly, and this is probably more important, they may result in the prices charged by the nationalized industries being higher than they otherwise would be. For the prices of nationalized industries, products and services, are in general averaged over the whole range of their operations. In the case of coal, the continuation of uneconomic services must either raise the price charged for coal generally or increase the loss or reduce the profit of the National Coal Board, or both. The continuation of the uneconomic railway services must have the same kind of effect. And in so far as these railway services are in competition with coastal shipping or road services, they may be hindering possibly other more economic activities—that is economic in the national interest—and you cannot easily find out whether there is or is not a subsidy.

Where the Government with Parliament's support wishes uneconomic services to be carried on, the additional cost of these should be provided in advance out of public funds. We recognized that it was quite impossible to discontinue uneconomic pits or discontinue uneconomic railway services, or any other, uneconomic, service abruptly without causing social damage and perhaps indirect economic damage quite out of proportion to the gain which would result by their termination. But it seemed to us that the judgment of this should be the judgment of Parliament and the Minister, and not the judgment of the Boards and their Chairmen.

The Government's answer is different. It is set out in the White Paper on the *Financial and Economic Obligations of Nationalized*

Industries.[1] Instead of providing the nationalized industries responsible for these services with money out of public funds in advance, the
Government will adjust the financial objectives imposed on these
industries. This goes a little way to meeting the problem, but it does
not—and I regret this greatly—mark a clear-cut division of responsibility between the Boards and the Ministers. In considering the
question of uneconomic railway services there are two important
points Parliament must bear in mind. Firstly, the effect upon the
efficiency of the railways and the service they give to the public;
and secondly, the ability of Parliament to control the decision, which
ability is of course reduced if there is some confusion as to who is
responsible. The same principles apply to uneconomic services as to
interference by Ministers in the freight, fare and price changes.

CONTROL OF CAPITAL INVESTMENT

The last general point is about the control of capital investment, and
here I think the Select Committee has been of value. In their very
first major inquiry, on the Coal Board, they were able to persuade the
Ministry of Power and the Treasury to take a closer look at proposed
investment schemes and to inquire into the yield or return which the
scheme was designed to achieve. Previously, they had been looking
at the investment programme as a whole without breaking it down at
all.

Obviously there is a limit as to how far the lender of money should
go in interfering in industry's decisions. The view we took was that it
was not possible to lay down very precisely how far the Government
as lenders ought to go, but when they were lending money to an
industry making large losses they clearly ought to go further in their
inquiries than when they were lending money to an industry making
large profits. Furthermore, as our inquiries developed over the years,
we did show how large sums of money were apparently being committed for projects which appeared to have great advantages but
without a very close analysis of the return that would be achieved
being made. Most of us were conscious that one of the problems of
Britain's economy in recent years has been not so much the quantity
of investment but the quality of it. The Select Committee cannot
claim to have been alone in the advice they were giving to the Government on these matters, but they can claim and do claim to share
general satisfaction that the Government have restated the financial
and economic principles which the nationalized undertakings should
observe.

The rest of what I have to say is aimed first at answering the

[1] Cmnd 1337, April 1961. See *Public Administration*, Autumn 1961, pp. 263–72.

question—What has the Select Committee achieved so far? And then at the end I will dangerously peer into the future.

What has been achieved?

(1) The House of Commons has been provided with a full report each year about one of the nationalized industries, setting out in a readable way the main facts and problems of that industry. This has been done without setting up a large office and without incurring any odium of investigation. The reports have improved the quality of debates, but they may have reduced their number by reducing controversy.

(2) Party political controversy has been absent in the Committee. There has, in all this time, been only one division in the Committee. That was in 1957, on the suggestion that imported coal should be sold at the price it cost, and on that occasion the Committee did not divide exactly by Party membership. Anyway, the point of that division seems rather strange now. The reports have been unanimous, mainly because the facts as gathered from the evidence have been allowed to speak and to dictate logically the conclusions drawn. But it should not be forgotten that until the Select Committee began to function, the activities of the nationalized industries were themselves controversial and the idea of a Select Committee itself was an idea of high political controversy.

(3) It is now generally accepted that the nationalized industries cannot contract out of their own economics—or out of national economics either. Market conditions changed in the mid-1950s from a sellers' market to a buyers' market. But the fact that the reports of the Select Committee propounded a doctrine of economic and financial discipline cannot have failed to have helped those responsible for nationalized industries, and the Treasury too.

(4) The influence of Ministers and the full effects of their decisions and requests within and beyond their statutory powers, has been discussed and explained objectively and I think fairly. Greater attention has been given to the importance of a clear-cut division of responsibility between Ministers and Boards. This too must have greatly helped for the future, though there is still more to be done.

(5) The atmosphere of the relations between Parliament and the Boards of the nationalized industries has been improved. Several Chairmen of the Boards have deliberately expressed

their pleasure in having a chance of explaining their problems fully and calmly. One at least has acknowledged the advantage to him and his colleagues of having to think things out in new ways to satisfy our friendly but probing curiosity. There is no ground for thinking that as a result of this Committee's work executives will look too much over their shoulders or that the weeds of the pernicious doctrine in industry of safety first will be more abundant or more flourishing.

In short, the Parliamentary experiment, as Mr Butler put it five years ago, has worked.

THE FUTURE OF THE COMMITTEE

The future of the Committee is no longer for me, but I cannot end without looking forward. Many of the members who served with me are still on the Committee and they have a most able new Chairman in Sir Richard Nugent. They may not all agree with what I shall say but they will know why I say it. The members of the Labour Party on the Committee have no official leader, but throughout my four years as Chairman, Austen Albu, the Member for Edmonton, greatly contributed both to the effectiveness and the unanimity of the Committee. It is good that he is still there. Continuity of thought, but not I hope any blind adherence to past practices, is further secured by the fact that the new Senior Clerk of the Committee has already served a year there.

In looking forward, my first thoughts are about the importance of keeping to the facts and the big issues, and of avoiding trying to manage in detail. In these investigations as much as anything else in my experience, the Greeks' advice of μηδεν αγαν (nothing too much) should be firmly followed. The Committee has but to unravel the facts and point the moral. Others take the action. That does not mean that the Committee should not probe—nor that they should not follow up their reports to see what has been done. But my present feeling is that the Committee will best serve the House of Commons and the public is they continue to take one industry each year and study it really thoroughly. Electricity and the rest of transport—excluding British Railways, but including London Transport—have still to be so covered.

At one time I thought we could usefully investigate some more general questions such as Consumer Councils, or price fixing in nationalized industries. But I learned to doubt the wisdom of that. There really is very little in common in these industries except that they are nationalized. An attempt to reach conclusions affecting any of them without having fully studied all the relevant facts in that particular industry, would be likely to jeopardize discussion and certainly its objectivity.

I have been considering whether the Select Committee could not help the House in its annual examination of the proposed investment expenditure of these industries. Certainly it would be wrong to rule out the possibility that the House might wish to refer such a question to the Select Committee for quick investigation. But here again there is a danger in quick inquiries. And so, not surprisingly, I am driven to defend the idea that the practice of the last five years should be continued. This would mean that the National Coal Board and the other nationalized industries will be investigated about every seven years. A long time, perhaps, but just about right because the Committee will be able to inquire thoroughly without feeling it is imposing too much on those who have the executive responsibility for running these industries. But let us all be careful at prophesying what will be or what should be. Much has changed in attitudes since 1955. Any further change in circumstances and opinions will certainly require changes in the Select Committee's methods, but sufficient unto that day.

55. WHAT KIND OF REPORTS?*

CONSIDERATIONS IN DESIGNING A STANDARD PATTERN

What would be a suitable form of Report to facilitate Parliament's task in making some assessment of an industry's efficiency? The first point to consider is whether a sharp division should not be made between past results and policies for the future. Such a distinction would seem to be justified, because in any effort to assess efficiency, it is necessary to ask the two questions: 'Have past results been good?' and 'Will current policies secure the best results over, say, the next ten or twenty years?'

Closely related to these questions is the extent to which the Report should describe ends and means. It is reasonable to assume that any industry that could demonstrate to Parliament that its past record was outstandingly good would not need to go into great detail about the means it employed. The ends achieved would be sufficiently eloquent in themselves. When a past record does not show such a result, some reasons and explanations, all of which may be perfectly valid, are necessary and justified. This does not imply, however, that all the means employed in running the industry must be laid bare.

* From Raymond Nottage: 'Reporting to Parliament on the Nationalized Industries', *Public Administration*, Vol. XXXV, Summer 1957, pp. 155–63. Reprinted by permission of the author and the editor of *Public Administration*.

When, however, one comes to consider the question of future efficiency, one is thrown entirely into the realm of the means to be employed. Reference may certainly be made to current and recent experience. This will often be a good guide to the future, but it may not be infallible and the extent to which it will need modification will always have to be considered.

In the cause of clear and logical exposition, therefore, it is suggested that a distinction between past results and policies for the future has much to commend it, and one of the important supporting reasons for this distinction is that it helps to secure a proper balance between the records of ends and of means. The National Coal Board, it is to be noted, already employ this form to some extent.

If this suggestion is accepted, the next question to be decided is the information that should be included in the record of past results. Here the Reports of the National Coal Board and British Overseas Airways Corporation give a lead. Both these Boards set out in tabular form at the beginning of their latest Reports salient operational indices and the financial results for the last year and also for the eight preceding years. One feels that in tables of this sort the reader can get the quintessential story of these industries, and in a way that would never be practicable by a report in text.

If this is so, it would be a service to Parliament if every Board printed at the beginning of its Annual Reports a summary of its operational results, in tabular form, as do the NCB and BOAC. Such a summary, it is suggested, could usefully follow these precepts:

(*a*) It should start with details of the physical operations.

(*b*) It should proceed in a logical order, e.g. an order of descending magnitude of importance.

(*c*) It should end with the financial results, which are the consequences of the physical operations.

(*d*) It should provide adequate comparisons with past years so as to reveal long-term trends.

For some Boards the production of such tables would involve little more than the collation of material already included in the Reports. For others, however, it might demonstrate that the information at present placed before Parliament is not as complete as it could usefully be.

THE SELECTION AND PRESENTATION OF INDICES

A reasonable way of selecting the operational indices would be to try and provide the essential information to answer the three following questions:

(*a*) Quantity of output—is it sufficient?

(*b*) Quality of output—is it adequate?

(*c*) Real cost of product—is it being reduced, and at a fast enough rate?

For some industries it would not be necessary to prepare elaborate indices to answer the first two questions. It is a matter of common knowledge, for example, that the gas supply is generally adequate and that, except in the very coldest weather, the electricity supply maintains its standard voltage and frequency. The more general publication of indices to measure the adequacy of the service being provided, both in terms of quantity and quality, would be helpful, however. For example, the Airways Corporations might indicate their latest accident rates and the trends of these over recent years. At the moment they publish no regular index of this important quality factor in their services.[1]

The Non-Financial Index

With regard to indices of cost, it is desirable that these should be given as far as possible in physical terms and no more than is necessary in money terms. The first reason for this is that in a time of persistent inflation, such as we have experienced since the last War, it is extremely difficult to appreciate the significance of the trend of financial costs, and to decide the allowance to be made in any particular case for the decline in the value of money. The second reason is that physical indices can often be prepared with much less trouble than those expressed in money terms and are, in fact, frequently the bases from which financial costings are derived—with a good deal of labour and expense.

The coal industry provides a good illustration of the advantage of the non-financial index. The following table shows the labour cost of a ton of coal in work and in money terms for the years 1951 and 1955 in comparison with 1947, the first year of public ownership of the coal industry:

Cost per Ton	1947	1951	1955
Man-hours[2]	7.45	6.61	6.53
Money[3]	26s 10d	32s 1d	41s 7d

[1] The Ministry of Transport and Civil Aviation publish 'Statistics of accidents on regular passenger-carrying services of UK operators' in an annual publication, *A Survey of the Accidents to Aircraft of the UK* (HMSO). They include such indices as passengers carried per passenger killed, passenger miles flown per passenger killed, and fatal accidents per 10,000 stage flights, all per year. No figures are given, however, for individual operators. The US Civil Aeronautics Board publish similar information to that issued by the Ministry.

[2] The costs in man-hours have been computed from the 'tons per manshift' figures for all workers given on page 3 of the NCB Report for 1955. A manshift,

The work index shows that there was a perceptible increase in labour efficiency between 1947 and 1951, but that the progress since then has been only slight. The money index shows a continuing and substantial decrease in labour efficiency, unless one subjects it to certain adjustments. Given the money index alone, how much should be allowed for (i) the general decline in the value of money, and (ii) the higher bid that has to be made for mining labour in conditions of stable full employment? An estimate can be made for the first—albeit a rough one—but the second involves a highly imponderable factor. One could never, in trying to assess the trend of efficiency of labour in the coal industry, produce through financial indices an answer which has anything like the certainty and validity of the index of output per manshift or per man-year.

The Ingredients of Production

All the industries being considered in this article have three principal ingredients of production: Men, Machines and Materials. It would be reasonable, therefore, for each industry, in selecting and developing its indices of real cost, to try and demonstrate the efficiency with which each of the ingredients of production is being used.

Men

An example has already been given from the coal industry indicating the value of an index measuring men's work.

Attention has also been drawn to the variation in detail of the numbers of staff employed. What is needed, generally, is an analysis of staff according to the work which they perform, and an indication of the volume of output achieved within each of those functions. Indeed, it should surely be the duty of the Boards not only to develop work measurement to a substantial degree for purposes of internal management, but also to report to Parliament the most important work measurement indices they normally use. The National Coal Board, it has been indicated, publish some such indices, as do BOAC and British European Airways. Most of the Boards, however, could usefully present a good deal more information of this sort than they do.

which is statutorily defined as '7½ hours *plus* one winding time', has been taken as an average of eight hours. The figures shown are thus 8—tons per manshift.

[3] The costs in money have been computed from the average earnings per manshift worked (all ages)—including the value of allowances in kind, details of which were published for 1947 in Table 37 of the 1948 Report, and for 1951 and 1955 in Tables 38 and 28, respectively, of the Annual Reports for those years. The figures shown are average earnings per manshift ÷ tons per manshift for all workers.

Machines

An important index in measuring the effectiveness of the utilization of machines is the 'load factor', which is broadly the ratio of remunerative work obtained from a machine to that which might have been secured if the machine could have been employed to the maximum possible extent. It is used by the Airways Corporations to show the load-ton-miles carried to the capacity-ton-miles offered, and for both corporations is now about 62 per cent. It is used in the electricity industry to show the ratio of the total amount of electricity produced or supplied during a given period to the total amount which would have been produced or supplied had the maximum demand been maintained throughout the period. Central Electricity Authority's load factor over the past few years has averaged about 45 per cent.

In the transport industries the potential speeds of the vehicles used and the average speeds actually achieved in operating them are, of course, important efficiency factors.

With regard to indices in relation to machines, there is probably scope in some of the industries for the development (or perhaps merely the publication) of measurements in regard to capital expenditure. At the moment, large sums of money are being spent, but the Reports contain little information which can enable the outsider to judge with what acumen. Presumably, when the Airways Corporations decide to buy a new aircraft, they know what the capital cost is in relation to certain basic operational units. Likewise, when Central Electricity Authority order generating equipment, they must know the probable cost per megawatt of installed capacity, and they no doubt have some knowledge of the average cost per route mile of extensions of their major distribution networks. Since the capital costs of these items of equipment are extremely high, Parliament would no doubt be interested to learn of the trends of cost in suitable unit terms, and of the resulting benefits. Indeed, it is essential to do so in any broad assessment of efficiency. Such indices can, of course, be produced most easily for industries using equipment in large and relatively standardized units, or for which average costings can be made without too high a proportion of them being subject to wide variation.

Materials

The electricity industry, with its index of thermal efficiency, provides a good illustration of the method of measuring the effectiveness with which materials—in this instance, coal—are used. Thermal efficiency is defined as 'the ratio, expressed as a percentage, between the heat energy contained in the fuel consumed, and the heat energy in the electricity sent out from the station', and Central Electricity Authority have increased it from an average of 20.91 per cent in 1947–48 to 24.35 per cent in 1955–56.

The gas industry also uses the index of thermal efficiency to assess the efficiency of its utilization of coal. In this industry, however, there are two ways of computing the index, depending upon whether one assumes that the main purpose of the industry is to produce gas and that the by-products, e.g. coke, are merely incidental, or that gas and the by-product are equally important. The Ridley Committee on *National Policy for the Use of Fuel and Power Resources* thought that the former method, which produces a relatively low figure, e.g. 55 per cent, was to be preferred; but the latter method, which produces a relatively high figure, e.g. 80 per cent, is the one used by The Gas Council in their Annual Reports.

Order of Presentation

As has been said, a logical order of presentation of information will greatly assist the layman to grasp its significance. One way of approaching this problem of presentation is to find out, and to explain to the reader, what are the proportions of the various ingredients to the total cost. According to a diagram in the 1955–56 Report of Central Electricity Authority (page 70), the cost of a unit of electricity is made up approximately as follows:

Fuel Costs	.575d
Capital and Related Charges	.425d
Other Costs	.390d

Thus it would be reasonable for Central Electricity Authority to present their operational indices for generation in the order of (i) materials, (ii) machines, and (iii) men.

Financial Information

While it may be said that, on the whole, the present Reports are deficient in work measurement indices, and unnecessarily so, they contain a plethora of financial details, and the question arises whether this emphasis on financial statements of one sort and another has not been overdone. Are a tithe of those submitted ever scrutinized, even in the most cursory fashion, and used in any way? The nationalized industries are generally required by statute to keep their accounts in 'a form which shall conform with the best commercial standards'. But in certain important respects, these industries are in radically

[1] Cmd 8647. See also The Gas Council's publication, *Thermal Efficiency in Gas Production and Utilization*, by J. E. Davis (1952).

different positions from privately-owned commercial companies, and one cannot help wondering whether they employ unnecessarily some of the detailed practices of commercial accounting. Be that as it may, in any determined attempt to make the Reports shorter, simpler and at the same time more illuminating, it might well be found that a good deal of the financial information at present included could be safely omitted. Some of this information is perhaps necessary for internal management purposes, but this does not mean that it should be included in Reports to Parliament.[1]

NEED FOR ADEQUATE COMPARISONS

In matters of administration and management there are no absolute standards of efficiency. One organization may be more efficient than another, but even the better one may fall short of its own ideals. Efficiency can be assessed only through a process of comparison and, if the Reports of the nationalized industries are to provide the best basis for such an assessment, they must make all the relevant comparisons they can, and present them in a systematic way. Such comparisons can be of three kinds:

(*a*) Over different periods of time.

(*b*) Between different parts of the organization.

(*c*) Between one organization and another.

With regard to the first of these comparisons, it has been pointed out that the National Coal Board and British Overseas Airways Corporation publish a table of results over the past few years, and there seems to be no reason why the other Boards should not do the same.

On the second, the National Coal Board, Central Electricity Authority and The Gas Council already submit a good deal of information on a Divisional and Area basis, and current practice in this regard probably needs no improvement. No doubt the British Transport Commission will do the same for the railways when their reorganization is complete.

With industries in national ownership, comparison with other organizations must often mean with those of other countries. The bases for comparison are no doubt rather limited, but it is open to question whether everything practicable is already done in this respect, and whether the Boards have made the fullest possible use in

[1] For some discussion on the question of whether or not the accounts of a nationalized industry can reveal the degree of efficiency achieved by that industry, see the Minutes of Evidence of the Select Committee on Nationalized Industries accompanying the Report of July 23, 1953 (235); in particular, the evidence given by Sir Frank Tribe, Mr T. B. Robson and Sir Harold Howitt, and Sir Edward (now Lord) Bridges.

their Reports of the internationally compiled statistics that are already available. For example, the United Nations' Economic Commission for Europe have made surveys of the efficiency of electricity supply systems in Western Europe and the USA, and the *World Airline Record* (published by Roadcap and Associates, Chicago) contains a good deal of information about the operations of the world's major airlines, including BOAC and BEA, compiled from replies to a standard questionnaire.

Once a set of operational indices is established for an industry as the basis of its record of past achievement, one may assume that, generally, not a great deal of comment need be added to explain or justify the results the indices reveal. In any event, if the indices are clearly presented in a logical order, and the comment is then directly related to them, it should be a simple matter for the reader to assimilate the information presented to him and to grasp its significance.

REPORTING ON FUTURE PLANS

The basic framework on which it has been suggested that past results should be recorded will also be suitable for reporting on plans for the future, since it will be desirable to know:

(*a*) In what quantity the goods or services of the industry will be required, or in what measure it is proposed to supply them;

(*b*) What variations, if any, in the quality of supply are in view; and

(*c*) What steps are planned to reduce the cost of the product.

With regard to the quantity, estimates may show that demand is rising. In this event, Parliament will need to be told how far this increased demand will be met by existing resources, and how far by extensions of plant. Estimates of the future may show, however, a declining demand, as with canals and the telegraph service, in which event Parliament will need to know the extent to which contraction is planned to avoid financial loss or rises in charges.

Where the quality of the service or product can be a variable factor, and especially where it is likely to influence the demand, it is reasonable for Parliament to be told what changes are proposed, the reasons for them, and the effects they are thought likely to produce.

The expected trend of future costs will inevitably be of great interest to Parliament, and it will clearly be helpful to express these costs as far as possible in real terms, so that when the actual costs come to be checked with the estimates, the comparison will not be invalidated by any changes which may have occurred in the value of money. Trends of costs may to some extent have speculative bases, and they may be falsified by events. That is no reason, however, for not advising Parliament of the assumptions on which the Boards are proceeding. The Boards clearly have to make some assumptions, and Parliament will no doubt allow for some margins of error as an inevitable feature of business activity.

The future efficiency of practically all the existing nationalized industries will depend predominantly on two factors:

(*a*) Rate of capital investment.

(*b*) Rate of technological progress.

Capital investment can serve three purposes. It can (i) maintain existing plant, (ii) buy extra plant to meet increased demands, and (iii) replace existing plant which is worn out or inefficient by modern standards. If Parliament is to be given the best possible indication of the trend of future efficiency, it will need to be told what part of proposed capital expenditure is going to each of these purposes. The first of them, maintenance of existing plant, is generally likely to lead to only minor improvements in efficiency. The second, new plant to meet extra demand, will help to raise the average efficiency, but the third, plant replacement, will generally make the biggest contribution to higher efficiency. In the latter connection it will be useful to know what are the general replacement rates for the principal items of equipment used by the industry concerned.

With regard to the rate of technological advance, this raises difficulties, as far as Annual Reports are concerned, for two reasons. First, because the Boards are not the only parties with an interest in research into, and development of, the plant and processes used in the industry with which they are concerned. The equipment manufacturers are also vitally affected, and no well-defined division of responsibility for research and development between the privately-owned manufacturers and the publicly-owned users seems as yet to have been publicly debated and promulgated. Second, research programmes generally extend over periods of longer than a year and, for this reason, are not always easy to report on each twelve months.

There is no reason, however, why the Boards should not describe the operating characteristics of the latest plant brought into service, and the improvements in these characteristics which plant soon to be introduced or shortly to be ordered is expected to produce.

ADVANTAGES OF A STANDARD PATTERN

The foregoing suggestions for a standard pattern of Annual Report would be largely applicable, it is thought, to all the present nationalized industries. Experience might show that they could be improved upon. But that a standard pattern could be constructed, to which all the Boards could broadly conform, if they felt inclined to do so, can hardly be doubted.

To have such a standard pattern would bring at least three advantages. First, for the Member who acquainted himself with that pattern, it would greatly facilitate initial reading and comprehension, and subsequent reference. Second, it would help Members to understand what are the salient factors that must concern the Boards themselves in running their industries. Third, it would serve to direct Parliament's consideration and discussion to the big issues and away from matters of less importance. Indeed, if they were able to obtain a clearer understanding of the major problems of the industries and the ways they are being tackled, MPs might feel less anxious than they are at present to debate the industries' affairs or ask Questions about them in Parliament. As Sir Ivor Jennings has said: 'Members are always curious until they have means of satisfying their curiosity.'

It may be argued that a Report of the type proposed, no matter how well it was constructed or how carefully its indices were selected and presented, would not be able to give the complete answer to the question: 'Is this industry being run with the maximum possible efficiency?' It would not be able to answer this question any more satisfactorily than can the shareholder who, when receiving an increased dividend, wonders whether, if the sales force had been more energetic and the production manager more ingenious, the increase might not have been even greater. A logical and standard method of selecting and presenting material would, however, have real advantages not offered by the present diverse methods of reporting. It would reveal the largest area of really significant information and, in so doing, limit the scope for conflicting interpretation and argument.

Improved reports for Parliament would not, of course, obviate the need for periodical detailed enquiries like those carried out by the Fleck and Herbert Committees in the coal and electricity industries. They might, however, help Parliament to decide when such enquiries should be undertaken. In any event, Parliament can never do the work of such specialized bodies itself.

CHAPTER IX

Consumers' Consultation

As a feature of post-1945 nationalization, the statutory consumers' council has given little satisfaction. Opinion differs whether this is due to the inherent defects of the device or to correctable faults in its existing structure. Since Mr J. W. Grove's comparatively early article on the subject (*Public Administration*, Vol. XXVIII, 1950, p. 221), few students have undertaken any analysis of consumer council organization and performance. A notable exception is the article by Messrs. Mills and Howe, from which *Extract 56* is taken.

On the other hand, there has been no lack of proposals for reform, many of which suggest that local authorities should be used as the 'base' of a redesigned structure. Outstanding among such proposals are those of Professor J. A. G. Griffith, made in 1950 (*Extract 57*). Other proposals have come from Professor Sargent Florence and Mr Henry Maddick (*Extract 58*). These authors, after criticizing the defects of the existing system, suggest that consumers' representatives ought to be permitted to participate in the taking of 'general decisions on the price level and structure, and on the quality of goods and services'.

56. CONSUMER REPRESENTATION AND THE WITHDRAWAL OF RAILWAY SERVICES*

An issue which attracted considerable attention in the post-war debates on the nationalization Bills was that of consumer representation. The nature of the representation ultimately included in the various Acts varied in detail from industry to industry, but a universal feature was that the consumer should not collaborate in the making of policy. This remained the prerogative of the Board of each industry, although a system of Consumer Committees was created from which the views of the consumer could be sought. In the early years of nationalization several studies of the various Committees

---

* From G. Mills and M. Howe: 'Consumer Representation and the Withdrawal of Railway Services', *Public Administration*, Vol. XXXVIII, Autumn 1960, pp. 253–62. Reprinted by permission of the authors and the editor of *Public Administration*.

were made, each expressing some doubts about the ability of the Committees, as constituted, to play any significant role.[1] A decade of experience of the working of the Committees now permits a further examination.[2]

This paper attempts to assess an important aspect of the work of the Consumer Committees in surface transport. Section 6 (7) of the Transport Act, 1947, empowers the Transport Consultative Committees to consider 'any matter (including charges) affecting the services and facilities provided by the [British Transport] Commission'. It was always intended that the Committees, as representatives of the consumer, should have some influence upon policy;[3] in fact, a major part of the work of the Committees has been the consideration of proposals made by the Commission to withdraw railway services and facilities, and it is only this issue which is examined here.

PROPOSALS FOR THE WITHDRAWAL OF SERVCES

The withdrawal of unremunerative services is not merely a post-war phenomenon. A number of services proved to be unremunerative as soon as they were opened, and, consequently, were promptly withdrawn. But despite increasing competition from road transport, the rate of withdrawal remained modest until nationalization, except for a short period from 1929 to about 1932. Section 3 of the nationalization Act required the British Transport Commission to provide 'an efficient, adequate, economical and properly integrated system of public inland transport' and to charge fares which would be 'sufficient for making provision for the meeting of charges properly chargeable to revenue, taking one year with another'. In prescribing objectives which differed from those of the railway companies, the advocates of nationalization hoped to continue the unremunerative services in, for example, the rural areas, by spreading the cost over the whole railway system.[4] By Section 25 of the Transport Act of 1953, how-

[1] See, for example, A. M. de Neuman, 'Consumers' Representation in the Public Sector of Industry', *Manchester School*, Vol. XVIII, 1950, pp. 143–62; J. A. G. Griffith, 'The Voice of the Consumer', *Political Quarterly*, Vol. XXI, 1950, pp. 171–83; F. Milligan, 'The Consumers' Interest', in W. A. Robson (ed.), *Problems of Nationalized Industry*, London, 1952, pp. 144–70; Acton Society Trust, *Relations with the Public* (Nationalized Industry Study No. 12), 1953.

[2] A comprehensive study of the machinery of consumer representation in the electricity industry was made by the Herbert Committee; see *Report of the Committee of Inquiry into the Electricity Supply Industry*, Cmnd 9672, 1956, Ch. 20. This study concentrated on the working of the machinery in investigating complaints, rather than in influencing policy.

[3] The Act for surface transport was the first to embody the term 'consultative committee', and the first to give a Board the statutory right to consult the committees on issues of policy.

[4] See 431, *H.C. Deb.*, 5s, Col. 1623.

ever, the duty of the Commission was changed to that of providing only such services as might appear expedient, due regard being had to efficiency, economy and safety. Concurrently with the increase in the financial difficulties of the Commission, the modernization plan of 1955 was drawn up. This envisaged the toleration of many unremunerative services on the assumption that the introduction of modern methods would ultimately make them remunerative. Since 1955 various reappraisals of the plan have been made and it is now accepted that the financial problems of the Commission are unlikely to be solved as rapidly as was previously assumed. In keeping with this, the view now is that the problems of unremunerative services can be tackled only by a more rapid rate of withdrawal.

The following table shows that the annual rate of complete closure has varied since nationalization:

CLOSURE OF STANDARD-GAUGE PERMANENT WAY,
BRITISH RAILWAYS, 1949–59

Year	Route miles closed	Year	Route miles closed
1949	11	1955	92
1950	102	1956	40
1951	117	1957	64
1952	90	1958	118
1953	56	1959	289
1954	72		

Source: British Transport Commission, *Financial and Statistical Accounts*, 1949–59.

Sometimes, the passenger service is withdrawn from a line while the freight service remains. Hence these figures refer only to cases where both types of service are withdrawn simultaneously, or where a line with one type only is completely closed. The total length of route open at the end of 1959 was about 18,565 miles. Thus the annual rate of total closure represents only a modest part of the total, and the corresponding proportion for the rate of withdrawal of passenger services only, is not significantly greater. British Railways have forecast that in the period 1959–63 about 1,850 route miles will be completely closed.[1] Though this indicates an increased rate of withdrawal, the rate remains a modest proportion of the total, namely about 2 per cent per annum. So far most of the services withdrawn have been on rural branch lines or on cross-country routes, while closure of individual stations has occurred also on main and suburban lines.

The initiative in the withdrawal of any service comes from the

[1] Cf CTCC *Annual Report for 1959* (HMSO, 1960), para. 5. This forecast may be revised in the light of the 1960 re-examination of the future role of British Railways.

railway management. Under the recent decentralization policy, the authority to propose a withdrawal now rests with district or line management.[1] In at least one district the profitability of all services is considered twice a year at a district management conference and selected services are then subjected to a more detailed cost analysis.[2] The selection is based largely upon economic criteria although consideration of possible public protest may occasionally have some influence. After the detailed analysis the management may recommend withdrawal. For all major proposals the approval of the BTC has to be obtained although the authority for minor proposals is now wholly with the regional managements. The proposal is made public and persons and organizations wishing to object are invited to write to the relevant Consultative Committee, if a satisfactory arrangement cannot be reached directly with the railway management.

THE CONSULTATIVE COMMITTEES—STRUCTURE AND COMPOSITION

The transport consultative machinery is two-tier. Section 6 (3) of the Transport Act, 1947, established a Central Transport Consultative Committee for Great Britain (CTCC) and Transport Users' Consultative Committees for Scotland, and for Wales and Monmouthshire. Also, it directs the Minister to create as many area Transport Users' Consultative Committees (TUCCs) as might be necessary to cover the whole of England. By 1952 the present structure of nine such Committees had been completed.[3] The area Committees per-

---

[1] The extent of decentralization, and the terminology used, varies from region to region. See British Transport Commission, *Annual Report for 1957* (HMSO, 1958), paras. 65–71.

[2] On the other hand, in the Western Region, in which there has been relatively little decentralization, there is a Branch Lines Committee to keep such services under review, and this committee makes recommendations to the regional management. See *The Economist*, London, January 24, 1959, p. 335.

[3] Scotland and Wales are not divided into smaller areas. For full details, see CTCC, *Handbook on Transport Users' Consultative Committees*, London, no date, pp. 10–11. The Transport Act, 1947, Sections 76–81, also created the Transport Tribunal (whose decisions are binding unless set aside by the Minister) to confirm, modify or reject charges schemes proposed by the Commission. The relationship between the CTCC and the Tribunal is not made clear in the Act; although the Consultative Committees have authority to consider charges, and although the Commission has submitted to the CTCC details of various charges schemes, the CTCC has usually chosen not to concern itself with such issues. Thus in 1951, the CTCC declined to comment on a scheme 'in view of the exhaustive nature of the public inquiry into the matter by the Transport Tribunal' (CTCC, *Annual Report for 1950* (HMSO, 1951), para. 16). The CTCC has considered charges on at least one occasion, however: in 1952, the Minister directed the BTC not to implement increases in charges which had been approved by the

form the detailed work of hearing objections to withdrawal proposals, bodies less remote than the CTCC being necessary partly because of the extensive services provided by the Commission and partly because of the personal nature of the contract between the supplier and the user of transport. In special circumstances, the CTCC has itself heard objections, but usually the role it plays in any particular case is confined to reviewing the minutes and recommendations of TUCCs.

Members of the Committees are appointed by the Minister. The number of members is left to his discretion and a membership of about twenty persons seems to be favoured for the CTCC and for each of the TUCCs. The composition of membership of all the Committees follows a similar pattern, namely, an independent chairman; members representative of agriculture, industry and commerce, shipping, labour and local government, chosen by the Minister from panels of names submitted by organized bodies; two members nominated by the Commission who are transport managers, one of whom shall be, in the case of the CTCC, a member of the Commission itself; and not more than two additional members appointed by the Minister. The Minister has not appointed two such members in every case; thus, at the time of writing, the TUCC for the East Midlands Area has only one. These additional members are intended to be representatives of the public at large. As members are part-time and unpaid,[1] however, it is to be expected that the appointments will generally be of public spirited persons rather than of persons qualified to speak for the public at large; one such member, for example, is a representative of the Federation of Women's Institutes. The additional members appointed to the CTCC have always been the chairman of the Scottish and Welsh TUCCs.[2]

Transport Tribunal, and asked the CTCC to consider the implications of the increases. In the main, the CTCC's report upheld the decision of the Tribunal, but the Minister did not reverse his directive. See *The Economist*, April 19, 1952, p. 142; April 26th, p. 207; June 21st, p. 799; or British Transport Commission, *Annual Report for 1952*, HMSO, 1953, pp. 54–5.

[1] Members may, however, be compensated at the discretion of the Commission for loss of earnings or out-of-pocket expenses in accordance with a scale approved by the Minister. Expenses are also paid at the discretion of the management of the industry in gas and electricity; but in coal, the Minister, and in civil aviation, Parliament, are *obliged* to make such payments.

[2] There is an interesting comparison with the Railway and Canal Commission, set up in 1873 and remodelled under the Railway and Canal Traffic Act, 1888. This Commission had five members. Two were appointed on the recommendation of the Board of Trade, and one of these was required to be 'of experience in railway business' (S. 3); these appointed Commissioners were paid a salary. The other three were *ex officio* members, who were required to be judges of a superior court, one from each of England, Scotland and Ireland. In general it would appear that only one *ex officio* member attended any particular hearing. The Commission was a court with full judicial powers over matters concerning charges and

THE EXAMINATION OF WITHDRAWAL PROPOSALS

The objections to any proposal are heard by the TUCC of the area in which the service is located. If a service passes through two areas then either the TUCCs concerned may hear objections jointly, or one of the Committees may hold a hearing and subsequently consult the other. The proposal is submitted by the Commission in a form which was devised during consultations between the Commission and the CTCC in 1958.[1] Representatives of the local railway management may be invited to the hearing to give further details of the proposal. Although Parliament has not given guidance on the form of procedure to be adopted at hearings, a fairly standard pattern has been developed, with an emphasis upon informality.

There is some difference of opinion, however, as to whether the Consultative Committees are to act as impartial advisers, or to represent only the views of the users.[2] The intention of the Government when promoting the Transport Bill in 1947 is clear: according to the Minister of Transport, the Committees would provide users, for the first time, 'with a real means of making their views felt'.[3] The CTCC, however, while stressing that it does not conduct arbitration proceedings,[4] has been guilty of ambiguities. Thus the Committees are bodies to which the user who cannot obtain satisfaction from the Commission 'may appeal and get an impartial hearing', but 'this appeal is not to a detached judicial authority but to an influential body of transport users'.[5] A reason for the difficulty may be that the Committees undertake two kinds of work of a differing character, namely the hearing of individual grievances and the review of policy; impartiality may be thought sensible in the former if not in the latter. Certainly more in line with the intention of the promoters with regard to policy matters is the view that the Committees' role is 'to represent users of all kinds and to convey their views to the Minister and to the British Transport Commission'.[6]

the provision of services, an important aim being to prevent the railway companies from discriminating between traders, etc. Thus while the purpose of the Commission had something in common with the Consultative Committees—namely, protection of the interests of consumers—the structure of the Commission was quite different. The Commission lost its jurisdiction over charges in 1921, and was abolished in 1949. See also O. Kahn-Freund, *The Law of Carriage by Inland Transport* (London, 1956), pp. 44–7 and p. 58, and D. N. Chester, *Public Control of Road Passenger Transport* (Manchester, 1936), p. 193.

[1] The form is laid out in the Appendix of CTCC, *Annual Report for 1958* (HMSO, 1959).

[2] J. A. G. Griffith and H. Street, *Principles of Administrative Law*, 2nd edition, London, 1957, pp. 313–4.

[3] 437, *H.C. Deb.*, 5s, Col. 128.

[4] CTCC Handbook, *op. cit.*, p. 7.

[5] *Ibid.*   [6] *Ibid.*, p. 1.

M

In considering proposals to withdraw services, the Committees have had to decide how best 'to represent transport users of all kinds', without any statutory guidance. The Committees have chosen to approve such proposals whenever 'the hardship of particular members of the public does not outweigh the general public advantage of closing a line or withdrawing a facility which is losing money'.[1] The intention of the Committees therefore is that the hearings shall provide a forum for the ventilation of cases of alleged hardship as a consequence of withdrawal. Although it is invariably the case that criticism of British Railways' figures of the savings that would follow withdrawal constitutes one of the more popular objections to the proposal, the Committees do not regard it as part of their function to allow those figures to be examined at the public hearing.[2] Indeed, questions raised by objectors upon the validity of figures have on occasion been ruled out-of-order.[3] An objector has the right to submit written objections only; having done this, he may be invited to attend Committee meetings, at his own expense, to give oral evidence.[4]

AMOUNT AND SOURCE OF INFORMATION

The amount of information in support of the proposal which is released to objectors is limited.[5] The extent of the information released is governed by the 1958 agreement between the Commission and the CTCC. That the amount of information provided is so limited reflects the view of the Commission, which is upheld by the CTCC, that, since the Committees 'themselves sufficiently represent and guard the public interest . . . there is no need to provide information for anyone else, particularly regarding figures of savings, costs or losses, which can only be explained with difficulty to those unfamiliar with them, and can be distorted by facile but unsound reasoning'.[6] Objectors have no right to cross-examine representatives of the Commission in an effort either to question the validity of the figures or to supplement the information available to them. The source of further information to objectors is the Committee, which usually takes the view that it is only necessary that the members of the Committees shall be satisfied that the figures are correct.[7]

[1] CTCC Handbook, *op. cit.*, p. 4.
[2] CTCC *Annual Report for 1958*, para. 20.
[3] For an example, see *Hunts Post* (Huntingdon), April 16, 1959, p. 13.
[4] Some committees have established the rule that all persons who submit written objections shall be invited to give oral evidence also.
[5] See CTCC *op. cit.*, Appendix, for the form in which the figures of savings estimated to accrue from withdrawal is released to objectors. A similar statement is commonly released to the Press, before the hearing.
[6] CTCC *Annual Report for 1957*, para. 7.
[7] See, e.g. *Hunts Post, op. cit.*, p. 13.

The individual Committee is also the source of information for the Press; it has discretion either to bar or to admit the Press, and, if the latter, to admit the Press either to the whole or to only part of the proceedings. In some cases the Press and the public have been excluded on the grounds that 'the full, frank and free discussion that takes place across a table would often be impossible if those taking part knew that everything they said was public property'.[1]

The hearing is generally brief and is usually followed by a short, private deliberation, which is not always held on the same day as the hearing. The recommendation of a TUCC, and the minutes of the hearing, are passed to the CTCC, which body may then either make its own recommendation to the Minister and to the Commission, or require the TUCC to rehear the case. The Minister acts as intermediary between the Consultative Committees and the Commission;[2] he can direct the Commission on issues raised in the CTCC's recommendation as he thinks fit and the Commission is obliged to carry out his directions. But, as far as withdrawal proposals are concerned, the Minister's powers of direction have not yet been used because the Commission has so far acted upon the recommendations of the CTCC in every case.[3]

THE EFFECTIVENESS OF THE CONSULTATIVE MACHINERY

In assessing the work of the Consultative Committees, their *effective* role is considered first. Despite the protestations of the CTCC to the contrary, the Committees appear, at first sight, to serve as *de facto* arbitrators. On the one hand, there is no effective course of action open to any member of the public who may disagree with a Committee decision: letters to the Press provoke only a statement from British Railways to the effect that the proper process of consultation has taken place, and that there is no ground for further complaint;[4] if the matter is raised in Parliament, the Minister places equal faith in the consultative machinery. On the other hand, British Railways have so far invariably accepted the recommendations of the CTCC. Thus the decision is clearly binding on the consumer and appears effectively to bind the Commission. But it must be pointed out that in only a very few cases have the CTCC refused to support the withdrawal of

[1] CTCC Handbook, *op. cit.*, p. 7. The public are admitted more freely to hearings in the gas and electricity industries but, there, the hearings are more usually to hear individual grievances rather than to review policy.

[2] By statute, the CTCC must submit an annual report to the Minister.

[3] Cf. CTCC Handbook, *op. cit.*, p. 6. See also footnote 3, p. 351 above.

[4] For an example, see the correspondence in the *Manchester Guardian*, June 10 and 12, 1959.

Nationalization

services;[1] hence, while the Commission at present accepts the decisions of the CTCC, it is not certain that it would continue to do so should the opinions of the two diverge to any significant extent.

The early commentators[2] criticized Consumer Committees generally on several counts: not advertising their existence to the public at large; holding meetings infrequently and often *in camera*; appearing to be subservient to the industry concerned, and passing 'the producer's point of view to the consumer, rather than the consumer's to the producer';[3] and so forth. In the case of the Transport Consultative Committees, little has changed to meet these criticisms, either in the legislation governing the structure, composition and arrangements of the Committees, or in the attitudes and acts of the Committees themselves. It is true that the Committees have endeavoured to become better known to the public, but, as shown above, the Committees still feel that the public are not to be trusted with a full knowledge of their work. The objectors are often not satisfied with the manner in which hearings are conducted; regrettably, the proceedings sometimes become acrimonious. The Committees are still provided with accommodation by the BTC, rather than by the Minister (as in the case of the corresponding Committees in the coal and civil aviation industries), and this continues to prevent justice from being seen to be done.[4]

The Technical Issues

A major criticism of the Committees is that they still lack the technical ability necessary for the assessment of the complex issues of costs and revenues presented to them. Since discussion of these issues is effectively restricted to the private deliberations of the Committees, informed opinions can come only from members of the Committee. The members appointed to represent organized bodies of consumers and the public at large are not chosen for their expert knowledge *per se*, and it seems that only rarely are such representatives specially qualified in this field. On the other hand, the Commission's representatives are chosen from the higher ranks of its own management and hence are usually much more knowledgeable on the major

[1] Some critics regard this as evidence of the subservience of the Committees to the Commission; however, the existence of an agreed economic criterion for evaluating proposals generally discourages British Railways from submitting proposals for which a strong case cannot be made.

[2] See the references given in the first footnote.

[3] de Neuman, *op. cit.*, p. 159.

[4] Also undesirable in this respect is the growing number of cases in which the Commission has acted in anticipation of a favourable Consultative Committee recommendation. For an example, see 606, *H.C. Deb.*, 5s, Col. 201.

technical issues. As a consequence, independent expert opinion will rarely be available.[1]

The agreed scheme of presentation of costs and revenues is much simpler than that used, for example, at the Lewes-East Grinstead inquiry, where there was considerable confusion over accounting technicalities.[2] Indeed the CTCC now feels that the Committees, 'as reasonable men and women',[3] without any particular expertise, e.g. in accountancy, are able to arrive at a sound decision. But, even if the criteria used in the agreed scheme are acceptable,[4] their application rests partly on the personal judgment of the British Railways' experts who prepare the estimates.[5] The Committee has neither the time nor the knowledge to make a full check either of this preparatory work or of the many courses of action alternative to complete closure. Thus it still seems to be desirable that the Committees should include some experts, or be assisted by qualified advisers.

In seeking to suggest ways of improving the situation, the second alternative seems to be the more promising. A research team of experts could be set up either in the Ministry of Transport or elsewhere in the Civil Service (e.g. in the Department of Scientific and Industrial Research), thereby ensuring a considerable degree of independence of view. The services of the group could then be made available to the Consultative Committees. In particular, the group could advise the CTCC on the form of the criteria to be used for estimating savings upon withdrawal, and for estimating the costs of alternative ways of providing rail services. Subsequently, members of the group could carry out checks on the application of these criteria in particular cases, and be present at hearings and meetings of the TUCCs to give expert advice from their own independent viewpoint. This scheme should ensure that the examination of withdrawal proposals is competent, and also help to convince objectors on this point.

Social Hardship

If the technical issues were removed from the province of the TUCCs, they would be left with the task of weighing social hardship. It is doubtful whether any acknowledged expertize constitutes a qualifica-

[1] It seems likely that because of their greater knowledge, the repesentatives of the Commission may unduly sway the Committee on these matters.

[2] CTCC, *Report on the Proposed Withdrawal of Train Services from the Lewes-East Grinstead Branch Railway*, Cmnd 360, February 1958; and the Minutes of Proceedings of the Inquiry.

[3] CTCC, *Annual Report for 1958*, para. 19.

[4] For an argument to the contrary, see M. Howe and G. Mills, 'The Withdrawal of Railway Services', *Economic Journal*, Vol. LXX, 1960, pp. 348–56.

[5] *Ibid.*, p. 350.

tion for this work, but obviously it is desirable that the Committees should be able to recognize the emotion and ambiguity which is frequently a feature of individual objections.[1] The main issue is the nature and extent of alternative public transport. If the research group were suitably constituted, it could carry out, on behalf of the TUCC, a factual survey which would be more thorough than that commonly undertaken at present. The research group could also follow up a closure by later studying the changes in the use made of transport facilities of all kinds consequent upon the withdrawal of the rail service in question.[2] Such studies would provide valuable experience, and would give the Committees a clearer idea of the social hardship likely to follow future withdrawals.

Policy and the Consultative Committees

In comparing the monetary valuation of social hardship consequent upon closure with the savings which would be made by closing the line, the Committees must be influenced by national policy. Now, although they have lacked firm and consistent guidance on how national policy is to be related to individual unremunerative lines, it is also fair to say that they have developed no vigorous views of their own. There does not seem to be anything in the legislation which would prevent the Committees from fulfilling the hopes expressed in 1948 by Mr Herbert Morrison (now Lord Morrison of Lambeth): 'I want them to be critically minded in every good sense of the term and I want their reports to Ministers and the public to be frank. They must be ready to fight when it is necessary for them to fight. These bodies can become important if they are properly run and the consumers' representatives are sufficiently active and vigorous.'[3] Thus their failure to do so must be largely of their own choice. In particular, they have failed to exercise initiative in developing any policy to represent the consumers' views on unremunerative services.[4] Since

[1] '. . . it has always been recognized by those who have studied the matter that consumer representatives . . . require certain special knowledge . . . [for example] methods of consumer research.' Acton Society Trust, *op. cit.*, p. 23.

[2] For example, at the hearing into the proposal to close the Eden Valley line, British Railways stated that they intended to carry certain freight across the Pennines by a longer alternative route and claimed that the delivery time would not be appreciably increased. (See *Cumberland and Westmorland Herald*, Penrith, February 27, 1960, p. 1.) Should this line be closed, this assertion could be tested by the research group. A more thorough method of investigation would be required than that reported, for example, in 'Closing of Branch Lines', *The Economist*, January 24, 1959, p. 335. A recent, more comprehensive investigation is by D. St John Thomas, *Report on Rural Transport*, Dawlish, 1960.

[3] Quoted in de Neuman, *op. cit.*, p. 144.

[4] The CTCC regards policy matters as being outside the proper sphere of a part-time organization; see CTCC Handbook, *op. cit.*, p. 7.

the 1953 Act the policy of the Government has been that the railways should endeavour to cover their total costs, or at any rate that they should do so after the completion of the 1955 modernization plan. At the same time, the Consultative Committees were prepared in principle to recommend the retention of those unprofitable services where, in their opinion, the social hardship outweighed the economic cost. Also at this time, the system as a whole was not earning enough revenue to cover its costs.

The CTCC could have made some attempt to resolve the contradiction by putting forward some policy of its own to represent the views of users. Detailed policy could have followed one of three general courses: (*a*) withdraw most, or all, unremunerative services; (*b*) subsidize specific services; (*c*) regard the railways as a whole as a public service, and grant a general subsidy. But the CTCC has not put forward any such suggestions, and it is significant that in the debate in the early part of 1960 on the future of the railways, there was no suggestion that the CTCC be consulted, even though, by statute, both the Minister and the Commission have the power to initiate Consultative Committee deliberations. Thus the effect of the consultative machinery on policy making in this respect has been negligible. Indeed it is conceivable that if the Consultative Committees had not existed, the various groups of consumers would have had a better chance of making effective representations, by approaching a Minister who could not then have avoided responsibility by transferring the problem to the formal consultative machinery.

57. THE VOICE OF THE CONSUMER*

We have suggested that that machinery is effective which persuades the public that a nationalized industry is being run for its benefit. This means that the body to whom complaints and representations are made must be easily accessible and strong in the consumer's cause, ready and able, if necessary, to cross swords with the administering corporations. The main defects of the present arrangements are as follows: First, the consumers' councils and committees are too closely linked to the administering corporations; everything then rests on the attitude which the consumers' body chooses to adopt. This is also the weakness of the suggestion that consumers' representatives should sit on the boards of the corporations. Second, there

* From J. A. G. Griffith: 'The Voice of the Consumer', *The Political Quarterly*, Vol. XXI, No. 2, April-June 1950, pp. 177–83. Reprinted by permission of the author and the editors of *The Political Quarterly*.

are too many different systems. This raises the problem of personnel, for the number of persons who have the time, energy and ability to do the kind of work which is required is limited. The country is becoming littered with advisory committees of one sort or another, and the standard seems to be declining. Above all, unity is strength and division is weakness. Third, the individual consumer suffers from being unorganized. An industry not only uses far more of the various services but is normally a member of a national organization. (Here, and below, we use the phrase 'individual consumer' to mean, in the case of gas, electricity and coal, the ordinary householder or small trader and, in the case of transport, the passenger or small trader; we use the phrase 'industry' to include those who use the services on a large scale for their business purposes.) The individual consumer is much too easily brushed aside, whether intentionally or not; indeed, he often feels so helpless that he does not trouble to make his complaints. He needs a champion—someone over whom he has some influence. We suggest that this role can be filled by his local authority (by which we mean his urban, rural, borough or county borough council). Fourth, the present consumers' bodies are too inaccessible to the individual consumer. This is particularly true in the case of coal, and seems likely to be true for transport also. The alternative method of applying to officials employed by the Ministry or the administering corporation is contrary to the whole conception of adequate representation of consumer interest.

To meet these defects, it is suggested that one hierarchy of authorities should be established to represent the consumer and user of services and facilities provided by *all* nationalized industries. At the top a Cabinet Minister without departmental responsibilities should represent consumers' interests. The most obvious choice would be the Lord President of the Council. There should be one central consumers' council and, at the lower level, one county consumers' council for each county and county borough area. In addition there should be a central consumers' tribunal and county consumers' tribunals.

The county consumers' councils would be composed of representatives of consumers. In a county, each district and borough council would nominate one of its members; other seats would be filled by an equal number of nominees of industries and associations in the county recognized by the Cabinet Minister for this purpose; in addition, the county council would nominate five of its members. In a county borough, the number of borough council members who sat on the county consumers' council would be equal to the number of other nominees. The central consumers' council would be composed of one delegate from each county consumers' council and would therefore number about 150. A county consumers' tribunal would have as its chairman an experienced lawyer appointed by the Lord Chancellor and two members. One member would be appointed by the Cabinet Minister referred to from a panel nominated by and drawn from the members of the county consumers' council; the other member would be appointed by the Minister of Fuel and Power (for gas, electricity or coal cases) or by the Minister of Transport (for transport cases), and would be a person experienced in the administration of the commodity concerned. The members of the central consumers' tribunal would be nominated in the same way except that the 'consumers' member' would be drawn from the central consumers' council.

Representations and complaints are, broadly, of three kinds. The first is *general* and concerns a whole area. The area affected may be as small as a county district or a ward; it may, in the case of gas and electricity, be the area of an area board; it may, in the case of transport, be the entire country. The complaint may be that the standard prices and rates in the area for the particular service are excessively high or that the facilities are inadequate or that the commodity supplied is generally poor. The train service may be thought insufficient, the gas pressure too low, electricity charges excessive, the amount of available anthracite inadequate. The second kind of representation or complaint is *particular* to an individual. A particular delivery of coal may be below the normal standard; there may be a complaint of undue preference or injustice; there may be a dispute about a differential rate; or about the attitude of a particular official or local office of an administering corporation. The third kind is a *legal* complaint. It covers short-weight deliveries, overcharging, negligent installation resulting in damage, and generally duties which are imposed on the administering authorities by common law or by statutes other than those which specifically establish and govern the administering corporations. These three kinds of complaint are not capable of being dealt with by the same bodies. Legal complaints must be particularly distinguished. It would be possible to grant to the consumers' tribunals referred to jurisdiction to deal with legal complaints, but there is no advantage in removing these matters from the ordinary courts. The liability of the administering corporations in these matters is not on a footing different from the liability of private persons and private corporations. The settling of legal complaints should therefore be left to the ordinary courts.

General representations and complaints made by industries (as defined above) would be made direct to the county consumers' council. Those made by individual consumers would be made to the local authority (urban, rural, or non-county borough council in a county, and county borough council in a county borough). The local authority would then decide whether to adopt the complaint and present it to the county consumers' council. If the local authority received ten or more representations or complaints on the same subject, it would be obliged to adopt and present. The object of requiring the individual consumer to approach the consumers' council through his local authority is twofold. First, it strengthens his position if his case is adopted and, secondly, it makes use of a representative body which the individual knows at first hand and which is responsible to him. A local authority would not have to wait for a subject to be introduced by an individual consumer; any ten of its members could themselves make their complaints as individual consumers or, on motion by any member, the authority would be able to resolve that a certain matter be brought before the county consumers' council. General representations and complaints would in all cases be presented to the county consumers' council in writing and would be referred at once to the committee of that council which dealt with its subject (gas, electricity, coal or transport). The representative of the local authority (or one nominated representative in the case of a county borough council) or of the industry which presented the matter would appear before the committee and the matter would be debated. The committee would then recommend to its council whether or not the representation or complaint should be forwarded by the council to the administering authority (area board for gas and electricity; regional authority for coal and executive for transport). The council would debate this recommendation. If the council decided to forward the matter to the administering authority, a deputation of three members nominated by the council would arrange with the administering authority for a joint meeting where the matter could be discussed. If the county consumers' council was dissatisfied with the response of the administering authority, it would be able to forward its case to the central consumers' council which would be entitled to approach the central administering corporation (British Electricity Authority, Gas Council, British Transport Commission or National Coal Board) in the same way. Further appeal by the Central Consumers' Council would lie to the Minister of Fuel and Power or of Transport. Before this Minister made his decision, he would be required to consult with the Cabinet Minister representing consumers' interests.

Particular complaints by individual consumers or industries would be made in the first instance to the local office of the administering corporation. If satisfaction were not obtained, appeal would lie to the county consumers' tribunal, which would hear both parties. If the complaint alleged a substandard consignment, the tribunal could order replacement or compensation; if a refusal to perform a par-

ticular duty, the tribunal could order performance; if undue preference, the tribunal could order compensation and future compliance;
if the complaint were of the conduct of a particular official, the
tribunal could declare its findings of the facts of the case. Appeal
would lie on questions other than those of fact to the central consumers' tribunal. These instances are only meant as examples of the
tribunal's jurisdiction. Generally it would have power to consider any
case where it was claimed that the public corporation had in a particular case failed to carry out the duties laid on it by its constituent
Act, provided that the failure were particular and not merely one
instance of a general inadequacy. For example, low gas pressure
would normally be common to a district and should therefore be the
subject of a general, not a particular, complaint. The tribunal would
therefore be entitled on this ground to refuse to hear a case and would
indicate to the complainant the course which he should pursue.

What we have said above applies generally to gas, electricity,
coal and transport, but certain exceptions must be made in the case
of transport because of the important and powerful position occupied
by the Transport Tribunal. We have seen that this body has jurisdiction over many questions relating to rates, facilities and undue
preference. There would clearly be little to be gained and much to be
lost by transferring this jurisdiction *en bloc* to the tribunals we have
proposed. Representations and complaints relating to transport
rates, in particular, would continue to be made to the Transport
Tribunal, which would also retain its jurisdiction over charges
schemes and its advisory function during the transitional period
where the Minister is considering an increase in charges. Local
authorities are entitled to appear before the Tribunal to object to
charges; we would transfer this right to appear to county consumers' councils, acting either on their own initiative or as a result of
a representation or complaint. Undue preference complaints would
continue to be made to the Transport Tribunal. We suggest that
experience has shown that complaints of inadequate facilities,
especially when made on behalf of the general public of a locality, are
not best handled by an independent tribunal. The powers and practice of the Transport Tribunal (or its predecessor) have, in this
respect, been restricted in scope, and we would transfer the making of
such general complaints to the hierarchy of local authorities, consumers' councils and Ministers which we have outlined above.

An industry or industrial consumer which is complaining may be
so large that it extends over the area of more than one county or
county borough. This is, of course, particularly true of the public
corporations themselves. In such cases, complaints and representations would be made direct to the central consumers' council or the

central consumers' tribunal. Either council or tribunal would have power, in cases of doubt, to instruct the industry to take the matter first to a specified county consumers' council or tribunal.

The consumers' councils and their committees would have other functions. Both central and county consumers' councils would be entitled to initiate representations and complaints to the administering corporations at their own level and would be able, on motion of any member, to debate any question relating to consumers' interests. They would also be available for consultation with the administering authorities on the latter's initiative. The Minister of Fuel and Power and the Minister of Transport would be required to forward to the central consumers' council drafts of all statutory instruments affecting consumers and users of gas, electricity, coal and transport and to consider any amendments which the council might recommend before making the final instrument. On laying the instrument before Parliament, the Minister would be required to indicate in what way and for what reason he had failed to adopt any recommendations of the council. A similar requirement would apply to general directions given by the Minister to the administering authority; it would be necessary to provide that these directions should be laid before Parliament. Following the precedent of the Transport Tribunal, where a gas or electricity area board or the National Coal Board wished to increase its standard charges, it should be required to prove its case. The body to hear this case and the objections to it would be the central consumers' tribunal. The consumers' councils and tribunals would make annual reports to the Cabinet Minister and the Lord Chancellor respectively, who would lay them before Parliament.

Members of central and county consumers' councils would be entitled to allowances as are members of local authorities today. The chairmen and members of Consumers' Tribunals would be paid, whole-time or part-time. These bodies would need staffs and accommodation; at the county level, the co-operation of county and county borough councils would result in some saving of expense.

Under these proposals, there would be no place for the existing consumers' bodies, with the exception of the Transport Tribunal. The Coal Consumers' Councils are largely advisory in fact, and this function would be taken over by the central consumers' council; the same is true of the Central Transport Consultative Committee. The functions of the present consumers' bodies for gas and electricity would be taken over by the county consumers' councils.

These suggestions have their own difficulties, and are necessarily presented in barest outline. But they attempt to meet the principal weaknesses in the existing system and to enable the voice of the consumer to carry further and more strongly down the corridors and into the rooms of the administering corporations.

58. A NEW DEAL FOR THE CONSUMER *

Decisions on general policy, as the Webbs, Professor Lewis, and many others have already said, are more difficult to make than interpretation of existing policy. They are also, perhaps, more important to the welfare of the whole community. The rest of this article will be devoted to the question how far the Consumers' Councils, as at present constituted, are likely to safeguard and promote the consumers' interest not by expeditiously handling individual place-by-place grievances, but by participating in the more general decisions on the price level and structure, and on the quality of goods and services.

Participation of Consumers' Councils in some general decisions has already occurred. But lack of research staff, or lack even of a staff that knew what ought to be researched into, and what evidence to call for, is likely at present to make participation rather ineffective.

Thus the consumers' Central Transport Consultative Committee accepted in March 1952 the British Transport Tribunal's 'conclusion upon the revenue aspect' (from raising fares),[1] having expressed their doubts as to the advisability of this step in the previous December.[2] Is it any more likely that a Gas Consumers' Council, faced with a proposed rise in prices, can put forward a convincing case for meeting increasing costs by compensating economies?

For the whole community as distinct from the consumer with specialized interests, it must be the broad policy decision, both the plans and the decisions to implement them, that cause the greatest concern; but the community lacks informed guardians capable of critically approving or suggesting alternatives to the Board's official proposals. These proposals, in themselves, may be admirable, but not the only possibility. Practicable alternatives may have been discarded because of prejudice or the momentum of the Board's existing activities, though as capable of successful conclusion as the proposal then being followed, and, perhaps, even more acceptable *to the consumers*. Policy decisions are rarely between the right and the wrong but between alternative possibilities and the community

* From P. Sargant Florence and H. Maddick: 'Consumers' Councils in the Nationalized Industries', *The Political Quarterly*, Vol. XXIV, No. 3, July-September 1953, pp. 266–71. Reprinted by permission of the author and the editors of *The Political Quarterly*.

[1] Cmd 8513, para. 7.
[2] *H.C.* 79, 1951–52, para. 58.

at large should have some say in the choice to be made, in the policy formation stage.

If this is agreed, then it must be admitted that Consumers' Councils, as at present constituted, are inadequate for the purpose; that the parliamentary guardians of the consumers' interest are often ill-informed depending, as they must do, upon the Board's annual reports which frequently leave out important questions[1] and which are often less of an honest confession of the ups and downs of the industry, than a window-dressing operation. As for the minister and his department, it has been suggested that they have not the 'technical knowledge necessary to judge the British Transport Commission . . . or to stand up against it on any matter other than some outstanding popular issue'.[2] The glaring error is likely to be detected easily enough, but then is it likely to be made?

There has been advocacy of the Parliamentary Select Committee, served by a skilled staff in the same way as is the Estimates Committee—but the objection to this, as to continual parliamentary questions on the administration of individual industries, seems to be overwhelming. There can be no way of preventing such an enquiry from cramping individual initiative and increasing the official records, leading to the consultation of every interest at every occasion in that vain search for the perfectability of every policy and each decision. It would be appalling to find a nationalized industry that *never* made a mistake! What may be a desirable aim in a government department is certainly a handicap in an industrial organization. In addition, by the time Parliament is reached, debates on the industry become involved in party political sniping at the responsible minister, a process that does not add greatly to the clarification of pressing problems.[3]

Another proposal often mooted for the consumers' benefit is that of a septennial royal commission, and here a comparison is drawn with the enquiries into the BBC. The comparison, however, is misleading. The BBC's technical decisions are small in scale and hardly affect the national economy; its policy decisions regarding programmes have a greater flexibility than investment programmes of nationalized industries and can be easily reversed. Furthermore, an *ad hoc* commission seems *prima facie* to be a less effective than an

---

[1] Neither the BTC in its 1951 report nor the Coal Board in its report prior to 1949 made any reference to the acute shortage of certain types of manpower. See pp. 14ff of the Acton Society Trust pamphlet, *Relations with the Public*.

[2] D. N. Chester, *Three Banks Review*, December 1952, p. 38.

[3] Discussing the backbench pressure for an enquiry into the Coal Board, *The Economist* wrote: 'It is ironic that a Conservative minister should thus find his reputation and possibly his job, depending on the success of a nationalized industry' (2, 5, 1953, p. 291).

expert body constantly in touch with the problems and decisions, constantly available to give informed criticism of these actions which affect the consumer individually or in groups, as well as the nation as a whole.

It has also been suggested that 'an efficiency unit in which would be employed first-class industrial consultants' would perhaps provide these requirements.[1] This unit should have more required of it than 'the investigation of snags of a serious character',[2] and should not be only the instrument of a Board requiring advice nor of a minister with a problem. Such a unit should be harnessed to a body which represents the consumer as far as possible, has a contact with the actual conditions prevailing and which could link expert opinion with that of the informed amateur experienced and interested in the problems of the industry in relation to the consumer and to society.

To achieve this, we suggest the setting up of a Central Consumers' Council to concern itself with all the nationalized industries. A small number of members, five to seven, must be full-time, and the Council must have a research unit adequate for its purpose. This national council would have, as its counterpart in each of the regions, one Consumers' Council to cover *all* the nationalized undertakings, which would be concerned with policies primarily regional or on which some expression of regional opinion would aid the national council. The regional body consisting of the chairmen of the district committees and representatives of major interests within the area, would be represented on the Central Council by its chairman. To this national body, other members up to, say, twenty might be co-opted to represent particular interests[3] not otherwise represented.

The full-time members should be responsible primarily over the whole field but each, also, would be selected for his expertness in a particular topic—such as finance, production, sales, raw materials, administration;[4] and each might have to make a special study of a particular industry—gas, coal, electricity, land transport, aviation and so on. The research staff should consist of efficiency experts, statisticians, experts in the broad considerations involved and in the problems of the particular corporations. This permanent staff would have to be supplemented in some of the specialized problems by

[1] Rt Hon. Herbert Morrison, MP, H. Houldsworth and others, *Efficiency in the Nationalized Industry*, p. ii (Allen and Unwin, 1952).

[2] *Ibid.*, p. ii.

[3] The present composition of the Central Transport Consultative Committee is an example of this bringing together of interests.

[4] A somewhat similar proposal is made by S. J. L. Hardie (first Chairman of the Iron and Steel Corporation) in the *Nationalized Industries*, 1952, p. 11, but his 'authority is to supervise the other nationalized industries to ensure that they function properly' and does not consider the consumer especially.

drawing on consultants from industry and commerce, from the universities, and from the public service. The responsibility of the full-time members with the research staff at their back would be to adduce facts and develop arguments supporting or criticizing the Boards' attitudes and policies *vis à vis* the consumer and also to provide material for purposeful discussion by the whole council, whose part-time members would bring to it wide practical experience based upon different occupations and interests, in different areas. Then and only then would the consumers' representatives be able to stand up to the Board.

This Central Consumers' Council would be empowered to investigate, as they saw fit, all matters referred to it by the ministers, by the Boards, by the Regional Consumers' Councils, or by any interested consumer or body of consumers, or to carry out any investigation which they considered desirable. Their enquiries and subsequent reports might cover one industry or any number of industries where the subject was a matter of common interest, for instance staff training; or was a matter of concern to all, such as methods of traction related to fuel economy, or to long-term finance. On any one of these subjects Parliament and the public needs a co-ordinated report and not a report concerned only with the problems of one industry.

On the wider problems of the nationalized industries—the problems fundamental to the Board's pricing and policy decisions—the Central Committee would probably have to adopt the methods used by the Select Committee on Estimates in handling complex problems in organizations of some size—splitting up into sub-committees, each of which would handle a particular topic, reporting back. The reports of the Council should be published, together with the supporting material, and minority reports, if any, should be included.

The minister, Parliament, and the public would, in this way, have some cause to feel that the problems of the nationalized industries, individually and collectively, were under unbiased review, and that in trying to decide on the merits of a case (which are often not political) they had access to other opinions, alternative policies, and that criticisms of the Boards' policies and decisions had been put and searchingly followed up.[1] These objects can only be assured by the provision of an independent Council provided with the means to carry out investigations in order that the public and its representative may not feel themselves helpless in the face of the Boards' expertise.

[1] You cannot of course make the horse drink. 'In the seven-hour debate on the [proposals for] the decentralization of the Railways and the denationalization of Road Haulage, only one direct reference to the previous year's annual report was made' (Acton Society Trust, *op. cit.*, p. 17).

This Council would be more suitable than quasi-judicial tribunals, such as the Transport Tribunal, to examine the case for an increase in charges. The decision between the Council's viewpoint and the Board's viewpoint should be made by the minister as additional considerations may arise, concerned with political and social policy, strategic issues and so on, rather than with questions of efficiency.

Where costs are affected by considerations of social policy, as, for example, an isolated community whose railway line is to be shut down because of losses, or the refusal to extend Oxford gas works on its present site in view of the injury to amenities, a statement of the potential social gain and the financial loss needs to be set side by side. The decision, as in the case of defence requirements overruling the covering of costs, can only be made by the minister responsible to Parliament, but it is desirable that a statement by such a body as this should precede any discussion in the House.

Such a council would provide a check on the efficiency of the various industries and would have the advantage of being able to compare problems which are common to all the industries because of their sheer size. In addition it would come to an assessment of efficiency, not in terms of utopian standards of perfection, such as the civil service strives for, but in terms of the business attitude (many of the Council members would be business men) summed up by the Chairman of the British Electricity Authority, Lord Citrine: 'We will accept a percentage of mistakes. We will not tell you what that percentage is. We will not guarantee that we will excuse a particular mistake, but we do not expect perfection.'[1]

Was it naïve or merely politically expedient for the Minister of Transport recently to say 'no inquiry was necessary to establish that monopoly control of rail and long distance road-haulage was detrimental to the public interest'?[2] A central Consultative Consumers' Council, as is suggested here, could go a long way to establishing facts and then leave the judgment to be made *when the facts are known*. At the present time, the community or its representatives in these matters, are left to accept the recommendations of the only experts, the Board's, because they are unable to contravert them. The machinery at present available for consumers' participation in policy must be admitted to be little more than an elaborate but ineffectual device. Possibly it is worse than having nothing because today it is easy for the Board to say 'this is approved by the Consumers' Council', or for the minister to lean on the Council's report,

[1] *H.C.* 332, Select Committee on the Nationalized Industries, October 29, 1952, p. xxii.
[2] *Hansard*, April 28, 1953, col. 1976. Such an answer can satisfy few save the dogmatist and the ardent party supporter.

or the Board to use the Council as a further public relations device.[1] Either the public is deluded into thinking that its Council has the means to carry out a proper examination or else it loses confidence even in those few cases where a critical assessment is possible and, in fact, has been made. It is vital to the nation's economy that effective machinery should be created to investigate impartially the policy and efficiency of the nationalized industries. The machinery suggested here should have both the qualities of efficiency and impartiality.

What use might be made of its findings is another matter. That they would be significant is beyond doubt for, in the absence of competition between products, there would be the stimulus of a competition between ideas—the ideas of the consumers and the ideas of the Board. The public sector of industry is so basic and important to the rest of the economy that neither its management nor the public, its owners, can afford to be complacent. It 'demands continuous vigilant scrutiny',[2] both from within and without and nothing should be taken for granted nor regarded as the last word. It is for this reason above all others that we suggest this institutional mechanism of one Consumers' Central Consultative Council—properly manned, efficiently served, adequately clothed with authority, and serving as a focus for similarly unified Consumers' Councils at the district and at the regional level. Thus armed, the community could, if it wished, make decisions with knowledge of facts and alternatives.

[1] L. Hardern, *Problems of Nationalized Industry,* ed. Robson, p. 180, 1952.
[2] Lord Latham in *Efficiency in the Nationalized Industries*, p. 31.

CHAPTER X

Industrial Relations

Another disappointing feature of nationalization is its failure to effect that transformation of the relationships between employers and employed which was expected of it by many trade union and Labour enthusiasts. The reasons for this disappointment, together with the special problems confronting trade unions with members employed in the nationalized industries, are clearly explained by Mr B. C. Roberts, of the London School of Economics, in *Extract 59*.

As is well known, the trade union movement was formerly committed to schemes of 'joint control' through which it hoped, by securing workers' representation on managerial bodies, to raise the status of its members and end the 'dictatorship' of the employer. Serious doubts about this policy were first expressed in the late 1920s, and during the 1930s there were heated debates at the TUC and the Labour Party Conferences between the advocates of joint control and those of joint consultation. To illustrate the nature of this controversy, which is by no means dead, we reproduce in *Extract 60* the rival statements of Mr John Cliff, of the Transport and General Workers' Union, and Mr Herbert Morrison, which were juxtaposed in a 'Labour Party Study Guide' published in 1933.

In its *Interim Report on Post-War Reconstruction*, published in 1944, the TUC came down firmly on the side of joint consultation, and the provisions of the subsequent nationalization Acts passed by the Labour Government gave effect to most of the views there expressed under the heading of 'Workers' Representation in Public Industry and Selection of Workpeople's Representatives' (*Extract 61*). By 1953, the TUC felt that the time had come to review the working of these provisions, in view of 'the continuing dissatisfaction of many workpeople with the structure of the nationalized industries'. The section of 'Public Ownership, an Interim Report' dealing with this aspect of nationalization is reproduced as *Extract 62*.

Pessimism about the working of joint consultation, as expressed in Mr Roberts's article and reflected in the TUC's Interim Report, may be less justified than many are prone to imagine. In electricity, at least, it has achieved rather more than a modest success. To document the intelligent approach to joint consultation that this industry has adopted we reproduce, as *Extract 63,* nearly the whole of a very circumstantial and keenly analytical account by Mr R. D. V. Roberts, Deputy Industrial Relations Adviser to the Electricity Council, and Mr H. Sallis, a member of his staff. In reading this article, the 'commitment' of its two authors should be borne in mind.

The issue of workers' participation in management cannot be regarded as finally settled, and recently we have seen attempts by a group of intellectuals on the left wing of the Labour Party to re-state the old guild socialist case. One such attempt, stimulated by the failure of the Labour Party's policy statement on Public Enterprise (1958) to envisage anything more radical than the existing system of joint consultation, is the subject of *Extract 64.*

59. TRADE UNIONS AND NATIONALIZATION*

The almost uncritical enthusiasm for public ownership displayed by the trade unions before 1945 has given way to cautious approbation and a reluctance to support the taking over of further industries by the State. There is a group of unions, some communist dominated, others with a strong, old-fashioned socialist tradition, that is still determined to see public ownership as the panacea for all social problems, but the report presented by the General Council and adopted by the 1953 Trades Union Congress, illustrates the doubts of the majority.[1] This report analysed the trade union approach to public ownership, the experience of public ownership in the major industries nationalized since 1945, the current economic background against which further proposals for nationalization had to be seen, and the criteria for the future taking over of industries. Its conclusions were, in its own words, 'nearly all tentative and procedural in character'. The only exception related to water supply, where in the opinion of the General Council, 'There is a clear case for the complete public ownership of the industry, in order to provide a universal service and eliminate waste'. The change in the attitude of the unions is a fundamental one; they are not prepared, at this stage, to recommend that nationalization should be carried much further, and it is worthwhile considering why they have reached that conclusion.

The appeal which the public ownership of industry has made to the trade unions in the past was both an ideological and a practical one. Ideologically, the public ownership of industry was viewed as

* From B. C. Roberts: 'Trade Unions and Nationalization', *Progress,* Vol. 44, No. 245, Winter 1954–55, pp. 114–18. Reprinted by permission of the editor of *Progress.*
[1] Interim Report on Public Ownership. TUC 1953.

the vital step to a new type of society; a society free from the hardships which working men and women had been compelled to endure for centuries; which would be co-operative rather than competitive; an El Dorado which would fulfil the dreams of everybody. Practically, it offered the hope that the unions might be able to secure higher wages and better working conditions through the abolition of profits; the maintenance of full employment through the more direct control of the State over the operations of industry; and a say in management through the greater influence of the unions and even the direct representation of the unions on boards of management.

To what extent have the objectives of the unions been achieved by the nationalization of the basic industries? Ideologically, so far as the great mass of trade union members is concerned, nationalization has been a failure. No one, in any of the industries, is wildly enthusiastic about the results, and the general attitude of most members is, to a very large extent, one of indifference. Yet there have been some important improvements in wages and conditions of employment.

It is estimated by the TUC that wages rose by about 70 per cent per manshift in coal mining between 1946 and the middle of 1953.[1] In the gas and electricity industries, they have increased at about the same pace as the rise in average earnings. But railway employees have lagged behind since nationalization, and the increase in their earnings has been only about three-fifths of the general average. Thus from the point of view of the pay packet, workers in nationalized industries have gained no startling advantage except in coal mining, where they have moved up from about the eightieth rung of the ladder to practically the highest. Wages would, however, have risen significantly in mining whether the industry had been nationalized or not, owing to the severe coal shortage in the post-war years, and the scarcity of miners. Certainly, in the other nationalized industries the more extravagant hopes have not been realized. The union leaders recognize that increases in wages are only one aspect of the success or failure of public ownership—experience has shown, says the TUC report, that 'nationalization cannot open the door to unlimited wage increases'.[2] But this is still a fundamental test for the majority of ordinary workers.

If wages have not generally improved further than in privately-owned industry, considerable advances have occurred in other conditions of employment. There have been, for example, in the mining industry, immense advances in welfare provisions, safety and health measures, compensation and pension schemes, training and promotion opportunities. While the other nationalized industries cannot

[1] Interim Report on Public Ownership. TUC 1953.
[2] *Ibid.*

show quite such spectacular gains as the mining industry, conditions of employment have materially improved for most of their employees.

Public ownership has brought important gains to the unions as organizations. It was laid down in each of the Nationalization Acts introduced by the Labour Government that machinery should be established for the negotiation of wages and working conditions and for joint consultation on questions of safety, health, welfare, and the organization and conduct of the operations of the industries which might affect the workpeople employed. The negotiating machinery set up is based to a considerable extent on that which already existed at the time of nationalization, but, at the insistence of the unions, changes have been made, and they have secured the benefit of more centralized and uniform procedures. Although the recognition of a particular union is a matter for the National Boards, the status of the established unions is assured, since any new union must satisfy the condition that it represents a substantial proportion of the workers employed. In the mining industry, organizational security is assisted by the 'check off' system—the National Coal Board deducts union contributions from wages—which helps the union to maintain membership with the minimum of effort on the part of the local officers. Perhaps the most significant aspect of all these changes is that the representatives of the unions have access to management whenever they need it; they no longer feel on the defensive as they did in the past, and often the roles are reversed, with management being more afraid of the unions than *vice versa*.

In spite of the gains made by workpeople in their conditions of employment and the increase in the power and influence of the unions, there does not seem to have been a commensurate improvement in the climate of industrial relations. There is in every nationalized industry a feeling among rank and file workers that no fundamental change has occurred. The behaviour pattern of the unions does not appear to be significantly different from what it was under private enterprise, and many observers are disappointed at what seems to them to be the failure of the unions to grasp their opportunity to contribute towards making nationalization a success.

There are a number of reasons for this state of affairs. In the first instance, the advances made under nationalization have not matched expectations. It is clear now that this was bound to be the case, since there was relatively little discussion during the period when public ownership became the core of the Labour Movement's objectives, of the problems that would arise when an industry had been nationalized. There were, of course, discussions of some issues, for example in the early 1930s and again in 1944, when the TUC published its statement on Post-war Reconstruction. While the trade unions may be criticized for not having prepared more detailed plans to deal with the problems that were likely to occur, they were caught, as all advocates of root and branch reform are caught, in a dilemma. Nationalization could not be advocated as the key to a new society and at the same time attention be drawn to the difficulties that would arise, without weakening the ideological appeal of public ownership. As a result the mass of the supporters of the Labour Movement expected far more than was ever possible of achievement, and, most important of all, failed to realize that nationalization would involve sacrifices by not only the former owners, but also by the unions, which had grown up out of private capitalism.

EFFECT OF FULL EMPLOYMENT

The maintenance of full employment, which has had little or nothing to do with nationalization and would have been achieved in the post-war years whether or not industries had been taken over by the State, has nevertheless had an effect on the attitude of workpeople to their unions. Full employment and the inflationary economic pressures that went with it have made the gains secured in the nationalized industries look less significant. The relative security of employment which a nationalized industry might have given has become less attractive. Comparatively, wages and working conditions in many private enterprises have improved as rapidly, and in some cases more rapidly than in the nationalized industries. Should a depression return, then conditions of employment are likely to deteriorate much more slowly in the nationalized industries, but it does not follow that further nationalization would be the means of restoring prosperity. A great deal could be done by the government of the day through fiscal, financial and trade policies, to achieve recovery, but the return of full employment might well be dependent on factors outside British control, which in any case could not be altered by the public ownership of industry. Thus one of the main reasons for the support of public ownership by the unions has no longer any validity.

In the 1944 *Report on Post-war Reconstruction*, the participation of the unions and workpeople at all levels of control was stressed as being of vital importance. At that stage it was admitted that the problems which would be raised could perhaps not even be foreseen. One point was, however, made quite clear, that it would not be in the 'best interests of workpeople of a nationalized industry to have, as directly representative of them, members of the controlling board who would be committed to its joint decisions. It will be essential, not only for the maintenance and improvement of the standards and conditions of the workpeople, but because of the power of independent criticism that they can exert, that the trade unions shall maintain their complete independence. They can hardly do so if they are compromised in regard to board decisions which are not considered to be in their members' interests by the fact of their representatives' participation in them'.[1] To avoid this danger, when trade unionists were selected for membership of the boards they ceased to have any connection with their own union.

CLASH OF SECTIONAL AND PUBLIC INTERESTS

This procedure has not, however, solved the problem. Ex-trade union leaders are expected by the rank and file to behave as though they were still employed by the union. Such men as W. P. Allen, Ebby Edwards and others, have encountered a great deal of criticism because they have had to represent the boards to which they belonged on policy matters over which there was a clash with the union concerned. By the very nature of their work as members of the boards, it is quite impossible for any outsider to know to what extent they have used their influence to forward policies desired by the unions. Also, as members of the boards, their first duty is to the public, not to any sectional interest, and from all the overt evidence they have put that duty first. Therefore, while the appointment of trade unionists to the boards of nationalized industries is a recognition of the status of the unions, it does little or nothing to solve the basic problem which arises out of the clash of sectional and public interest.

The nationalized industries must be efficient and pay their way; this the trade unions accept as necessary—but the demands which they have made for subsidies and price increases indicates that their interpretation of these principles may be different from that of those whose prime duty is to the general public. Under private enterprise, the unions pay little attention to the problems of the employer in meeting a wage increase, unless it is very obvious that the members of the union will directly and immediately suffer as a consequence. When an industry is nationalized, they cannot escape the consequences quite so easily. It is not a simple matter for a publicly-owned industry to raise prices; it may involve major political problems and it is sure to arouse a far greater amount of public criticism than a rise in prices made by private enterprise. Moreover, there are no profits to be squeezed, and though it is sometimes suggested that compensation paid to stockholders should not be a charge on the industry, this is not a satisfactory method of providing funds to meet wage increases. Public ownership does not, therefore, make it any easier for a trade union to secure higher wages; indeed the contrary may prove

[1] *Post-war Reconstruction*, TUC Annual Report, 1944, Appendix D.

true. On the other hand, it must be noted that with the political influence which the unions now exercise, they may, through direct pressure on the government, secure improvements over the heads of the boards. The five-day week policy in the mines, and two wage increases in the railways have been decided in this way—by the influence of ministers. There is a very great danger in this development, since if it were to go very far—as it certainly might if more industries were nationalized—wage policy in publicly-owned industries would become a political matter. The ultimate consequences of such a development require no stressing; they ought, perhaps, to be given even greater weight by the unions.

The attitude of the unions as it has developed is to move away from expecting much from the appointment of trade unionists to the boards of nationalized industries. Recent statements of the leaders of the mineworkers have been to emphasize the independence of the union and that its first duty is to secure higher wages and better conditions for its members. The attitude of the railway unions has been precisely the same. When it has come to accepting decisions designed to make the industry more efficient, but involving a sacrifice of the short-run interests of their members, they have been extremely reluctant to agree. In practice then, the behaviour of the unions is largely determined by collective bargaining advantage. Admission of wider responsibilities necessarily involves the unions in difficulties which cannot easily be resolved without undermining the basic reason for the existence of the union.

The most powerful motivating force of trade unionism is sectional interest. Unions are organized on this basis and they reflect in their policies the occupational and industrial interests of their members. Since the duty of a union is to protect the wages and working conditions of its own members first, it naturally follows that conflict with management—and with other unions—is inevitable. The unions cannot, of course, simply ignore all other interests but their own, but how far can they take into account the public interest without destroying their main function and hence their organization? In any concrete instance, this question may be answered in several ways, but what is clear from post-war experience is that even in the nationalized industries, on which they staked so much hope, the unions are not prepared to put other interests first.

It does not, of course, follow that the unions have no interest in promoting the efficiency of the nationalized industries, any more than similar attitudes displayed in private industry indicate a lack of concern about the efficiency of private enterprise. They have such an interest, and they have shown it in many practical ways, because they are well aware that future employment, wages and working conditions of their members depend upon the more efficient use of existing resources and technological advance. But the wider interests of the unions stem from the narrower ones. That is to say, any responsibility which they accept will be based upon the extent to which it furthers the interest of their members. If to any particular union the disadvantages seem to outweigh the advantages to its members, it will not agree to accept the policy concerned if it can avoid it. Collective bargaining is not, however, a one-sided affair, and the policy which a union follows will be its response to the policies of management, the policies of other unions and the general social and economic conditions which prevail.

It was thought at the time when the basic industries were nationalized, and it still is the view of many people, that the unions would be able to participate more freely in matters which concerned the running of industry if a line were drawn between negotiation and consultation and separate machinery set up for each purpose. When the TUC formulated its policy for post-war reconstruction, it supported this idea and recommended that to enable workpeople to contribute to the efficient operation of industry joint consultative committees should be established which would be untrammelled by questions of wages and working conditions, thus allowing those sitting on them to think in terms of industrial efficiency rather than bargaining advantage. Although the type of machinery to be established for negotiation and consultation in the nationalized industries was left to agreement between the boards and the unions, implicit in the legislation was the assumption that there was a significant distinction between negotiation and consultation, and naturally the question arose as to whether, in order to keep the functions quite separate, it would not be wise to set up separate committees.

The course adopted was not uniform; in the coal and electricity industries the policy has been to keep them separate, in road and rail transport to combine them; while in the gas industry separate committees were established at the local level, but not at area and national levels. In each industry it was agreed with the trade unions that they should be empowered to nominate representatives to the consultative committees at regional and national level; where the committees combined the functions of negotiation and consultation, they naturally already had this right. At the local level, representation in theory is directly from the employees, but in practice representation is largely determined by the local union organization. In the mining industry, nomination for election to the Colliery Consultative Committee is by agreement confined to the Lodge of the Mineworkers' Union; in addition, the Lodge Secretary and Area Agent are ex-officio members of the Committee.

JOINT CONSULTATION PROBLEMS

Whether negotiation or consultation is carried on through the same committee, or by separate bodies, in theory an attempt is made to keep the two functions apart. The underlying principles involved are that in negotiations the committee is one of two sides, and if deadlock is reached, it may be resolved either by arbitration, or by any further action which either side might desire to take. In consultation, the committee is supposedly acting as an advisory body seeking an answer to problems in the interest of the industry as a whole. The committee has no power to enforce its decisions. It is not an executive body, and management has the final responsibility of deciding whether to act on the decisions of the committee.

It is the opinion of many union officers and management officials that joint consultation, as so conceived, is a failure. The difficulty is to attain a permanent agreement between management and men as to the function and purpose of joint consultation. However much lip service might be paid to the idea that there should not be two sides, that the committee should operate in the common interest, in fact there are two sides, and each is seeking to achieve its own ends. If, as Clausewitz said, war is but politics continued by other means, joint consultation might be said to be nothing more than collective bargaining continued under another name.

Unfortunately, it is not even that. In collective bargaining the two sides, no matter what they might say of each other in the course of negotiations, are prepared to come to an agreement and honour it. Under joint consultation, the unions are often not interested in arriving at an agreement, and there is no certainty that if they do it will be carried out.

The unions fear that in joint consultation they may be called upon to accept responsibilities which they cannot really undertake. The difficulties experienced in the coal industry and on the railways clearly establish this point. In each case, major concessions were made to the unions in return for vague undertakings that they would, through joint consultation, co-operate with management to make these industries more efficient. In both cases, the results so far have been negligible. The unions have simply not been prepared to accept the consequences of the policies which managements have wanted to pursue.

Nevertheless, joint consultation at the national and regional levels in the nationalized industries has some value, even though the meetings of the committees are reported to be badly attended by union officers, who have in any case, little time to give to studying the papers involved.[1] It does mean that the unions have access to information which would enable them to make a much bigger contribution to the efficient running of the nationalized industries should they feel able to do so in the future.

WEAKNESS AT LOCAL LEVEL

It is at the local level that the joint consultative committees seem to be weakest. There the problem is further complicated by the fact that the committees—except in the coal industry—are not formally a union responsibility, even though mainly union members are appointed. The unions have done little to ensure that union members are properly equipped to make an effective contribution; they have not arranged special conferences or meetings of joint consultative committee members; nor have they made any effort to see that there is adequate reporting back to the membership. There is a widespread ignorance among the majority of workers about the work of these committees, and those who serve on them are, more often than not, cynical about their value. The problem here, as at the higher level, is that on issues which are of importance to the members the workers' side wants not merely the right to have information and to offer advice, but an agreement with management that certain things will be done. In other words, their attitude is that of bargaining agents, but they are often not in a position to bargain effectively since they lack authority to arrive at agreements. A greater readiness on the part of the unions to devolve responsibility to the local level, and to integrate their representatives at the work-place into the structure of the unions would lead to a more serious attempt to grapple with these issues.

What, then, has happened under nationalization is that the scope of collective bargaining has been widened to embrace such questions as redundancy, the manning of jobs, new methods of working, seniority, promotion, discipline and so on. These are all matters on which workers expect the union to defend their interests, and the unions are not prepared to look at them merely from a consultative point of view; they are also, however, matters which vitally affect the efficiency of industry, and it is vital that effective agreements should be made.

The attitude of the leaders of the unions is one of desiring to see the efficiency of nationalized industries improved, but at the same time being reluctant to sacrifice their members' immediate interests to secure that end. This ambivalence has led to severe criticism of the unions, but they could not, in fact, have behaved otherwise without

[1] See *The Future of the Unions*, Acton Society Trust, 1951.

exposing their organizations to internal stresses which they could not have sustained. So long as the unions remain democratic organizations they cannot carry out policies which do not command the support of their members. They may be legitimately criticized for not having done more to educate their members, and for not having put their own house in order by making changes in their internal organization, and by improving communications between the different levels of leadership. But here again, they run up against fundamental issues. Unions cannot shrug off the facts of their history, and reshape their attitudes, basic structure and methods of organization as if they were starting from scratch.

Further changes will come, but only slowly as the unions cautiously adjust themselves to the new aspects of their industrial situation. This is the price which has to be paid in a society in which power is wielded by large collective organizations. It is a price, it should be remembered, that is perhaps far less high than the community might have to pay if trade unions and management of large scale industry, whether publicly or privately-owned, were in such close harmony that they always acted in unison. The domination of society by the interests of producers would then be certain. The safeguard against this danger is that management manages, and trade unions remain sufficiently free from association with the policies of management to be able to defend the interests of their members. Though it may be that the interests of the public are not always protected, the damage sustained from conflicts between unions and management is less than it would be if the conflict were between the public and a combination of unions and management.

60. JOHN CLIFF VERSUS HERBERT MORRISON,

1933*

I. BY JOHN CLIFF

With the development of Trade Union Organization, Industrial Workers have secured an increasing measure of control over, and determination of, their conditions of employment.

By the exercise of power obtained through collective action, they have insisted upon the Employers entering into agreements regulating the rates of wages, the number of hours to be worked, and the

* From *The Workers' Status in Industry*, Labour Party Study Guide No. 5, 1933, pp. 5–16. Reprinted by permission of the Labour Party.

conditions under which the work should be performed. The workers have also, in an increasing measure, limited the use of the power possessed by the Employers to dismiss them from their employment.

During the struggle to obtain increased power over their 'work-a-day' lives, and to secure a progressive increase in their standard of life, the workers have learned many important lessons, the most valuable of which is expressed in their demand for the Socialization of Industry.

One of the main objects underlying this demand is the abolition of servitude and the securing of free and full citizenship in Industry.

The Socialization of Industry must mean that Industry will be transformed into Communal Services, designed to meet the needs and requirements of the community, and its acceptance imposes upon all members of the community the obligation of service.

It may be, though it is by no means certain, that the application of the principles of Socialism will, in the first instance, be applied to a selected number of primary industries and services. In any event, the question arises:—how is the objective of the workers—the demand for Citizenship in Industry—to be met? The National Executive Committee of the Labour Party, in its Report on the National Planning of Transport (page 15, para. 47), makes an interesting declaration on this question, as follows:

'Workers in the Industry'

'At the same time, it must be a primary object in any publicly-owned industry to give the workers the fullest share in its organization compatible with effective service to the Nation. Thus, in Transport, the widest facilities should be given for education in transport economics and management, and it should be a duty imposed on the Board to provide such facilities. The internal organization of the industry should be such that adequate opportunities are given for consultation and discussion on management problems, and that in time an increasing measure of industrial self-government is built up. Self development and the expression of individuality are not mere phrases. It is not sufficient to know how to do a job; every worker should know why he does it, and how it fits into the general scheme of things.'

This declaration propounds:
(1) That it is the primary object of a socialized system of Transport that the workers engaged in Transport should have the fullest share in its organization, compatible with effective service to the Nation;
(2) That the widest facilities should be provided for the workers to be educated in transport economics and management;
(3) That adequate opportunities should be afforded to the workers for consultation and discussion on management problems;

a Socialist Order of Society, and even the present Order of Society, must grapple with and remove the burdens of Usury, or otherwise perish. In any event, the workers in a Socialized Industry must not be regarded as an 'Interest'; they will insist upon being regarded as Citizens engaged in rendering a service to the Community.

The workers in a Socialized Industry must, from the Doorkeeper to the Chief of Staff, be organized to serve some definite and prescribed need of the Community. Are they to be deprived of their undoubted rights to some form of self-government in the rendering of that service?

Any Scheme of Socialized Industry must provide the beginnings of a 'new Status' for the workers in that Industry. The bondage of Servitude must be exchanged for the freedom of Citizenship. A mere transfer from Private to Public Ownership, similar to that of a Municipal Service or the National Telephone Service, is insufficient.

The workers demand Power; Power to share the Government of the Industry in which they are engaged. They will accept the responsibilities and obligations imposed by the acquisition of that power. This has been demonstrated in the Movements which have been built by the workers, such as their Trade Union and Labour Organizations; their Friendly Societies; the Co-operative Movement, and the part they have played in International Labour Organization, and in Local and National Government.

II. BY HERBERT MORRISON

The issue between us is a fine one. It is not whether the workers shall enjoy an increasingly effective voice in the internal organization of the industrial activity to which they devote their working hours; it is not whether working class people shall be members of the Boards of Public Corporations (for paragraph 46 of the Transport Report would fully commit the Party): it is whether definite statutory provision should be made whereby the Trade Unions in the industry affected *alone* shall have the right to make nominations in respect of a certain number of seats on the Board. Such is the difference between us as it appeared on the Party Conference Agenda.

Socialism: A Classless Society

Let us keep in our minds throughout that the society of the Socialist Commonwealth will be a classless society. We surely seek to make of it a real co-operative brotherhood (and sisterhood) of workers by hand and by brain. Idle capitalists and landlords will be gone: all will be workers. The whole problem with which we are here concerned will be much simpler. The citizen-worker-consumers will be the State,

N

and the State will be the whole body of citizen-worker-consumers. Just as the means of production will no longer belong to the landlords and capitalists, so, for example, the transport system and the electricity undertakings—which are of concern to all, including the housewife who is sometimes forgotten in these discussions—cannot be regarded by the good Socialist as being the special property of the transport workers and the electrical workers (including in both cases the managerial and technical officers).

The Socialism of the Labour Party must not be confused with the Syndicalism which Mr Harold Clay came near to urging when he declared to the University Labour Federation at Sheffield (*Daily Herald*, January 9, 1933): 'I would submit as a general ruling principle that in a completely Socialist State the running of industry would be by the people within that industry.'

At the Point of Production

In contributing to the discussion as to the position of the workers in socialized undertakings, let us beware lest we start at the wrong end. The rank and file of industrial workers are most directly interested in their position at the point of production where their daily industrial life is spent, namely, in the workshop.

The Transport Policy Report opened up great possibilities in this direction. We must seek to make the workman a conscious part of the internal co-operative organization of industry and enable him to feel that he is enjoying the advantages and dignity of co-operation with his fellows, including the management. And, of course, there must be the fullest recognition of the Trade Unions. This policy, coupled be it remembered with opportunities for industrial and technical education, will give us an increasing number of workers able to take their place on merit on the Boards of the Public Corporations responsible for the management of industries or services for which the Public Corporation method is appropriate. But they will be there because of their competence and not as semi-delegates. And their job will be a different job, for management is a special task.

The Amendment Examined

Let us now examine the statutory right of the Trade Unions *in the industry* to nominate a proportion of the members of such Boards, remembering that the Transport Workers' amendment does not claim a majority. In any case, that would not be tolerated by the general body of citizen-consumers, so that a policy of majority control would be fatal to Labour's electoral success. We must realize at all times that we have not only to evolve socialization schemes that please *us*; they must also command the confidence of the millions of electors whose support we need and have not yet secured.

In the first place, I suggest that such representation would be unreal. If we take the national transport industry (which includes railwaymen of various grades, craftsmen in the railway shops, electricians working at sub-stations and on the tracks, and the clerical and administrative staff; the road transport drivers, van-men, conductors, regulators, mechanics, and motor-body repairers; canal workers; and various types of labour employed in docks and harbours); if we remember that these workers are organized in a considerable number of Trade Unions, and that their occupational consciousness would remain even if they were in one Union; and if we keep in mind that effective management requires us to avoid an unwieldy membership—we shall readily see that the limited number of seats available for labour in the industry would inevitably leave vast masses of transport workers with the feeling that their particular trade, calling or grade was not represented on the Board.

It is not even proposed that a nominal reality of representation should be secured by a ballot of the whole of the vast army of the workers in the industry for the persons to represent them on the Board. Even that expedient would not give the workers a real sense of having a voice in the supreme management, nor would it be calculated to secure the appointment of the best men available. It is proposed that the Trade Unions should nominate a panel to the Minister, and that he should be required to select from the nominations made by the Trade Unions. That would be an invidious task for the Minister.

Substantially the members of the Board would be jointly and severally responsible for all its actions, for the open Party rivalries and public votes and divisions obtaining in Parliament and the local authorities can hardly be the practice on the Board of Management of a Public Corporation.

The position of a Trade Union official or other delegate of the workers in the industry would be one of some difficulty. He would inevitably be regarded by his colleagues as a Trade Union delegate, and his influence on labour questions would tend to be weakened rather than strengthened as a consequence. He would tend to be held answerable at Trade Union gatherings for his conduct on the Board; efforts might be made to involve him in individual grievances, personal desires for promotion, appointments, etc., in ways that might be very embarrassing to him and contrary to those principles of equity and freedom from improper influence which should always govern these questions, besides weakening Trade Union action. In the case of a trade dispute involving the Board, his freedom of judgment would be restricted; he would be in an anomalous position in relation to official Trade Union negotiations with the Board; he would have divided loyalties between the Board and the Trade Unions which would probably involve him in difficulties on both sides. These were, no doubt, among the reasons which caused the Railway Unions to decline the proposal that they should be represented on the Boards of the Railway Companies.

The Question of Status

Compare the position of a Trade Unionist, Co-operator or Labour Party public administrator selected, not as a semi-delegate of the workers in the industry, but on grounds of personal competence, ability and loyalty to the socialized undertaking, a qualification which must apply to *all* the members of the Board. He would in status be the equal of his colleagues on the Board, appointed on merit and not as an act of statutory favour.

I suggest that a man so appointed has a higher status of dignity, equality and influence than a person who is selected by the workers in the industry as (at any rate in part) the representative of their interests, and that an appointment so made is far sounder judged by Socialist standards.

There is another consideration. The proposal that the workers in the industry should have a special statutory right of representation, at any rate tends, owing to the limited number of seats, to exclude able Trade Unionists associated with other industries, Co-operators experienced in the management and direction of considerable co-operative trading undertakings, and members of the Labour Party who have been more active on the political side of the Movement and who may have acquired considerable competence and experience in important fields of public administration. The proposal gives a privilege to a restricted section of the Movement; this seems to me to be unfair in itself, and to be contrary to the principle of getting the best man for the work. For all these reasons I think it is preferable for such appointments to be made in accordance with the pledge contained in paragraph 46 of the Transport Policy Report.

The Graver Consequences

But there is a much graver consideration to be faced. We are not living in the classless society of Socialism; we are living in that aggregation of classes and interests known as capitalism. Once the principle of statutory sectional representation is conceded in the transition period it is certain that we shall not be able to stop at labour in the industry. In that case we are led to a Board of semi-delegates thinking largely about the interests which appointed them, instead of a Board of ability acting in a corporate spirit for the communal well-being. And let us not assume that even a Parliamentary Labour Party—quite apart from the Conservative Party—*once the sectional principle is established*, would not be subject to the successful pressure of other interests.

It is highly probable that the Co-operative Movement, of which most of us are proud to be members, would follow the first concession with the demand for statutory representation, and whilst their demand could be resisted on grounds of general principle it would be exceedingly difficult to resist it when the principle had been given away.

Farmers and agricultural interests would stress the vital importance of transport to agriculture and would claim direct representation on the Board. Are we certain that Labour MPs (plus Tory MPs) representing rural divisions would not bring strong pressure to bear upon the Government to make concessions?

The manufacturing interests would make a specious case for representation, pointing out the great importance of transport to the manufacturers; they also would bring much powerful pressure to bear on sections of Labour MPs; the heavy industries, such as iron and steel and mining, whose commodities are principally carried by rail, would make a similar case, and as these industries are predominant in certain constituencies the Labour MPs concerned would find it very difficult not to support the claim.

The Associations of Local Authorities (all with non-Labour majorities) would make an attractive case as representing the general interests of local communities, and these associations would be powerful in the Parliamentary Labour Party for they would mobilize behind them the local authorities of the country.

And, finally, the stock-holders whose property had been transferred to the new Board, and who had probably been given transport stock in return, would command considerable public support in demanding that they should have a voice in securing the efficient management of the undertaking.

So at the end of it all, the 'statutory' Trade Union representative(s) would probably be snowed under by second-rate non-Labour 'representatives' sent to the Board largely for the purpose of keeping costs (including wages) down. Under Paragraph 46 of the Transport Report we can put able Trade Unionists on the Board without running these needless risks.

Socialism v. Capitalist Sectionalism

All these claims are typical of the sectional mentality of capitalism itself.

Socialists must put first Socialism and the well-being of the working class as a whole, the communal interest, the public interest. On the national economic body associated with the State planning of industrial production and economic planning as a whole in the Socialist Commonwealth, the Trades Union Congress, representing the workers, the Co-operative organizations, representing consumers, and the public industrial concerns, have a strong case for representation in order to deliberate on these matters in association with the Executive Government. But the sectionalizing of the *management*, the constitution of Boards of Management by the representation of sectional interests, is not a Socialist conception: it is characteristic of that insistence upon sectional interests which is one of the worst features of capitalist society.

61. THE T.U.C. AND WORKERS' REPRESENTATION*

WORKERS' REPRESENTATION IN PUBLIC INDUSTRY

90. In relation to publicly-owned industries, it is fundamental to any plan for the organization of a public service that the workpeople have the right to a voice in the determination of its policy. This right does not rest only on the fact that their labour is indispensable to industry and that they are the group most immediately affected by its policy, but also on the interest of the public in the efficient conduct of the industry.

91. There is today a conviction that given equal opportunity workpeople who have gained their experience in the day-to-day work and in the Trade Union organization of industry are as capable of undertaking administrative responsibility as those who have been assisted in its attainment by the possession of certain social advantages.

92. Beyond this, it is widely felt that private industry has not utilized the knowledge and experience of the workpeople on the job and that the full productive possibilities of public ownership will not be realized until this reservoir of capacity is tapped. During this war the right of workpeople to contribute to the conduct of industry and the value of their contribution has been widely recognized and it is imperative to constitute this as a necessary feature of any publicly-owned industry.

93. The right of its workpeople to a voice in the conduct of a public

* From Trades Union Congress: *Interim Report on Post-war Reconstruction*, 1944, paras. 90–104. Reprinted by permission of the authors.

industry must, therefore, find a formal place in its organization and operation. There must further be some guarantee that this expression shall be effective in the formulation of its policy. The problem has been to find a means of achieving this.

94. Effective operation demands that the managers of sections or departments of an undertaking shall be individually responsible for their efficient direction. The full-time administrator, so far as his professional function is concerned, must be representative of the policy of the directorate of the concern to which he must be personally accountable. The officials of a public undertaking should be selected solely by their technical and administrative competence though experience gained 'on the job' and in collective organization of the workpeople may well be regarded as an important factor in selection.

95. It follows that every worker should be afforded the opportunity to achieve managerial position. If the social division between management and workpeople is to be broken down, and the effectiveness of workers' representation to be continuously improved, continuous technical education should be accessible to workpeople irrespective of age up to the highest technical institutions. Access to higher technical qualification should be on grounds of capacity to benefit alone.

96. The execution of policy, however, should, not only as a matter of right, but in the interest of the efficiency of the industry, be subject to the continuous influence of those whom it directly affects. To secure this, consultative machinery, based on the collective organizations of the workpeople, will be required at all levels; a structure of works, regional or sectional, and national councils from the basic unit upwards to the Board itself will be necessary. Responsibility for the conduct of units should, however, be clearly defined; though the management must be under an obligation to consult these councils it does not appear that the latter can have any executive authority other than that agreed with the Board. There must, therefore, be some means of ensuring that the viewpoint of the industry's workers receives adequate consideration at the level at which the policy of the industry is in fact determined.

97. On the means by which the expression of the workpeople's viewpoint is to be made effective in the determination of policy a a thorough discussion took place between 1932 and 1935 in the Trades Union Congress and the Labour Party. The position originally taken up in the 1932 Reports to both bodies was that the appointment to the Boards of public industries should be 'solely on the grounds of ability to fill the position' and not as representative of particular interests. This was subsequently modified and a statement was

accepted by the 1935 Margate Trades Union Congress which claimed statutory provision for the representation of workpeople through their organizations in the direction of public industries.

98. There was, however, no decision at the time as to how this principle should be implemented and the reformulation of T.U.C. policy makes it important that this problem shall be examined in the light both of the general need for public control of economic life and of the position of the Trade Unions in relation to this control.

SELECTION OF WORKPEOPLE'S REPRESENTATIVES

99. It does not seem by any means certain that it would be in the best interest of the workpeople of a nationalized industry to have, as directly representative of them, members of the controlling board who would be committed to its joint decisions. It will be essential, not only for the maintenance and improvement of the standards and conditions of the workpeople, but because of the power of independent criticism that they can exert, that the trade unions shall maintain their complete independence. They can hardly do so if they are compromised in regard to Board decisions which are not considered to be in their members' interests by the fact of their representatives' participation in them.

100. Moreover, unless a workers' representative participates in responsibility for, and thereby authority over, the direction of the industry his status is likely to be in fact advisory or consultative. The tendency will be, however, for effective authority in administration to lie in the hands of those appointed as full-time directors of the industry. Members of the governing body cannot at the same time answer to the workers of the industry as their representatives and bear responsibility to the Minister for its administration. To attempt to lay such a double duty on them may well result in making the governing body in a sense a negotiating committee, in which the workers' representative will be in an ambiguous position.

101. Ultimate control over the policy and direction of a public industry must be exercised by Parliament as representative of the community in general. Public control must be secured by the definite responsibility of a Minister to Parliament for the industry's affairs. This in turn, must be ensured by placing the administration of the industry in the hands of persons responsible to the Minister for that administration.

102. The governing Board of a public industry will thus be required to determine and administer its policy solely in the public interest and should be accountable to the public through a Minister responsible to Parliament for its administration. It appears therefore that the

persons composing that body should be selected by their competence efficiently to administer the industry in that sense.

103. It is apparent that in this respect experience gained in the collective organization of Labour is a strong qualification. Apart from people with this background, however, it seems probable that the field of selection for the members of controlling boards will in the main be limited to those who have acquired their qualification in the service of the State or of private industry, and in relation to this there is a certain fear that the administration of public industry will be in the hands of individuals indifferent to the viewpoint of its workpeople. In the interest of the efficiency of the industry itself, therefore, and particularly in the context of the continuance of a wide range of private interests whose existence will to some extent condition its policy, it appears important to secure that there shall be on the governing body people who, though in no way accountable to any other interest than the public for their decisions, shall ensure that the views of the industry's workers on its management receive full consideration.

104. This might best be secured by nomination by workers' organizations of candidates from whom the Minister shall select a number of the Board members. The TUC as representative of the viewpoint of organized workers in general, might well serve as the best channel for this particularly since, in cases where a number of separate unions each have a substantial membership in the industry, it would be difficult to determine the responsibility of the Minister concerned to the different Unions. The TUC would, of course, consult with the appropriate Unions on the list of nominations. On the other hand, while those appointed should hold office for a definite period, it seems proper that they should surrender any position held in, or any formal responsibility to the Trade Union.

62. SECOND THOUGHTS*

SOURCE OF CRITICISMS OF EXISTING ARRANGEMENTS FOR WORKERS' PARTICIPATION IN CONTROL

112. The continuing dissatisfaction of many workpeople with the structure of the nationalized industries, and with the limited extent to which they can influence the policy of the industries in which they work springs from a number of sources.

* From Trades Union Congress: *Interim Report on Public Ownership*, 1953, paras. 112–125. Reprinted by permission of the authors.

Minority Opinion

113. Sometimes traditional ideas of what constitutes industrial democracy lead to criticism of the existing structure of nationalization. Only one or two unions are now officially committed to support of 'workers' control', although within many of the others there are sections of the rank and file who disagree with the official policy of their organizations. The source of these minority viewpoints is usually to be found in the syndicalist conceptions prevalent in the early part of this century. Although only a comparatively small number of trade unionists may hold such views, their influence at branch and workshop level is important, as many of them are the active members who hold trade union offices and who serve on the consultative and negotiating committees at their places of work.

114. It is not sufficient to wait for time to work an alteration in such opinions. Trade unionism is not learnt out of a book, and the great majority of the active trade unionists who do the day-to-day work of the Movement learn their trade unionism from older men in the workshop. Out of date ideas about industrial relations can thereby be propagated for generations. A determined effort ought therefore to be made by education and propaganda to explain current policy more fully than has hitherto been done.

Limits of Joint Consultation

115. Joint consultative machinery is essentially advisory as distinct from executive in its scope. In the last resort, and after full discussion with their employees, the responsibility for policy decisions must rest on the Boards concerned. This limitation, which is inherent in the policy of Congress, must be recognized and accepted, and joint consultative machinery must not be expected to give executive power to workers' representatives. In instances where too much has been hoped for the results have been disappointment and frustration and, what is perhaps even more important, subsequently the machinery has not been used adequately for its intended purpose.

General Economic Problems

116. Some of the criticisms expressed by trade unionists in the nationalized industries arise more from the general economic problems of those industries than, for example, from shortcomings in the machinery for consultation or in the administrative structure. 'Workers' control', it may be urged, would enable wages to be raised and would solve painlessly the problems of redundancy which sometimes occur during the reorganization resulting from nationalization.

These arguments derive from wishful thinking and from the desire to avoid unpleasant or difficult economic and industrial problems for which public ownership, no matter what its form, does not provide an automatic solution.

Administration

117. All the major post-war nationalization Acts laid an obligation on the Boards to establish joint consultative machinery. This machinery has now for the most part been set up, and the various Boards have expressed their wish to develop consultation. These general statements, however, depend for their implementation upon the way in which managers at different levels interpret the Boards' policy. At the time of our 1949 survey a number of difficulties at area and local levels were mentioned by the unions concerned, and there was wide agreement that although there had been improvements since nationalization many managers (and, incidentally, workers) had failed to adjust their outlook to the needs of successful consultation. What improvement has taken place subsequently, and what more can be done to improve relations at lower levels, are two of the questions on which we intend to consult the unions concerned.

118. Criticism of a somewhat different kind which is levelled against the administration of some nationalized industries takes the form of accusations of bureaucracy—'too many bosses', or 'too many non-manual staff'. It is almost invariably difficult to pin down such accusations to actual cases. The size of the administration in nationalized industries is often exaggerated, and in fact compares well with large privately-owned concerns. In the main these complaints seem to arise partly from the sheer size of the nationalized industries, partly from the suspicious attitude of some manual workers towards technical and non-manual staffs. In some industries —notably coal mining—there is, indeed, an urgent need for more, not fewer, technicians. It is nevertheless important not only to avoid the growth of 'bureaucracies', but also to persuade workpeople that this is not happening. The fullest possible information about the number and functions of staffs should therefore be given to trade union representatives and passed on to their constituents. It might be useful if unions developed means of exchanging information between representatives in different units and areas on this and other topics of relative efficiency.

ORGANIZATIONAL PROBLEMS OF JOINT CONSULTATION

119. Some of the criticisms which have been outlined above are probably an indication that all is not well in the consultative arrange-

ments within the industries concerned. The General Council therefore intend to discuss with the unions concerned whether industrial
relations might be improved by adjustments in the organizational
framework of the consultative machinery. There are in particular
four problems which appear to merit consideration, bearing in mind
that investigation of these problems will probably disclose others of
equal and perhaps even greater significance for good industrial
relations.

Consultation and Negotiation

120. It has been questioned whether it is desirable for the same
bodies to undertake both consultative and negotiating functions. At
the present time practice varies—in electricity and coal mining, for
example, the two functions are kept separate, while on the railways
and, at area and national level, in the gas industry the same
machinery is used for both negotiations and joint consultation. The
suggestion has been made that where the same bodies do both jobs
there is a tendency for a negotiating and bargaining spirit to be introduced into discussions of common problems, where it is out of place.
It is argued that these functions are better separated so as to ensure a
less contentious atmosphere for the discussion of common problems.
Whilst recognizing that what works well in one industry may not be
applicable in another, an exchange of experiences between unions in
this respect might yield useful results.

Centralization of Consultative Machinery

121. A further complaint is that the consultative machinery is too
centralized, and that matters are too often referred from local to
regional and national levels, with consequent delays and lack of local
initiative. It is sometimes alleged that, because of their wish to secure
uniformity of treatment even on detailed matters, unions press them
to the national level; on the other side some managers are reluctant
to commit themselves without the approval of their superiors.
Another criticism of the same type, but coming from the top levels, is
that local committees are unwilling to show initiative, and have to be
stimulated by action from above. These types of criticism are almost
bound to arise when joint consultative machinery covering hundreds
of thousands of workers is being established, but we intend to discuss
with the unions concerned whether these problems are diminishing in
importance and what is being done to solve them.

Organization and Personnel of Unions

122. The existence of the problems outlined in the last two para-

graphs emphasizes the need to consider whether it may be necessary in time to modify union organization to conform more closely to the nationalized industries. In this connection the 1944 report said that trade unions 'will have to develop a form of organization appropriate to the altered context of their operations'. The General Council recognize that the question of trade union organization has long been the subject of controversy in the Movement, and that it is an issue which does not lend itself to generalization but has to be discussed industry by industry: nevertheless they consider it of sufficient importance to warrant the most careful consideration by the unions concerned.

123. Involved with the problem of trade union organization is the question of trade union personnel. Consideration should be given to the possibility of associating a greater number of lay members with the consultative machinery at its higher levels. Not enough is being done to give workers' representatives the kind of training which would enable them to be more effective on consultative bodies—a training which should go beyond an elementary training in production and managerial techniques and should include a knowledge of the economic context of the industry concerned, and some study of the techniques of consultation. At the present time the trade union members of joint consultative Committees are, in the main, the people who are responsible for negotiations. Whilst recognizing that the wide and varied knowledge which is derived from participation in negotiations is often invaluable in the process of joint consultation, it is worth considering whether this twofold duty does not sometimes lay too great a burden on the officials concerned, and whether the industry and the union membership would both benefit if a greater degree of specialization were possible.

124. Finally more needs to be done to increase the flow of workers from the shop floor to supervisory and managerial positions. This avowed objective of nationalization necessitates not only extended training facilities, but also a change of attitude on the part of some rank and file trade unionists to those of their colleagues who accept promotion. This, too, calls for education in the position and responsibilities of trade unions within the nationalized industries.

Inter-union Relations

125. The fourth of the main group of problems is that of Unions whose members are a small minority in a nationalized industry and who therefore cannot secure independent recognition at all stages of the consultative process. It is unlikely that this can be overcome by changes in the formal machinery of consultation, as it is part of the

wider problem of securing effective co-operation between different unions at the place of work. Another aspect is the large number of unions in certain of the nationalized industries which sometimes makes it difficult for any one of them to give a positive lead, particularly when unpopular decisions have to be taken.

63. JOINT CONSULTATION IN THE ELECTRICITY SUPPLY INDUSTRY*

ORIGINS OF THE JOINT CONSULTATIVE SYSTEM

Under section 53 (1) of the Electricity Act, 1947, the Authority were enjoined to make agreements with the appropriate trade unions for the establishment and maintenance of machinery for:

(a) the settlement by negotiation of terms and conditions of employment of persons employed by electricity boards, with provision for reference to arbitration in default of such settlement in such cases as may be determined by or under the agreements; and

(b) the promotion and encouragement of measures affecting the safety, health and welfare of persons employed by electricity boards and the discussion of other matters of mutual interest to the boards and such persons, including efficiency in the operation of the services of the boards.

Also in section 2 (2) of the Act there was reference to joint consultation on education and training.

Section 53 (1) of the Electricity Act, 1947, was repealed by the Electricity Act, 1957, but the wording which replaced it is almost exactly the same. Since January 1, 1958, the Electricity Council has taken over the responsibility for making the agreements with the trade unions and has become a party to the current agreements. From the same date the Electricity Council and the Generating Board have been represented on the machinery for joint consultation in place of the Authority.

The Authority and the nine trade unions[1] in the industry (seven of which have members in other industries) met informally before the

* From R. D. V. Roberts and H. Sallis: 'Joint Consultation in the Electricity Supply Industry 1949–59', *Public Administration*, Vol. XXXVII, Summer 1959, pp. 116–33. Reprinted by permission of the authors and the editor of *Public Administration*.

[1] The nine trade unions were: Amalgamated Engineering Union, Electrical Trades Union, National Union of Enginemen, Firemen, Mechanics and Electrical Workers, National Union of General and Municipal Workers, Transport

vesting date. Although they were initially preoccupied with establishing or re-establishing negotiating bodies covering all grades of employees, except a small number of senior executives, there were nevertheless discussions between them in 1947 and 1948 on the implementation of section 53 (1) (b) of the Act. On January 1, 1949, an agreement was signed which provided for one comprehensive system of joint consultation to cover all employees—manual, clerical, administrative, technical and managerial—in the industry.

The main principles which were agreed and, where appropriate, embodied in the constitutions of the joint bodies were these:

(a) The councils and committees to be established were to improve communications between management, on the one hand, and the trade unions and employees on the other, to facilitate the exchange of views on matters of common interest to both groups, and more generally to provide a means through which management might gain the co-operation, understanding and participation of employees in the work of the industry.

(b) The councils and committees were to be consultative in character and have no explicit executive authority.

(c) Nationally and at the district levels, the councils were to be made up of union officers and top representatives of the electricity boards. At the local level, the trade union representation should be replaced by directly elected representatives of employees of all grades working in the locality. This last point was agreed to by the trade unions on condition that all employees standing for election to local committees had to be members of the appropriate trade unions, although all employees had the right to vote in these local elections.

(d) The only subjects having a bearing on the progress of the industry and the well-being of employees which were to be excluded from the terms of reference of the councils and committees should be those which related to the negotiated agreements on terms and conditions of employment. The terms of reference of the councils and committees were taken directly from section 53 (1) (b) of the Act.

During the preliminary discussions leading to this agreement the only major point of difference between the electricity boards and the trade unions concerned the unions' desire that the councils and committees should be given executive authority. The boards pointed out to the unions that responsibility for managing the industry had been

and General Workers' Union, Clerical and Administrative Workers' Union, National and Local Government Officers' Association, Association of Managerial Electrical Executive. Later the National Federation of Building Trades Operatives became a party to the Agreement.

placed squarely on the boards' shoulders and that, even if they wished
to do so, they had no authority to share that responsibility with
anyone else. The electricity boards nevertheless understood the
trade unions' anxiety that the work of the councils and committees
should be effective and this was one of the reasons why they agreed
that at each of the three levels at which the councils and committees
were to operate—nationally, in the twelve districts, and in the local
management units—top management should be members and act as
chairmen.

In January 1949 a National Joint Advisory Council was set up. It
consisted of members of the Authority, with the Chairman of the
Authority as its Chairman, chairmen or deputy chairmen of the area
boards, controllers of the generating divisions, and representatives
of the trade unions. Since January 1958 the Chairman and certain
Members of the Electricity Council and the Generating Board have
replaced the Authority's representatives and the Chairman of the
National Joint Advisory Council is the Chairman of the Electricity
Council. In June 1949 twelve district joint advisory councils were set
up in England and Wales, each covering the area of an area board
and the corresponding division of the Authority, now of the Generating Board. Each council consisted of senior representatives of the
board and division and district representatives of the trade unions. In
October–November 1949 the local joint consultative bodies
(local advisory committees), consisting of management members
and elected representatives of all the employees, were created and
met for the first time. There were initially some 400 of these committees (there are now 484), each covering a local management unit
such as a power station or a distribution district or a small compact group of such stations and districts.

THE NATIONAL JOINT ADVISORY COUNCIL

The National Council has now been in existence for ten years. It has
been concerned mainly with two functions: the development of the
industry's personnel policies (other than those dealing with terms
and conditions of employment), and the development and revision
of the joint consultative system as a whole.

When the National Council began its work in 1949, it was functioning in relation to a nation-wide organization which had been
created only eight months previously and which had taken over 540
electricity supply undertakings with very different types of organizations, standards of employment, and outlooks on personnel policy.
It is not surprising therefore that, in its first five years, the National
Council spent most of its time formulating schemes of education and

training, safety, and health and welfare and recommending them to the electricity boards for adoption. In this period it made over one hundred major recommendations covering such subjects as an employees' suggestions scheme; safety rules for the whole industry; the provision in power stations of amenities of certain minimum standards; a correspondence tuition scheme; an educational incentives scheme, including a university scholarship scheme; and training programmes for many categories of staff, including craft and student apprentices, graduate trainees, engineers, supervisors, power station operatives, chemists, jointers, accountants, and secretaries. All the recommendations made by the National Council during this period were accepted by the Authority and most were accepted by the area boards, which inform the National Council of the steps they take to implement its recommendations.

The preparation of these recommendations was done by the various standing committees of the Council, and to assist them the officers of the Authority responsible for education and training, safety, health and welfare attended the meetings as advisers. But while it is true that the committees leaned on such specialist officers for factual information and advice, the schemes themselves were invariably a product of detailed consultation, often continued over a number of meetings, in which both the electricity boards' members and the trade unions' members played a full part. There was no question of the National Council merely rubber stamping schemes which had been devised outside the committee room. In the first few years the subjects of what were later Council recommendations were no more than item headings originating with the Authority, but later a gradually increasing proportion of the subjects began to come up from the district councils and the local advisory committees after these bodies had done preliminary work on them.

With regard to the National Council's second main function—that of developing and revising the joint consultative system as a whole— we should point out that nothing really comparable to the local advisory committees (LACs) had existed in the industry before. Although before 1948 there had been in some parts of the industry works committees representative of managements and manual workers, these committees rarely dealt with matters other than those associated with the negotiated wage agreements. Experience in other industries suggested that, in their first few months, the LACs would spend much of their time acting virtually as welfare-cum-complaints committees. That proved to be the case, and the National Council, in 1950 and 1951, made a number of decisions aimed at speeding the committees' progress through this phase. Thus, they recommended that $4\frac{1}{2}$-day training courses for LAC members and secretaries should be arranged at the two residential training centres, and since then over 200 courses attended by over 4,500 members and secretaries have been held. They also recommended that the chairmen of the local committees—who are also usually the local managers—should present progress reports on past and future work and welfare activities at each meeting of their committees. Again, they arranged conferences of LAC members to discuss the reports of the two teams from the industry which, in 1949, visited the United States to study the public utility industry there.

A number of other recommendations of the same kind were made in 1952, but by 1953 the number had fallen and an interesting change had occurred in the National Council's policy towards the local committees. Instead of thinking up ideas of its own for stimulating the LACs, it began to pick up ideas developed by individual committees and bring them to the attention of all the committees. This was done first of all by means of specially prepared papers on specific subjects, but the National Council later came to rely much more on two publications—an eighty-page annual report and a thirty-page six-monthly publication entitled *Joint Consultation*—which are sent to members of the local committees and are discussed at their meetings. This development is of course a healthy one; it would have been regrettable if, after the first few years, the LACs had continued under the tutelage of the National Council.

The National Council has initiated two reviews of its own work and the work of the district councils and local committees.[1] The first review was undertaken in 1951 when the LACs were less than two years old, and the second in 1955 after about six years' experience. These reviews were undertaken in the belief that, in this important new field, self-criticism and self-examination were most desirable.

The first review, which was based on the written comments of members of the National Council, of the DJACs (district joint advisory councils), and of some of the LACs, did not lead to more than one or two small constitutional changes, but it called attention to the need to arouse interest in and understanding of the local committees among employees generally. The main recommendation made was that the district councils should encourage the LACs to arrange meetings of employees at six-monthly intervals at which the work of the local unit and of the local committee should be described and discussed. These meetings were to be held at least partly in the employees' own time.

The second review was made in 1955–56 by a sub-committee of the National Council and arose from an analysis of questions and dis-

[1] See the British Electricity Authority's Annual Report for 1951–52 and the Central Electricity Authority's Annual Report for 1955–56.

cussions at eight regional conferences on joint consultation attended by representatives of the National and district councils and the local advisory committees. The sub-committee made a number of recommendations which were accepted by the National Council. Most of these recommendations required constitutional changes and a revision of the original agreement between the electricity boards and the trade unions. The new agreement was signed in March 1957 and the new constitutions came into force on April 1st.

The main change concerned the memberships of the National and district councils. These councils consisted of electricity boards' representatives and official representatives of the trade unions. The electricity boards had for some time held the view that direct employee representation should be added to the existing memberships at the district and national levels and had first proposed it in 1950. They wanted this mainly because it would provide a direct link between top managements at national and district levels and the men on the shop floor. This has now been achieved. On each of the twelve district councils there are now, in addition to the previously existing members, ten elected representatives drawn from the local committees in the district concerned, six of them manual, two clerical and administrative, and two technical staff representatives. In addition, the previous membership of the National Council has been supplemented by twelve LAC elected representatives—six manual, three clerical and administrative, and three technical staff representatives—one being drawn from each district council.

Another change related to the spheres covered by the LACs and has had the very satisfactory effect of restricting the coverage of all but a handful of the local committees to single local management units. The remaining constitutional changes have made provision for (*a*) the holding of an annual conference on joint consultation in each district (several districts had already organized them); (*b*) the regular presentation of progress reports to their committees by LAC chairmen (85 per cent of them had already done this); (*c*) the organization by LACs of at least one local employees' meeting each year (over 50 per cent had already done this); and (*d*) the preparation by LACs of annual reports (about 35 per cent had already done this).

It is too soon to make any useful comment on the full effects of these changes, although it can be said that most of the LAC elected representatives on the National and district councils have taken a full part in the councils' work. There are several advantages in having full-time trade union officials on the councils: they can thereby be kept informed of what is going on in the industry; they demonstrate to employees the unions' support for joint consultation; they bring a breadth of experience to the work (they are usually members of negotiating bodies in other industries); and they have an independent position. But at the same time, they usually are not themselves directly affected by the outcome of their work on the councils and they have not the same detailed knowledge of local conditions as those who work in the industry. It is precisely these limitations which are being overcome by the presence of the LAC elected representatives on the councils.

It could not be expected that the National Council would go on indefinitely turning out schemes with the vigour and intensity that it showed in the first five years and in the last few years, particularly in 1957 and 1958, the emphasis of its work has changed. New technical developments—this is a very rapidly developing industry—have led to the necessity to modify and expand existing schemes for the safety, health and welfare, and education and training of employees and this is being done. But increasingly it is becoming a forum for the whole industry, a role for which it is uniquely suited since it is the only place where the top managements of the electricity boards, the leading trade union officials, and directly elected employees' representatives can meet to discuss questions affecting the whole industry. Almost since the Council's inception, its chairman has presented a report on the industry's progress at each meeting, while the annual consolidated accounts of the electricity boards are each year the main subject of one entire meeting. In addition, more specific topics of major importance now make up the agenda. Thus in the last two meetings subjects discussed included safety in nuclear power stations, safety precautions in the construction of power stations, current problems of area boards, planning and research, present and future financing of the industry and the industry's university scholarship scheme. These meetings represent an advanced kind of joint consultation in industry, although it is possible to visualize still further developments in the Council's work in the coming years.

THE DISTRICT JOINT ADVISORY COUNCILS

We do not propose to say much about the work of the district councils—not because this work is unimportant, but because much of it is similar to that of the National Council. The main respects in which their work has differed have been that (a) they have examined how National Council recommendations approved in principle by the electricity boards could best be carried out in the districts concerned, and (b) they have been directly in touch with LACs in their districts and have directly stimulated their development. Perhaps we should emphasize two facts: firstly, the district councils have the same terms of reference (although their spheres are of course smaller) as the

National Council and that they do not have to wait for the initiative to be taken on any subject by the National Council; secondly, although they receive the minutes of all the LACs in their districts, this is solely so that the district councils may assist their development and deal with any recommendations which are addressed to them. The councils do not approve the local committees' minutes and local action on them can be taken immediately after LAC meetings. Over 95 per cent of items discussed by LACs are of mainly local interest (this is not to say that they are of minor importance) and a similar percentage of their total recommendations are addressed to local managements.

THE LOCAL ADVISORY COMMITTEES

At the foundation of the joint consultative system in the industry are the local advisory committees, since it is their work which most directly and decisively affects the quality of human relations in the industry. There are now nearly 500 committees, nearly all of them identified with a single local management unit, usually either a distribution district or a power station. Normally the membership of a committee consists of about fifteen people, of whom five or six are nominated representatives of management, with the local manager in the chair, and nine or ten elected representatives of the manual, clerical and administrative, and the technical staff. Manual workers almost always predominate in numbers. The secretary is appointed by the committee and is not a member. In nearly all cases he is a local clerical or administrative employee and servicing the committee is a job which he fits in with his normal departmental duties.

It is possible to see four phases in the development of the local committees over the past ten years and it is useful to examine their development by reference to these phases.

(i) *The First Phase*

In their first eighteen months or so—to mid-1951—nearly all the committees worked in a restricted way. Under their constitution they must meet once every two months, and although they might have chosen to meet more often, very few did so. The agendas were short and consisted largely of requests by elected representatives for improved amenities at the work-place, a fact which perhaps was not surprising since in some places the provision of such amenities was poor by modern standards and many employees expected such improvements to be one of the first benefits of the new organization. Few meetings lasted more than an hour and many were even briefer. Few standing or *ad hoc* committees were established. The prevailing conception of the LAC was that it was a welfare-cum-complaints committee. The management representatives tended therefore to think that the fewer the items and the shorter the meetings the more satisfactory things must be, while the elected representatives tended to think that the more complaints they could think of to bring to the committees the greater the success they were making of joint consultation. Many management representatives were apprehensive about these new bodies which in their view had been thrust upon them. They vaguely regarded the LACs as a threat to their traditional rights and status as managers and were inclined therefore to interpret strictly the committees' terms of reference and to seek to define those questions which the committees might legitimately consider and those which they could not because they were part of the 'managerial prerogatives'. Many elected representatives, for their part, regarded the LACs as additional negotiating committees and went to the meetings having had 'side meetings' beforehand at which the line to be taken on the various items was settled. Such approaches were at variance with both the principles and the aims of joint consultation.

(ii) *The Second Phase*

By about the middle of 1951, many local managers and employees had begun to settle down in the new organization of the industry and to the work of the local committees. The response of the electricity boards to requests for improved amenities had been sympathetic and this was recognized by many employees. The ground had therefore been prepared for an advance in joint consultation and the period from mid-1951 to mid-1954 marked a definite phase in its development. Many old suspicions and misunderstandings among managers and elected representatives were partly, though not entirely, dispelled and by the end of the period the predominant conception of the LACs was that they were an important communicating link between management and employees and a means through which people in the industry might be made more aware of underlying common interests and common purposes.

There was, in this phase, a gradual increase in the length of LAC meetings until, by the end of it, few were lasting less than two hours. A number of committees met monthly and about 200 standing sub-committees were set up, mostly on safety or accident prevention and the operation of canteens.

The agendas were no longer dominated by welfare amenities items. At the start of the phase there had been few items on education and training and efficiency, but by the end items on efficiency had become fairly common and there had been some increase in education and training items. Except in so far as the chairmen's progress reports dealt with questions of efficiency, nearly all items of this kind originated with the elected representatives. Typical items on education and training consisted of reports by individual employees on training courses they had attended, usually at one or the other of the two residential training establishments; requests for information on available education and training courses; questions concerning the training of craft apprentices; and the selection of employees to attend the spring and summer schools which are held each year at Oxford and Cambridge. Frequently recurring efficiency items related to waste prevention; the provision of adequate tools and materials in stores; the effective use of transport; the siting of meters in consumers' premises and the efficient reading of meters; means of increasing sales of electrical appliances to consumers; and improved methods of handling equipment. Most local managers, although they did not themselves bring forward such items, encouraged employees to do so and for the most part dealt with them quite well. Many agenda items originated in the national and district councils; most of these consisted of reports of meetings and requests for information and for local views on subjects being discussed by the councils.

But this was above all a phase when safety or accident prevention became the main subject of discussion, when large numbers of chairmen began to present progress reports to their committees, and when the committees themselves began to tackle that most intractable problem of arousing interest in and understanding of the work of local committees among employees generally.

By the end of this second phase the great majority of the LACs were discussing safety or accident prevention at every meeting and doing it in a most methodical and practical manner. Many of them had set up safety sub-committees and instituted safety suggestion books, and in 1953 about a dozen committees followed the initiative of one by organizing a local safety week. The rapidly increasing interest in this subject is not of course surprising. Nobody likes accidents: everyone has an obvious interest in reducing them; and safety discussions on joint consultative committees need not raise any fundamental issues concerning management-employee relationships. In the history of joint consultation in the industry the significance of this very extensive and rapid development is that it gave the LAC members a chance to get to know each other by working closely together on a job of unquestioned value and to learn techniques of joint consultation which could be applied in other, more controversial, fields of LAC activity. Furthermore, this subject involved many more employees than sit on the LACs in activities directly associated with the committees through their co-option to work on safety sub-committees, their appointment as voluntary safety wardens, and their attendance at such functions as safety weeks.

It is doubtful if, in mid-1951, twenty LAC chairmen all-told presented progress reports to their committees, but by mid-1954 well over 300 of them were regularly doing so. Nearly all these reports consisted of factual accounts of local technical and commercial activities. Much work was put into them and their preparation implied recognition by many managers of the importance of keeping employees informed of technical and commercial problems and progress; but it is a fact that although the reports were usually listened to attentively and were appreciated, they rarely led to many questions or much discussion, or to the making of recommendations to local managements.

It was also in this second phase that a fair proportion of the committees first began to give serious attention to informing employees generally about what they were doing and to quickening their interest in joint consultation. Before this the minutes of the meetings had usually been very brief and largely unintelligible to employees not attending the meetings and few copies were sent to people not attending the meetings. Some progress was made toward remedying these defects and in particular many committees saw to it that middle managers and supervisors received copies of the minutes. Indeed additional representatives of these grades, particularly first-line supervisors, were brought on to the committees at this time as management representatives. Many, though by no means all, the elected representatives acquired the habit of reporting back orally to their 'constituents'.

In 1952 a beginning was made with meetings of employees, most of which were held partly in the employees' own time and at which the work of the local units and of the LACs was described and discussed. In 1953–54, at least 250 of these meetings were held, most of them quite successfully. Several LACs (though probably still less than fifty) began producing annual reports, and by 1954 about sixty committees had followed the lead of one or two committees which in 1951 had begun producing or sponsoring local magazines or news-sheets. These ranged over many local activities and employee interests and usually included sections on LAC work.

Many other techniques were devised by individual committees and all of them together certainly had some impact on employees as a group. But it could not be claimed that the impact was anywhere either very solid or sustained, except where employees were directly brought into some LAC activity such as the work of a sub-committee, the editing of a local magazine, or the organization of a power-station open day.

We might sum up the position in mid-1954 by saying that, when things were going fairly well, most employees thought very little about the LACs, but when things were going wrong they asked what the LACs were doing about it. The fact that they thought about the LACs in any circumstances was something of a triumph for committees which at that time had been working only for three and a half years.

(iii) *The Third Phase*

It is not suggested that the LACs underwent any sudden radical change in 1954, but from about that time significant changes began to occur in which an increasing number of committees became involved. These changes concerned not only the attitudes of many members towards their committees, but also the subjects discussed by the committees, as well as the way in which some of these subjects were handled.

Changes of attitudes were most pronounced among the most able and progressive local managers. By 1954, these managers had long ceased to regard the LACs as a threat to their managerial status and authority. Rather, they had acquired a positive view of the role of the committees, based on a conception of the power stations and distribution districts as social institutions as well as production units. They had begun to see the potentialities of the committees as bodies through which human relations might be improved and employees induced to co-operate more closely with management in the development of the industry. If such managers were still in a minority in 1954 they were already influencing the attitudes of many of their colleagues and today their numbers have greatly increased. The proof that these managers' attitudes have changed substantially may be read in the initiative they now take on their committees, the thoroughness with which they prepare for meetings, the skill with which they get the most out of their members' experience, the time they devote to this work, and the speed and decisiveness with which, as local managers, they deal with the committees' recommendations.

Many elected representatives have responded to this lead and have increasingly shown a willingness not only to cast off their earlier doubts and misconceptions, but also to commit themselves positively to this still comparatively new system of consultation. It cannot be said that by any means all of them prepare as thoroughly for meetings as is desirable or that there is no longer room for improvement in the manner and extent to which they report back to their 'constituents', but it is nevertheless impressive to see the keenness and understanding of many elected representatives and their readiness to accept the responsibilities which membership of these committees often involves.

These gradual adjustments of attitudes have been reflected in the steady growth in the volume of LAC work and in the growth of what might be called the orthodox types of LAC work. In 1958–59 130 of the committees met more often than bi-monthly, most meetings lasted half a day, and there were about 770 LAC sub-committees besides. Most of these sub-committees are concerned with problems of accident prevention, the operation of the canteens, and power station maintenance, and most are very active. Many LACs now organize safety weeks and open days and in 1958–59 they organized a total of 580 local meetings of employees. Outside the committee room the members spend much time explaining the committees' work to employees, encouraging them to apply for the industry's university scholarships, technical college study under the industry's manual worker traineeship scheme, attendance at spring and summer schools, enrolment in one of the industry's correspondence courses, participation in arts and crafts exhibitions, fire-fighting and first-aid work, and so on.

It was in 1954 that more than a handful of LAC chairmen first began to produce progress reports of a new type. Whereas in the earlier phases these reports had been straightforward accounts of technical and commercial progress made since the previous meeting, many now included references to new local developments planned or likely to be forthcoming in the following months, prospective changes in the organization of sections of work and, though less commonly, references to specific managerial problems to which solutions had not yet been found. The reports also ranged occasionally over major developments in the industry such as the construction of the 275-kV 'Super-Grid', the nuclear power programme, rural electrification, and the annual reports of the electricity boards. Further, the LAC chairmen began to include in their reports sections on social activities, educational successes of employees, achievements of individuals and groups in overcoming work problems, and the welfare of sick, injured, and retired employees. In other words, the chairmen, in preparing their reports, were increasingly asking themselves what the employees were most likely to be interested in and attempting to relate such interests wherever possible to the activities of their fellow employees, the future work of the local units and the problems of management. Today this development has gone so far that most reports presented by chairmen do, from time to time, contain such items. They usually lead to discussions, some of which have been of high quality.

In spite of the existence of an employees' suggestion scheme under which, since it was established in 1951–52, nearly 16,000 suggestions have been submitted and well over 5,000 awards made, the committees have, during this third phase, spent more time than formerly discussing items relating to the efficient operating of the local units. Mostly, however, these items are of the same type as were raised by (far fewer) committees in the previous phase, are still of a comparatively minor character and are still raised mostly by elected representatives. Such items are now actively encouraged by most local managements and are examined carefully by them. Although it cannot be said that any great number of important efficiency recommendations has been forthcoming, the discussions on efficiency items have had a definite value. They have helped employees to see more clearly how their own and other people's jobs fit into the local organization; they have been part of that educative process which is necessary in any rapidly changing industry; and they have induced managements to think more carefully of the human implications of decisions which they make on ostensibly technical matters.

Perhaps the most valuable work of the power station committees associated directly with efficient operations has been done in connection with the annual overhaul of boiler plant. This is the major maintenance job in power stations and often has to be done quickly and in accordance with a divisional plant outage programme. It is inherently complex and involves co-ordinated work by many employees, often under difficult conditions. Recently an investigation was made into the value of the work of a cross-section of the boiler overhaul sub-committees which exist in about fifty of the large stations, and two definite conclusions were reached: that the sub-committees had contributed to the smoother working of overhauls in the sense that friction had been reduced, misunderstandings avoided, and the co-ordination of jobs improved, and also that the sub-committees had helped to improve human relations on the stations concerned.

The LACs are now spending more time than formerly discussing education and training. While it remains true that these discussions have been mostly of the rather superficial kind already referred to, there are now numerous examples of committees assisting in the preparation of training courses for various categories of local employees, and helping to apply locally education and training schemes prepared in general terms by the district and national councils.

But the distinguishing characteristic of this third phase has undoubtedly been the growing number of committees which have been involved in the processes of technological, methodological, and organizational changes which have, since 1954, been taking place rapidly in the industry.

By mid-1954 the industry had been organized in its existing form for six years and some of the electricity boards were beginning to examine, in the light of these six years' experience, the question of whether the managerial organizations which they had set up were still suited to the requirements of a rapidly expanding industry. Since then, changes have been introduced which have affected important sections of the Authority (and since January 1, 1958, the Generating Board) and several area boards. In 1954, for example, the Authority decided, as an experiment, to amalgamate two of its divisional organizations, and this led to changes affecting many employees. In that and the following years, several of the area boards have amalgamated and otherwise changed the boundaries of their local management units. One area board, for example, in the last few years has reduced the number of managerial units in its area from fifty-six to twenty-two with consequent extensive changes not only in organization but in the distribution of functions and responsibilities. At present, another board is undertaking an equally radical transformation. There have, in addition, been some major changes relating to specific functions of area boards and divisions. For example, extensive mechanization of the methods used to compile consumers' accounts has led to the centralization of this and related functions and to a considerable reduction in the number of employees engaged in this work.

In many of the power stations even more striking changes have been going on. Between 1948 and 1954 most of the power stations were carrying heavy loads throughout the year, but since then, with the construction of new stations and extensions of existing ones, the loads on many stations have fallen, with loads at off-peak periods being carried by a small number of highly efficient modern stations based on the coal-fields. These changes in load distribution have given rise to several human relations problems. Many power station employees have been faced with reduced opportunities for overtime and promotion, with periods in the year when they have not had their normal operational work to do, and with anxiety about their future employment. The Authority, for its part, wanted to transfer men temporarily from older stations to modern stations to give them training on modern plant and enable them to undertake relief work there. At first this aroused suspicion at some modern stations and a good deal of apprehension among men at the older stations. This particular problem is not a temporary one; on the contrary, with the commissioning of nuclear power stations, which have to be run almost continuously if they are to be economical, the problem is likely to grow in the coming years.

Increasingly in the last four years the LACs have been consulted on the many changes occurring in the industry. Before then such isolated changes as took place had usually been introduced after little more than prior information had been given to the committees, but today the situation has been transformed, as may be seen from the following three quite typical illustrations drawn from recent experience.

The area board already referred to which is now embarking on a full-scale rearrangement of its local management organizations, after deciding in broad outline what it wanted to do, informed the district joint advisory council of its intentions. The council then sent this information to all the area board LACs with the invitation to discuss it and to make any comments and to ask any questions they wished. Senior officers of the board attended many local meetings and many committees sent in written questions and suggestions which were dealt with in detail by the board, which then gave its answers in a paper presented to the district council and subsequently sent to all the LACs. The local committees arranged meetings of employees throughout their localities to explain and discuss the board's proposals. Without question, the board's employees were fully consulted on the changes and in a form and at a time when this could do most good. Indeed, as a result of a recommendation of one of the LACs the board decided to increase the number of districts decided upon under its reorganization plans from twelve to thirteen.

The Authority developed a policy for dealing with the effects of changing load conditions on employees. This policy covers not only procedures to be adopted when the Authority (now the Generating Board) decides to close an old station, but measures to be taken to maintain the morale of employees in stations with falling loads. The policy, which was introduced through the National Joint Advisory Council, is geared to the work of the local advisory committees. No station may be closed without giving a year's notice to the district council and the local committee involved, after which action is taken (if it had not begun before) to resettle employees elsewhere in the industry, preferably in the same or a neighbouring locality. Whenever stations with falling loads must continue to operate for some years the LACs are enjoined to tackle the problem of maintaining the morale of employees by a variety of activities, and many of the committees are responding to this lead. Some years ago, when men were temporarily transferred for training and work from old to modern stations, serious objections were raised by some employees at the modern stations, but now such temporary transfers are being carried out in the summer months on a large scale and without serious disturbance. Everywhere this has been done after the support of the LACs has been gained.

Operational research has been introduced into the power stations only after full explanations have been given to the LACs by management. At a few stations managements have not been able to convince some of the manual workers' representatives that operational research is not another name for time and motion study, but such cases have been few. In most stations the introduction of operational research has been supported by the LACs and there have even been cases of employees asking managements to 'bring in operational research teams to assist them with specified work problems.

Some three years ago the Chairman of the Authority wrote in a publication which was circulated throughout the industry that the way in which operational research was introduced into the power stations 'is how the Authority will always proceed when they propose introducing major changes affecting employees. They will do so because they think it is the right and the intelligent thing to do. By consulting on changes months before they are to be introduced there is time and opportunity to discover the best methods of introduction, there is the opportunity for those affected to adjust themselves to change and there is the likelihood that the disturbance will be reduced to an absolute minimum'. There are strong grounds for the belief that this promise will be lived up to not only by the Authority's successor, the Generating Board, but by the area boards as well. And if, as many people believe, the crucial test for joint consultation is the way in which it deals with the human consequences of technological change, there can be no denying that joint consultation in the electricity supply industry rests on firm foundations.

(iv) *The Fourth Phase*

Many local committees, in their activities and in the attitude of their members, fall a long way behind the best, and even the best of them still have their problems. There is still great scope for improvement, particularly in the fields of education, training and efficiency. Also there is everywhere a gap waiting to be filled between the levels of information, co-operation, and understanding achieved on the committees themselves and those levels attained by the great bulk of employees on the shop floor.

In the past year or so a substantial number of LACs have been approaching their work in such a manner as to improve its quality and to encourage the participation in it of a greater number of local employees. The method which they are adopting is sufficiently distinctive to suggest that these LACs may now be initiating a fourth phase of development. It might be termed the phase of LAC planning and it requires some explanation.

The agendas of most LAC meetings have, in recent years, looked rather alike in broad outline and have been compiled in very much the same way. There have been the formal or procedural items common to almost every type of meeting; a number of reports and publications and requests for information; the Chairman's progress report; minutes of standing committees, and three or four items raised by management and elected members on such matters as arrangements for employees' meetings, suggestions arising from the job and proposals for making some alteration of organization or method.

The agendas are, of course, prepared by the LAC secretaries and the committees worked through the different items with more or less effectiveness. But they rarely asked themselves, as committees, whether the items on the agendas were the ones which they ought to be devoting their time and thought to. And this is precisely the question which, at the present time, these committees (which are still a minority) are asking themselves. And they are attempting to answer this question by reference to the needs of local employees and the efficiency of the local unit.

This is the seed of LAC planning, which might be defined as the deliberate choosing, by the LAC, of some of the things it intends to do over a period of time and of the methods it is going to adopt. The approach has obvious merits and is being worked out in the following terms. At one meeting the LAC decides what is to be the planned subject for discussion at the next meeting. Between these two meetings members of the committee think about the subject and the elected representatives discuss it with their 'constituents'. Publicity material has, in some cases, been prepared and it has been made plain to local employees that their own ideas on the subject will be welcomed by the committee and that they should pass them on to their representatives. By such means many more employees are more actively associated with the LACs' work, the LAC members come to meetings having prepared themselves more adequately, and the committee deals with at least one subject which has meaning in the daily lives of local employees. Among the many subjects so far tackled by LACs in this way have been the training of apprentices; communications and co-ordination between departments; the adequacy of tools and equipment to do the jobs intended for them; waste prevention; matters which should be included in the Chairman's progress reports; problems resulting from reduced loadings on older power stations; stores layout and stores handling and documentation; problems of providing light work for unfit employees; the rehabilitation of disabled employees, and the issue and care of tools.

While it is impossible to predict how the committees will develop in the coming years, it is at least reasonable to expect that many more of them will come up to the level of achievement of the best and, in particular, that more will adopt a planned approach to their work.

CONCLUSIONS

We have given an account of joint consultation in one of the basic industries of this country and drawn attention to the speed with which the local committees in this industry transferred their attentions from fringe interests and activities to the main problems affecting the industry's efficiency and well-being of its employees. We have shown that, in a recent phase of their development, the local committees became deeply involved in examining and dealing with the consequences for employees of the many recent changes in organization and techniques in the industry, and that they have done some of their most valuable work in this area.

What are the main reasons for the progress which was made? It is impossible to isolate and identify all these, but we would point to the continuous support given to joint consultation by top managements, and the steadily growing support of the trade unions, the integratio of the joint consultative system with the industry's manageria organization, the fact that the industry has been growing in siz efficiency and prosperity, and the fact that its history has not bee clouded by acute labour-management conflicts. It is not possible to say whether progress in joint consultation would have been so rapid if the industry had been nationally organized but privately owned, or what would have been the trade unions' attitude to joint consultation in such conditions. But we would underline our belief that successful joint consultation does not depend fundamentally on the character of industrial ownership and also the fact that the Trades Union Congress has repeatedly declared (and acted upon) its faith in the value of joint consultation in both the nationalized and the privately-owned sections of industry.

What then are the main grounds for opposition or indifference to joint consultation, in so far as it exists, on the part of management, the trade unions, and employees generally?

Opposition or indifference on the part of managements is usually based on the belief that joint consultation undermines their status and authority, takes up too much of their time, leads to difficulties with supervisors, and is a poor alternative to day-to-day informal consultation on the shop floor.

It is difficult to see how these beliefs can be sustained. Some managers have a tendency to exaggerate and misunderstand the extent and nature of their authority ahd to forget that, in any industrial organization, decisions are not only made by themselves but are made at all levels, and indeed that most well-rendered answers grow out of the facts when once assembled. It is surely not the actual making of decisions that presents the greatest difficulty for managers, but rather the securing of acceptance throughout the industry or firm of those decisions and of executive authority. To be effective, decisions must be understood and accepted by those who have to carry them out and it is here that joint consultation is of the greatest value to management. In making use of joint consultation managements demonstrate not their weakness but their wisdom, and only limit their right to make final decisions where the joint consultative committees have misunderstood their terms of reference. This is something which need never arise and does so only through lack of skill on the part of those involved in the work.

It is true that an effective committee will take up a good deal of a manager's time. But it is no more reasonable to assert dogmatically that it takes up 'too much' of his time than it is to say that machines should not replace men because they are 'too expensive'. Both joint consultation and machines are investments in indirect means of production, and before reaching any conclusion about their value, one must consider the return from joint consultation, just as one considers the return from machines.

There is no reason why a proper relationship should not be worked out between supervisors and joint consultative committees. Firstly, firms should arrange that employees' complaints and suggestions should so far as possible be disposed of between the employee or his representative and the immediate supervisor. Secondly, when subjects which concern supervisors are to be discussed the supervisors should be told about them and be given the opportunity either to express their view to higher management or to attend the meeting itself. Thirdly, supervisors should be directly represented on the joint committee. And finally, they should be given copies of agendas and minutes and should be informed immediately after meetings of any discussions or recommendations which concern them.

The argument that informal consultation is preferable to joint consultation in committee begs the question. It suggests that there is some conflict between the two methods, whereas in fact informal consultation is stimulated by formal joint consultation and cannot be adequate without it. For informal consultation has several serious limitations. It does not necessarily take place with the appropriate representatives of the employees, it seldom involves higher management, it is not clearly related to rights and procedures which are understood throughout the firm, and it does not take place in conditions suitable for discussing important subjects affecting other than small groups of employees.

o

Some national trade union leaders and workers' leaders in the factories are hesitant about participating fully in joint consultation for fear that they may compromise their freedom in wage negotiations. These leaders must make a fundamental decision about their relationships with management. They must decide whether they are to be a permanent opposition group in industry, taking no part in management decisions outside the area reserved for collective bargaining, or whether they are to consult with managements on matters of mutual interest and at the same time retain the trade unions' independence. Irrespective of the form of industrial ownership which may prevail, the second alternative is, in our opinion, the only one which will benefit employees, industry, and the whole community. Such co-operation is essential to increased industrial efficiency and productivity. Also, it will enable the unions to influence not only the character of managerial decisions but also the attitudes of managers to their own jobs and to those of their employees. This in turn can lead to changes in relationships which will enable managements and employees to identify and enlarge the areas of common interest and consent in industry. It should lead to an increase in the satisfaction which employees get from their work and free managements from the depressing and inhibiting sense of working with an indifferent or even hostile body of employees. If, on the other hand, the alternative of opposition is preferred, the unions and the local leaders in the factories will be admitting that they are neither able nor willing to give their members rights and responsibilities and an enhanced status in industry comparable with those they have gained in the political community. If joint consultative committees are to be successful they need the attention of the ablest leaders of the unions and of the local employees and a system of communication and consultation within the unions which is as effective as those demanded by employees within the factories themselves.

With regard to employees generally, they often share the doubts of their leaders, are sometimes reluctant to shoulder the responsibilities which inevitably accompany the right to joint consultation, and may feel conflicts of loyalty to their representatives, to their supervisors, and to the primary working groups to which they belong. It is a necessary condition for successful joint consultation that, in arranging the electoral units, full account should be taken of the existence of primary working groups. The electoral structure should enable the natural leaders of these groups to be elected to the committees, for in this way any conflicts of loyalty will be reduced to a minimum. This point has been forgotten time and again and yet it requires only careful thought and planning in the initial stages to avoid the more obvious pitfalls.

Effective joint consultation cannot be achieved simply by imposing a committee or system of committees on an existing organization and hoping for the best. It must be carefully integrated into the organization of the firm or industry as a whole. Neither should it be assumed that those who participate in the work are necessarily expert at it or can become so in a short while. Training and experience and active measures are required to increase understanding, the most important measure probably being to bring management and employees' representatives together to discuss their differences and to get to know each other's point of view.

From our experience in the electricity supply industry over the past ten years we would argue confidently that, if the conditions which we have postulated are fulfilled, there is no reason why joint consultative committees should not prove effective throughout British industry. These committees have a substantial contribution to make toward creating and maintaining those co-operative attitudes which are the foundation of successful industrial enterprise.

64. A PLAN FOR 'INDUSTRIAL DEMOCRACY'*

Where do we stand now?

Public Enterprise sees industrial democracy burgeoning from the mutual respect and liaison between the public sector executives and the trade union leaders.

But this intimacy between the two power centres in each Corporation is completely without significance on the shop floor.

The storm signals are visible throughout the public sectors; the active trades unionists are no longer prepared to accept responsibility without authority.

Mr Hugh Gaitskell wrote recently:

'It may be said that nationalization has not so far lived up to expectations in this matter precisely because too much power is left in the hands of managements and not enough given to the workers. Certainly most of us would like to see a greater degree of "workers' control"; and there will be general agreement on the desirability of creating a greater sense of partnership and participation. But the very hesitations and doubts which assail the Labour Movement on "workers' control" at the moment show how much more complicated the issue of "power" is than at first sight appears.'[1]

* From Clive Jenkins: 'Retreat: The Labour Party and the Public Corporations', *Universities and Left Review*, Winter 1958, Supplement 'The Insiders', pp. 59–60. Reprinted by permission of the author and the *New Left Review*.
[1] *Socialism and Nationalization*, Fabian Tract 300, July 1956.

Since the Corporations were set up, few precise ideas on the devolution of power have been evolved.

The unions have been completely involved in short-run problems of industrial organization and their economic consequences. And when a Conservative Government was returned, practical negotiators treated the issue as academic in the face of Ministerial attacks.

But now that the Labour Party is preparing for its return to power, discussion of specific suggestions based on experiences of the unions since 1946 is essential. These propositions are advanced in the first instance:

(1) Workers in an industry are entitled to a voice in workshop management and in higher policy making.

(2) Their authority at local level should be absolute in such questions as working arrangements, hiring and dismissals.

(3) They should be allowed to select their own supervisors (providing these are technically qualified).

(4) Workers' representatives should sit on the Managing Board for their industry.

(5) This scheme of sharing in power (while operated by the joint union organizations within the corporations) should be manned by employees only and *not* full-time trade union officers, who should remain primarily responsible for the negotiation of wages, conditions, and grievance settling.

A modern industrial society could not tolerate each industry's workers dominating their own Board and bargaining with the community. It could not have the easily-automated industries distributing large benefits and shorter hours to its own employees only.

It must, therefore, make clear that a corporation's workers have substantial—but demarcated—powers.

They are entitled to a block of Board seats, but not a majority. Consumers and technicians will also require to be heard.

And, extremely important, representatives of the national planning organization will have to be seated.

A Socialist Government should have, as a priority, the drawing up of plans and targets for each branch of the economy which are aimed at rapidly and substantially increasing the standards of life for all sections of the community.

The planning machine of the 1945 Labour Ministers was plainly too weak for the job. This deficiency should have been recognized by now and technical means devised for unifying the development programmes of the public institutions—in a positive and leading way.

A workmanlike way of providing worker-directors would be to split industries into occupational constituencies, e.g. of clerks, supervisors, managers, labourers, technicians and all the appropriate grades which bulk differently in each industry. This is suggested because there is frequently more enduring identity of interest between men of a similar trade in different parts of the country, than between men of different occupations in the same factory.

Each constituency would elect an agreed number of representatives to an 'Electoral College' which would, in turn, select the persons to sit on the Board.

The advantages of this method are these.

Workers are enabled to vote for someone with a common language and viewpoint in a group with which they identify themselves—as opposed to a geographical constituency.

The Electoral College will become a stable forum which will, in time, have opportunities of measuring individual performance at the job in hand and so be better equipped to pick the best qualified worker to go on the Board.

All Board background papers and situation-appreciations can be circulated to Electoral College members who will thus be enabled to quiz their Board members and better able to fulfil their reporting-back function. And if they are dissatisfied with the representation they are getting, they can recall a Board member—by due process—and replace him by another Electoral College member without loss of representational efficiency.

These suggestions may be unsuitable or needing radical amendment.

But the need now exists for the defeatism over workers' representation to be finally rejected.

The Labour Party is essentially, and above all else, the vehicle for the aspirations of the British working class, and based firmly on the industrial workers. It should not blur its historic role by protestations that the existing public corporations meet the desires of the organized trades unionists who work every day within them.

The National Executive Committee must realize that the outworn owner-worker relationship has been carried over into the public corporations.

It can only be uprooted by a Socialist Party deliberately placing its trust in the workers and effecting a shift in the balance of power. When this is done the Party will witness a release of productive energies which will transform our society into one of which the British people can be proud.

CHAPTER XI

The Measurement of Efficiency

The development of techniques for the measurement of efficiency is important in all large-scale organizations, industrial and non-industrial, public and private. In a nationalized industry it is particularly important, in view of the fact that the test of profitability may be of very limited significance.

The results of efficiency-measurement are primarily of interest to management, as control-data, but they also provide the means whereby supervising authorities, such as the Minister and the legislature, may form more reliable judgments of performance than would otherwise be possible.

In *Extract 65*, M. Gabriel Ardant, formerly Secretary-General of the Central Committee of Inquiry into the Cost and Output of the Public Services in France, emphasizes the need for efficiency measurement and proposes certain methods by which he considers it may best be effected. The use of comparative statistical data by the Select Committee on Nationalized Industries to assess the performance of British airlines is the subject of *Extract 66*. This is also dealt with, in more general terms, by Sir Toby Low in *Extract 54*, Chapter VIII, above. In *Extract 67* Sir John Elliot, in a lecture to the British Institute of Transport, deals with certain special problems of defining and measuring efficiency in transport undertakings.

65. MEASURING PRODUCTIVITY IN STATE UNDERTAKINGS*

PRINCIPLES ON WHICH THE METHOD IS BASED

The main fault that supporters of private enterprise have to find with state management—in whatever field—is the disappearance of the profit motive and of the rational pricing of goods and services. There

* From Gabriel Ardant: 'The Measurement of Productivity in State Undertakings and Public Services', *Annals of Collective Economy*, Vol. XXIV, 1953, pp. 81–7. Reprinted by permission of the *Annals*.

is, however, no real reason why part of this machinery should not be retained in state undertakings and services, or rather certain equivalent processes substituted for it. The complete argument would exceed the scope of this article, but we propose to show here that by measuring output it is possible to make use of one essential factor of the system of private enterprise—competition—which may at first seem quite out of place in a system of state management.

A publicly owned undertaking is composed of a number of basic units. For example, in France the tobacco monopoly consists of twenty-two factories, the National Stud Farms have twenty-one stables of stallions, the national aircraft construction corporations, of which there were four some years ago, each consists of several factories. These units are further subdivided into workshops and warehouses. On the whole, and bearing in mind major reservations, each basic unit performs the same kind of operations as the others. It would therefore seem natural to compare costs in each unit, factory, stable or workshop. Such a comparison would automatically take place if each plant were a private undertaking; in so far as competition entered into play, the plant with the lowest costs might try to increase sales by lowering prices, thus compelling other undertakings to lower their profit margins, reduce costs or go out of business. This, of course, is an ideal picture in view of all the phenomena of imperfect competition to which contemporary economic analysis and observation have drawn attention.

Competition survives to a certain extent, however, and there is no reason why it should not be utilized in the operation of a publicly owned undertaking consisting of a number of factories, depots or warehouses. The machinery will not work as automatically as it does when there is a free market, with its ultimate sanction of bankruptcy, i.e. the elimination of the unfit or at any rate the unsuccessful. The head of the undertaking will have to apply considered decisions based on conclusions drawn from observed differences of costs.

He must decide whether excessively high costs in a particular factory are due to the incompetence or negligence of its manager. If so, and a warning does not suffice, the dismissal of the manager will have to be contemplated. Or it may be that the organization of the factory is at fault and that the manager, warned of the inadequacy of his results (as a private enterpreneur would be by decreased profits or falling sales), may be able to put things right by reorganizing methods of work. It may be that the equipment is at fault, for which the manager of the factory is not necessarily responsible, in which case it falls to the general manager to draw the conclusions and decide whether to scrap the old equipment and plan an investment programme.

It may also be that the factory is too small to be profitable. The law of non-proportional returns needs no mathematical proof here; in general, returns increase with increasing production, because of the spreading of fixed costs over a greater volume of production. After a certain figure is reached, returns begin to decrease for many reasons, particularly the difficulties of managing efficiently an undertaking of more than a certain size. Every establishment thus has an optimum size corresponding to maximum returns. The economic law is well-known in principle, but only observation can indicate the optimum size of establishment for a given production. In private enterprise the operation of the market enables it to be determined to a certain extent. In practice it leads to the closing down of undertakings which are too small to be profitable or the collapse of certain mammoth undertakings. The process of natural selection is responsible, in a large number of industries, for the concentration which is so characteristic of the modern economic world. In state-run industries it may be replaced by a comparison of costs in the various basic units. Output tables show at once which factory workshop or depot is the most satisfactory size. It may be useful to quote some examples from the work of the Central Committee of Inquiry into the Cost and Output of the Public Services, which has been using the method described here for several years past. In the National Stud Farms, the comparison of the net cost per stallion on the books of each farm shows that the small farms have a relatively high net cost as a rule. The cost falls as the farm increases in size. Beyond a certain number of stallions, about 300, the net cost again becomes relatively high. These figures have to be interpreted, of course, since the farms are not all concerned with the same type of stallion. This is, however, a definite fact to go on which may be taken as the basis for a regrouping plan, and it was as a result of these findings that the Committee of Inquiry proposed that six farms should be shut down, under certain conditions, and within various periods. Under free market conditions the result would have been the same; it is up to the state to make a considered decision where such conditions do not exist.

The inadequacy of the output of a works or service is not determined only by its size or the efficiency of its management. It may be that some establishments are badly located or that transport costs are too high. The influence of natural conditions is obvious in the case of a mine, where costs are closely linked to the quality of the seam. It is well known that in the case of communication routes and transport services working conditions are different for mountainous or flat country, for clay or limestone areas, etc. In comparing the efficiency of works or local managers these differences must be taken into account; the minimum costs attainable with management of average quality must be determined for each establishment, and differences between these costs should be accounted for only by differences in natural or working conditions and the quality of the equipment. If it then appears that costs in a particular establishment are, and must remain, higher than for the others, the question arises of its elimination or conversion to other uses.

There are obvious problems involved in closing down a works whose costs are too high. The state is more reluctant to do so than a private entrepreneur would be, because of its greater responsibility towards its employees. This means that the state must either try to resettle the workers and find them other jobs by converting a works or establishment to other uses, or gradually reduce activity by not replacing employees who leave or are retired. It is nonetheless essential to find out which works are, and must remain, too costly, in order to make preparations for shutting down or reconversion.

As in the case of the natural operation of the market, the deliberate decisions suggested here may, therefore, result in two different kinds of elimination or selection. One is the selection of management by a process such as bankruptcy: in private enterprise the head of an undertaking who fails is eliminated, though the works may continue to exist and operate under the management of a more skilful entrepreneur; in the public sphere such elimination must be effected by the transfer or dismissal of a works manager who is unable to turn his establishment to good account. The second is the elimination of organizations where the costs are appreciably higher than in others, even when well managed. The closing down of private undertakings must be paralleled in the public sphere by the planned regrouping of works or improvement of communications, plans which comprise both cutting down and building up and which must be carried out under conditions worthy of the state.

The method suggested for local works and management can, and must be, applied to the sub-units, workshops and depots. Results must be measured at all levels. For instance, the measurement of productivity leads to the question of whether tobacco depots should be maintained in a large number of districts or whether fewer and better located depots would not provide an appreciable economy in management expenses.

OBSTACLES AND OBJECTIONS

The suggested procedure seems so simple that it may be wondered why it has not been universally applied. Such a system of management is not entirely unknown, as is proved by the example given below, but it is often more or less inadequately carried out according to circumstances. Even where costs are determined, their systematic utilization for purposes of comparison is not sufficiently widespread. It may thus be useful to point out some of the difficulties in the way of applying such a method and the objections that may be raised.

In the first place, it must be admitted that it is not always easy to determine average cost per unit. One of the main difficulties is the allocation of common costs between the various different products manufactured in one establishment. But these are well-known problems, and industrial accounting has its own commonsense rule for dealing with them.

An example will show that such difficulties can be overcome, given a will to do so. Tobacco manufacture presents fairly complex problems.[1] Each factory makes several types of cigarette and the materials change weight from one workshop to another, owing to variations in the amount of water they contain. The SEITA (State Match and Tobacco Monopoly) has developed a number of processes, the details of which need not be described here, for overcoming these difficulties. The initiative was provided by the report of the Sergent Committee set up in 1925 to study ways of improving the revenue of the tobacco monopoly. A report submitted by A. Citroen proposed in particular the calculation of the cost of each product manufactured. The accounting system was improved and the costing carried through but it remained too slow and too approximate. For some years past, SEITA has been making efforts to improve the system and has succeeded in perfecting a reasonably accurate method of costing which now enables the factory cost per packet to be calculated for the most popular brand of cigarettes, *Gauloise bleues* (*caporal ordinaire*).[2] The results are shown in the table below.

The method used allows the calculation of possible economies both in materials and labour. Complete costing is carried out once a year, but monthly variation indices can be established in order to follow the development of results more closely. It has also been possible to calculate the optimum cost for each factory, taking into account various circumstances, particularly the quality of its machinery. Two sorts of conclusion may be drawn from these figures: the comparison of a factory's actual and optimum costs is an index of the quality of its management and particularly of the works manager; and the comparison of optimum costs for different factories can be used to determine to what extent an improvement could be achieved

[1] Cf. Pierre Berend: 'Le prix de revient et le controle de la gestion dans les manufactures de tabac du SEITA', in *Revue Economique*, July 1952.

[2] Factory cost at inventory value of stock. The weighted average cost per packet for the industry as a whole after inclusion of overheads is 7.57 francs.

by modernizing equipment or having greater specialization in certain factories, or by the regrouping of factories.

Factories		Cost per packet in 1949 (francs)
Bordeaux		7.34
Châteauroux		6.73
Dijon		6.72
Issy		6.69
Le Mans		7.06
Lille		6.78
Lyons		6.82
Marseilles		7.24
Morlaix		6.45
Nancy		7.28
Nantes		7.04
Nice		8.35
Orleans		6.85
Pantin		6.89
Strasbourg	A	6.99
	B	7.19
Riom		6.69
Tonneins		7.38
Toulouse		7.37

This example has been emphasized in order to show that accounting difficulties can be overcome—the difficulties in this instance were considerable.

There is also a second class of obstacle, due to fear on the part of employees that 'competition' may lead works managers to require that work be speeded up to an exhausting extent. Is there not a danger that the reintroduction of 'capitalist' processes may lead to the re-creation of capitalist abuses? The answer would seem to be that the highest costs are often connected less with the effort of the employees—which may in some cases be inadequate—than with the organization of work, the nature of the equipment, the routing of materials and products and the arrangement of works and offices. The observations of the Central Committee established to inquire into government-owned industrial establishments in France are significant in this respect.

A concrete example will show better still the kind of reform on which productivity depends. In a number of financial departments or establishments, such as nationalized commercial banks, the Bank of France, treasury departments, etc., it became apparent that one of the departments with the highest deficit was the department dealing with stocks and bonds. One of the main reasons for this was the existence of bonds and coupons of extremely low value, due to the habits of French savers and above all to the devaluation of the currency. The handling of such bonds was found to be costly. The Committee of Inquiry therefore suggested that it was of prime importance to eliminate operations which were too small to be profitable by means of an accelerated policy of bond regrouping, fixed minimum nominal values, etc. Many examples of this kind could be given.

The argument should be carried further. Measurement of productivity is not only the measurement of the quantity of the product made in a given space of time, but the determination of the total cost of manufacture; industrial risks and sickness are also elements of cost. The proportion of industrial accidents and sickness, even the mortality rate among the employees, should be calculated for each factory, and these elements should figure alongside costs in the output tables by which the efficiency of the managerial and supervisory staff and the profitability of establishments are judged.

THE MEASUREMENT OF PRODUCTIVITY AND ITS EFFECTS ON INITIATIVE AND RESPONSIBILITY

The measurement of productivity has another advantage, which is really only a different aspect of the one indicated above, namely, the restoration of the spirit of initiative which nationalization tends to restrain. An official with the interests entrusted to him at heart finds it difficult not to compare occasionally the many restrictions which hedge his action with the relative freedom he would enjoy if he were managing a private undertaking. This is in part illusory and arises from the comparison of dissimilar situations, but the feeling is not without a certain basis in fact. This being so, observers of the extension of state control who expect further extensions—and particularly those who would like to see such extensions—must face this question of its possible restrictive effects on freedom or the sense of freedom, as well as on productivity, and the consequent risk of initiative becoming paralysed.

The measurement of output is the only way of avoiding such consequences. The general manager of a public undertaking can only be granted wide powers of discretion if the results of his trusteeship can be gauged. The balance sheet should reflect the quality of his management as accurately as possible. To this end the granting of budgetary independence is not enough. The undertaking must be debited with the taxes paid by private undertakings, the cost of services rendered by government departments, and the interest on capital provided by the community. Conversely, it must be credited with the services it renders to other government departments. These principles appear obvious, but they are far from being applied in full.

The process should be taken even further: some undertakings benefit from a monopoly which may enable profits to be made having no relations to the quality of management; this portion of their profit margin should be deducted in the same way as the taxes which in certain circumstances are levied on the profits of private undertakings.

Subject to these various conditions it should be possible to judge from the balance sheet of a public undertaking whether the management is good or bad. Similar principles should be applied in examining the basic units or works which go to make up the undertaking as a whole. The calculation and comparison of costs is just as necessary for developing the freedom of action of works managers as for increasing productivity. If the efficiency of their management is judged by results, they can be left fairly free to choose methods, and decentralization of management should be able to proceed as techniques for establishing factory costs are worked out and improved. The same evolution should be possible within the works, a greater freedom of action being inevitably granted to shop and gang foremen and even to the workers, as it becomes possible to check results with greater accuracy.

The measurement of output in public undertakings has other aspects which it would take too long to go into here. We believe, however, that the possibility of reintroducing competition and through it responsibility and initiative must be the basis of any real reform of management in publicly owned industrial, commercial or financial establishments. It is a condition without which nationalization cannot succeed. It is also essential to an efficient socialist system.

66. AIRWAYS MUST DO BETTER*

OPERATIONS OF THE AIRLINES

125. In earlier examinations of nationalized industries, Select Committees have been hampered by the difficulty of making a comparison between the industry and its rivals or competitors overseas. On this occasion, Your Committee have been able to compare the results achieved by the nationalized air corporations with those of foreign airlines, as a result of the information published in their Reports, or in the annual statistical bulletin published by the International Civil Aviation Organization. For the extraction and assembling of these statistics, Your Committee are indebted to the

* From *Report from the Select Committee on Nationalized Industries: The Air Corporations*, May 1959, HC 213, paras. 125–77.

Ministry of Transport and Civil Aviation (Appendices A and B to this Report; also Appendices 20 and 21).

126. In making comparisons between these figures, several qualifications must be borne in mind. For one thing, the figures do not always relate to the same period of time—some of them being for the calendar year 1957, some of them for the financial year 1957–58. Secondly, the figures should not be isolated from other results being achieved at the same time by the Corporations: thus in 1957 BOAC were introducing new types of aircraft into service, and the disruption is reflected in their statistics (Q. 1357–8).

127. Allowance should also be made for the fact that the different airlines are of different sizes, and the scale of operations of each should be remembered when comparisons are made. The different total capacities, in millions of ton-miles,[1] of airlines in question in 1957 were these:

Swissair	Scandi- navian Air Services	KLM	Air France	Pan American Airways	Trans World Airlines	Sabena	BEA	BOAC
116	254	316	363	826	861	131	160	329

128. Another important distinction that must be made when comparing results lies in the fact that the different companies are catering for different kinds of services. BEA, for instance, stress that their results reflect throughout the fact that journeys made by their aircraft are, on average, very much shorter than those made by their competitors. They are indeed the only major airline in the world that concentrates on short-haul operations, and has no long-haul business. The difference between a short-haul carrier, like BEA, and a long-haul carrier, like BOAC, is a factor which must be reckoned with constantly in these comparisons. The average passenger journey lengths of some of the airlines are given, in statute miles, in this Table:

SAS	KLM	Air France	PAA	TWA	Swissair	BOAC	BEA
671	1,313	763	1,306	893	489	2,929	329

129. Provided these various qualifications are made, the statistics

[1] This figure, hereafter called 'c.t.m.', is a measure of transport production. The capacity ton miles produced by a flight are the capacity for payload of the aircraft, measured in short tons, multiplied by the miles flown. (This definition, and others that follow, are taken from or based on definitions given in the BEA Annual Reports.)

provide a valuable point from which to start to assess the results of the British air corporations.

BEA Operations

Passenger Load Factor

130. A vital factor in the financial results of an airline is the extent to which it can sell the seats it has on offer; the unoccupied seats in an aircraft can be used as a measure of failure. The standard of measurement used is called the Passenger Load Factor, which is defined as 'the percentage relationship of passenger miles to available seat miles'. The Passenger Load Factors achieved by the various airlines in 1957–58 were these:

Swissair	SAS	KLM	Air France	PAA	TWA	Sabena	BOAC	BEA
61.7	55.7	59.5	68.5	67.0	62.9	60.0	63.3	68.5

131. All Passenger Load Factors are expected to show a decline in 1958 (Q. 1094–5), but BEA expect that the year's results will continue to show them in a good light (Q. 1099, 2442). Your Committee agree that BEA have achieved a satisfactory load factor on international routes (Q. 1091–2).

Aircraft Utilization

132. Of no less importance than the proportion of seats occupied in each aircraft, is the number of revenue-hours that that aircraft can achieve in a given time; thus a good Passenger Load Factor is of little value unless each aircraft can spend a high proportion of its time earning money. The average number of hours of revenue-earning flight performed by each aircraft on the days when it is available for revenue service, or is unavailable only by reason of routine maintenance, is called the Aircraft Utilization; and the Utilization achieved by the major airlines in 1956 or 1956–57 is shown in these statistics:

Swissair	SAS	KLM	Air France	PAA	TWA	BOAC	BEA
6.77	7.88	7.50	6.77	8.59	7.70	7.62	5.11

In 1957–58, the figure for BEA dropped to 4.74 (Appendix B).

133. The Ministry pointed out that BEA's Utilization was low because of the comparatively short distance of their flights, and because so much of their traffic is seasonal; the aircraft, which may be very full in summer, will be idle in winter (Appendix A). BEA

themselves stressed very strongly that their low Utilization figure was
due entirely to the fact that they were 'the only purely short-haul
airline of comparable size in the world' (Q. 1051). After a short
flying-time, the unavoidable time spend embarking and disembarking
passengers and re-fuelling is comparatively large. Furthermore,
passengers on short journeys will for preference travel by daylight,
so that there is little utilization of aircraft through the hours of
darkness (Q. 1052, 2431).

134. Your Committee agree that, in these circumstances, they
would expect BEA's Utilization figure to be considerably lower than
that of their competitors. But while their figure for a year may not be
properly comparable with that of other airlines, it should be comparable with their own performance in previous years. What disturbs
Your Committee is the fact that the figure has been declining:
5.11 in 1956–57, 4.74 in 1957–58. BEA ascribe this to the fact that,
on the whole, they are flying faster aircraft now; the flight time is
quicker, but the time of turn-round may be the same, or longer, and
accordingly the Utilization figure drops (Q. 1053, 1057). They add
that, as the number of a particular type of aircraft in service declines,
the Utilization figure of the remainder diminishes rapidly; this has
been the case with their Elizabethans (Q. 1055), and the total average
consequently also dropped.

135. But, with faster aircraft, there are occasions when those
aircraft can make more flights per day (Q. 1056), and this should at
least balance the lower Utilization that comes with increased speed,
as a witness from BEA agreed (Q. 1057). The reliability of the type
of aircraft in use is a considerable factor in Utilization (Q. 1085) and
BEA, with their Viscounts and Pionairs, may have the most reliable
fleet in the world (Q. 1088). Over the previous few years their
Utilization had been rising despite the fact that they must have been
introducing faster aircraft then. There has also recently been an
increase in the number of night services at cheap fares and this
should have been reflected in better Utilization.

136. For all these reasons, Your Committee think that, while
BEA's Utilization is bound to be very much lower than a medium-
haul or long-haul carrier, it should not have been declining, and they
were pleased to hear that recent results have been better (Q. 2429).

C.t.m. per Employee

137. The quotient of the airline's capacity and the number of its
employees acts as a rough gauge of the output being achieved by the
airline's staff; but considerable reservations must be made before
comparisons are drawn. Thus the airlines differ very considerably in

the amounts of work they contract out, and the amounts they undertake for other operators or for third parties; BEA, for instance, must
keep at London Airport enough staff to handle the aircraft of
twenty-six other airlines (Q. 1110). Moreover, in countries such as the
United States, where labour is expensive, it is more rewarding to
have a higher degree of mechanization (and in consequence less employees, and a higher resultant ratio of c.t.m. to employees) than in
other countries. Long distance routes and routes of high traffic
density give the highest returns per employee. The introduction of
new aircraft into service has an adverse effect on output. Air lines
with highly seasonal traffic will appear at a disadvantage to those
which cater for a steadier demand (Appendix A). For all these
reasons, the figures for c.t.m. per employee must be viewed with
caution. The figures are:

	Swissair	SAS	KLM	Air France	PAA	TWA	Sabena	BOAC	BEA
1957	25,600	23,100	18,400	19,000	37,700	44,100	12,800	16,400	14,600
1956	24,200	21,200	16,900	19,500	34,200	39,300	11,500	14,800	13,200

138. It was pointed out that most of the factors, mentioned above,
are at present working to BEA's disadvantage; and consequently the
Chairman of BEA made a spirited attack on the worth of any conclusions that might be drawn from the figures (Q. 1107–10).

139. Your Committee do not want to make too much of this comparison, since like is not being compared altogether with like; but
BEA acknowledge that the figure is significant when a comparison is
made with the equivalent figure they themselves achieved in previous
years (Q. 1113). Your Committee agree with them and were pleased
to note that BEA's improvement in 1957–58 was in step with the
improvements made by SAS, KLM, Sabena and Pan American
Airways, and was much better than that made by Swissair (10.6,
compared with 1.7 per cent).

Operating Cost per c.t.m.

140. An index of an airline's efficiency can be given by the cost of
its operations; and the measure which is generally used is the amount
spent in carrying one ton of payload for one mile. The amounts, in
pence, spent by the various airlines are these:

	Swissair	SAS	KLM	Air France	PAA	TWA	Sabena	BOAC	BEA
1957	34.5	33.2	34.0	39.5	30.9	26.7	38.4	39.1	39.6
1956	38.2	33.6	31.3	44.8	31.5	28.2	37.8	39.9	39.7

141. The first point that emerges from this is that BEA's costs are considerably higher than most of their foreign competitors; but allowance must be made for the fact that they operate on journeys that are so much shorter and quicker than others. Each passenger on one of their very short journeys requires as much documentation, etc. as a passenger flying the Atlantic (Q. 1064); so administrative costs must be comparatively high.BEA aircrew costs are high too, because, with short journeys, the amount of waiting at either end is comparatively great; on the London–Paris flight, for instance, the crews will fly for less than half the time they are on duty (Q. 1079–80). Further, with landings being made so much more frequently than those of long-distance airlines, their total landing fees are greater, and the costs of handling and turn-round are proportionately more heavy (Q. 1063–4). In these circumstances, BEA consider their figure to be 'quite creditable' (Q. 1063), and Your Committee agree.

142. What appears to be less creditable is the second point that can be made from a study of the figures: while most of the other airlines have been cutting down the ratio of their costs to their c.t.m., BEA have stood still. Indeed, they say that the figure has even been increasing slightly in recent months (Q. 1104–5). The five significant factors in their operating costs were defined by their Chief Executive as being wages, fuel, landing-fees, aircrew utilization and aircraft utilization (Q. 1075). Of these, landing-fees cannot be reduced in total so long as BEA maintain or increase their present services. Total wages—which by reason of wage rates, should place BEA at an advantage compared with the Americans, roughly on a par with Swissair, and at a disadvantage with KLM (Appendices 29 and 30, Q. 1040–2)—are not likely to be reduced, especially as BEA are taking on more staff (Q. 1121). Fuel costs could be lowered significantly only by a change in tax (see paragraphs 212 to 214) and BEA can do nothing about this. It follows that, if BEA are to improve their cost/c.t.m. ratio, it must be by improving either aircrew utilization or aircraft utilization or both.

143. While BEA are not complacent about these matters, they believe that they are unlikely to be able to do much better in the future (Q. 1077); but it seems to Your Committee from the evidence of BEA themselves that there is room for improvement in aircraft utilization and in maintenance costs, and that, with improved aircraft performances, BEA can and will do better.

BOAC Operations

Passenger load factor

144. BOAC's Passenger Load Factor in 1957–58 was slightly above

the average for the group of airlines being considered. In 1956–57, it was well above average.

	Swissair	SAS	KLM	Air France	PAA	TWA	Sabena	BEA	BOAC
1957	61.7	55.7	59.5	68.5	67.0	62.9	60.0	68.5	63.3
1956	64.4	57.2	61.5	68.6	66.0	64.0	59.4	70.3	66.0

145. It will be seen that most of the Passenger Load Factors dropped in 1957, but that BOAC's drop was slightly greater than the average. The reason for this was that world affairs prevented the growth in traffic which had been expected and for which BOAC had introduced more capacity (Q. 1460). The same disappointing results continue to come from the Eastern and African routes this year, but there has been a recent small improvement on the Atlantic route due to the new Economy Class: over all, the load factor should remain about the same (Q. 1462). It appears that the unsatisfactory Passenger Load Factors on the Eastern route were partly due to the reputation for unpunctuality which the Britannia's record on introduction gave the Corporation (Q. 1462).

146. BOAC aim to increase their Passenger Load Factor; but they are alive to the possibility of getting more revenue from a lower load factor combined with higher Utilization. The two are closely related and are both important; neither should be viewed for too long in isolation. There is some reason to believe that, as BOAC admit, they have in recent years laid too much emphasis on load factors and not enough on Utilization (Q. 2378–9).

Aircraft Utilization

147. It does not necessarily follow that the airline with the longest average stage-length will achieve the best Utilization of its aircraft; more important than the size of this average is the proportion of its operations that an airline can undertake at night. In this respect BOAC argue that they are not necessarily at any advantage over competitors who may be operating routes which are, on average, shorter (Q. 1389).

148. Utilization figures (*see* paragraph 132) for 1956 or 1956–57 were these:

Swissair	SAS	KLM	Air France	PAA	TWA	BEA	BOAC
6.77	7.88	7.50	6.77	8.59	7.70	5.11	7.62

In 1957–58 BOAC'S figure fell to 6.71. This fall was explained by the fact that BOAC were beginning to introduce the new Britannia aircraft at the time. There is always a drop in Utilization when a new aircraft comes into service, and in this particular case the effect was more pronounced as a result of the Britannia's icing troubles (Q. 1370–1). A host of later troubles have continued to add to the total effect (Q. 2310), and the result has been low Utilization over the last two years (Q. 2306–7).

149. The average number of hours in a year which an aircraft can fly is related very closely to the number of hours it must spend in workshops for maintenance or repair. Thus the problem of Utilization is bound up with that of Aircraft Maintenance, which is discussed in paragraphs 160 to 177 of this Report. But as a result of the steps BOAC have already taken in their engineering organization, their Utilization figure is on the increase; it is already, they say, no worse than that of comparable airlines (Q. 2322). Furthermore, they have made plans which should lift their average Utilization from 6.71 hours in 1957–58 to 9 or 9½ hours when the new aircraft are fully in service (Q. 1397). These plans are already bearing fruit (Q. 2308–9).

150. Your Committee believe that although Utilization has not been good in recent years, the steps that BOAC have taken and are taking should improve results. They believe that BOAC should publish figures for Aircraft Utilization in their Annual Reports, so that the improvement can be watched.

Operating cost per c.t.m.

151. BOAC's costs have been high, as this Table shows (the figures are in pence):

	Swissair	SAS	KLM	Air France	PAA	TWA	Sabena	BEA	BOAC
1957	34.5	33.2	34.0	39.5	30.9	26.7	38.4	39.6	39.1
1956	38.2	33.6	31.3	44.8	31.5	28.2	37.8	39.7	39.9

BOAC's figure has been on the level of about thirty-nine pence for four or five years now (Q. 1361). It was comparatively high in the years under examination because, as mentioned above, the Corporation were in a period of re-equipment. New aircraft were not fully in service, but were being fully amortized; so it was a period when BOAC were at a disadvantage compared with some of their competitors (Q. 1360).

152. Whilst allowing for that, Your Committee pursued a comparison between BOAC's operating costs and those of another long-haul airline, Pan American Airways. In 1957, Pan American Airways' figure for their world-wide operations was 30.9 pence per c.t.m., while that of BOAC was 39.1 pence—more than a quarter as high

again. BOAC asked that the comparison should be limited to PAA's Atlantic Division, whose operations most closely resembled those of BOAC. The figure for the Atlantic Division was 33.4 pence per c.t.m. If allowance were now made for the different proportions of first-class and tourist seats that each airline offered, BOAC's figure would be 37.5 pence, and the gap between the two would be halved. Nevertheless, the gap is still a substantial one, and BOAC recognize that their own costs are much too high (Q. 1641).

153. If the composition of these costs is studied, it is found that aircraft maintenance costs BOAC something in the nature of ten pence per c.t.m. For PAA, the amount is about half that (Q. 1363–4). If BOAC could lower their maintenance costs to the level of those of PAA, their figure of operating cost per c.t.m. would be the better of the two (Q. 1642); and this is what BOAC hope to effect (Q. 1598).

154. This whole subject of aircraft maintenance, and the steps being taken to reduce its cost, are examined later in this report. At this point, Your Committee merely draw attention to the fact that the cost of BOAC's flight operations, too, is rather above average (Appendix 23).

C.t.m. per employee

155. As mentioned above (paragraph 137), the ratio of c.t.m. to the number of employees is not always a fair basis of comparison between airlines. In BOAC's case, the comparison is, they say, particularly unjust, because they probably try to do more things for themselves than their competitors do: they run their own coaches, they overahaul all their own engines (and a great many more for the US Air Force), they try to save dollars by repair work on spare parts, and they contract out only very little of their work (Q. 1428). As a result, their ratio of output (in c.t.m.) to staff is a low one, as this Table (referring to 1957, or 1957–58) shows:

Swissair	SAS	KLM	Air France	PAA	TWA	Sabena	BEA	BOAC
24,600	23,100	18,400	19,000	37,700	44,100	12,100	14,600	16,400

156. Although there are so many qualifying factors in the case of BOAC, their witnesses did not deny the general impression these figures give; namely, that BOAC do not get enough output in relation to the large number of people they employ (Q. 1445–8). The major reason for this is, again, the existence of maintenance engineering practices that have required the employment of more staff than are needed. This subject is discussed below, in paragraphs 160 to 170.

157. But there are other contributory reasons. One of these is the fact that aircrews have not been utilized as much as they theoretically might have been (Q. 1403). This arises from the fact that, as mentioned above, this has been a time of re-equipment for BOAC; their whole fleet is being changed, so that it will take some three years before aircrew utilization returns to normal (Q. 1404). To begin with, the crews which had been flying Constellations had to be trained to fly Britannias, and a course of this kind would keep them off service for a period of about four months (Q. 1419). But, as a result of the early troubles of the Britannias, many of the crews had to be re-trained to fly Constellations, and then, after a period, trained once more to fly Britannias (Q. 1407); each of these re-conversion courses took at least a week (Q. 1415). Once the new types of aircraft have been fully introduced into service, aircrew utilization should rise again to a high, steady level (Q. 1403); as it is, BOAC claim that some of their crews are already approaching the maximum possible flying time (Q. 1423).

158. Another reason why BOAC's ratio of output to staff is lower than that of the American airlines lies in the fact that BOAC employ larger flight crews (Q. 1508, Appendix 27), partly as a result of their more widespread operations (Q. 1511), and partly because the British safety regulations are more stringent in this respect than are those of the Americans (Q. 2387–8); BOAC do not dispute the need for these extra precautions, and accept them as a vaulable help to safety and efficiency (Q. 2388). Generally speaking, the size of BOAC cabin-crews is the same as that of comparable airlines (Q. 1699–1700).

BOAC Operations: Conclusion

159. Whatever qualifications are made when these operating statistics are considered, it is clear that, in recent years, BOAC have been operating with less efficiency than most of the airlines to which they can be fairly compared. Account must however be taken of some special factors—the effect of the sudden removal from service of the Comet I, the considerable loss in efficiency they have sustained as a result of the defects that developed in the Britannia aircraft. Further, the years under examination have seen BOAC in the middle of an ambitious programme of re-equipment, during which their operations are bound to appear temporarily less effective than those of their competitors. But a major part of their difficulties has been caused by over-staffing, especially in their workshops. At the heart of the problem posed by BOAC's indifferent results in the last few years lies another problem: how can BOAC improve their aircraft maintenance?

AIRCRAFT MAINTENANCE

BOAC aircraft maintenance

160. In their Annual Report for 1957–58, BOAC say that they had been concerned for some years at the apparently high level of their engineering costs. In the second half of 1956, their Chief Engineer appointed an expert team to investigate engine overhaul procedures. As a result of the changes recommended by the team, the time taken for an engine to pass through the overhaul shops was cut by approximately half during the year 1957–58.

161. In June, 1957, after bringing the matter to the notice of the local joint panels and consultative committees established under the National Joint Council procedure, the Chief Engineer instituted a further enquiry by a committee of management (Q. 1599) into comparative methods, with a view to establishing the relative efficiency of the Corporation's procedures for the overhaul and maintenance of aircraft. After a close study of the organization of three other airlines whose aircraft operations and standards are similar to those of the Corporation—Pan American Airways (Pacific Division), KLM and United Air Lines of America (Q. 1520)—it was established that the Corporation's engineering organization and methods required fundamental revision (*H.C. 239* of 1957–58, pp. 10–11).

162. The conclusions reached by the team corroborated the views which were by then held by the Board of BOAC (Q. 1520). They bore out, indeed, the opinions which had been expressed to the Board, unavailingly, by the financial side of BOAC as far back as 1952 (Q. 1581). In these circumstances, it surprised Your Committee that the major investigation by BOAC into their excessive engineering costs should not have begun until mid–1957, although the annual statistics published by IATA and ICAO had some while previously shown that something was wrong (Q. 1520, 2275). Their explanation was that they had decided to deal only with engine overhaul at first, as a certain amount of information had already been assembled on that point; when that preliminary inquiry was complete, it was intended that the major investigation should begin. But, at that moment, the icing troubles of the Britannia, and the consequent problem of whether or not to introduce that aircraft into service as planned, intervened, and the Chief Engineer was preoccupied with this. When the Britannia eventually went into service in February, 1957, the illness of the Managing Director caused a further three-month delay, and the investigation did not begin until June of that year (Q. 1707). Your Committee think that neither of these reasons in any way justifies the delay in an organization of this size.

163. The team reported in December, 1957 (Q. 1522), and its find-

ings were unequivocal. BOAC's aircraft maintenance costs were nearly twice as high as those of Pan American (Q. 1594–5). In their engineering workshops, BOAC were employing 3,000 more staff than they needed (Q. 2350). They employed more than twice as many staff per aircraft or per flying-hour as did the others (Q. 1520); they employed between four and six times as many inspectors and supervisors as did the other airlines investigated (Q. 1522). In all these assessments, there were no compensating factors—such as better workshop equipment—which could account in any significant way for the disparity that had been revealed (Q. 1520).

164. The roots of this problem go back many years; practices which originated in different conditions are still being maintained, despite the better results being achieved by other methods employed in the airline industry abroad (Q. 2073). Too much reliance has been placed on repeated inspection and supervision at too many levels, instead of allowing the mechanic himself more responsibility (Q. 1522). Your Committee considered whether any of the blame for this could rest on the shoulders of the Air Registration Board, which lays down the standards of airworthiness and safety to which the Corporations must conform; but they are satisfied that this is far from being the case (Q. 2073, 2075, 2080–3). The responsibility for what happened in the past must rest inside the Corporation.

165. In their Annual Report, BOAC say that they are taking the necessary measures to achieve the 'fundamental revision' of their organization and methods that is necessary (*H.C. 239* of 1957–58, p. 11). Your Committee asked what these measures were, and what progress was being made in implementing them. They were told that the revision was to be made in two stages: first, a reorganization of the structure of the engineering department, and secondly a re-allotment of the jobs which each class of technician can undertake (Q. 1522). This is a recognition of the fact that BOAC have been using a method of quality control which is now out of date; an indication of the scope of the changes they must make is given by their target of reducing their inspectorate to a third of its present size (Q. 1583). This will be done by giving the mechanic more responsibility; he will himself see that the job is completed satisfactorily, and there will not be the need for the amount of inspection and control that is at present customary. As a result of this change, there is bound to be a considerable reduction in the responsibilities of the present inspectors and supervisors (Q. 1522); this will not in any way run counter to the requirements of the Air Registration Board (Q. 2082), but it will rightly engage the interest of the Trade Unions involved.

166. The change of structure in the engineering department has now been completed. It took six months to effect (Q. 1522). Combined

with it, other improvements have been made in the last year or so: for example, the centralization of all engineering functions in the one set of buildings, at London Airport, has allowed a more efficient system of control to be employed (Q. 1539–40). As a result of these, considerably better results have already been achieved by BOAC; the time taken for a major overhaul for a Stratocruiser, for instance, has in the last few years been reduced from three weeks to eleven days (Q. 1584). Whereas in 1957 one in three of the Corporation's aircraft was, at any given moment, in the hangars for overhaul and maintenance, the figure now is one in four and in 1960 is likely to be one in five. The overhaul time for spare engines, which was seven to eight weeks in 1955, had been reduced to four weeks in 1957; now it is down to three weeks (Appendix 37). Maintenance, which cost BOAC 8.2 pence per c.t.m. in 1957–58, is estimated to cost 6.6 pence per c.t.m. in 1959–60 (Q. 2336).

167. This estimate makes no provision for any economies in manpower that might be made by then (Q. 2334); it makes, in other words, no allowance for any improvements that may result from the second stage of BOAC's 'fundamental revision' of their organization. This involves the Corporation in discussions with the Trade Unions in an attempt to define afresh the 'job descriptions' covering the scope of work which a particular category of workman is allowed to undertake. These discussions have already started, but it is estimated that it may be mid-1960 before the whole reorganization is completed (Q. 1522).

168. Your Committee believe that the House wishes them to keep clear of matters normally dealt with by collective bargaining between workers and management, such as wages and conditions of employment. In order, however, to explain the present stage of the reorganization by BOAC of their maintenance arrangements it is necessary to understand the practice and customs which have grown up in the nationalized airlines in matters concerning relationships between management and the Trade Unions. By statute the Corporations, like other nationalized industries, are required to make agreements with the Unions concerned on (*a*) the settlement by negotiation of terms and conditions of employment, and (*b*) the discussion of matters affecting safety, health, welfare and efficiency.

169. In other industries these matters are discussed in separate committees; but in the Air Corporations, consultation and negotiation have become merged together. This is because a complex system of councils and panels has been set up at national and local level, and matters which would normally be settled at local level have sometimes become the subject for consideration at national level (where usually negotiations only on terms and conditions of employ-

ment take place) (Appendix 39). The way this system has been operated has undoubtedly involved delays when changes in methods and job descriptions are proposed, and this is why BOAC believe that it will take them another year to negotiate the changes they now believe to be necessary (Q. 1522).

170. It is not the duty of Your Committee to comment on these arrangements, on which they took no evidence from the Trade Union side. But they must point out that a state of affairs which was believed to be unhealthy in 1952, and which was proved to be unhealthy in 1956, may not be healed until the middle of 1960. It is clear that, however rigid the negotiating procedure may have become, it is the responsibility of the management of BOAC to achieve at a very early date a drastic improvement in the productivity of their aircraft maintenance department. Until this has been done, BOAC cannot expect to compete on even terms with the other airlines of the world.

BEA aircraft maintenance

171. Since BEA were set up in 1946, they have not experienced the accretion of staff that had gone on in BOAC since before the war (Q. 2118). They introduced a bonus incentive scheme into their workshops in November, 1948, which has been very effective in increasing efficiency (Q. 1351).

172. Yet the system of inspection raises the same problems for each Corporation (Q. 2107): indeed, the proportion of inspectors to hourly-rated staff is considerably more for BEA than it is for BOAC (Q. 2116, 2118). This stems from their bonus incentive scheme, which reduces the actual number of direct workers, but requires the inspectors to be more quickly available. A large inspectorate has to be in waiting all the time, and this, combined with the reduction in direct labour, increases the proportion of inspectors on the shop floor (Q. 2118); at BEA's main base, there is an average of one inspector to every 3.2 hourly-rated staff (Q. 2100) (which compares with BOAC's average of one to seven—Q. 2116).

173. A measure of the extent of over-inspection that occurs in both Corporations is given by the contrast between BEA's inspection system at their main base, with that at their other bases. At these outside bases, they do not employ inspectors, but rely entirely on clearance by licensed maintenance engineers (Q. 2104). As a result, the ratio of inspectors to hourly-rated staff (1 to 3.2 at their main base at London Airport) is, over all, one in ten (Q. 2100). When asked why then they did not extend this system to their main base as well, the BEA witnesses indicated that they had not so far been able to achieve an agreement with the Trade Unions on this point (Q. 2078, 2105).

174. Evidence was given by BEA that the degree of mechanization in their workshops was much less than that of the American airlines (Q. 1315). BOAC on the other hand claimed that, with the exception of those at Treforest, their workshops were as highly mechanized as any of those of their competitors (Q. 1534). The extent to which labour-saving plant and machinery should be installed is obviously a matter of commercial judgment, and there is evidence to show that neither Corporation is prevented from exercising this judgment as they think fit (Q. 1316, 2092).

175. Against this background BEA's maintenance costs, expressed as a percentage of traffic revenue in 1956 or 1956–57, have been slightly above average. The equivalent percentages of various airlines are shown in this Table (Appendix 32):

Swissair	SAS	KLM	Air France	PAA	TWA	BOAC	BEA
18.5	14.5	14.0	28.0	17.0	16.6	23.7	18.7

Figures for the foreign airlines in the following year were not available, but BEA's costs dropped in 1957–58 to 16.5 per cent. (Q. 1043). Bearing in mind that other airlines take on other engineering work which helps to improve this figure for them, BEA argued that their figure was already very close to the lowest level of expenditure practicable (Q. 1280).

176. Their engineering costs are, moreover, still proportionately falling. Expressed this time as a percentage of their total costs, BEA's engineering costs in the last few years are shown thus (Q. 2056):

		Per cent
1955–56	..	19
1956–57	..	18.25
1957–58	..	16.55

There has in these years been a general, unspectacular improvement in maintenance efficiency (Q. 2057–8). Costs may go up temporarily as new types of aircraft are introduced into service (Q. 1305), but the general trend is for them to be reduced; for instance, by taking over from a private company the maintenance of their Dart engines, BEA expect to cut their expenditure on engine overhaul by 16 per cent in the next few years (Q. 1286–7).

177. To sum up: BEA's maintenance costs are now approximately equal to those of their competitors, and are all the time being steadily reduced. However, as they agree, they still have a good deal to learn (Q. 1306), and they are constantly comparing their own practices with the way other airlines operate (Q. 1300). Their inspectorate is at

present much too large, and it is possible that they could benefit from
more mechanization, so there is room for further improvements.
When these have been made, BEA should be in a strong position.

67. EFFICIENCY VERSUS COST IN
PUBLIC TRANSPORT*

In public transport as in other industries, efficiency can mean different
things. It all depends on which side of the fence you are standing,
whether you are the public or the operator, a private or a State-
owned business; and here I must emphasize, that in this short paper
I do not propose to deal with efficiency from the purely statistical
point of view.

First we have to remember that private enterprise puts a rather
different emphasis on the word efficiency compared with a publicly-
owned operator. There are some people who feel (and say so publicly)
that there should be no such difference, but a moment's thought will
show that a like-for-like comparison between the two types of undertaking is unrealistic. The ultimate object of private enterprise in doing
business (and properly so in my view) is to earn the best return on the
capital employed, always assuming, as we do in these enlightened
days, that staff welfare has been taken into account. Of course, the
other objective of private enterprise companies is to study public
needs—the market. If they did not, they would never make profits,
but equally they cannot lose money indefinitely in pleasing the public
or their business will have to fold up. On the other hand, the major
objective of a publicly-owned transport undertaking like British
Railways, on which I have spent most of my working life, and London
Transport where I have been for nearly five years, is bound to be
different, because Parliament has laid down in the Transport Acts
that it is the provision of an 'adequate service' that must be the first
objective. In return for that, so far as London Transport is concerned,
a monopoly of public passenger service in Greater London is reserved to it and to British Railways passenger trains; note that
Parliament did not define 'adequacy'.

Leaving aside the question of comparisons with private enterprise
for a moment, let us look at the public on the other side of the fence.
The user of public transport, State or privately-owned, naturally
takes the view that an 'efficient' service is one that takes him or his

* From Sir John Elliot: 'Efficiency versus Cost in Public Transport', *The Journal
of the Institute of Transport*, Vol. XXVII, No. 10, May 1958, pp. 334–7. Reprinted
by permission of the author and the Council of the Institute of Transport.

goods from point A to point B at exactly the time he wants it, as quickly and cheaply as possible, and with a high degree of reliability. If he does not get all these, then he can and often does make other arrangements which may be more or less efficient in terms of real cost, but which give him the special kind of service he wants. People buy cars, motor-bikes, scooters and cycles, and once the traffic is lost it is very difficult for public transport to regain it. The enormous increase in the number of 'C' licence vehicles in the country since the war is proof of this fact, though it is also true that some firms run their own 'C' licence transport for other reasons, e.g. publicity, and even in some cases, politics, i.e. downright dislike of State ownership. All this of course they are fully entitled to do.

Now, what is the true cost of providing 'efficient' service? It is here that we come to the problem which faces all public transport. I need hardly mention the unprofitability of the peak traffics, whether they be daily, weekly or seasonal. In all cases, large sums of capital are tied up in equipment which is only in use for a very short time, and in addition to this, crew operating costs are disproportionately high. To give just two examples from London Transport: about 33 per cent of our 8,500 buses and trolleybuses are in service during the peak hours only—the rest of the day they are idle in the garages. Similarly we have trains on the Underground which only do one trip of about twenty miles in the morning and one in the evening, five days a week. But that one trip is essential.

By operating standards, this is highly uneconomic and therefore inefficient, and if we were simply out for a profit regardless of all else, we should have to cut some of the peak services to ribbons. But the loads in the rush hours must be carried, profit or not, so we must strive to keep the factor of cost inefficiency as low as possible, and to balance it by the best use of our crews and rolling stock in the off-peak hours, midday, evening, and week-ends. We have to weigh our pursuit of efficiency with our statutory obligations to the public, the user, a riddle which vastly intrigued the competent Chambers Committee of Enquiry into London Transport in 1954.

These obligations, as I have said, are laid down by Parliament, but to make the problem more complex, it added a clause to the effect that we must play our way, i.e. run the business commercially and pay the modest interest on the capital invested. Now if we are to discharge both these obligations it is obvious that we must indulge in a certain amount of tight-rope walking. That was one of the principles behind the creation of the London Passenger Transport Board in 1933 by Lord Ashfield and Mr Herbert Morrison. Monopoly of the paying services must ensure the provision of those that no one else will run, yet must be run if the public is to be served.

In this touchy business, London's Underground and over half the bus services, fail to earn enough to cover all costs, including finance charges. Even so, it seems likely that in 1957 the business as a whole just earned its allotted net revenue (largely due to extra traffic during the Suez petrol rationing), the profitable routes covering the losses elsewhere. I wish it always did.

It is essential for a public transport undertaking to cost out each of its services and try to put them on an economic basis—if we did not we should soon be looking for another job. On the other hand we should be in the same position even more quickly if we withdrew all the services that did not pay their way. It is in the reconciliation of these two apparently conflicting tasks that management must be skilful, determined, and patient.

Here are one or two illustrations of the sort of thing I mean:

First there are the services operating through areas which have very high peak loadings, usually in one direction only, with few people travelling at other times. In many of these, the difference is so great that it is impossible for the service to cover its cost.

Second there are the services which carry good traffics even during the off-peak hours but on which it is only possible to use single-deck vehicles because of low or weak bridges. It is a fact that every one of our single-deck bus routes loses money and there are 122 of them out of a total of 521. Yet they all provide essential services of one sort or another, or we should not run them.

Third there are the services which we have to provide in the new towns and housing estates, particularly during the course of the development of the area concerned. These are not always uneconomic, and much depends on the location, size, etc., of the individual town or housing estate, but the fact remains that these services must be provided if the new town is to live and grow, and they are often highly unprofitable.

The fourth example, which is more applicable to our Underground railways, where a certain number of staff have to be on duty regardless of the frequency of the service, is the early morning and late evening service which makes the traffic day too long to be staffed by two shifts. (This also applies to a certain extent on the road services.) If we were to cut our services so that the first train or bus ran at 6.0 a.m. (at present we start at about 5.30 a.m.) and the last at 11.0 p.m. (at present the last trains leave the Central Area at about 12.30 a.m. and the last bus a little earlier) we could materially improve our financial results. But thousands of people have to get to work around 6.0 a.m., and does anyone seriously suggest that public transport in a great city like London should shut down at 11.0 p.m.?

Services or groups of services may be uneconomic for a variety of reasons, but I should add that while one service may not pay its way taken on its own, it is sometimes part of a group of services which taken together are profitable, or at least cover their direct costs and make some contribution to the overheads. So it may be that if such services are withdrawn, the finances of the undertaking as a whole will suffer rather than improve.

ADEQUACY AND CONSISTENCY OF SERVICE

These are some examples of unprofitable service which we must provide. In addition, we receive many requests for services which we have to turn down on the grounds that not only are they certain to lose money, but in our view there is insufficient traffic demand to justify such loss. You may well ask me on what basis does London Transport decide whether a service should be provided or not, and how in effect do we define the word 'adequate'?

We use no scientific formula for this, although such things are not unknown—for instance, several public transport systems in North America have a definite minimum service obligation laid down by their governing body, expressed in terms of seats per passengers offering in a given period of time. We are not burdened with such a definition in London Transport, and whether we provide a frequent or infrequent service or no service at all must be a question of judgment which can only be based on long experience. The tests are the degree of hardship involved if we do not provide the service, the amount of loss if we do, and the volume of other public service available in the locality.

It is very important, too, that as far as possible we should be consistent in the provision of services in all the parts of the area we serve and in which, with minor exceptions, on the fringes we have a monopoly. For example, we ought not to say that because a bus service for one housing estate is likely to pay it should be provided, whilst a service for another estate which is likely to lose money should not be. (This was an actual case with two estates in our area situated about eight miles apart, but with dissimilar characteristics. Our estimates were proved correct, and we provided a service in both cases.) Similarly we ought not to refuse to run additional buses on a route on which people were regularly having to wait in queues for too long, simply because it would be uneconomic, if at the same time we are doing all we can elsewhere to reduce the queue waiting to half the time. Obviously we cannot apply exactly the same traffic criterion in every case. Each must be judged overall, on its merits and demerits.

If we do not keep our balance on the tight-rope there will come a time when the number of unprofitable services is so large that there are insufficient paying services to support them. Management is then faced with three alternatives, assuming of course that the services themselves are being provided as efficiently as possible. It can seek approval to raise the fares; it can reduce or cut out some or all of the unpaying services; or it can reduce the general level of service provided, with a view to making the profitable routes more profitable and the losing services less so. The first is sometimes the right answer and both private and publicly-owned companies have had to increase charges; the second must be tackled, but up to a point only, or we shall not be providing an adequate service; the third must be used with discretion, because if we reduce the paying services too much the waits will be too long and they will become losers because people will find other means of transport.

'This is all very fine,' you may say, 'but how can you be sure what the public wants?' Well, as I have said, our Traffic Managers have had long experience in these matters and we have a highly organized Public Relations Department which keeps its finger on the pulse of public opinion in all sorts of ways, and passes that information on to the management daily. Our Public Relations Officer or his assistant attends all the regular meetings which the Traffic Managers have with their officers, and ensures that the public's views are kept to the fore when services are being planned or adjusted. Also keeping a watchful eye on us are the 138 Members of Parliament representing constituencies in Greater London, plus the numerous ratepayers' and other similar associations, who are never slow to remind us of our obligations and our shortcomings. On top of all these thermometers, we have the Press, national and local, which is studied carefully, and our own letter-box, which is never empty.

One of the main difficulties facing the passenger transport operator in recent years has been that whilst there has been virtually no decrease in the number of passengers travelling in the height of the peak, traffic has been declining steadily at nearly all other times. You will see therefore that whilst we can trim our services to match reductions in off-peak demand and thereby reduce our expenses marginally, no major savings can be made without touching the peak hour service, which must have some effect on queue waits at this time. It is for this reason that in the past we have preferred to raise fares rather than cut mileage, and it is worth recalling that the Chambers Committee, to which I referred earlier, went on record as saying that rather than face heavy cuts in services, Londoners would be better advised to pay more for those they now enjoyed. A spartan doctrine which human nature rejects in every language under the sun!

SHOULD TRANSPORT PAY ITS WAY?

I said at the beginning of my paper that Parliament had laid it down that public transport should pay its way. Let us examine this vital matter briefly. Was Parliament right or was it wrong? In other words, is it in the national interest that public transport should be required to pay its way? There are all sorts of answers. The public transport systems of some European cities incur heavy deficits almost entirely because they are not allowed to make realistic charges for their services (i.e. their fares have generally been pegged at low levels for political reasons despite heavy increases in working expenses). There are plenty of examples in America also, and in Australia and New Zealand.

It may be said: 'Well, why not? The public gets cheap transport and likes it.' In fact, they may also get unnecessary and wasteful transport because, if management need not pay its way, no one need care how much it loses until the bill comes in. Then the whole picture becomes blurred, and no one knows the real reason for the losses, or the solution. Management gets criticized, staff irritated.

It is my belief that there is nothing as effective as the yardstick of income versus expenditure to ensure that an undertaking is run efficiently, and management and staff kept on their toes. If there is no driving necessity to make ends meet, it will be difficult, and sometimes impossible, to get the same careful watch on expenditure as there must be if there is a budget to balance at the year's end.

Still, if a public transport undertaking does not, cannot, or is not allowed to pay its way, then the question arises who *is* going to foot the bill, and we come to the controversial question of subsidies. The first thing to go overboard is always transport economics. In general I believe that subsidies create more problems than they solve, and, in particular, they open the door for those providing the subsidy to try to dominate the undertaking themselves and for decisions to be based on political or other motives and not on our sound old friend, 'the rider must pay the cost of his ride'. Subsidies are also unjust, because they compel people who do not use the services to pay by rates and taxes for those who do, whilst the riders pay less, often far less, than the cost of the transport they use. And a subsidized show is open to pressure by every kind of crackpot.

All that is something different from profitable services paying for those which are essential but which are, and must be, unprofitable, as in London Transport. In an area like Greater London a passenger may, and often does, travel on profitable and unprofitable routes every day, without knowing one from the other—that is an internal subsidy, as opposed to a public one. In the imperfect world in which we live, we must accept certain inconsistencies.

P

Because the path to be trodden between surplus and deficit is very narrow, it is not to be expected (as it would be expected in most purely commercial operations) that deficits can always be avoided. The Act, with its reference to 'taking one year with another' acknowledges this. Moreover, during periods of heavy capital expenditure, such as that in which British Railways are involved at this time, it becomes necessary to take a longer view still. But the driving necessity to make ends meet of which I have spoken ought to persist even though the time taken to make them meet has to be longer.

CHAPTER XII

The Future of Nationalization

To summarize and adequately illustrate the continuing debate about the future of nationalization is impossible in the space available. We therefore limit ourselves to two extracts from comparatively recent documents. The first (*Extract 68*), taken from the last chapter of a booklet published by the Federation of British Industries, sees no advantages whatever, and many disadvantages, in the further extension of the public sector. The second (*Extract 69*) represents the Labour Party's latest thoughts on the subject, from *Signposts for the Sixties*, the policy document adopted by the 60th Annual Conference in 1961. It will be noted that this heavily emphasizes the alleged contribution that an extended public sector can make to the achievement of a higher rate of economic growth, and envisages a considerable variety of forms of public ownership. No specific promises of further nationalization are made (except for the *re*-nationalization of iron and steel), but the areas in which a future Labour Government would consider the extension of the public sector are clearly, if generally, indicated.

68. NO MORE NATIONALIZATION*

INTRODUCTION

1. A programme of nationalization affects both individual industries and the working of the whole economy. Whatever may be thought of the wisdom of past measures of nationalization, for the economy as a whole the spread of nationalization would undermine the foundations of its efficiency. (Paragraphs 1–4.)

2. The system of free enterprise is efficient and dynamic because it provides the incentives which make it so. Hence it provides high and rising standards of living, produces the individual self-reliance which is essential to a free society, and yet is capable of adjustment to the exercise of important and expanding powers by the State. (Paragraphs 5–8.)

* From Federation of British Industries: *Report on Nationalization*, November 1958, pp. 50–56. Reprinted by permission of the Federation.

3. This report does not make a case for the denationalization of industries already nationalized, but the country ought not to be content with their performance so far. Even the threat of further nationalization jeopardizes the country's prospects of prosperity. (Paragraphs 9–10.)

THE ARGUMENTS FOR NATIONALIZATION

4. The Labour Party's constitution contains words implying that all private ownership of capital produces 'exploitation' and this has been supplemented by the argument that free enterprise is inherently inefficient. This must imply the eventual nationalization of all industries. (Paragraphs 11–13.)

5. But a policy of gradualness and hence of selective nationalization having been adopted, industries have been chosen for nationalization because they are thought to be 'basic' or because they are alleged to be inefficient, to be monopolistic, to suffer from bad labour relations, or to be unable to raise capital for development. (Paragraphs 14–16.)

6. In 1957 the Labour Party produced a new policy statement (*Industry and Society*) which advocated the renationalization of steel and long-distance road haulage, the nationalization of any industry found to be 'failing the nation', and the State acquisition of equities in other industries. This last proposal was founded on the view that the functions of the private shareholder have decayed, that the State should reap the capital gains of equity ownership in order to reduce inequality of incomes, and that State ownership of equities would facilitate economic planning. In 1958 a further policy statement (*Plan for Progress*) advocated the special supervision of the investment programmes of large companies and the establishment of a National Investment Board to keep investment policies under permanent review. Apart from the fact that some elements in the Labour Party wish nationalization to extend well beyond the limits suggested by these two statements of policy, the arguments which have been applied to particular industries continue to be enveloped in a general hostility to profit and alleged 'exploitation'. (Paragraphs 17–28.)

THE RECORD OF NATIONALIZATION

7. The record of nationalization cannot be the sole basis of answers to questions concerning the wisdom of further nationalization, but it will assist the finding of such answers by throwing light

on the differences between free and State-owned industry. (Paragraphs 29–30.)

8. Parliament has laid upon the Boards of the nationalized industries obligations concerning operation, pricing and finance, and labour relations; in operation, efficiency (but expressed in various vague forms); in pricing and finance, the earning of revenue to meet outgoings 'taking one year with another'; and in labour relations, the promotion of the welfare of employees. (Paragraphs 31–39.)

9. Efficiency of operation must be measured by financial as well as technical success, and so the operational obligation merges with the financial one. Taking the field of nationalization as a whole, the financial obligation has not been met, for the Boards have fallen far short of covering their outgoings if depreciation is calculated on a replacement basis. (Paragraphs 40–47.)

10. Apart from the inadequacy of depreciation provisions, the failure to cover outgoings has been partly due to a mistaken belief that the national interest is served by low prices irrespective of cost or to postponement by Governments of proposed price increases, and partly to weakness in the control of costs. (Paragraphs 48–53.)

11. The large capital expenditure of the public corporations has been met only to a minor extent from funds set aside by them. The major part, if not to be a cause of inflationary Government borrowing, has had to be raised from the savings of private individuals and firms or from the proceeds of taxation. (Paragraphs 54–58.)

12. The nationalized industries have taken a more than proportionate share of the total funds used for investment in the economy but there is no conclusive test by which to determine whether this has been justified. The use of capital under free enterprise has to pass the test of the market; in the nationalized industries it has not or has not to the same extent, and decisions as to the amount to be used have been clouded by political considerations. (Paragraphs 59–60.)

13. Nationalization had produced no discernible improvement in labour relations; it has indeed made them more difficult by destroying the worker's choice of employer within his industry, by bringing the Government into the ring in important cases of dispute, and by disappointing the expectation of some workers that it would produce workers' control. (Paragraphs 61–64.)

14. The Acts of nationalization set up statutory bodies to represent consumers in their dealings with the Boards and to safeguard their interests. They have not been effective and it has not been possible to make them so. (Paragraphs 65–66.)

15. The authors of the Acts of nationalization intended the Boards to be made accountable to the nation for the discharge of their obligations. Parliament has not been able to devise methods for

bringing them effectively to account; the Parliamentary system is unsuitable for the efficient control of industry, and accountability without control is meaningless. (Paragraphs 67–70.)

16. The record of the nationalized industries makes clear that they have not fulfilled the nationalizers' expectations of outstanding progress and improvement. (Paragraphs 71–72.)

FREE AND NATIONALIZED INDUSTRY CONTRASTED

17. The purpose of economic activity is to provide the goods and services on which we live. The problem is to use the limited available resources as efficiently as possible to produce the things that people want. (Paragraph 73.)

18. Free enterprise attacks this problem through the process of competition. This selects the most efficient producers and provides a yardstick of success in profitability. It also causes the resources of the community to be led into the production of what consumers want, and for this purpose it enables those who run business to have the authority as well as the yardstick necessary for successful operation. Further it provides both the stimulus for the expansion of the economy and also, if not hampered by fiscal or other deterrents, the capital necessary therefor. (Paragraphs 74–80.)

19. It is true that 'what consumers want' means 'what consumers are able and willing to pay for' and that wants are therefore supported by differing degrees of purchasing power. But the free economy will adapt itself to any pattern of purchasing power as long as the incentives to seek out and satisfy wants are not destroyed. (Paragraph 81.)

20. In the free enterprise system the task of solving the problems of costs, prices, consumer protection and accountability rests with the market. The market produces flexibility, adaptability and a constant pressure for innovation, and where these features of economic activity are especially necessary free enterprise has no peer. (Paragraphs 82–83.)

21. This account of the free enterprise system has long been thought by many to represent its ideal, not its reality, on the grounds that even where competition is clearly to be seen it is not perfect, and that it is sometimes weakened by monopolies. The first objection is based on a misunderstanding; competition does not need to be perfect to be effective, but competition is the dominant climate in which free enterprise works. (Paragraphs 84–85.)

22. As to the second, in cases such as the public utilities where economic necessity makes monopoly inevitable, the choice between public and private ownership is an empirical one and the balance of

advantage will vary from case to case and from time to time. In manufacturing industry and commerce monopoly can never be complete and permanent. In any case nationalization is no remedy; if needed this is to be found in existing legislation. (Paragraphs 86–88.)

23. The 'industry' is a mere concept of classification of firms. The nationalization of an 'industry' runs counter to the natural growth of firms and hinders efficiency. (Paragraph 89.)

24. Efficiency requires tests and inducements. A monopoly must find tests other than those of the market, but engineering and accountancy techniques cannot fully take the place of the tests of the market. As for the inducements of the market nationalization replaces them by political control and the principle of conforming to some ill-defined notion of the 'public interest', and thus it deprives industry of a clear yardstick. In sum the effect of nationalization is to make efficiency elusive first by extending monopoly, secondly by subjecting it to political control, and thirdly by removing the yardstick of profitability. (Paragraphs 90–95.)

25. Nationalization is advocated as a means to facilitate central economic planning. In fact in a substantially free society it does not do so and a Government can plan better by influencing and assisting the activities of private firms. (Paragraphs 96–97.)

26. Further nationalization would jeopardize Britain's export performance. Export success calls for a high measure of initiative, flexibility, adaptability, readiness for risk, and quickness of decision, which are pre-eminently features of free enterprise. Furthermore nationalized undertakings would meet with resistance or suspicion overseas and this would be especially serious for overseas branches or subsidiaries of British firms. (Paragraphs 98–103.)

27. The threat of further nationalization must have an adverse effect on investment by other countries in Britain, on the position of the City of London and on the strength of sterling. This effect would be intensified by the formation of the European Free Trade Area, which also will make the need for free enterprise qualities of initiative, flexibility and efficiency even greater than it now is. (Paragraphs 104–107.)

28. The comparative analysis of free and nationalized industry enables us to review the arguments for the nationalization of particular industries.

(*a*) There is no need to nationalize an industry simply because it is 'basic'. It will not be made more efficient or more fitted for national planning.

(*b*) The monopoly argument applied to manufacturing industries is false because technical change may reintroduce competition, because political control does not enhance efficiency or accountability, and because existing legislation provides for the correction of any abuses.

(c) The inefficiency argument is founded either on misrepresentation or on a misunderstanding of the nature of efficiency.

(d) Nationalization does not improve labour relations; it may make them more difficult.

(e) There is no justification for the proposal to renationalize the steel industry or long-distance road haulage. Apart from the direct effect on these industries, the indirect effect on the rest of industry must be profound. Notably the steel-using industries cannot afford the slightest loss of flexibility; nor can the country afford a further upheaval in the steel industry. (Paragraph 108.)

THE ACQUISITION OF EQUITIES: NATIONALIZATION BY THE BACK DOOR

29. Equity-acquisition by the State is advocated to facilitate planning and to reap capital gains, and is said to be justified by the alleged need to solve the problem of 'social power' and by the alleged decay of the functions of the shareholder in the large company. The shareholder, it is said, no longer bears risk, supplies capital, or controls management. Hence company boards are alleged to have become self-perpetuating oligarchies. (Paragraphs 109–114.)

30. The shareholder's functions have not decayed as alleged. First, boards are subject to his ultimate veto which is sufficient for his purposes because competition supplies a day-to-day control. Secondly, the shareholder still has an active part in the supply of capital. Thirdly, risks have not been extinguished for holdings in large companies. (Paragraphs 115–120.)

31. If equity-acquisition is intended to produce Government control of industry it will produce problems similar to, but more difficult than, those already thrown up in the nationalized industries. If it is intended to give the Government ownership but not control, it will not succeed because the Government will find itself drawn or propelled into control. (Paragraphs 121–124.)

32. The acquisition of equities would radically change the climate for shareholders and managers in industry. Steps would be taken to avoid Government interference and this might stifle enterprise and growth. (Paragraphs 125–126.)

33. The aim of acquiring a share in capital gains rests partly upon a recognition of the efficiency of private industry and partly on the allegation that they are undeserved by private shareholders. Capital gains are partly a protection against inflation, which forms of property other than equities have; and partly they are the result of the

reinvestment of profits. The argument that they are undeserved is therefore ill-founded. (Paragraphs 127–130.)

34. In any case the State cannot turn capital gains into cash; or if it did it would lose the control for which equities were acquired. Nor is it clear that the State can gain by investment in 'growth' stocks as against 'non-growth' stocks. (Paragraphs 131–133.)

35. The purchase moneys for equities must be drawn from the public if they are not to be newly created and therefore to cause an enormous inflation. This must increase either taxation or Government debt, but if the Government prizes equities above its own debts it is unlikely to be able to borrow the money from the public. Nor could it borrow from the banks except by methods which would be as inflationary as the creation of currency. Furthermore the replacement of Government securities by equities in the hands of Government departments would blunt or break one of the instruments regulating the gilt-edged market and the volume of credit. (Paragraphs 134–138.)

36. The new proposal to supervise the investment programmes of large companies is based on the belief that they set the pattern and tempo of investment for the whole economy. There is both truth and error in this; but the true reason why the control only of large companies' investment is advocated is that the authors of *Plan for Progress* are obsessed by a picture of Boardroom timidity and sluggishness in large companies which they can blow away. Thus, it is thought, they will do enough to cause the whole economy to expand. (Paragraphs 139–141.)

37. No explanation is provided of how the Government would in practice exercise its investment supervision. As the proposed National Investment Board is to be only an advisory body the executive responsibility appears to be left with Whitehall. How monumental its task would be is shown by the one example given in *Plan for Progress*, namely the dovetailing of steel-using into steel-producing programmes. This is not a manageable task for a single authority except under totalitarian or wartime planning. (Paragraphs 142–143.)

69. THE PUBLIC SECTOR IN A PLAN FOR EXPANSION*

If Britain is to regain her place in world production and recover her export markets, we must have a plan for economic growth. A national plan, with targets for individual industries—especially the key sectors

* From *Signposts for the Sixties:* a statement of Labour's home policy accepted by the Sixtieth Annual Conference of the Labour Party at Blackpool, 2–6 October 1961, pp. 13–18. Reprinted by permission of the Labour Party.

which produce the tools of expansion—would enable every industry and undertaking, publicly or privately owned, to plan its own development with confidence in the future.

PREPARING THE PLAN

The preparation of such a plan would require the creation of a National Industrial Planning Board, integrated with the Government's own planning machinery and in close touch with both sides of industry. The central directive of this Board would be to ensure speedy and purposive industrial investment.

In consultation with industry, the Board would work out the expansion plans of the basic sectors of the economy and see that the resources are there to meet them. In consultation with the Government departments concerned, it would direct the industrial expansion to areas where labour is available and where new work is needed.

Once the plan has been laid down, the full resources of the Government would be needed to make sure that it was carried out, industry by industry. Financial policies must be directed to seeing that the investment programme is fulfilled. Tax policies encouraging new investment and the speedier writing off of capital expenditure, guaranteed orders where appropriate, and, where private industry manifestly cannot meet the need, new publicly owned undertakings— all these will be needed. But it is not enough to decide that more money must be spent on capital investment: the necessary money must be channelled into the investment programme. The investment of Budget surpluses and State superannuation funds; a greater control over the investment policies of pension funds and private insurance companies—these, too, will be required.

Since these measures would generate a powerful head of steam behind the investment drive, it would be necessary to have some orderly control over the timing of major industrial and commercial projects. This would ensure that priority developments could go ahead first: it would also be a means of steering new factories into the areas where they are most needed.

SCIENCE IN INDUSTRY

Of equal importance with new plant and machinery is the application of science to our industries. The scientific revolution presents British industry with a tremendous opportunity. One important reason for the failure of so much of our industry to modernize itself is the reluctance of British businessmen to invest in research and development and the refusal of the Government to make good this deficiency. In the application of science to industry, we face formidable competition, not only from the Communist bloc but also from the United States, Germany and Japan. Yet, while the nationalized industries and some private firms have a fine scientific record, there are key industries in which scientific research hardly exists.

The little that has been done owes a great deal to State initiative. It has been the State which has financed the greater part of industrial research. Today over 60 per cent of all research in Britain is paid for by the Government. In the vital work, too, of translating research into finished industrial products, public enterprise has played a leading role. Britain leads the world in the peaceful application of atomic energy—the work of the publicly-owned Atomic Energy Authority. Jet aircraft would not have been produced without a massive investment of public money, or television without the joint enterprise of the Post Office and the BBC.

The National Research Development Corporation, set up by the Labour Government, has sponsored the industrial development of scores of new inventions, among them the Hovercraft and advanced electronic brains and digital computers. From the modernization of the cotton industry to the building of the new Queen liner and the erection of modern steel plants in Wales and Scotland, the story has been the same. In case after case the progress of private industry depends on public money.

NATIONAL RESEARCH AND DEVELOPMENT

How can Britain make up the lost ground in the scientific revolution? The first thing to be done is to reconstruct and greatly to enlarge the existing National Research Development Corporation.

In its new form, the Corporation should be authorized to engage in production, either in its own establishments, through the creation of subsidiary productive undertakings, or by joint enterprises with private companies which have the expertise to develop new products but lack the resources.

The Corporation could also be used for mobilizing the under-used talents of groups of scientists by placing research or development contracts with them. In the past such contracts have been used at great cost and with inadequate financial control by Defence Ministries to develop new types of aircraft or guided missiles.

For a fraction of the cost of one of the missile contracts, the National Research Development Corporation could stimulate research directed towards promoting new developments in civil industry, for example, for new advances in textile machinery, shipbuilding techniques, machine tools or electronics. Encouragement could be given to young scientists to form research and development teams to work on particular programmes.

The third function of the reconstructed Corporation would be to help in revitalizing and modernizing existing industries which are declining or backward. This would not mean the acquisition of an entire industry, for to do so frequently means paying large sums as compensation for assets of very doubtful value. In machine tools, for example, our aims will probably best be realized by means of competitive public enterprise—the establishment of new, publicly owned plants, specializing in the types of machine tools which existing firms are not producing satisfactorily.

NATIONAL PLAN FOR APPRENTICESHIP

But increased investment and greater development of science will not of themselves solve Britain's problems. In the last resort our industrial effort depends on the nation's human resources, the workers by hand and brain in every sector of industry. To train them and, having trained them, to give the fullest play to their talents: these are among the top priorities for our industrial system today. Yet private industry has failed either to provide more apprenticeships or to modernize the system of training the apprentices in industry.

The nationalized industries are making a magnificent response. But too many private firms react in a way associated with the traditional laws of capitalism. Why should they spend money on the costly job of training apprentices if the young men, when trained, are then snapped up by other firms who made no contribution to their training? From the narrow, balance-sheet point of view of the individual firm, this may appear sense: the consequence for the industry as a whole, and for the nation, is a dangerous shortage of men with the right kinds of skill.

Here is a problem which can only be resolved if both sides of industry recognize past failures and accept responsibility for putting them right. Apprenticeship is a national responsibility and what is now needed is a national scheme for apprenticeship and training. It should be worked out by the trade unions and employers concerned, but with much greater help in providing finance and facilities.

Active Government help will also be required for encouraging industries to develop other common services, covering research, design, education in management, export promotion and other activities. This would be of particular assistance to the medium-sized and small firms, who usually cannot afford specialist services. In the power to set up Development Councils in the Industrial Organization and Development Act, 1948, we already have a valuable statutory framework.

THE ROLE OF PUBLIC OWNERSHIP

So far we have discussed how the Government, through central planning, can stimulate the whole economy, private as well as public, to the rapid expansion the nation requires. What role will public ownership play in this development? We have already described one new application of it, in our account of the job to be done by the reconstructed National Research Development Corporation. Once this Corporation was firmly established, the public sector would be able to advance where it is most needed—at the growing points of the British economy and in the new industries based on science.

THE CAPITALIST BEGGING-BOWL

Another field where public ownership may well have to be extended is in those private industries which, through the receipt of subsidies or loans, are dependent on the State for their continued existence.

A Labour Government would insist on much more austere tests for the expenditure of public money in buttressing this so-called private enterprise. Where national assistance is required by manufacturing industry, it should be made conditional on public participation in the enterprise—the setting up, for example of a joint venture, with the State as at least an equal partner.

The position of those industries which are largely dependent on State purchasing programmes should also be reviewed. The National Health Service spends over £80 million a year on pharmaceutical products and there is clear evidence of waste and profiteering.

Why should we not protect the taxpayer by arranging that it should meet its requirements increasingly from public enterprise, either through new, publicly owned undertakings or by the acquisition of existing ones?

There is a similar problem in the aircraft industry, where a number of firms owe their continued existence to research and development grants and contracts awarded on a cost-plus basis. Exhaustive enquiries by the all-party Public Accounts Committee have made it clear that the taxpayer cannot be protected against waste—running into tens of millions of pounds a year under the present system of awarding contracts. Here too new forms of State participation will be necessary, if the taxpayer is to be protected.

The structure of the existing nationalized industries must also be reviewed, with particular attention to the problems of finance, public accountability and worker-management relations.

Meanwhile the scope for public enterprise should be extended by removing the anomalous restrictions which at present prevent public corporations from undertaking many useful and profitable develop-

462 *Nationalization*

ments. Britain will never have an economic transport industry until the publicly owned transport authority is free to extend its road services wherever it can usefully do so.

Restrictions on the ability of the publicly owned industries, such as coal, gas, electricity and the railways, to develop the equipment and machinery they need, within the framework of a national plan, should also be ended.

Finally, we must consider what may well be the most important contribution that public ownership can make to the nation's economic revival. We have already called attention to the menacing growth of private monopoly and the consequent concentration of economic power in irresponsible hands. The giant corporations or private financial empires which dominate so much of the British economy, and which decisively influence its total performance, grow each year larger, fewer and yet more closely interlocked. It is the Tory view that they should be free to conduct themselves exactly as they like, responsible to no one but their directors and financial controllers: free to be bought or sold like lots at an auction sale: free to swallow each other up, or even to be swallowed up by foreign firms. Conservatives, who have always opposed the idea that the British people should own their own industries, have no objection to seeing valuable productive enterprises pass into the control of London or Wall Street financiers: the only body which is excluded from making takeover bids is the community itself, whose work has created these great economic empires and whose service is their ultimate justification.

The British people cannot be asked much longer to subscribe to this curious and fundamentally unpatriotic doctrine.

Where vast concentrations of economic power have created monopolies, the Government, on behalf of the people, has the right to insist that such economic empires be made accountable to the public interest. That is our case for renationalizing steel. Where competition creates not efficiency but chaos in a key sector of the economy, there too an expansion of public ownership may be necessary to put things right. That is our case for creating an integrated and publicly owned transport system.

Where major changes of ownership and control in a vital industry are threatened by takeover bid or merger, the State must be free to intervene, either by vetoing a proposed transaction or by stepping in itself and asserting the rights of the community through an extension o, public ownership.

To achieve these different purposes, the forms of public ownership will, of course, vary widely. Already we can see it developing in various forms—nationalization of a whole industry or firm. State participation in industrial companies on a partnership basis, the establishment of State-owned undertakings competing with private concerns, municipal enterprise and, finally, Co-operative ownership. All these kinds of social ownership have their part to play in meeting the dangers of monopoly, in achieving a fair distribution of the national dividend—and, most important of all, in helping to fulfil our national plan for economic growth.

The success of that plan is vital for Britain's future—for full employment, for the direction and improvement of our social services, for improving our living standards and for the contribution we must make in the war against want in the underdeveloped areas of the world.

The fulfilment of the plan, therefore, must not be sacrificed to the dictates of private profit, to the selfish whims of speculators, to outmoded financial techniques, or to unpatriotic manoeuvrings in foreign exchange. Neither great industrial combines nor monopoly institutions must ever be allowed to become the masters of our economic policy. If Britain is to survive, a Government responsible to a democratically elected Parliament must take full responsibility for the nation's economic destinies.

TABLE OF SOURCES

Page

EDWARDS, R. S. 'The Finance of Electricity Supply', *Lloyds Bank Review*, October 1960, pp. 14–30.   247

ELLIOT, SIR JOHN. 'Efficiency versus Cost in Public Transport', *The Journal of the Institute of Transport*, Vol. XXVII, No. 10, May 1958, pp. 334–7   444

FLORENCE, P. S. and MADDICK, H. 'Consumers' Councils in the Nationalized Industries', *The Political Quarterly*, Vol. XXIV, No. 3, July-September 1953, pp. 266–71   365

GAITSKELL, H. *'Socialism and Nationalization'*, Fabian Tract 300, 1956, pp. 5–7 and 31–36   23

GREAVES, H. R. G. 'Public Boards and Corporations', *The Political Quarterly*, Vol. XVI, No. 1, January-March 1945, pp. 69–77   297

GRIFFITH, J. A. G. 'The Voice of the Consumer', *The Political Quarterly*, Vol. XXI, No. 2, April-June 1950, pp. 177–83   356

HUGHES, J. *Nationalized Industries in the Mixed Economy*, Fabian Tract 328, October 1960, pp. 8–11   269

JENKINS, C. 'Retreat: The Labour Party and the Public Corporations', *Universities and Left Review*, Winter 1958, Supplement 'The Insiders', pp. 59–60   419

LABOUR PARTY. *The Workers' Status in Industry*, Study Guide No. 5, 1933, pp. 5–16   381

LOW, SIR TOBY. 'The Select Committee on Nationalized Industries', *Public Administration*, Vol. 40, Spring 1962, pp. 1–15   322

MILLIGAN, F. 'Ministerial Control of the British Nationalized Industries', *Canadian Journal of Economics and Political Science*, Vol. XVII, May 1951, pp. 179–83   282

MILLS, G. and HOWE, M. 'Consumer Representation and the Withdrawal of Railway Services', *Public Administration*, Vol. XXXVIII, Autumn 1960, pp. 253–62   348

MOLSON, H. 'Nationalized Industries: Select Committee to Secure Parliamentary Control', *The Times*, September 8, 1949   311

NOTTAGE, R. 'Reporting to Parliament on the Nationalized Industries', *Public Administration*, Vol. XXXV, Summer 1957, pp. 155–63   338

REID, SIR CHARLES. 'The Problem of Coal, III—New Structure proposed for the Industry', *The Times*, November 24, 1948   120

ROBERTS, B. C. 'Trade Unions and Nationalization', *Progress*, Vol. 44 No. 245, Winter 1954–55, pp. 114–18   372

ROBERTS, C. A. 'The National Coal Board and the Fleck Report', Appendix, *Public Administration*, Vol. XXXV, Spring 1957, Paras. 1–32   130

ROBERTS, R. D. V. and SALLIS, H. 'Joint Consultation in the Electricity Supply Industry 1949–59', *Public Administration*, Vol. XXXVII, Summer 1959, pp. 116–33   398

ROBSON, W. A. 'A New Deal for the Post Office', *The Political Quarterly*, Vol. 32, No. 2, April-June 1961, pp. 139–45   98

SIMON OF WYTHENSHAWE, LORD. *The Boards of Nationalized Industries*, Longmans, Green, 1957, pp. 13–33   184

SMITH, J. H. 'The Rise of a Bureaucracy', *Transactions of the Third World Congress of Sociology*, Vol. II, pp. 56–70   159

WADE, E. C. S. 'The Constitutional Aspect of the Public Corporation', *Current Legal Problems*, Vol. 2, 1949, pp. 173–7   110

INDEX

Abel, Deryck, 35n–46
Accounting procedure for nationalized industries, 213
Acton Society Trust, 349n, 366n, 380n
Admiralty Dockyards, 12
Agricultural Mortgage Corporation, 12, 64
Air corporations, British, *see* British air corporations
Air Registration Board, 440
Albu, Austen, 337
Allen, W. P., 376
Ammon, Lord, 83
Anglo-American Council for Productivity: Iron and Steel Team, 62
Anglo-Iranian Oil Company, 84
Ardant, Gabriel, 422n–429
Area Gas Boards, *see* Gas Boards, Area
Ashfield, Lord, 445
Assheton, Ralph (now Lord Clitheroe), 324n
Associated Electrical Industries, 186
Associated Portland Cement, 186
Atomic Energy Authority, 65, 104n–106, 459
Attlee, Rt Hon. Earl, 36, 98

Baillie Committee (1937), 173
Baldwin, Rt. Hon. Samuel, 82
Bank of England Act, 36–37
Bank of England, Issue Department, 263, 266
BEA, *see* British European Airways
Beeching, Dr Richard, 176–184
Bell, R. W.: on manpower in nationalized industries, 198n–205
Berend, Pierre, 426n
Best, R. Darcy, on Atomic Energy Authority, 65, 104n–106
BOAC, *see* British Overseas Airways Corporation
Bowman, Sir James: Chairman of Third Coal Board, 190
Bridgeman Committee on the Post Office, 64, 95n–97, 297, 299
Bridges, Sir Edward (now Lord), 316, 344
BBC, *see* British Broadcasting Corporation

British Airways, 12
British air corporations: Ministerial responsibility for, 281, 288n–289; Select Committee Report on BOAC and BEA, 326; national prestige of airlines, 332; aircraft accidents, 340n; aircraft utilization, 431–444; airlines efficiency measurement, 422, 429n–444
British Broadcasting Corporation, 12, 459; as forerunner of present Boards, 81–83; recruitment to, 301; control of revenue, 302; Ministerial responsibility for, 323; foreign services, 303; listeners' enquiries, 366
British Council: and recruitment, 301; control of revenue, 302
British Electricity Authority, 113; pithead power stations, 173; accounting and costs, 212–213
British European Airways: operating costs, 38, 430–438; Ministerial responsibility, 289; Select Committee Report on, 326; fares, 328; maintenance costs, 442–444
British Iron and Steel Federation: (alliance with Import Duties Advisory Committee), 43
British Overseas Airways Corporation: amalgamated with British South American Airways Corporation, 12; Ministerial responsibility for, 289, 302; comparing aircraft maintenance costs, 327; operating costs and maintenance, 430–444; Select Committee Report on, 326; information contained in Annual Reports, 339, 344
British Petroleum Company, 12, 64
British Railways Board, 107–108
British Railways, 18; organization and management, 114; decentralization, 115, 106–110; structure of, 154n–159; Treasury and Ministry control, 210, 278n–280; Ministerial responsibility for, 289–297; fares and charges, 293–294, 328, 333; Select Committee Report on, 326; comparison with Continental railways, 327; closure of permanent way, 350;

GEORGE ALLEN & UNWIN LTD
London: 40 Museum Street, WC1

Auckland: 24 Wyndham Street
Bombay: 15 Graham Road, Ballard Estate, Bombay 1
Buenos Aires: Escritorio 454–459, Florida 165
Calcutta: 17 Chittaranjan Avenue, Calcutta 13
Cape Town: 109 Long Street
Hong Kong: F1/12 Mirador Mansions, Kowloon
Ibadan: PO Box 62
Karachi: Karachi Chambers, McLeod Road
Madras: Mohan Mansions, 38c Mount Road, Madras 6
Mexico: Villalongin 32–10, Piso, Mexico 5, DF
Nairobi: PO Box 4536
New Delhi: 13–14 Asaf Ali Road, New Delhi 1
São Paulo: Avenida 9 de Julho 1138-Ap. 51
Singapore: 36c Princep Street, Singapore 7
Sydney, NSW: Bradbury House, 55 York Street
Tokyo: 3 Kanda-Ogawamachi, 3-Chome
Toronto: 91 Wellington Street West

NATIONALIZED INDUSTRY AND PUBLIC OWNERSHIP

WILLIAM A. ROBSON

Professor Robson's new book is primarily an inquiry into the working of the British nationalized industries during the past ten years. He examines, with the aid of a wealth of material, the organization and management of these industries, how far they are subject to competition, their labour relations, their financial policies, their research and development programmes, their consumer councils, their relations with Ministers and Parliament, the political influences to which they are subject, and their general performance. He considers also the ideas and proposals which have recently been put forward about the manner in which publicly owned industries should be run and the aims they should pursue. The final chapter discusses some of the alternatives to nationalization which have been advanced.

Nationalized Industry and Public Ownership stands in a class by itself, for although the author makes no attempt to conceal his own views, his main object is to present a fair and accurate account of the nationalized industries. The reader will find here no simple story of success or failure, but an honest account of achievements and shortcomings, of difficulties overcome and of problems still unsolved.

This is an indispensible book for everyone who wishes to be properly informed on the subject.

Small Royal 8vo.   *50s net*

ECONOMIC EXPANSION AND STRUCTURAL CHANGE

Edited and translated by T. L. JOHNSTON

A TRADE UNION MANIFESTO FROM
L O (Landesorganisationen i Sverige—The Swedish Confederation of Trade Unions)

L O enjoys an international reputation as a trade union movement with exhilarating ideas on wages policy and collective bargaining. In the past generation the Swedish labour market has been remarkably active in evolving codes of conduct and successful in avoiding demarcation disputes. The present 'manifesto' is a systematic exposition of recent Trade Union thought in Sweden on the problems of economic growth and on the structural changes for which it will call.

Demy 8vo.   *About 25s net*

MONEY, TRADE AND
ECONOMIC GROWTH
SURVEY LECTURES IN ECONOMIC THEORY

HARRY G. JOHNSON

This book surveys a broad range of subjects in a brief space, but it has all Professor Johnson's originality and incisiveness. The first part deals with international trade and economic growth: Professor Johnson discusses the Balance of Payments, seen nowadays as a policy problem, the modern theories of comparative costs and commercial policy and the new developments in the theory of customs unions or preferential groups—a highly topical subject.

The second part is concerned with modern monetary theory and a re-examination of Keynes after twenty-five years. In the third part Professor Johnson discusses the roles of planning and the market in economic development, and makes some original contributions to the economic theory of the 'affluent society' and the theory of its social policy—a field which he is convinced will yield interesting and fruitful applications of economic analysis.

Demy 8vo. 25s net

PRICING AND EQUILIBRIUM

PROFESSOR ERICH SCHNEIDER

Allen and Unwin have already published an English version by Mr Kurt Klappholz of Volume Three of Professor Schneider's famous *Introduction to Economics* under the title *Money, Income and Employment*. Volume Two has already appeared in English under the title *Pricing and Equilibrium*, translated by Professor T. W. Hutchison from the first German edition.

His version has been out of print for some years and Mr Bennathan's new edition is based on the greatly enlarged sixth German edition. This volume analyses the economic planning of households and firms, i.e. their economic dispositions. Using partial equilibrium analysis, it describes the equilibria corresponding to various dispositions and the effects of changes in dispositions, ending with an exposition of the problem of general micro-economic equilibrium in a stationary economy.

Translated by E. BENNATHAN.

Demy 8vo. 45s net

PRODUCTIVITY AND ECONOMIC INCENTIVES

J. P. DAVIDSON, P. SARGENT FLORENCE, BARBARA GRAY AND NORMAN ROSS

This book gives the results of 'fieldwork' investigations in factories, laundries and Co-operative shops, conducted by members of the Faculty of Commerce and Social Science at the University of Birmingham. By means of statistics of output before and after a change in methods of wage-payment and of interviews with the individual workers actually concerned, it was found that the productivity of labour, so important to the national economy, can be very greatly increased, together with an increase in earnings, without workers complaining of undue strain. The conditions are given in detail under which the increase in productivity was obtained, varying from 7 per cent to over 200 per cent and resulting in lowered cost of production. These conditions include the procedures, found so necessary, for obtaining the workers' consent. P. Sargent Florence, now Emeritus Professor, supplies an introductory chapter reviewing to date productivity studies, in many of which he has, since 1913, participated, and also discusses the extension of piece-rates to jobs where hitherto they have not been applied.

Demy 8vo. 35s *net*

A PHILOSOPHICAL INTERPRETATION OF ECONOMICS

J. K. MEHTA

Professor Mehta is an economic theorist of the highest class and brings to bear on the subject a knowledge of mathematics as well as a wide acquaintance with eastern and western philosophy. In this challenging book he explores the philosophical foundations of the subject and western economists will find it most salutary to see how arbitrary and unexamined a great deal of accepted theory can be made to appear. For economics tends, in the hands of many, to degenerate into a collection of facts and an enumeration of half-baked principles, but in this book there is a real attempt to raise it to its dignified position as a true science.

Professor Mehta covers such subjects as methodology, production, distributive shares both absolute and relative, statics and dynamics, the quantity theory of money, philosophy of disguised unemployment, the acceleration principle and other topics of immediate interest to students. As against the ordinary run of books on economics it is, however, outstanding in its demand that economists should not offer a system of simultaneous answers to questions which cannot be simultaneously asked, and which imply contradictory views of the human condition. As Professor G. L. S. Shackle has written of it, 'This is a beautiful, moving and most deeply interesting book, and it is superbly well-written. It deserves to become a classic.'

Demy 8vo. *About 35s net*

THE THEORY OF
ECONOMIC INTEGRATION

BELA A. BALASSA

This is an excellent exposition of a complex and far-reaching topic. It will interest economists in Europe by reason of its subject and treatment, but it is also a valuable and reliable textbook for students tackling integration as part of a course on International Economics and for those studying Public Finance.

In offering this theoretical study, the author builds on the conclusions of other writers, but goes beyond this in providing a unifying framework for previous contributions and in exploring questions that in the past received little attention—in particular, the relationship between economic integration and growth (especially the inter-relationship between market size and growth, and the implications of various factors for economic growth in an integrated area). Among these are: economies of large-scale production, competition, technological change, uncertainty and the allocation of investment funds. The last four chapters cover the problems of economic policy in an integrated area.

Medium 8vo.   28s *net*

A NEO-CLASSICAL THEORY OF
ECONOMIC GROWTH

J. E. MEADE

Much attention is now paid to problems of economic growth. What is it that makes real income grow rapidly in come economics and only slowly in others? Political and social factors play a major role in the answer to this question, but purely economic considerations remain of great importance. Many economic theorists have used entirely new methods of economic analysis to deal with this question. But in this short book Professor Meade has outlined the way in which classical economic analysis may be developed for application to the problem of economic growth. This is a book for the student of economic theory; but the basic theory is expounded in the main text of this book in a way which does not demand any extensive familiarity with mathematical techniques.

Demy 8vo.   *2nd edition.* 28s *net*

GEORGE ALLEN & UNWIN LTD

DATE DUE

GAYLORD | | | PRINTED IN U.S.A.